The Eliade Guide to World Religions

The Eliade Guide to World Religions

MIRCEA ELIADE

IOAN P. COULIANO

With Hillary S. Wiesner

HarperSanFrancisco

A Division of HarperCollins*Publishers*

 For information address HarperCollins Publishers, 10 East 53rd Street, New York, NY 10022.

FIRST EDITION

TEXT DESIGN BY RICK CHAFIAN

Library of Congress Cataloging-in-Publication Data

Eliade, Mircea.
The Eliade guide to world religions / Mircea Eliade, Ioan P. Couliano, with Hillary S. Wiesner.
p. cm.
Includes bibliographical references.
ISBN 0–06–062145–1
1. Religions. I. Couliano, Ioan P. II. Wiesner, Hillary S. III. Title.
BL80.2.E415 1991
291—dc20 90–56452
CIP

91 92 93 94 95 RRD(H) 10 9 8 7 6 5 4 3 2 1

This edition is printed on acid-free paper that meets the American National Standards Institute Z39.48 Standard.

FOR CHRISTINEL ELIADE

I say that He, in His wisdom, was not disposed
to give more and that He did not want to give more.
Why He did not want it I do not know. Yet He knows it.
Albert the Great (1206–1280), *Opera* xxvi 392

Kāna fiʾl-imkān abdaʿ mimmā kān.
What may be is more marvelous than what is.
Al-Biqāʿī (1404–1480), *Tahdīm al-arkān*, fol. 48a

Contents

Note to Readers

The Eliade Guide to World Religions is designed for easy, practical use and can fulfill a multiplicity of functions.

Following the model of the *Encyclopaedia Britannica*, it is divided into two parts: Part I, a "Macro-Dictionary" containing complete surveys of thirty-three religions, numbered from 1 to 33 and divided into paragraphs and subparagraphs; and Part II, a "Micro-Dictionary" containing both short entries on more significant topics and simple references to the Macro-Dictionary (references indicate numbered items and internal divisions in the Macro-Dictionary).

The Micro-Dictionary works as a regular dictionary, with the difference that some topics are only covered in the general part or Macro-Dictionary. The Macro-Dictionary works both as a dictionary of different religions and clusters of religions, *and* as a readable yet thorough presentation of the most important world religions. In other words, the reader can either consult this book as a dictionary, or read it as an updated digest of the history of religions in comparative perspective and according to an advanced cognitive methodology.

Preface to the World English Edition

Formulated by Mircea Eliade in 1975, the project of a guide to world religions took shape in 1983 when a first contract was signed; I was involved in the project from the onset. We did not actually start work on it until the spring of 1986, when I was affiliated with the University of Chicago as a visiting professor and Hiram Thomas Guest Lecturer. At the time, Mircea Eliade had given up his long-cherished idea of condensing into one volume his *History of Religious Ideas;* therefore, his wish now was to make the guide into a readable compendium, in which—somewhat unusually—the major religions would be separately arranged in alphabetical order and the wealth of data made available by the Macmillan *Encyclopedia of Religion* under his general editorship could be profitably drawn upon. If he was not to write the whole "novel" of the history of world religions, at least he would provide a number of "short stories" on the major individual religious traditions, the number of which, after considerable deliberation, was set at thirty-three. After Mircea Eliade's death on April 22, 1986, I scrupulously continued the original project, with the assistance of H. S. Wiesner (Harvard University), whose knowledge of Near Eastern languages and religions was most helpful. In addition to Eliade's own *History of Religious Ideas,* we perused the new *Encyclopedia of Religion* and the basic bibliography of each religion, a process that took more time than initially planned.

In this guide, we will use an *H* hereafter to refer to the *History of Religious Ideas* and *ER* to refer to the *Encyclopedia of Religion.* We gratefully acknowledge the hospitality of the Netherlands Institute for Advanced Study at Wassenaar in 1987, and of Dorothy and Kurt Hertzfeld of Amherst, Mass., for two extended periods in 1988 and 1989; we are also indebted to the Royal Library in The Hague, the Regenstein Library in Chicago, Widener Library in Cambridge, Massachusetts, and the libraries of Amherst and Smith colleges.

Many scholars have been extremely helpful over the years in acquainting me with the history of different religions or with different perspectives on the study of religion. The following list is incomplete: Gösta Åhlstrom, Moshe Barasch, Dieter Betz, Ugo Bianchi, Jerry Brauer, Adela and J. J. Collins, Carsten Colpe, Wendy Doniger, Umberto Eco, Mircea Eliade, Giovanni Filoramo, Jacques Flamant, Chris Gamwell, Florentino García Martínez, B. Gladigow, Gherardo Gnoli, Robert Grant, Ithamar Gruenwald, David Hellholm, Moshe Idel, Hans Jonas, Hans Kippenberg, Joseph M. Kitagawa, Jacques Le Goff, Gerard Luttikhuizen, Grazia Marchianò, Martin Marty, Bernard McGinn, Michel Meslin, Dean Miller, Arnaldo Momigliano, Aryeh Motzkin, Michael Murrin, Frank Reynolds, Giulia Sfameni-Gasparro, Jonathan Z. Smith, Michael Stone, Guy Stroumsa, Larry Sullivan, Herman Te Velde, David Tracy, Maarten Vermaseren, Hans Witte, Tony Yu, Elémire Zolla, and many others. I have learned much from many of my students at the University of Chicago over my years of teaching here. To all those mentioned above and to those not named, my heartfelt thanks.

Since 1973, the journals *Aevum, Journal for the Study of Judaism, Journal of Religions, History of Religions, Revue de l'Histoire des Religions, Revue d'Histoire et de Philosophie Religieuses, Studi e Materiali di Storia delle Religioni,* and others have published many of my book reviews on religion; this relentless and rather unrewarding job of reviewer, which I have continued as editor in chief of *Incognita* (Brill, Leiden), showed its advantages for the first time during the work on this guide.

As Mircea Eliade undoubtedly would have done, we dedicate this work to his courageous wife, Christinel.

Ioan P. Couliano

Chicago, March 4, 1991

The Eliade Guide to World Religions

Introduction: Religion as System

What *is* religion? Why do rational, practical people still buy into it? Why do all religions of humankind, at all times, show striking similarities with each other? Why do genetically unrelated myths and rituals have similar narrative plots or ritual sequences?

All these seem naïve questions, and therefore no serious scholar, after a long training in some philologies and the history of religions, would ever dare to ask them. And yet, they are the basic questions of the discipline, those questions—still unanswered—that practically called the discipline of the history of religions into being.

Is it possible to answer such questions at all? The claim of many scholars whom we define today as "cognitive" historians is that *the unity of everything mental must necessarily lie in the unity of the human mind.* This perspective, adopted here, has been used before by such scholars as Mircea Eliade and Claude Lévi-Strauss to account for common yet unrelated mythical patterns in different geographical areas. Contrary to Lévi-Strauss, who used cognitive presuppositions at the *microlevel* of mythical narratives, Eliade used them at the *macrolevel* involving large units of belief: *religious systems.*

According to Eliade, religion is an *autonomous system.* Both words need to be defined. *System* means that all phenomena pertaining to a single unit are interrelated and integrated into a complex structure that generates them. Being a mental process, this system follows the tracks created by the computational rules of the mind. This is its only "logic" (which may not be "logical" at all according to the standards of formal logic).

Autonomous is opposed to *heteronomous* and means that religion in its origin and function is not the by-product of other systems (i.e., economy or society), does not depend on them, and does not generate them.

Eliade was not alone in emphasizing the mental and systemic character of religion. In his quest, he was preceded and accompanied by several scholars, such as Émile Durkheim, Marcel Mauss, Georges Dumézil, and Claude Lévi-Strauss. Yet most of these scholars did not believe in the autonomy of religion. In his basic book *The Elementary Forms of Religious Life* (1912), Durkheim expressed the idea that the religious system is heteronomous, i.e., that it actually encodes another system, the system of social relations within a group. Like Durkheim, Georges Dumézil remained faithful all his life to the conception of myth as a "dramatic rendering" of the fundamental ideology of human society.[1] Yet he envisioned "ideology" as something more fundamental and quite different from systems of parenthood and even, though to a lesser extent, from hierarchical classification. Dumézil was trained in Indo-European linguistics under Antoine Meillet and began by considering myth and ritual among all Indo-European peoples as a way to access their pristine institutions, which in turn would open the magic door of history leading to a presumable phase (Proto-Indo-European, or PIE) when all peoples and languages were one. This Indo-European "dreamtime" was characterized, in Dumézil's view, by original simplicity. Its most basic structure was the so-called "tripartite ideology," responsible for the existence of three major social functions: the priestly, the royal, and the nutritive-productive.[2]

Ten years younger than Dumézil, and attracted by his thinking, the anthropologist Claude Lévi-Strauss acknowledged Dumézil's influence.[3] Yet, unlike both Durkheim and Dumézil, Lévi-Strauss emphasized the autonomy of myth, its relative independence from social structures. In a famous example—the myth of Asdiwal among the Tsimshian Indians of America's Northwest Coast—Claude Lévi-Strauss showed that myth cannot be envisioned as a dramatic rendering of Tsimshian society. Far from encoding social relations, Tsimshian my-

---

[1] See especially his *Heur et malheur du guerrier. Aspects mythiques de la fonction guerrière chez les Indo-Européens* (1985), p. 15. On the relationship between Dumézil and Durkheim, see especially C. Scott Littleton, *The New Comparative Mythology: An Anthropological Assessment of the Theories of Georges Dumézil* (1966), p. 6.

[2] See C. Scott Littleton, *New Comparative Mythology*, p. 6.

[3] See Guido Ferraro, *Il linguaggio del mito: Valori simbolici e realtà sociale nelle mitologie primitive* (1979), p. 51.

thology systematically distorts them.[4] On a more abstract level, Lévi-Strauss would reject what he believed to be Durkheim's confusion between logic and history, as well as the fictitious opposition between individual and society.[5] According to Lévi-Strauss's premises, the ultimate "system" is purely logical and works behind the screen of history; consequently, individuals are only actualizations of the "grammar" rules encoded in society.

At the end of the four monumental works bearing the generic title *Mythologiques* (1964–1971), Claude Lévi-Strauss seems to discover that one fundamental structure underlies all mythologies of North and South America, much in the same way as PIE underlies all Indo-European languages. And yet, whereas the explanation of the common traits of all Indo-European languages lies in their common origin, being therefore historical, Lévi-Strauss would rather emphasize the purely logical character of the ultimate mythical structures, thereby explaining their cross-cultural manifestation.[6]

Despite his insistence on the historical character of the study of religion, Mircea Eliade treated religion systemically. Unlike both Dumézil and Lévi-Strauss, Eliade did not approach religion either from a linguistic or from a sociological perspective. Well acquainted with the modern historiography of religion, he was influenced by the phenomenological school (especially of Gerardus van der Leeuw) and by the theory of "cultural cycles" of Wilhelm Schmidt and the Vienna School.[7] A blending of the two is sustained in his *History of Religious Ideas*.

Unlike Georges Dumézil, Eliade would emphasize the autonomy of religion and myth, whose structure does not depend on a more fundamental "ideology," but on the functioning of the "psyche" in a given environment. Although scholars like to oppose Eliade and Lévi-Strauss and to label their respective theses as irreconcilable, Eliade's main assumption sounds rather akin to Lévi-Strauss's hidden logical processes. There seems, however, to be a radical difference concerning the *level* at which the two scholars try to map the religious system.

Indeed, Eliade insists that overall maps of religion are possible and necessary. It is therefore not necessary to start from the most basic level

---

[4] See Claude Lévi-Strauss, *Paroles données,* (1984), p. 122 (*Anthropology and Myth: Lectures 1951–1981,* translated into English by R. Willis, [1987]).

[5] See Sandro Nannini, *Il pensiero simbolico,* (1981), p. 24–25.

[6] See Ferraro, *Il linguaggio del mito,* pp. 51–56.

[7] See I. P. Couliano, *Mircea Eliade,* (1978).

in order to understand higher levels of the religious system. One can begin instead at the highest and most primary generative level of religion, where the rules that produce it are relatively simple. Yet, in order to perceive these rules, scholars need more than just information: they need *complex* information. Only when apparently chaotic instances multiply is it possible to understand their hidden structure, the computational "logic" that secretely organizes them. The reader will be confronted with a multitude of such phenomena in the pages of this guide, and especially in the analysis of more complex religious systems. Let us give here a simple example.

What is reincarnation? Many people, both in the Western world and outside it, still believe in reincarnation, and recently the therapeutic technique of "past lives regression" has turned into a profitable business. The modern discipline of history of religions was the product of a good number of German scholars, flanked by other European colleagues such as the great Belgian philologist and archaeologist Franz Cumont. Cumont tried painstakingly to reconstruct the historical and local "origin" of the idea of reincarnation, and its passage to Ancient Greece, where it was held by Pythagoras, Empedocles, the Orphics, and perhaps others, and became extremely influential with Plato.

Cumont spent a long time trying to demonstrate that all belief in metensomatosis came from India, and the Greek Pythagoreans had received it, strangely enough, via Iran (where it had left no trace at all).[8] Had Cumont consulted any of the anthropological surveys available before his time, he would have discovered that Indians and Pythagoreans were not the only ones to believe in reincarnation. They shared this idea with quite a few others: in Africa, with the Swas of Kenya, the Wanikas, the Akikiyus, the Bari of the White Nile, the Mandingo, the Edo, the Ibo, the Ewes, the Yorubas, the Kagoro, the Akan, the Twi, the Zulus, the Bantus, the Barotse, the Ba-ila, and the Marovi tribes of Madagascar; in Oceania and Malaysia, with the Tahitians, the Okinawans, the Papuans of New Guinea, the Melanesians, the Marquesans, the Indonesian tribes, the Solomon Islanders, the Sandwich Islanders, the Fijians, the Dayaks and other Borneo tribes, the Balinese, the Poso-Alfures of Celebes, the tribes of New Caledonia, and the New Zealand Maoris; in Asia, with the Andaman Islanders, the Santals of Bengal, the Dravidians and Nayars of southern India, the Khonds of eastern India, the Anagami Nagas of Assam, the Changs of the Naga

---

[8] Franz Cumont, *Lux perpetua* (1949), p. 143ff; see my *Psychanodia I* (1983), pp. 29–30.

Hills, the Karens of Burma, the Semang of the Malay Peninsula, the Giliaks, Yenisei Ostyaks, and Buriats, the Cheremiss of Central Russia, and a few others; in North America, with the Algonquins, the Dakotas, the Hurons, the Iroquois, the Mohave, the Moqui (Hopi), the Nachez, the Nutkas, the Tacullis, the Kiowas, the Creeks, the Winnebagos, the Ahts of Vancouver Island, the Denes, the Montagnais, the Tlingit, the Haidas, the Tsimshians, the Eskimos, the Aleuts, and the Athapaskans; in South America, with the Caribs, Mayas, and Quiches, Patagonians, Peruvians, Sontals, Popayans, Powhattans, and Tlalacans of Mexico, the Icannes and Chiriquanes of Brazil, and undoubtedly more.[9]

Even if—as we will see shortly—views of reincarnation may differ very widely, they all start from a common premise, an *inevitable premise,* we may add, upon which any human mind, anywhere and at any time, would stumble, should it begin from the commonly shared assumption that we have a body and a mind experienced as a three-dimensional screen that can by no means be identified with the body. This duality is inherent to all humans and may easily lead, as it actually did, to the idea that the mind performance is separable from the body. In many traditions, the mind performance is known as "soul" or equivalents, and is supposed to exist independently from the body.[10] This, of course, was perceived as a great discovery at a certain stage of introspection of humankind, perhaps tens of thousands of years ago, and as a great secret ever since.

As soon as the human mind admits that beings (humans, animals, all sentient beings) consist of soul and body, then the problem of the relation soul/body arises immediately. Only a few solutions are available, stemming from two major dichotomies:

1. The soul preexists the body vs. the soul does not preexist the body;
2. The soul is created vs. the soul is uncreated.

That souls are created and preexistent is a very common view shared by Hindus, Platonists, some gnostics, Origenists, and many others. That souls are created and do not exist before their bodies is a combination of views held by orthodox Christians approximately since Augustine. That souls do not preexist their bodies and are not created

---

[9] The list, approximative as it may be, comes from Joseph Head and S. L. Cranston, *Reincarnation in World Thought* (1967).

[10] About the theories concerning the opposition between "free soul" and "body soul" in the works of the Swedish school of anthropology, see I. P. Couliano, *Out of this World: A History of Otherworldly Journeys* (1991).

is a doctrine called Traducianism, held by Tertullian of Carthage and quite orthodox in his time.[11] According to it, souls are generated from the psychic copulation of the parents in exactly the same way as bodies are generated from their physical copulation. The fourth hypothesis, that souls preexist bodies without being individually created, is held by many North American peoples who believe in a permanent tank of soul stuff from which individual souls come and to which they revert, and by the twelfth-century Muslim Aristotelian of Spain, Averroes, who likewise believed that the Universal Intellect is one: individual intellects are reabsorbed into it after death.

Metensomatosis, Creationism, and Traducianism are not only the three main doctrines the scholar stumbles upon all over Late Antiquity; they are *necessarily* three of the most common logical solutions to the question of the relation between mind and body. As such, they are atemporal and ubiquitous. They do not "originate" in India and "cross" Iran; they are present in all human minds that contemplate them by contemplating the problem. May this serve as a clear illustration of our view of "genesis" and "cognitive transmission" of ideas, as opposed to the view of a certain elementary historicism.

If the idea of religion as a system seems to be widespread and legitimate, how can it be used in a work of reference like this guide, a work in which the reader expects to find an epitome of the history of every particular religion, together with succinct information concerning religious events, ideas, and personalities? Let the reader be reassured: all this is indeed present in our guide. Yet in those articles that deal with a complex wealth of data—such as the articles on Buddhism, Christianity, Jainism, Judaism, or Islam—we are able to show some of the systemic lines along which religion functions. We hope that it becomes immediately apparent that the "history" of these religions is the outcome of the interaction of many mental systems. Readers who would bring in their own knowledge from other fields such as economy or social history of a world area or a certain period in time would probably be surprised how all this holds together: for it is the same human mind that produces religion, society, and artifacts, and in the mind the productive processes are inseparable. We somewhat artificially distinguish among different systems, all of them a flowering of mind. The unexpected conclusion of this *cognitive* view of religion is that a

[11] See Tertulliani, *De anima,* edited with Introduction and Commentary by J. H. Waszink (1947), p. 27.

change in the system of religion would immediately affect all other systems that create history, and thus religion actually has an enormous impact on all other human activities.

This guide aims to combine methodological sophistication with popular accessibility, and the fact that it was selected as "Great Book of the Month" in France shortly after being in print means that it succeeded in combining these two apparently opposite goals. The reason for its success consists, I believe, in the seamless way that its cognitive methodological presuppositions are integrated into the concentrated presentation of each religion or group of religions. It is left to the reader to discover, for example, that beliefs about the soul, or beliefs about Christ, are "systems" generated by the human mind, systems that tend to cover all logical alternatives offered by the terms of a certain problem. In other words, *all* religions are maps of the human mind. This explains the basic question we asked at the inception of this Introduction: Why do religions have so many things in common? The answer is: because any two maps of the human mind must by necessity overlap, at least in some corner. And the larger the maps, the more do they have in common. Religions like Christianity and Buddhism, based on monastic institutions that freed large numbers of human minds of daily cares and set them to think for extended periods of time over thousands of years, would tend to create complex maps of reality that coincide in many ways.

Therefore, what the reader will find in the pages of this book is confirmation that, no matter how bizarre some religions may appear to us at first sight, they can ultimately be understood as the dwelling of human minds on certain hypotheses concerning nature and existence, wrestling with the perennial mysteries of life, death, good and evil, human purpose, justice, and so forth. This is ultimately what our minds also do. The fundamental unity of humankind does not reside in a unity of *views or solutions,* but in the unity of the *operations* of the human mind.

This leaves us, however, with one question unanswered: What is the relevance of religion? A "guide to religion" should attempt to assess the importance of its subject matter to humankind. If indeed religion acts like "software" or a "program" within human society, then it may only be to the message of religion that society is able to respond; thus, there is hope that by transformations in the sphere of religion the impending future of societies or social groups might be reprogrammed.

Ioan P. Couliano

PART ONE

The Religions

1

African Religions

1.1 CLASSIFICATIONS. Humankind was born in Africa about six million years ago. Today the continent shelters many peoples, who speak over 800 languages, of which some 730 have been classified. The inhabitants of Africa themselves have been submitted to other classifications as well, according, for instance, to their "race" or to "cultural areas." The inadequacies of these criteria have been demonstrated over the past three decades. Although the delimitations of languages are not precise, the linguistic classification is by far preferable to any other.

In 1966 Joseph H. Greenberg proposed a division of the African continent into four large linguistic groups, composed of several families. The most important is the group called Congo-Kordofan, whose main family is the Nigero-Congolese. The Bantu languages are a subfamily of the latter. The Congo-Kordofan area covers central and southern Africa.

A second linguistic group, including the languages of the Nilotes, of western Sudan, and of the Middle Niger area is the Nilo-Saharan group.

Afro-Asian languages are spoken in North and Northeastern Africa. They include the Semitic languages of western Asia, Coptic, Berber, the Kushite languages, and the languages of Chad, such as Hausa.

The fourth group contains the languages popularly called "click," from four characteristic sounds of the language of the Bushmen. Their principal speakers are the Bushmen and the Hottentots, and their scientific name is the Khoisan languages.

Religious borders often do not follow linguistic borders. The northern countries have participated in the long history of Islam, in its Egyptian and Berber varieties, both permeated by women's possession cults, which have repeatedly been compared with the ancient Greek Dionysiac cults, and by African magic. In this Afro-Islamic syncretism, the *marabout*, receptacle of *baraka*, or spiritual force, is the main character. Before Islam, some Berber tribes had embraced Judaism, but most of them belonged to African Christianity. The moral rigorism of the Donatists fought by Augustine (354–430 C.E.) was already manifesting the particularism of the Berbers, which consists of choosing a form of religion that never coincides exactly with that of their dominators.

In West Africa the situation is different. Senegal is divided among autochthonous cults, the cross and the crescent. Moving south, African religions become dominant. In Guinea, Liberia, Ivory Coast, Sierra Leone, and Benin, syncretism prevails. The Mandés are Islamicized, but this does not apply to the Bambara, Minianka, and Seniufo. In the Nigerian confederation, African cults are powerful. The religion of the Yoruba is one of the most important of the region.

Equatorial Africa and the south, evangelized by the Portuguese and by British and Dutch Protestant missions, are prevalently syncretistic. Eastern syncretism among the Bantus is dominated by the banner of the Prophet. The Lake tribes (Azande, Nuer, Dinka, and Masai), in spite of British missionary activity, are still practicing the religion of their ancestors.

Confronted with such diversity, historians of religions have to make an uneasy choice. They can take an aerial view, without landing anywhere, as B. Holas did in his *Religions de l'Afrique Noire* (1964); they can deal with the subject phenomenologically, without giving any importance to geographic and historical divisions, as was done by Benjamin Ray in his *African Religions* (1976); or they can pick up a few representative religions from different areas and describe them individually and contrastively, as was done by Noel Q. King in his *African Cosmos* (1986). Each one of these options has its advantages and disadvantages. We will here borrow elements from the three of them.

Before proceeding any further, however, we must ascertain that two traits, although not universal, are shared by many African religions: the belief in a Supreme Being, often a *deus otiosus* (inactive deity) who withdrew from human affairs and consequently is not actively present at human rituals; and divination in two forms—by spirit possession and by varying geomantic methods that seem to come from the Arabs.

1.2 RELIGIONS OF WESTERN AFRICA.

1.2.1 The religion of the Yoruba, practiced by over fifteen million people in Nigeria and the surrounding countries such as Benin, is probably the largest African religion. Its inexhaustible subtleties have recently been explored by a relatively fair number of scholars.

At the beginning of the century the Yoruba community was still dominated by a secret brotherhood that nominated the highest representative of public power: the king. Before his nomination, the king was not aware of the proceedings, for he was not a member of the Ogboni brotherhood.

Being a member of this exclusive club means talking a secret language not understood by the uninitiated and practicing forms of hieratic and monumental art that have little in common with exoteric Yoruba art. Cloaked by the secret of initiation, the internal Ogboni cult remains mysterious. It is centered around Onile, the Great Mother Goddess of *ile,* that is, the elemental world in its chaotic state, before having been organized. The *ile* is opposed on the one hand to *orun,* heaven as an organizational principle, and on the other to *aiye,* the inhabited world, which stems from the intervention of *orun* in *ile.* Whereas everyone knows what the inhabitants of the *orun* look like, as well as the *orisa,* who are the object of exoteric cults, and likewise the *deus otiosus* Olorun, who has no cult, the presence of *ile* in Yoruba life is mysterious, troubling, and ambivalent. The goddess Yemoja was fecundated by her own son Orungan, and the products of the incest were numerous gods and spirits. Yemoja was the mistress of the Yoruba witches, who took her as a role model because of her extraordinary, tortuous life story. Infertility, represented by the goddess Olokun, wife of Odudua, is likewise associated with witchcraft.

The organized world stays away from *ile.* The creator god is Obatala, whose specialty is shaping the embryo in the maternal uterus. Together with him, the *orun* has sent into the *aiye* the oracular god Orunmila, whose divination tools are present in every traditional Yoruba house. *Ifa* divination is a form of geomancy stemming from the Arabs. It has sixteen basic figures, whose combinations give the forecast. Diviners are not supposed to interpret the verdict. They simply recite verses belonging to a traditional repertory, not unlike the commentaries of the *I Ching,* the ancient book of Chinese divination. The more verses he knows, the more the diviner is repected by his customers.

Another important *orisa* is Esu the Trickster, small and ithyphallic (with erect penis). He provokes laughter, but he is a great cheater. It is important to have him on one's side, and therefore the Yorubans propitiate him with animal sacrifices and offerings of palm wine.

The patron of blacksmiths, whose status throughout Africa is very special, implying at the same time isolation and suspicion but also ambivalent magic powers, is the warrior god Ogùn. The same ambivalence surrounds twins. In numerous African worldviews, the anomaly of twin birth is either interpreted as a breach in the harmony of the universe, in which case one or both of the twins might be suppressed, or as an exceedingly auspicious event, in which case twins are venerated. The Yoruba combine these two positions by saying that their original attitude was suppression of twins, but an oracle enjoined them to bestow special reverence on them.

If Obatala makes the body, it is Olodumare who blows into it the spirit (*emi*). At death, the components of the human being return to the *orisa,* who allot them to newborn infants. Some components are, on the other hand, everlasting, for spirits can come back to the earth and take possession of an Egungun dancer. The latter delivers the message of the deceased to the living.

Combining joy with fright, the Gelede dance is performed in the marketplace in honor of women ancestors, the terrifying goddesses who need to be placated and propitiated.

1.2.2 The religion of the Akan. The Akan, neighbors of the Yoruba, speak a Twi language, belonging like the Yoruban language to the Kwa group. They form a dozen independent kingdoms in Ghana and Ivory Coast, among which the most important is the kingdom of the Asante, or Ashanti. Their clanic structure, consisting of eight matrilineal units, does not coincide with their political structure. Like the Yoruba, the Asante have their heavenly *deus otiosus,* Nyame, who flees the human world because of the unbearable noise made by women while beating yams into a paste. At Asante houses, Nyame has his own little altar on a tree. As a creator god, he is constantly invoked in prayer, together with the earth goddess Asase Yaa.

The Asante worship both the personal divinities called *abosom* and the impersonal ones called *asuman,* and call upon their ancestors (*asaman*) with the aid of special wooden stools blackened with blood and other matters. The royal house has its own black stools that receive periodic offerings. The royal institution of the Asante consists of a king (Asantehene) and a queen (Ohenemmaa), who is neither his wife nor his mother, but simply the representative of the matrilineal group that cuts through the political structure.

The central religious festival of all of the Akan kingdoms is Apo, a time of reflection on the ancestors, accompanied by purifying and propitiatory ceremonies.

1.2.3 The Worldview of the Bambara and Dogon of Mali. Germaine Dieterlen wrote the following in 1951, in her *Essai sur la religion bambara:*

> At least nine peoples of unequal importance (the Dogon, the Bambara, the Blacksmiths, the Kurumba, the Bozo, the Mandingo, the Samogo, the Mosi and the Kule) share the same metaphysical, if not religious, background. They have in common the theme of creation through an initially immobile Word, whose vibration slowly determines first the essence and then the existence of all things; and the same applies to the conic spiral movement of the universe. They have the same conception of the person as well as of primordial twinhood as an expression of perfect unity. All of them believe in the intervention of a hypostasis of the divinity who often takes the shape of a Redeemer and world ruler who appears among all these peoples in identical form. All of them believe in the necessity of universal harmony, as well as in the internal harmony of all beings, the two being connected. One of the consequences of this notion is the subtle mechanism producing the disorder which, in absence of a better word, we call impurity, matched by a well developed set of cathartic practices.

In the cosmogony of the Dogon, the archetypes of space and time are first a numerical code in the bosom of the heavenly god Amma. Actual space and time are brought into being by the Trickster Yurugu, the Pale Fox. In another version, the universe and human beings were created by a helicoidal (spiral-like) vibration expanding from a center at a rate indicated by seven segments of increasing length. The Dogon worldview is defined by two parallel operations: cosmicization of the human being and anthropomorphization of the universe. Consequently, as G. Calame-Griaule asserts in her *Anthropologie et language,* "[T]he Dogon looks for his own reflection in all the mirrors of an anthropomorphic universe in which every blade of grass and every beetle are carriers of a human 'word' (*parole*)." The word has paramount importance among the Bambara, as Dominique Zahan emphasizes in his *Dialectique du verbe chez les Bambara:* "The word (*verbe*) establishes . . . a connection between humans and their God as well as a link between the objective, concrete world and the world of subjective representation." Pronouncing a word is like giving birth to a child. Several operations and instruments serve to ease the birth of the word through the mouth: pipe and tobacco, cola nuts, the filing of the teeth, tooth rubber, and tattooing of the mouth. Giving birth to the word is no safe endeavor, for it breaks the perfection of silence. Silence, leaving secrets unspoken, has initiatory value. In the beginning, language was not necessary, for all that existed was integrated into an "unheard word," a continuous drone passed by Bemba, the rude, phallic, treelike creator of the origins, to the refined, celestial, and water-related Faro. Muso Koroni, Bemba's wife, who had borne him the plants and the animals, became jealous of her husband, for he would have intercourse with all the women of the human race created by Faro. This is why she betrayed him in her turn, and for this Bemba pursued her and, catching her, choked her in anger. Out of this violent treatment inflicted on his adulterous wife by the adulterous husband, language itself—resounding silently yet continuously into the present—is intermittently *choked* so that the sonorous stream is cut into pieces and thus words are born. Like the Dogon, the Bambara believe in a process of decay of humankind, a process of which articulate language is only one of the signs. In every individual the decay is made manifest by the *wanzo,* disorderly femininity connected with witchcraft. The perfect human being is androgynous. The visible support of the *wanzo* is the foreskin. Circumcision deprives the androgyne of femininity. Lacking femininity now, the male goes in search of a wife: this is how community comes into being. Physical circumcision takes place during the *n'domo,* the first initiation of childhood. The last among the six *dyow* or initiations, the *kore,* is meant to restore the man's spiritual femininity, making him androgynous again, and thus perfect. The *n'domo* marks the access of the individual to social existence; the *kore* marks the retreat out of society, in order to join divine wholeness and spontaneity. The Dogon and the Bambara have built on their myths and rituals a complete "architecture of knowledge," subtle and complex.

1.3 EAST AFRICAN RELIGIONS. The East African area has one hundred million inhabitants belonging to the four main linguistic groups previously mentioned (1.1) and forming over two hundred different societies. A simplified Swahili serves as *lingua franca,* yet most natives speak Bantu languages. This applies to the Ganda, Nkore, Soga, and Gisu in Uganda, to the Kikuyu and Kamba in Kenya, and to the Kaguru and Gogo in Tanzania. The religions of the Bantu people have a few traits in common, such as the character of *deus otiosus* of the creator, who, with the exception of the Kikuyu, is viewed as a remote figure who does not have any part in everyday events. Consequently, his presence in ritual is generally reduced. The active divinities are the heroes and the ancestors, often consulted in their sanctuaries by mediums who are supposed to communicate with them in a state of trance. In principle, spirits of the dead can likewise possess a medium. This is why it is imperative to placate them by making periodic offerings to them. Certain rituals are meant to rid society of states of impurity contracted through the willing or unwilling transgression of norms that make up order.

Divination by simplified geomancy occurs among most peoples of eastern Africa. It is practiced in order to help make decisions consisting of a binary choice (of the yes/no type), to find a culprit, or to foretell the future. Witchcraft is supposed to cause death, sickness, and bad luck. Divination also serves to determine the author of witchcraft in order to punish him or her. The study of the anthropologist E. E. Evans-Pritchard on the Azande shows the relationship between witchcraft and oracles.

All East African peoples know the institution of puberty initiation. Male initiations are in general more complex than female initiations. Most Bantu peoples practice circumcision and clitoridectomy and/or labiadectomy. Advanced initiations into groups of warriors are often meant to cement the unity of secret organizations, such as the Mau Mau among the Kikuyu of Kenya, which played a role in gaining Kenyan independence.

Among the Nilotic peoples of eastern Africa are the Shilluk, Nuer, and Dinka of the Republic of Sudan, and Acholi of Uganda, and the Ino of Kenya. The religion of the Nuer and Dinka is particularly well known, thanks to the extremely valuable works of E. E. Evans-Pritchard and Godfrey Lienhardt. Like other inhabitants of the Lakes (e.g., the Masai), the Nuer and the Dinka are transhumant cattle herdsmen. This ecological circumstance is important in their religion; the first human beings and the first bovine animals were created together. Close to humankind are the spirits, who can be conjured up, and the ancestors.

In both societies the role of communicating with the invisible forces falls to the specialists of the sacred: the Leopard-Priests among the Dinka and the Masters of the Harpoon among the Nuer, who perform ox sacrifices in order to deliver the collectivity from pollution and the individual from illness. The Nuer and Dinka prophets are characters possessed by the spirits.

1.4 RELIGIONS OF CENTRAL AFRICA.

1.4.1 Religions of the Bantu. Some ten million Bantu live in central Africa, in the Congo river basin, covering an area that stretches from Tanzania in the east to Congo in the west. Among them the best known are the Ndembu and the Lele, due to the work of Victor Turner (*The Forest of Symbols*, 1967; *The Drums of Affliction*, 1968) and Mary Douglas (*The Lele of the Kasai*, 1963).

At the center of Bantu religions are spirit cults and propitiatory magical rituals. Connected to the former are the secret initiatory societies among such people as the Ndembu, but also the more widely spread institutions of the royal oracles and "cults of affliction," which consist of the ritual exorcism of "afflicted" spirits who possess human beings. Often spirits of marginal individuals belonging to other ethnic groups, they would ask the medium to speak their language. Witchcraft as a women's institution is not universal among the Bantu.

The creator god, who is beyond gender, has usually become a *deus otiosus*. Consequently, he has no cult, but is called upon as a witness and warrant of oaths.

1.4.2 The Pygmies of the tropical forest form three main groups: the Aka, the Baka, and the Mbuti of Ituri in Zaire, studied in the famous works of Colin Turnbull, of which the best known is *The Forest People* (1961). Aroused by Father Wilhelm Schmidt's (1868–1954) conviction that all illiterate peoples have originally monotheistic beliefs, many Catholic missionaries and anthropologists affirmed the existence, among the three groups of Pygmies, of a creator who had waned to the status of *otiosus*. But Colin Turnbull denies the belief in a creator god among the Mbuti: for them, god is the environment, the jungle. A certain poverty of ritual prevails among them, in the sense that they have no priesthood and do not practice divination. They do have rites of passage, associated with circumcision in the case of young boys and with the isolation of girls at their first menstrual period.

1.5 RELIGIONS OF SOUTHERN AFRICA. The Bantu migrated toward the south in two waves: one between 1000 and 1600 C.E. (the

Sotho, Tswana, Nguni [to which the Zulu belong], Lovendu, and Venda) and another one in the nineteenth century (the Tsonga). According to the German Africanist Leo Frobenius (1873–1938), the foundation of the ancient kingdom of Zimbabwe was connected with the ancestors of the Hungwe, coming from the north.

As portrayed in a Karanga myth, the symbolic function of sacred kingship was to realize a balance of contraries between heat and humidity, symbolized by the princesses of the wet vagina and the princesses of the dry vagina. The former were supposed to have intercourse with the great water snake, who, often under the name of Rainbow Serpent, is a supernatural being present in many mythologies of western and southern Africa. The princesses of the dry vagina were the vestals in charge of the ritual fire. In time of drought, a princess of wet vagina might be sacrificed in order to make rain.

Male initiation rites at puberty are more complex than female initiations. Circumcision is not the general rule and clitoridectomy is not practiced, although the ritual may entail simulating excision. Initiatory symbolism is based on the passage from night to day, from darkness into sunlight.

1.6 AFRO-AMERICAN RELIGIONS originated among the West African slaves of the Caribbean archipelago, of the eastern coast of South America (Surinam, Brazil), and of the eastern coast of North America.

1.6.1 The Afro-Caribbean cults are, together with the Afro-Guyanese religions, authentically African, despite the fact that they borrowed from Catholicism a number of names and notions. Haitian Voodoo, whose role in the winning of that country's independence is well known, is a possession cult centered around deities (*lwas*) of Fon and Yoruba origin, whereas the spirits conjured up in Cuban Santería and Trinidadian Shango are the Yoruban *orisas* (1.2.1). In all three cases, bloody sacrifices and ecstatic dances culminating in trance are performed, serving as a means of communication between humans and gods. The gods sometimes have African names, sometimes names of Catholic saints, yet always authentically African traits. The network of Voodoo covers the whole of Haitian society, with its witchcraft and counterwitchcraft, with its secrets and its occult fame.

The ancestors are worshiped in many syncretistic cults such as the Kumina, the Convince, and the Kromanti dance of the Jamaican maroons (fugitive slaves), the Big Drum Dance of the islands of Grenada and Carriacu, the Kele of Santa Lucia, and so forth.

In several other cults, such as that of the Jamaican Myalists, the Shouter Baptists of Trinidad, and the Saint-Vincent Shakers, the Christian component prevails over the African.

The Jamaican Rastafarians are in the first place a millenarian movement. They are usually identified through dreadlocks, reggae music, and the use of marijuana, grounded in a philosophy that has many adepts in Western as well as in African countries.

Taking inspiration from Psalm 68:32, some Afro-Jamaicans discerned in Ethiopia the Promised Land, and their movement became political when the Ethiopian prince (Ras) Tafari (whence "Rastafarian") was crowned emperor of Abyssinia in 1930 under the name of Haile Selassie. With time, and especially with the death of the emperor, the movement broke into several groups that share neither ideologies nor political hopes.

1.6.2 Afro-Brazilian cults originated around 1850 from a mix of sources, yet contain true African elements such as possession by the *orixa* deities and ecstatic dances. In the northeast the cult is called Candomblé; in the southeast, Macumba. The Rio de Janeiro Umbanda has become very popular since 1925–1930. Originally forbidden, possession cults today represent a vital component of Brazilian religious life.

1.6.3 The Afro-Guyanese religions appeared in Surinam (former Dutch Guyana) among the Creole population of the coast and likewise among the maroons who had fled to the interior of the country. The religion of the coastal Creoles has the name Winti or *afkodré* (from the Dutch *afgoderij*, "idolatry"). The two preserve ancient and authentic African beliefs.

1.6.4 African Americans. The religious life of the Africans of the United States of America is particularly known for its intensity. However, subject to an evangelization that was more intense and efficacious than elsewhere, the African Americans did not keep intact much of their African religious heritage. The idea of a return to Africa was successfully preached among them by the American Colonization Society starting in 1816 and, in different tones, by several black churches from 1900 on. While many black churches today are marked by a vivid spiritual and ritual life, and by effective social activism, numerous African Americans, disappointed by past and present Christian church attitudes, have embraced other religious faiths such as Judaism and especially Islam. Today two principal Muslim denominations exist among African Americans, both stemming from the Nation of Islam founded by Elijah Muhammad (Elijah Poole, 1897–1975) in 1934, originating in an organization called into being by a Muslim (Wallace D. Fard) and also benefiting from the favorable climate created by another parallel organization, the Moorish Science Temple of Noble Drew Ali (Timothy Drew, 1886–1929), and by the missionary propaganda of the Indian Ahmadiyah, begun in 1920. In 1964 the splinter group Muslim Mosque of Malcolm X (Malcolm Little, 1925–1965) detached itself from the Nation of Islam and became independent. After the death of Elijah Muhammad in 1975, his son Warithuddin (Wallace Deen) Muhammad changed the Nation of Islam into an organization affiliated with orthodox (Sunnite) Islam, under the name of American Muslim Mission. The Nation of Islam, led by the Chicago minister Louis Farrakhan, continues in the direction traced by Elijah Muhammad.

1.7 BIBLIOGRAPHY. On African religions in general, see B. C. Ray, "African Religions: An Overview," in *ER* 1, 60–69; E. M. Zuesse, "Mythical Themes," in *ER* 1, 70–82; B. Jules-Rosette, "Modern Movements," in *ER* 1, 82–89; V. Grottanelli, "History of Study," in *ER* 1, 89–96. See also B. Holas, *Religions du Monde: L'Afrique Noire* (1964); Benjamin C. Ray, *African Religions: Symbol, Ritual, and Community* (1976); Noel Q. King, *African Cosmos: An Introduction to Religion in Africa* (1986). A good collection of African religious texts has been assembled by L. V. Thomas and R. Luneau, *Les religions de l'Afrique Noire: Textes et traditions sacrées*, 2 vols. (1981).

On West African religions, see H. A. Witte, *Symboliek van de aarde bij de Yoruba*, (1982); Marcel Griaule, *Dieu d'Eau* (1966); M. Griaule and G. Dieterlen, *Le Renard Pâle* (1965); G. Dieterlen, *Essai sur la religion bambara* (1951); Geneviève Calame-Griaule, *Ethnologie et langage: La parole chez les Dogon* (1965); Dominique Zahan, *La dialectique du verbe chez les Bambara* (1963); D. Zahan, *Sociétés d'initiation Bambara: Le N'domo, le Koré* (1960).

On East African religions, see W. A. Shack, "East African Religions: An Overview," in *ER* 4, 541–52; B. C. Ray, "Northeastern Bantu Religions," in *ER* 4, 552–57; J. Beattie, "Interlacustrine Bantu Religion," in *ER* 7, 263–66; J. Middleton, "Nuer and Dinka Religion," in *ER* 11, 10–12; E. E. Evans-Pritchard, *Nuer Religion* (1956); E. E. Evans-Pritchard, *Witchcraft Oracles and Magic among the Azande,* (1980, 1937); Godfrey Lienhardt, *Divinity and Experience: The Religion of the Dinka* (1961).

On central African religions, see E. Colson, "Central Bantu Religion," in *ER* 3, 171–78; S. Bacuchet and J. M. C. Thomas, "Pygmy Religion," in *ER* 12, 107–10; Colin M. Turnbull, *The Forest People: A Study of the Pygmies of the Congo* (1962).

On southern African religions, see M. Wilson, "Southern African Religions," in *ER* 13, 530–38; L. de Heusch, "Southern Bantu Religions," in *ER* 13, 539–46.

On Afro-American religions, see G. Eaton-Simpson, "Afro-Caribbean Religions," in *ER* 3, 90–98; Alfred Métraux, *Le vaudou haïtien* (1958); A. J. Raboteau, "Afro-American Religions: An Overview," in *ER* 1, 96–100; A. J. Raboteau, "Muslim Movements," in *ER* 1, 100–102; Y. Maggie, "Afro-Brazilian Cults," in *ER* 1, 102–5; R. Price, "Afro-Surinamese Religions," in *ER* 1, 105–7.

2

Australian Religions

2.1 ABORIGINAL RELIGIONS. In the northern regions of Australia, in Arnhem Land, and in the center of the continent, the aboriginal religions have resisted acculturation. They show numerous common traits.

The aborigines know a creator god who withdraws into the distant realm of heaven, where human beings cannot reach him. He does not leave his mysterious dwelling except to be present at the most sacred initiations. Consequently, the aborigine does not call upon this *deus otiosus* (inactive diety) in the circumstances of daily life, but on the cultural hero and on the autogenous beings of the "dreamtime," the time of the beginnings (*alchera* or *alcheringa*). These beings are celestial and circulate freely between the earth and the sky, using to this effect a ladder or a tree. They are the authors of a "second creation," i.e., of the inhabited world. The geography of this world is sacred. Each human being can still see, in a rock or in a tree, the traces of the presence of these primordial beings, who subsequently disappeared either in the bowels of the earth or in the sky, withdrawing the bridge between heaven and earth. These two levels of space, which are actually two different ontological realms, have thus been completely and irremediably separated.

The aborigines learn the world's sacred history during initiations and during meetings of the secret initiatory cults (the Kunapipi and the Djangawwul). Puberty initiations are not always connected with circumcision or subincision, but they invariably pass fundamental mythological knowledge on to the neophyte.

Puberty rites are more complex among boys than among girls reaching their first menstrual period. Although circumcision is not universal in Australia, the boy always meets symbolic death, accompanied by ritual wounds. Sprinkled with blood, he enters a state of lethargy during which he is supposed to remember, in a sort of anamnesis, the sacred origins of the world. The secret cult Kunapipi is generally based on the mythological cycle of the Wawilak sisters, who received secret knowledge from the great phallic Serpent. After the creation of the universe and the creation of the inhabited world, this was the "third creation": the creation of the cultural space of the aborigines.

The same scheme of ritual death and rebirth is more strongly emphasized in shamanic initiations. The candidate is "killed" and "operated upon" by the college of medicine men, who replace his internal organs with mineral organs that are not perishable. During this time the soul of the neophyte is supposed to be on a Dantesque journey through heaven and hell. Reassembled, the body of the new shaman enjoys special faculties.

In most mythical components of initiation, the Rainbow Serpent plays an important part. In the ponds where he lives, the Rainbow Serpent guards the quartz crystals from the dreamtime and the heavenly world, crystals that are supposed to replace the mineral organs of the new shaman. The Water Serpent Wonambi, in the western deserts, is supposed to kill the neophyte. In Queensland he dispatches into their bodies his stick or a piece of bone, which the medicine men extract a few days later, during the process of "reanimation" of the future shaman. The magical substances cross the distance from heaven to earth over the back of the rainbow. This is why it is forbidden to bathe in a pond or in a puddle over which the end of the rainbow has passed, for one could easily steal the magical crystals from the water.

Death among the aborigines is considered the result of witchcraft. The funerary ritual entails the punishment of the presumed murderer. The dead one, like the shaman, travels to heaven; yet, unlike the shaman, the dead one can no longer make use of the physical body.

2.2 BIBLIOGRAPHY. M. Eliade, *Australian Religions* (1970); A. P. Elkin, "The Australian Aborigines: An Overview" in *ER* 1, 529–47; C. H. Berndt, "Mythic Themes," in *ER* 1, 547–62; S. A. Wild, "Mythic Themes," in *ER* 1, 562–66; K. Maddock, "History of Study," in *ER* 1, 566–70.

3

Buddhism

3.1 THE VAST LITERATURE OF BUDDHISM can be classified according to the traditional division of the *tripiṭaka,* the "threefold basket" of sūtra (the *logia* [sayings] of the Buddha himself), *vinaya* (discipline), and *abhidharma* (doctrine). To these one should add the numerous *śāstras,* systematical tractates by known authors, the *jātakas,* or Lives of the Buddha, and so forth.

Three *tripiṭakas* are extant: the incomplete one of the Theravāda monks of Southeast Asia, composed in the Pali language; that of the Sartvāstivāda and of the Mahāsāṃghika in Chinese translation; and finally the Tibetan collections (the Kanjur and the Tanjur), which are the most complete. Many writings in Sanskrit have been preserved as well.

The Buddha had encouraged his disciples to use their own dialects. Pali, the language of the Theravāda canon, was one of these dialects belonging to the Avanti province, not the original language in which the Buddha taught. This is why the use of Pali terminology is not always justified over the use of Buddhist Sanskrit, a form of Sanskrit containing many Prakrit words.

3.2 THE BUDDHA, whose name means, in both Pali and Sanskrit, "The Enlightened One," was in all probability a historical character. Yet, in his Lives, or *jātakas,* mythology prevails to the point where it transforms the Buddha into a prototype of the "divine man" according to Indian tradition (18.3), who has numerous traits in common with perfect men in other religious traditions, for example, the Greek *theioi andres* or subsequent founders of religions such as Jesus, Mani, and others. It is, of course, impossible to detach the historical elements from the purely mythical ones. Yet quite a few data seem to be real. The Buddha was probably the son of a minor king of the Śākya clan of northwestern India. The dating of his birth varies between 624 and 448 B.C.E. Legend has it that his mother died a few days after delivery, yet not without having had all possible premonitions concerning the birth of a miraculous being. According to the docetic versions of the Buddha's origins, his conception and gestation were immaculate, his birth was virgin, and his body bore all the marks of a World King.

At sixteen, Prince Siddhārtha married two princesses and led a carefree existence in the paternal palace. Yet, venturing out of the palace three times, he encountered the three inescapable evils that afflict humankind: age, pain, and death. Emerging once more, he perceived their remedy: the peace and serenity of a begging ascetic. Awaking in the middle of the night, he received another lesson in the impermanence of the world, taught to him by the flaccid, corpselike bodies of his sleeping concubines. Horrified, the prince left the palace in haste and became an ascetic under the name of Gautama. After having abandoned two masters who taught him something akin to yoga philosophy and practice, he engaged in severe mortifications of the body together with five disciples. Having realized the uselessness of such relentless asceticism, he accepted a rice offering and ate it. His disciples saw in this gesture a proof of weakness and abandoned him. Sitting under a fig tree, Śākyamuni (the ascetic of the Śākya clan) decided not to get up before receiving the Awakening. He underwent the assaults of Māra, a character who united in himself the traits we might attribute to Death and to the devil. At dawn he defeated Māra, thus becoming the Buddha, now in possession of the Four Truths, which he taught in Benares to the same disciples who had abandoned him. The first Truth was that everything is suffering (*sarvaṃ duhkhaṃ*): "birth is suffering, decay is suffering, sickness is suffering," everything impermanent is suffering. The second Truth was that suffering originates from desire (*taṅhā*). The third Truth was that suppression of desire entails suppression of suffering. The fourth Truth was the revelation of the Eightfold Path (*aṣṭapāda*), or the Middle Way, which leads to extinction of suffering: correct (*samyak-*) seeing, view (*dṛsti*), resolve, determination, or intent (*saṃkalpa*), word (*vāk*), action (*karmanta*), means of existence (*ajiva*), effort (*vyayama*), attention (*smṛti*), and contemplation (*samādhi*). This seemed to be the form closest to the original message of the Buddha.

After this first sermon of Benares, the community (*saṃgha*) of converts grew spectacularly, attracting brahmans, kings, and ascetics. Too many of them, to the tastes of the Awakened One, who was pressed to open monasticism to women. He predicted on that occasion the decline of the Law (*dharma*). The Buddha was not spared the jealousy of rivals, nor absurd disputes between monks. According to certain sources, his cousin Devadatta tried to kill him in order to become his successor at the head of the *saṃgha*. Yet the Buddha escaped, to die at eighty of indigestion. Such details, insist the scholars, are too embarrassing to be invented. Consequently, they may be historically accurate.

3.3 SHORT HISTORY. After the funerals of the Buddha (*parinirvāṇa*), his successor became Mahākāśyapa and not the faithful disciple and secretary Ānanda, who, having been for twenty years in the direct service of the Awakened One, had never had the leisure to master meditation in order to become an *arhat,* that is, a Buddhalike being who has attained *nirvāṇa* and will never come back again into the cycle of metensomatosis, or reincarnation. When Mahākāśyapa invited the *arhats* to attend the Council of Rājagṛha, Ānanda is not included. Apart from the world, practicing in loneliness, Ānanda rapidly obtained mastery of the yogic techniques, becoming an *arhat.* He appeared at the council, reciting the sūtras, whereas another disciple, Upali, would commit to posterity the rules of discipline (*vinaya*) learned from the Buddha. Indian Buddhism, along with other rising ascetic movements, challenged the complacent and stratified Hindu society.

What, according to these venerable documents, was the original form of the Buddha's preaching?

Contrary to what many scholars have asserted, Buddhism is not "pessimistic." Originally, it was a doctrine unparalleled among all world religions, a doctrine in first instance *negative,* not affirmative. The way of the Buddha is the way of the annihilation of the Self and thus of the world of phenomena. All the certainties that the Buddha, in his exemplary mistrust of all metaphysics, would allow, are negative. This is why those who love logical rigor may have perceived a subtle kinship between his method and that of certain neopositivists, particularly the philosopher Ludwig Wittgenstein.

In this respect, one of the most enlightening examples is that of the monk Malunkyaputta (*Majjhima Nikāya,* sūtta 63), upset by the fact that the Buddha would preach at the same time "that the world is eternal and the world is not eternal, that the world is finite and that it is infinite, that soul and body are identical and that they are not identical, that the *arhat* exists after death and the *arhat* does not exist after death, that he both exists and does not exist after death, that he neither exists nor does not exist. . . . " Asking the Buddha to explain this puzzle, the monk obtained the following answer: "It is as if a man had been wounded by a poisoned arrow and, while his family and friends would all hasten to find him a doctor, this man would say: 'I will not have the arrow removed before I know if the one who wounded me is a warrior, a brahman, a vaiśya or a śūdra . . . ; his name and to what clan he belongs . . . ; whether he is tall, average or short . . . ; whether he is black, brown or yellow . . . ,'" and so on.

In the same way, when the itinerant ascetic Vaccha enumerated all the above-mentioned theses and their antitheses in an attempt to understand the doctrine of the Buddha, the Awakened One rejected both theses and antitheses, proclaiming himself "free of any theory." Confronted with the perplexity of Vaccha, who reasoned according to the terms of a simplistic logic (if A is not true, then non-A must be true), the Buddha asked him if he could answer the following question: Where did an extinguished fire go—east, west, south, or north? Upon the interlocutor's recognition of his own ignorance, the Buddha compares the *arhat* with an extinguished fire: any statement concerning his existence would be purely conjectural (*Majjhima Nikāya,* sūtra 72).

For the same reason that had led him to the rejection of all theories, the Buddha opposed the brahmanic doctrine of the Self (*ātman*) as an invariable element of the human compound, without thereby stating the opposite, that is, that death leads to the complete annihilation of the *arhat* (*Samyutta Nikāya* 22, 85). Like everything else, what we call *arhat* is a simple linguistic convention (cf. *Milindapaña* 25), having no real existence. This is why the only actors in the universe are Suffering and Extinction:

> There is only Suffering, there is no sufferer.
> There is no agent, there is only the action.
> *Nirvāṇa* exists, not the one looking for it.
> The Way exists, not the one walking on it.
>
> (*Visuddhi Magga* 16)

Managing not to be trapped in the dead end of philosophical speculation, the preaching of the Buddha aimed at salvation. In the law of "conditioned production" (*pratītya samutpāda: Samyutta Nikāya* 22, 90), the Buddha derived every cosmic process from ignorance (*avidyā*) and all salvation from the cessation of ignorance: "It is Ignorance which produces Innate Information (*samskāra*); it is Innate Information which produces Consciousness (*vijñāna*); it is Consciousness which produces the Names-and-Forms (*nāma-rūpa*); it is the Names-and-Forms which produce the six Sensory Organs (*ṣadatyayana*); it is Sensation which produces Desire (*tṛṣṇa*); it is Desire which produces Attachment (*upadana*); it is Attachment which produces Existence (*bhāva*); it is Existence which produces Birth (*jāti*); it is Birth which produces Old Age and Death (*jaramarana*)." The remedy for old age and death is thus the cessation of ignorance, whose equivalent is the adoption of the Buddha, of his law (*dharma*), and of his community (*saṃgha*).

After the second council held at Vaiśālī, the saṃgha split into two major groups, which through further splits led to the complex system of the Buddhist sects briefly examined below.

The emperor Aśoka (274/268–236/234 B.C.E.), grandson of Candragupta (ca. 320–296 B.C.E.), the founder of the Maurya dynasty, converted to Buddhism and sent missions to Bactria, Sogdiana, and Śri Lankā (Ceylon). The success of the last one was astonishing, for the Sinhalese have remained Buddhist until the present day. From Bengal and Śri Lankā, Buddhism conquered Indochina and the Indonesian islands (first century C.E.). By way of Kashmir and eastern Iran, Buddhism was propagated in Central Asia and in China (first century C.E.), in Korea and in Japan (552 or 538 C.E.). In the seventh century C.E. it put down roots in Tibet.

From 100 to 250 C.E. a new form of Buddhism appeared, which was advanced as a means of liberation superior to any previous doctrine. It proclaimed itself to be Mahāyāna, or the Great Vehicle, reserving to the Buddhism of the past the title of Hīnayāna, or Lesser Vehicle. Although originally slightly contemptuous, this *terminus technicus* can still be used in the chronology and taxonomy of Buddhism, provided it is exempt of any pejorative connotation. The process by which Mahāyāna Buddhism came into being is not entirely known, but a period of transition around 100 C.E. has produced many important texts. Toward the seventh century C.E., Mahāyāna Buddhism lost its vitality. It soon saw the rise of Tantric Buddhism, of which Vajrayāna, or Diamond Vehicle, was a variant. Tantrism reached China as early as 716 C.E.

Mahāyāna and Vajrayāna were taught in Indian university centers, of which the most important were Nālaṇḍā and Vikramaśīla. With the destruction of these centers in 1197 and 1203 C.E. by the Turkish conquerors, Buddhism practically disappeared from India. It is difficult to explain its withdrawal before Islam, when Hinduism and Jainism continued to exist. Yet, in the same way that Buddhism had undergone the strong influence of Hinduism, so Hinduism would assimilate numerous Buddhist ideas and practices. We will come later (3.7–10) to the destiny of Buddhism in Asia.

3.4 HĪNAYĀNA BUDDHISM. From a systemic viewpoint, Hīnayāna Buddhism is an extremely interesting case, which should be compared with other systems with multiple branching (or sect formation) such as Jainism, Christianity, and Islam. Needless to say, doctrinal conflict was a fundamental dimension of the system, the potentialities of which were latent, sometimes discernible, from the outset. Thus, it is hardly helpful to transpose it into an economic or sociopolitical key. Whatever its stake, the religious "program" preceded its result on the stage of human history, and perpetuated itself in religious terms. Its interlocking with other subsystems that are part of history was inevitable.

The system of Hīnayāna sects was complicated and several links are missing for a reconstruction. However, like the other religions we mentioned, Buddhism ended up establishing a dichotomy between a "poor" and a "rich" tradition, between an *anthropic* and a *transcendental* tendency. The first emphasized the human dimension of the founder, the second his divine dimension.

The first schism within Buddhism took place at Pāṭaliputra, after the second council of Vaiśālī and before the reign of Aśoka Maurya. At stake was the quality of the *arhat:* Was he beyond defilement, or was he still fallible? In the five contended issues, the "rich" tradition defended the fallibility of the *arhat*, whereas the "poor" tradition, more conservative, wanted the *arhat* to be perfect. Debated was whether the *arhat* was still subject to temptation in dreams, whether he still had residual ignorance, whether he had doubts concerning faith, whether he could be helped in the pursuit of truth, and whether he could reach ultimate Truth by the exclamation "Aho!" The two parties were willing to compromise on four of the five points under discussion, but the community split over the delicate issue of the *arhat's* nocturnal pollutions, the majority of the *saṃgha* (whence Mahāsāṃghika) maintaining that the *arhat* could still be seduced by goddesses in dreaming, whereas the "Ancients" (Sthāviras, whence Sthāviravādins) opposed this view. Thenceforth the Sthāviravādins represented the anthropic tendency and the Mahāsāṃghikas the transcendental tendency within Buddhism.

A further split occurred among the Sthāviravādins concerning the concept of "person" (*pudgala*) and its relation to the five agregates (*skandhas*) that compose the human being, namely: *rūpa* (qualities comparable to the Aristotelian "Forms"), *vedanā* (Sensibility), *samjñā* (Perception), *saṃskāra* (Innate Information), and *vijñāna* (Consciousness). The orthodox Sthāviravādins held *pudgala* to be a mere linguistic convention without any reality whatsoever, whereas the disciples of Vātsīputra (Vātsīputrīyas) asserted that *pudgala* was neither identical with nor separated from the five *skandhas,* neither among them nor outside them. Yet *pudgala* was a quintessence that transmigrated from body to body. Vātsīputra's opponents were entitled to claim that he surreptitiously reinstated the ancient brahmanic concept of *ātman* (soul), which the Buddha had repudiated.

Fifty years later, two other schools came out of the stem of the Mahāsaṃgha: the Ekavyāvahārikas, who believed that the Intellect was by its nature above any defilement, and the Gokulikas (several variants of their name exist), who believed the five *skandhas* to be nil.

It is possible that the last edict of Emperor Aśoka Maurya (237 B.C.E.), who took the part of the Sthāviravādins, alluded to the expulsion from the community of the Ancients of a few monks who formed the nucleus of one of the most important Hīnayāna sects: the Sarvāstivādins (from *sarvam asti,* "everything is"). In the Sarvāstivāda doctrine, all *dharmas,* or phenomena, be they past or future, had a real existence. On the contrary, the orthodox Ancients held both the past and the future as nonexistent, whereas a further division from the same branch, the Kāśyapīyas or Survasakas, held only those past actions as existent which had not yet produced their effects.

The proliferation of contradictory *abhidharmas* (commentaries to the sūtras) led to four new schools stemming from the Vātsīputrīyas: the Dharmottarīyas, the Bhadrayanīyas, the Sammitīyas and the Ṣaṇṇagarika. Only the *abhidharma* of the Sammitīyas has been preserved, holding *pudgala* for a mere concept.

Another debate concerning *abhidharmas* led to a split among the Gokulikas and to the appearance of two new sects: the Bahuśrutīyas, who already made the distinction, so important in Mahāyāna Buddhism, between Buddha's "earthly" teachings and his "transcendental" teachings; and the Prajñaptivādins (*prajñapti,* "concept"), for whom all existence was a mere concept.

Even closer to what was to be the Mahāyāna were the "Transcendentals" (Lokottara), who separated themselves from the Mahāsāṃghikas. The Buddha was a whole being, for them, was completely transcendental (*lokottara*); they professed a form of docetism. The system of Buddhist docetism had many points in common with the later Christian docetism.

There is no point in mentioning here the whole list of Hīnayāna sects. The famous Theravādins who settled in Śri Lankā around the mid-third century B.C.E., and whose name was simply the Pali version of the Sanskrit Sthāviravādins, were a branch of the Vibhajyavādins. It is impossible to reconstruct the whole system of sects: the information is scant and contradictory, and many links are missing. Yet, even in the absence of a complete picture, we may still discern that the historical sects were a projection of the logical relations implicit in the "packages of relationships" contained in the story of the Buddha, of the original community, and of the primitive doctrine stemming from his teachings. Other sects, which we left unmentioned, would activate such oppositions as Buddha versus *saṃgha*, *sūtra* versus *abhidharma*, transmigration versus nontransmigration of the *skandhas*, and so forth.

No matter how complex the whole system was, it is still possible to follow in it the logic of the two directions, the anthropic and the transcendental. At first sight, when they declared that the *arhat* must be beyond defilement (and not, like their opponents, that he actually *was* beyond defilement), the Sthāviravādins seemed to opt for the second tendency. But actually the Mahāsāṃghikas, in admitting the fallibility of the *arhat*, were not concerned with the humanity of the Buddha, showing that what matters was not to reach perfection by human means, but to understand that one was perfect *here and now*, in the present. It was according to this tendency that several schools of the Mahāsāṃghika evolved, in which most ideas sprouted, giving rise to the Mahāyāna.

3.5 MAHĀYĀNA BUDDHISM. The doctrine of the Mahāyāna first appeared in the literature of the Sūtras of Transcendental Gnosis (*prajñāpāramitā*), whose origins were around 100 C.E. The passage from Hīnayāna to Mahāyāna was actually a *change in the ideal of Buddhist perfection*. Whereas the aspiration of the adept of Hinayāna Buddhism was to become an *arhat*, a being who would never abandon the state of *nirvāṇa*, and never return into the abominable *saṃsāra*, or cycle of reincarnations, the adept of Mahāyāna wished to become a Bodhisattva, a being who, having reached Awakening, was nevertheless ready to sacrifice his own well-being for the benefit of all living beings and thus preferred to remain in the world instead of retiring. The Bodhisattva would never be a *Pratyeka Buddha*, a silent Buddha, one who had no message for fellow beings, but an Awakened Buddha who spoke up and actively assisted humankind in need. This was definitely a new perspective, perhaps influenced, as many scholars believe, by Hindu *bhakti* devotion.

If compassion for the human beings afflicted by ignorance seems to be the main trait of the Bodhisattva ideal, Mahāyāna doctrine is mainly interested in crafting a logic able to cope with the particular Buddhist need to operate with contradictory notions without incurring contradiction. This is often called "negative logic," but in reality it is simply a non-Aristotelian logic that does not recognize the principle of the excluded third, thereby transcending both affirmation and negation at the same time. One can easily understand why certain scientists in search of a religion have recently found in Mahāyāna logic a valuable model for understanding the paradoxes of modern physics, wont to operate with non-Euclidean geometries and with the conception of multiple dimensions of space. In reality, the overlapping of the two systems is more illusory: in the case of Buddhism, it is the rejection of the simple alternative *if not A then non-A* that leads to audacious speculations, whereas physics derives its fantastic topologies from non-Euclidean spaces and from the visionaries of the Fourth Dimension such as Charles Howard Hinton (1853–1907 C.E.).

The Buddhist logic of the "third included" has multiple expressions, starting with a text of the early Mahāyāna such as the *Saddharmapuṇḍarīka,* or Lotus Sūtra, in which the Buddha as an eternal being was said not to have experienced Awakening. Indeed, not only was he always Awakened, but there was actually nothing to awaken into, for *nirvāṇa* has no substance of its own. According to the Yogācāra school, the transcendental being who was the Buddha could multiply indefinitely for the salvation of humankind, during different epochs or even the same epoch. Besides an "absolute body" (*dharmakāya*), the Mahāyāna ascribed to him an "ethereal body" (*saṃbhogakāya;* literally, "enjoyment-body"), in which the Buddha "enjoyed" his own religious merits in the Pure Land Paradise, and also a third body, the "magic body" (*nirmānakāya*), in which he dwelt in order to save humankind.

The paradoxes already present in pre- and early Mahāyāna texts received extensive treatment in the work of the quasi-legendary Nāgārjuna (around 150 C.E.), creator of the Mādhyamika system. First of all, Nāgārjuna showed active skepticism concerning all traditional philosophical opinions (*dṛṣṭi*), scrutinizing them by reductio ad absurdum, or *prasaṃga.* Through this method, he rejected brahmanic essentialism, asserting that all things are deprived of individual essence; consequently, what is is empty (*śūnya*). This ultimate truth, which is opposed to the illusory truth of daily experience, equally implies the identity in emptiness (*śūnyatā*) of *nirvāṇa* and *saṃsāra,* of the existence of phenomena consolidated into karmic cycles and of the cessation thereof.

Around 450 C.E. the Mādhyamika school split into a branch that retained only the negative lesson of Nāgārjuna, the skeptics, or Prasaṃgika, and a branch that retained only his affirmative lesson, the Svatantrika. Mādhyamika Buddhism penetrated in China and in Japan, contributing to the appearance of Ch'an (Zen) Buddhism; it declined there in the tenth century.

The other main school of Mahāyāna, the Yogācāra, stemmed from such intermediate texts as the Laṅkāvatāra Sūtra and others, which held the universe as a pure mental construct deprived of any reality, however illusory. To a certain Maitreya, who was either a historical or a purely mythical character (Maitreya was the name of the eschatological Buddha to come), was ascribed a fundamental role in the appearance of Yogācāra. The propagation of the doctrine was the work of the brothers Asaṅga and Vasubandhu, who developed the idea of *citta matra*, "everything is thought," endowing it with a psychocosmical basis in the "ethereal consciousness" (*ālayavijñāna*), a psychic hidden tank in which experiences accumulated in the form of karmic litter that determined the successive existences of the human being. In the Western world, such had been the dominant theory of early Gnosticism (9.4), a trend in radical Platonism that flourished in the second century C.E. This theory was also adopted by the late Neoplatonists. East and West alike are confronted with the same problem: how to burn up the karmic bonds that attach us to the cosmos.

3.6 TANTRIC BUDDHISM. Born under the influence of popular Hinduism, Tantric Buddhism ended up challenging Mahāyāna in the seventh century C.E., and eventually supplanting it. Several schools of Indian Tantric Buddhism are known. The most important was the Vajrayāna, or Diamond Vehicle, whose name already implied the sexual symbolism (*vajra* = thunderbolt, symbol of the phallus) that pervaded the structure of Tantrism, its multilevel "secret language." Tantric concepts shared with the mythical serpent that bites its own tail the quality of changing incessantly one into another in such a way that every text is always open to at least a double reading. For example, *bodhicitta* literally means "thought of Awakening" but is at the sexual level the secret name of sperm, and Gnosis-Woman (*prajñā*) is the partner—concrete or imaginary—of ritual sexual intercourse and at the same time the central conduit of the medulo-spinal energies according to yogic physiology. Every Tantric text is thus subject to two exegeses: in one the referent is a secret ritual, often but not always leading to a sexual union whose purpose is to obtain Awakening, and in the other the referent is purely metaphysical.

3.7 BUDDHISM IN SOUTHEAST ASIA. The type of Buddhism that took root in Southeast Asia and in Indonesia (where Islam would eventually prevail) was Theravāda Buddhism, a variant of Sthāviravāda propagated by the missions sent by Emperor Aśoka. However, Buddhism in Indochina would remain eclectic up to the fifteenth century C.E., when Theravāda orthodoxy from Śri Lankā (Ceylon) was adopted by the countries of Indochina. Sinhalese Buddhism became politically influential in the eleventh century C.E. It is interesting to note that in Burma, Thailand, Laos, Cambodia, and Vietnam the Buddha is not primarily thought of as a preacher of world renouncement, but as the *cakravartin,* the one who turns the Wheel of Dharma, the World Sovereign. Buddhism lived in symbiosis with Indochinese politics. This explains the building of magnificent monuments with an edifying purpose, true encyclopedias made of stone, which summarize the doctrine and the initiatory path that led to Awakening.

Faced with Western colonialism, Buddhism was to confer upon the peoples of Indochina a strong sense of national identity, opposing at the same time the inevitable modernization of their countries. Engaged already in a process of slow erosion, Buddhism did not resist the shock of the communist revolutions that involved parts of Indochina. It is perhaps correct to assert that at the present time Southeast Asian Buddhism is moving through a critical period.

3.8 CHINESE BUDDHISM. About 130 C.E., the presence of Buddhism was already evident in Chang-an, the capital of the Han dynasty (206 B.C.E.–220 C.E.), where the dominant doctrine was a starched, scholastic Confucianism (8). In the beginning Buddhism was readily taken to be a strange Taoist sect, especially since the first correct Chinese translations of Sanskrit Buddhist texts did not appear before the end of the third century C.E., indeed making use of Taoist equivalents to translate the concepts of the new religion.

After the Huns conquered northern China, Buddhism continued to exist in the underpopulated south, among aristocrats and intellectuals like Hui-yüan (334–416), founder of Amidism (cult of Amitābha Buddha), or the Pure Land school. In the sixth century the emperor Wu Liang converted to Buddhism, which he favored at the expense of Taoism (30). But even before that period, first popular Buddhism and then Amidism returned north, in spite of the ferocious opposition from Confucianism (8). In the fifth century the great translator Kumārajīva settled down in North China.

Under the Sui and T'ang dynasties, in unified China, Buddhism prospered among all layers of society. Its pervasive expansion was the work of the Ch'an school (Japanese Zen; from the Sanskrit *dhyāna,* meditation), which taught the immanence of the Buddha as well as special techniques to obtain immediate awakening. Ch'an Buddhism claimed Bodhidharma as its founder, the twenty-fourth patriarch of Indian Buddhism starting from the Buddha himself.

Another influential school was T'ien-t'ai (Japanese Tendai), founded on the eponymous mountain in Chekiang by Chih-i (531–597).

The extraordinary vitality and prosperity of the Buddhist establishments fatally attracted the jealousy of the court, escalating into atrocious persecution in 842–845. Buddhism was suppressed, its sanctuaries were destroyed, its monks and nuns were obliged to join lay society. This event marked the decline of Chinese Buddhism, which continuously lost ground before Confucianism (8), which became state doctrine in the fourteenth century.

Eminent specialists of Chinese Buddhism have often noticed that a certain Sinology taking inspiration from the ideology of the Enlightenment often ignores the fundamental contribution of Buddhism to Chinese culture. An indication of the vitality of Buddhism well after the ninth-century persecutions and its loss of power before Confucianism was given by the novel *Hsi-yu chi,* or *Journey to the West,* often attributed to the sixteenth-century clerk Wu Ch'eng-en. If Paul Mus gave us a history of Buddhism in South Asia starting from the description of the Borobudur temple on the Indonesian island of Jawa, Anthony Yu, in his monumental integral translation of *Hsi-yu chi,* presented us with a complete history of Chinese Buddhism, of its Indian background and its extraordinary expansion among all strata of Chinese society. The plot of the novel concerns the exploits of the monk Hsüang-tsang, who left in 624 for India, in order to bring back to China authentic Buddhist scriptures. But Hsüang-tsang, who is often the target of the author's rather fond irony, is not the true hero of the story. The reader's attention is captured by Monkey, a semidivine ancestor in possession of illimitable magical powers. This character, majestic and ridiculous at the same time, embodies the two contradictory aspects of a mythical past: spiritual power and comical simplicity.

3.9 BUDDHISM IN KOREA AND JAPAN. Buddhism expanded from China to Korea as early as the fourteenth century C.E. The first

Buddhist monastery, in the country that well deserved the name of "kingdom of hermits," was erected in 376. After its introduction to Korea, local Buddhism remained in contact with its Chinese base, following, adopting, and adapting developments that took place in Chinese Buddhism. Much as in China, until the tenth century Korean Buddhist centers knew unbounded prosperity, at the expense of their spiritual message. Exasperated by their rigid scholasticism, the representatives of Shon Buddhism (Chinese Ch'an, Japanese Zen) constituted an independent faction. Yet this national schism was not followed by the same decline as that already mentioned in ninth-century China. Only later, under the Yi dynasty (1392–1910 C.E.), would Confucianism become state doctrine. Without being suppressed, Buddhism was submitted to strict regulations from 1400 to 1450, being formally organized into two branches, the meditational Shon and the doctrinal Kyo. During the modern period Korean Buddhism developed in harmony with Japanese Buddhism.

Japanese Buddhism has been, and remains, striking in its creativity. It was introduced to Japan from Korea during the second half of the sixth century, initially without success. The conversions of Empress Suiko (592–628 C.E.), who became a Buddhist nun, and of her nephew, Prince Regent Shotoku (573–621), mark the commencement of an epoch of prosperity for Buddhism, which was to continue during the period of the "Six Sects," in the capital Nara, founded in 710. Later on, when the capital was transfered to Heian (Kyoto: 794–868), Buddhism underwent rigorous state control. During the Kamakura shogunate (1185–1333), Buddhism spread among the Japanese population in the form of Amidism, or Pure Land (Jōdo) doctrine (shū). Pure Land was the Western paradise of Amitābha Buddha, whose name (*nembutsu*) represented a simple and efficacious meditation formula. The Tokugawa shoguns (1600–1868), who transferred their capital to Edo (Tokyo), were themselves adepts of Jōdo-shū, which they favored. Yet the Tokugawa *Ordinances* (1610–1615) identified Buddhism with official Shinto (27), setting it under complete state control.

During the Meiji epoch (1868–1912 C.E.), the peaceful coexistence of Buddhism and Shinto came to an abrupt and bloody end reminiscent of several episodes in the West, from the suppression of monasteries in Germany or England to the French Revolution and, more recently, to the Spanish civil war. Buddhism was suppressed and organized destruction was begun under the slogan *haibutsu kishaku:* "Kill the Buddhists and abandon the Scriptures." The call was followed: many Buddhist monks and nuns either perished or joined the lay population, and many sanctuaries were either destroyed or changed into Shinto temples.

The aforementioned intellectual creativity of Japanese Buddhism at the present time is not the result of a flourishing organization, comparable to the religious nonprofit organizations of the United States. Several reforms after 1945, as well as the radical modernization of the country, have largely deprived Buddhism of its traditional means of subsistence.

The proliferation of Buddhist doctrines in Japan followed in general the evolution of Chinese Buddhism, yet not without originality. Strangely enough, the problems faced by Japanese Buddhist thinkers overlapped strikingly with those faced during roughly the same period by their Western medieval colleagues, the Christian theologians.

In the ancient division of the Six Sects, we can still recognize the doctrinal debates that had produced the schools of Indian Buddhism (3.4). The Jojitsu, Kusha, and Ritsu sects belonged to Hīnayāna Buddhism; the Sanron, Hosso, and Kegon sects to Mahāyāna.

Tendai Buddhism (from the Chinese T'ien-t'ai), introduced into Japan by the monk Saicho (767–822), met with the favors of the Heian imperial court. The fundamental text of this school was the *Saddharmapuṇḍarika* in the translation of Kumārajīva (406 C.E.), its basic thesis being that all beings possessed Buddha nature and participate in his *dharmakāya*.

Shingon Buddhism (from the Chinese Chen-yen, which translates as the Sanskrit *mantra*) is a form of "right-hand" Tantrism (nonsexual, in opposition with "left-hand" Tantrism, which is sexual), systematized by the monk Kūkai (774–835), who traveled to China (804–806) and received instruction from an Indian master from Kashmir. Shingon iconography was particularly important in Japanese religious art.

A third school, Amidism, or Jōdō-shū, was founded by the priest Hōnen, or Genku (1133–1212 C.E.).

Finally, Zen (from the Chinese Ch'an, translating as the Sanskrit *dhyāna*), which had already produced several schools in China, came to Japan in two variants: Rinzai Zen, introduced by the priest Eisai (1141–1215), which would find numerous adepts among the samurai, and Soto Zen, more meditative and popular, introduced by the priest Dōgen (1200–1253). The social distinction betwen the adepts of the two schools was summarized in this Japanese formula: *rinzai shogun, sōtō domin*—Rinzai for aristocrats, Soto for peasants.

These four major schools of Japanese Buddhism took different positions concerning the problem of grace, which had led in the West to the debate between Augustine and Pelagius and would later oppose the Protestants to the Catholics. Tendai and Jōdō, against Zen and Shingon, showed a quietistic tendency. Awakening, asserted Tendai, was innate in us; we only had to find it again. Jōdō-shū, like Augustine in his polemic against Pelagius, asserted that the individual could obtain Awakening through his or her own efforts (*jiriki*), for all salvation came from Buddha's grace (*tariki*). Confronted with the same problem, Shinran (1173–1262 C.E.), disciple of Hōnen and founder of Jōdō Shinshu, or the True Sect of Pure Land, found a solution that we would perhaps call Lutheran if it did not lack one of the terms so fundamental in Luther's interpretation of Augustine: predestination. For Shinran, salvation was democratic, which led him closer to certain Anabaptists: the world was *already* saved; consequently, it was not necessary to follow the way of asceticism, and marriage was allowed.

On the contrary, Shingon Buddhism asserted the principle of *sokushin jobutsu:* one could *become* a Buddha in the immediate present, by performing certain Tantric rituals.

Zen likewise held that one could obtain Awakening through one's own efforts. Yet, whereas Rinzai favored shock treatments with an immediate effect such as the *koan,* a paradoxical utterance often accompanied by unexpected gestures, Soto knew one single rule: seated meditation (*zazen*).

Japan produced a national school of Buddhism, the sect of Nichiren (1222–1282), who started as an adept of Tendai but soon moved out of this environment, too narrow for his ambitious projects of monastic reform. Endowed with an intransigency both picturesque and extraordinary, Nichiren launched violent attacks against the Buddhism of his time, which he accused of decadence. These attacks were justified, in his eyes, by his personal rank in Buddhist heavenly hierarchy, for he himself was not one but several Bodhisattvas at the same time. Repeatedly exiled, condemned to death then pardoned, he never abandoned his crusade against the monks, the government, and the lax and petty period of time into which he found himself born. His messages, which he sent from just before the threshold of death pretending he had already crossed it, were sufficiently shocking to win him popularity. "I, Nichiren," he declared in his *Kaimokusho* (The Awakening to the Truth, 1272 C.E.), "have been beheaded between the hour of the Rat and the hour of the Ox, on the twelfth day of the ninth month of the last year, and the idiot in myself has died then. I came to Sado in spirit and, in the second month of the second year, I write this tractate in order to send it to my adepts. Since it has been written by a ghost, they may be frightened."

In the present day, Buddhism is fragmented into a number of schools that surpasses that of any other religious organization in Japan: 162 according to a 1970 census.

3.10 TIBETAN BUDDHISM. Indian monastic Buddhism, discipline (*vinaya*) of the Mūlasarvāstivādins, settled in Tibet toward the end of the eighth century C.E.. By the mid-ninth century, Tibetan Buddhism had undergone all sorts of influences, primarily from China and from Indian Tantrism. During the eleventh century, a renaissance of Tibetan Buddhism took place through a return to the original Indian sources. The Indian monk Atiśa, the guru (lama) par excellence, was invited to Tibet (1042–1054), where one of his disciples would become the founder of the monastic order Bka-gdams-pa. Marpa the Translator (1012–1096) traveled to India and brought back with him a form of Tantric asceticism taught to him by his guru, Naropa (956–1040), which he transmitted in turn to the famous Milarepa, guru of Sgam-po-pa, founder of the Bka-brgyud-pa order. A disciple of Sgam-po-pa, founder of the order Karma-pa (popularly known as "Black Caps"), established on esoteric grounds the succession of the Great Lamas. The same procedure was adopted by other orders, and in particular by the Dge-lugs-pa, or "Yellow Caps" (fourteenth century), whose chief, called the Dalai Lama, exerted civil authority in Tibet from the seventeenth century, spiritual authority devolving to another Yellow Great Lama living in the monastery of Tashilumpo.

Besides these orthodox orders and their multiple branches, two other orders took shape, one a mixture of Buddhism and pre-Buddhist Bon religion (32) called Bon-po, and the other, the Order of the Ancients (Rñin-ma-pa), who claimed the guru Padmasambhava (eighth century) as a founder, and whose doctrine and practices preceded, in most cases, the eleventh-century renaissance.

The Bon-po were frankly heterodox, excluded from the main body of the Buddhist orders dominated by the Yellow Caps. If their desire were to be part of it, it was because the doctrines of the Bon-po were clearly the result of a synthesis produced under the pressure of Buddhism. The Bon-po claimed to be more ancient than any other order, to derive their beliefs from the sacred mists of the mythical western land of Shambhala (Ta-zig), and to have their own Buddha, who was not the impostor Śākyamuni. Their shamanistic and magical practices had had a serious impact on the Ancients (the Rñin-ma-pas, or Red Caps, one of the two orders who have adopted this color), who were found to be rife with magical superstitions during the moral reform of the Yellow Caps founded by Tsong-ka-pa (1357–1419 C.E.).

Opposition to the doctrines of the Red monks was characteristic of the Yellow Caps, the most powerful among the orders of Tibetan Buddhism. The Yellow monks did not accept the authenticity of the doctrines of the Red, whereas other orders showed a more conciliating attitude. The situation was further complicated by the habit, common to the Ancients and the Bon-po, of revealing so-called *gter-mas,* or "buried treasures," i.e., apocrypha attributed to Padmasambhava himself or to other venerable masters and allegedly "dug out" from hidden repositories or simply from the unfathomed depths of the mind of some individual. The schools of Tibetan Buddhism can be classified according to their attitude toward the two extremes: the Yellow monks and the Red monks.

Lamaism became a state religion in Mongolia, where it arrived in two waves during the thirteenth and the sixteenth centuries.

3.11 BIBLIOGRAPHY. On Buddhism in general, see Eliade, *H* 2, 147–54, 185–90; F. E. Reynolds and Ch. Hallisey, "Buddhism: An Overview," in *ER* 2, 334–51; F. E. Reynolds, *Guide to the Buddhist Religion* (1981); Edward Conze, *Buddhism: Its Essence and Development* (1959).

On the Buddha, see F. E. Reynolds and Ch. Hallisey, "Buddha," in *ER* 2, 319–32; André Bareau, *Recherches sur la biographie du Bouddha dans les Sutrapitaka et les Vinayapitaka anciens,* 2 vols. (1963–1971).

On the history of Indian Buddhism, see L. O. Gómez, "Buddhism in India," in *ER* 2, 351–85; Étienne Lamotte, *Histoire du Bouddhisme indien des origines à l'ère Saka* (1958); A. K. Warder, *Indian Buddhism* (1970); John S. Strong, *The Legend of King Aśoka: A Study and Translation of the Aśokavadana* (1983).

On Hinayāna sects, see A. Bareau, "Buddhism, Schools of: Hinayāna Buddhism," in *ER* 2, 444–57; André Bareau, *Les sectes bouddhiques du Petit Véhicule* (1955); André Bareau, *Les premiers conciles bouddhiques* (1955); Nalinaksha Dutt, *Buddhist Sects in India* (1970).

On Mahāyāna Buddhism, see Nakamura Hajime, "Buddhism, Schools of: Mahāyāna Buddhism," in *ER* 2, 457–72; on Tantric Buddhism, see, A. Wayman, "Buddhism, Schools of: Esoteric Buddhism," in *ER* 2, 472–82.

On Buddhism in Southeast Asia, see D. K. Swearer, "Buddhism in Southeast Asia," in *ER* 2, 385–400; on the basic notions of Sinhalese Buddhism, see Nyantiloka, *Buddhist Dictionary: Manual of Buddhist Terms and Doctrines* (1952, 1972); on the symbiosis between Buddhism and royal power in Thailand, see Stanley J. Tambiah, *World Conqueror and World Renouncer: A Study of Buddhism and Polity in Thailand Against a Historical Background* (1976).

On Chinese Buddhism, see E. Zürcher, "Buddhism in China," in *ER* 2, 414–26; S. Weinstein, "Buddhism, Schools of: Chinese Buddhism," in *ER* 2, 482–87; Arthur F. Wright, *Buddhism in Chinese History* (1959); Paul Demiéville, *Le Bouddhisme chinois* (1970); Kenneth K. S. Ch'en, *The Chinese Transformation of Buddhism* (1973); W. Pachow, *Chinese Buddhism: Aspects of Interaction and Reinterpretation* (1980). The integral translation of the novel *Journey to the West* is the achievement of Anthony C. Yu (4 vols., 1977–1983); by the same author, see "Religion and Literature in China: The 'Obscure Way' of the Journey to the West," in Ching-i Tu (ed.), *Tradition and Creativity: Essays on East Asian Civilization* (1987), 109–54; and "'Rest, Rest, Perturbed Spirit!': Ghosts in Traditional Chinese Prose Fiction," in *Harvard Journal of Asiatic Studies* 47 (1987), 397–434.

On Korean Buddhism, see R. E. Buswell, Jr., "Buddhism in Korea," in *ER* 2, 421–26. On Buddhism in Japan, see Tamaru Noriyoshi, "Buddhism in Japan," in *ER* 2, 426–35; Araki Michio, "Buddhism, Schools of: Japanese Buddhism," in *ER* 2, 487–93; Joseph M. Kitagawa, *Religion in Japanese History* (1966); *Japanese Religion: A Survey by the Agency for Cultural Affairs* (1972); E. Dale Saunders, *Buddhism in Japan: With an Outline of Its Origins in India* (1964); *A Short History of the Twelve Japanese Buddhist Sects* (1886), translated from the original Japanese by Bunyin Nanjio (1979). On Shingon, see Minoru Kiyota, "Shingontsu," in *ER* 13, 272–78; on Shinran, see A. Bloom, "Shinran," in *ER* 13, 278–80; on Zen, see especially D. T. Suzuki's *Essays on Zen Buddhism.* A good collection of texts of the founders of Japanese Buddhism is Hōnen, Shinran, Nichiren and Dōgen, *Le Bouddhisme japonais: Textes fondamentaux de quatre moines de Kamakura,* preface and French translation by G. Renondeau (1965). Nichiren's *Kaimokusho* has been translated into English by N. R. M. Ehara, *The Awakening to the Truth, or Kaimokusho* (1941).

On Kukai, see Thomas P. Kasulis, "Reference and Symbol in Plato's Cratylus and Kukai's Shojijissogi," in *Philosophy East and West* 32 (1982), 393–405.

On Tibetan Buddhism, see H. Guenther, "Buddhism in Tibet," in *ER* 2, 406–14; D. L. Snellgrove, "Buddhism Schools of: Tibetan Buddhism," in *ER* 2, 493–98; Giuseppe Tucci, *The Religions of Tibet* (1980). For a new classification of Buddhist doctrines in Tibet, see Matthew Kapstein, "The Purificatory Gem and Its Cleansing," in *History of Religions* (1989). On Mongolian Buddhism, see W. Heissig, "Buddhism in Mongolia," in *ER* 2, 404–5.

4

Canaanite Religion

4.1 HISTORY. For thousands of years, migrations of peoples from the Syrian and Arabian plains were a continual and periodically dramatic process. A Semitic language–speaking population first appeared in Palestine somewhat before 3000 B.C.E., marking what we call the Early Bronze Age. Large-scale Amorite invasions about 2200 B.C.E. brought further mixing and restructuring of cultural patterns, as would the coming of the Israelites in the late second millennium B.C.E. Along the Mediterranean coast, agrarian fertility cults mixed with the celestial pantheon of the nomadic herders. Records of the religious traditions of these people, aside from excavated shrines and figurines, have previously been drawn from the (sharply polemical) accounts in the Hebrew scriptures and some Hellenistic and Roman authors, and extrapolated from tablet archives found to the east (Mari) and the southwest (Amarna). But more recently and successfully, we have turned for coherent documentation to a more timely (Late Bronze III, ca. 1365–1175 B.C.E.) and more centrally situated source, a single city representing a part of what we call the "Canaanite" tradition: Ugarit.

From the early second millennium B.C.E., Ugarit emerged as a trading port on the coast of modern Syria (Ras Shamra). About 1350 B.C.E. the first alphabetic script was formulated there, composed of cuneiform wedges pressed into clay. Religious dedications, spells, prayers, god lists, and above all myths of undetermined antiquity were copied in the new script until the invasions of the Sea Peoples destroyed the city about 1175 B.C.E.

4.2 THE PANTHEON. The Ugaritic pantheon was topped by the *deus otiosus* (inactive deity) El or Il, creator of the universe and father of the gods, transcendent and benevolent yet now rather distant and impotent and superseded by the rigorous Baal, called the Son of Dagan, a storm god like the Mesopotamian Adad. More than one El or Baal was recognized by the scribes and popular cult—indeed, their names are generically God and Lord—and some Els and Baals were probably linked to geographic locations or to qualities attributed to the deities. Baal was the Powerful, the High One, Rider of the Clouds, Prince and Lord of the Earth. In myths, he contended with Yamm (Sea), the evil "devourers," and Mot (Death), by whom he was temporarily conquered.

The wife of El was Athirat (Asherah), the queenly goddess with some sea attributes. More vivid was Anat, sister or consort of Baal but more importantly a potent love and war goddess sometimes depicted standing on a lion's back. Later unified as Ashtart wa-Anat, these grew into the later Syrian marine ferility goddess Atargatis, who was still worshiped into the early Christian period. Other gods who appeared in the Ugaritic lists included Ars wa-Shamem (Earth and Heaven), a moon god and goddess, some daughters of Baal, the morning and evening stars (Venus), Kothar the craftsman, Rashap (flame and pestilence), and some Hurrian and other imports. Ancestors, and especially the line of kings, were also deified and worshiped, and an assembly of lesser gods not individually enumerated.

4.3 CANAANITE WORSHIP. As findings of metal and terracotta figurines attest, worship in Ugarit often focused on two pairs: the regal pair, which was a force above the world, El and Athirat; and the pair of gods active in the world, Baal and Anat. Some figurines were left as votive deposits in sanctuaries. Ugarit is known to have had temples to Baal and Dagan, and probably others as well. Large temples possessing flocks and stores of oil and wine left more records than the small shrines of the popular religion. Records of the state cult show the king and queen at the top of the institution and active in rituals, festivals, and prayers for the protection of the city. Priests (*khnm;* cf. Hebrew *kohanim*) and a lower rank of religious officials (*qdshm*) oversaw temples and cult practices that included offerings, sacrifices (some burned), purifications, and care of the wooden image of the deity. A special group of men attended to the cult of the dead, whose primary rite was an orgiastic feast; funerary ceremonies were banquets as well, to propitiate the dead. Evidence for divination shows that a class of omen priests existed, and inscribed clay livers were found as guides for extispicy (divination through entrails) as practiced in Mesopotamia. Magic and appeals to particular deities for safeguarding were probably practiced by the populace.

4.4 MYTHOLOGY. Ugaritic mythology primarily tells of struggles for sovereignity: conflicts between El and Baal and between Baal and his adversaries. One of the best known of these is the battle of Baal and Yamm, a divine aquatic being pictured sometimes in human form, sometimes as a sea monster. Encouraged by his father El, the sea jockeyed for a superior position to Baal, who battled and defeated him with magical weapons supplied by Kothar the craftsman of the gods. The battle invites comparison with the defeat of Tiamat (the sea) by Marduk in the fourth tablet of the Babylonian *Enuma Elish,* and with images of Yahweh's defeat of the sea in certain psalms and in Job 26:12–13, perhaps echoed in Moses' parting of the Red Sea. In the next installment of the Baal cycle, Anat demonstrated her warlike prowess. Baal sent her a peace invitation, and he communicated his desire for a "house," a temple befitting his status (as in the *Enuma Elish*). She sought and obtained authorization for this from El, and a grand temple was fashioned. Baal next contended with Mot, Death, a rival son of El. In the balance of nature, it appeared that the reign of Baal meant plenty and the prevalence of Mot was famine and drought. After an exchange of messengers, who visited Mot in his residence of mud and filth, Baal agreed to descend to the underworld with his storm god entourage. When the broken text resumes, Baal was thoroughly dead, to the bitter laments of El and Anat, and no son of El was great enough to take his place on the throne. Some time after she had buried Baal, Anat met up with Mot and shred, winnowed, roasted, ground, and sowed him in the fields for the birds to eat. El then dreamed that Baal and prosperity had returned to the land, and indeed they did. Seven years later Baal decisively defeated Mot and eternal kingship was his destiny.

Two Ugaritic epic texts are the tales of Kirta and of Aqhat. Each begins with a royal and just man who sought to cure his unfortunate childlessness, a familiar Old Testament theme. Their predicaments were remedied by the gods and a series of human-divine intrigues begin: Anat engineered the death of Aqhat, the desired son, after he insulted her in her advances to obtain his magical bow. Kirta won a wife by warfare, but forgot a vow to Asherah and fell ill, later to be accused of injustice in kingship by one of his sons. Despite the often fragmentary preservation of this literature, it supplements our picture of the world—

historical, mythological, and religious—that the Israelites would come to occupy and transmit to Western culture.

4.5 BIBLIOGRAPHY. Eliade, *H* 1, 48–52; A. M. Cooper, "Canaanite Religion: An Overview," in *ER* 3, 35–45.

Translations are available in the work of Johannes C. De Moor, *An Anthology of Religious Texts from Ugarit* (1987).

5

Celtic Religion

5.1 POPULATION AND LANGUAGE. The Celts appeared in history during the fifth century B.C.E. and settled in an area stretching from the Iberian Peninsula, Ireland, and Britain, in the west to Asia Minor (the Galati) in the east. They were the carriers of the La Tène culture, or Second Iron Age. Their expansion was stopped by the Germans, the Romans, and the Dacians. In 51 B.C.E. Caesar conquered Gaul. Celtic tribes continued to exist, under foreign rule, in Britain and Ireland. Today Celtic languages are not spoken outside the insular zone (Irish, Gaelic, and Welsh) and French Brittany, (and there not, as one might expect, as a survival of ancient Gaul but as an import from Britain).

5.2 SOURCES. Unfortunately, the Druids were forbidden to commit their secret knowledge to writing. Due to this circumstance, there is no direct source concerning Gaulish religion, except for a relatively large number of monuments, heavily influenced by Roman art. Indirect sources, from Julius Caesar to Diodorus of Sicily, are numerous.

There is rich information on the insular Celts, but most documents are (late) medieval and have been influenced by Christianity and epic material. Several Irish twelfth-century manuscripts contain ancient traditions. Two famous collections of the fourteenth century, *The White Book of Rhydderch* and *The Red Book of Hergest,* contain Welsh texts such as the mythical stories known under the title *Mabinogi.*

5.3 THE RELIGION OF GAUL has come down to us in Roman interpretation. Caesar mentioned a supreme god whom he identified with Mercury and four other gods, identified with Apollo, Mars, Jupiter, and Minerva. Despite the controversial character of this testimony, archeology seems to confirm it. "Mercury" must be the god called Lugh by the Irish, many statuettes of whom have come down to us. His name occurs in many toponyms (place-names).

The Celts performed human sacrifices to three divinities (Teutates, Esus, and Taranis). Each one of them could be Caesar's Mars. Teutates seems to be a generic name, meaning "tribal god"; the Irish word *tuath* means "small tribal kingdom."

There were several competitors for the Apollo title; the choice among them is not easy. Over fifteen epithets, such as Belenus, Bormo, Grannus, and so forth, designated him.

The Gaulish Jupiter was the mythical ancestor of the Druids. He has not been identified so far.

Several local divinities may be interpreted as Minerva, as both her iconography and her votive inscriptions showed. One of these divinities was the Irish Brighid, associated with poetry, medicine, and technology. Both her mythical personality and her feast have survived under the guise of Saint Brigit (Brighid of Kildare).

Monuments have preserved the aspects and names of several other divinities, such as the sylvan gods Sucellus and Nantos and the god Cernunnos (Horned), who bears stag horns.

5.4 IRISH TRADITION preserves the record of the mythical history of the island after the great flood. The first immigrants had to repel the constant attacks of the Fomhoire, a malignant race of beings from beyond the sea. A new wave of immigrants brought to the island laws and civility of manners. They were followed by the Tuatha Dé Dananu, "the Tribes of the Goddess Dana," initiated into the knowledge of magic and possessors of several magic objects such as the spear of Lugh, which ensured victory in war, the fail-less sword of King Nuadhu, the inexaustible cauldron of Daghdha, and a stone that served to choose the only true ruler among contenders. The Tuatha Dé Dananu were led by the god Lugh himself to the battle of Magh Tuiredh against the Fomhoire, who, defeated, were forever banned from Ireland. After the Magh Tuiredh battle, the first Celts landed, coming from Spain. Their seer Amharghin used his occult power to neutralize the legitimate mistrust of the Tuatha Dé, and the newcomers were allowed to set foot on Irish ground. Henceforth, Tuatha Dé and Celts often fought against each other, and their relationship remained tense. Eventually, the Tuatha Dé withdrew into the underground world, leaving all visible space to the Celts.

5.4.1 The institution of the Druids was associated in Ireland with Uisnech, the center of the country, a sacred spot where the great seasonal festivals probably took place.

Irish kingship was sacred. It was conferred upon the king after he had sexual intercourse with the goddess who represented his kingdom or with a substitute of the Great Equine Goddess (the Welsh Rhiannon, the Gaulish Epona, etc.). In his *Topography of Ireland,* the twelfth-century author Gerald of Cambrai described the consecration of the Irish king, the principal scene of which consisted in the public intercourse of the future king with a white mare, whose boiled meat was then eaten by the audience.

5.4.2 The heroic cycle of Ulster had young Cú Chulainn as its protagonist. The setting was the Ulster court of King Conchobar. Queen Medhbh of Connacht sent an army to steal the brown bull of Cuailnge, and the people of Ulster, bewitched, were unable to mount any resistance. Cú Chulainn alone fought the enemy army. The epic closes with a terrible fight between the brown bull of Cuailnge and the bull of Connacht. Cú Chulainn's career was short, for his enemies killed him using witchcraft.

Another mythical hero was Fionn mac Cumhail, head of the Fian, a brotherhood of warriors. Like Cú Chulainn, Fionn had magical powers, which he used to rid the country of threatening supernatural forces.

5.5 WELSH TRADITION has chiefly come down to us as a collection of stories called *Mabinogi,* written down probably during the eleventh and twelfth centuries C.E.. Among the eleven pieces contained in the *Red Book of Hergest* (about 1325 C.E.), two are unimportant and three seem to summarize the plot of three Arthurian novels by the French twelfth-century author Chrétien of Troyes. The others contain what one scholar has called "a Celtic mythology in decline," whose characters were unclassifiable gods. One of them, Pwyll, had a curious relationship with the netherworld, where he actually reigned for one year. His wife was the equine goddess Rhiannon, a variant of Epona, who in Roman religious syncretism was identified with the Greek goddess Demeter-Erinys, who changed herself into a mare in order to escape Poseidon's advances. Yet Poseidon changed himself into a stallion (Poseidon Hippios), and from their union Persephone, the goddess of the underworld, and the horse Areion were born (Pausanias 8.25, 5–7). The Vedic variant (*Ṛgveda* 10.17, 1–2) indicates that the myth was Indo-European. In all three cases, the progeny of the goddess was both human and equine, a fact that finds confirmation in Irish mythology (*Noínden Ulad*).

Other Welsh tales contained traditions that a number of scholars have called "shamanistic"; their hero is Cei, later the gloomy steward Key of the Arthurian cycle. The Welsh prototype of Merlin was the poet-magician Taliesin, who claimed to know "all the magic arts of Europe and Asia." Other characters such as Math, Gwydion son of Dòn (the goddess Dana), Llwyd, and so forth were equally capable of extraordinary feats.

5.6 BIBLIOGRAPHY. Eliade, *H* 2, 169–72; P. Mac Cana, "Celtic Religion," in *ER* 3, 148–66.

On Welsh mythology, see P. K. Ford, *The Mabinogi and Other Welsh Tales* (1977).

6

Central American Religions

6.1 THE MESOAMERICAN REGION is the Americas' equivalent of the Fertile Crescent. It was the cradle of numerous advanced civilizations (Toltec, Olmec, Zapotec, Mixtec, etc.), of which the most remarkable are the Maya and the Aztec.

6.2 THE MAYA, possessors of a hieroglyphic writing that has been partially deciphered and of a complex and precise calendar now transposable into Common Era dating, are the heirs of the Olmecs, whose civilization flourished around 1200 B.C.E. The most ancient traces of the Maya do not precede 200–300 C.E. Effaced shortly thereafter by an invasion from Teotihuacán (today Mexico City), they resumed later and reached a climax under the extremely unfavorable conditions of the tropical forest. About 750 C.E. four important urban centers made their appearance (Tikal, Copán, Palenque, and Calakmul), around which extended a maze of towns and villages. Yet the existence of a centralized Maya state during that period is improbable.

For unknown reasons, of which the most plausible were invasion and religious war, between 800 and 900 C.E. the population left the cities, abandoning their magnificent monuments to the jungle. After this catastrophe, Maya culture was concentrated in the Yucatán Peninsula, where many urban centers appeared between 900 and 1200 C.E. Among them, Chichén Itzá was probably conquered by the Toltecs of Tollán, precursors of the Aztecs, who made it into one of their points of expansion. According to the legend, the mythical hero Quetzalcóatl-Kukulkán (Quetzal-feathered Serpent) himself in 987 led the exiles out of Tollán (Tula, north of Mexico City), invaded by the forces of the destructive god Smoked Mirror (Tezcatlipoca), to the Yucatán, where he founded Chichén Itzá. Abandoned around 1200, Chichén Itzá relinquished its splendor to the city of Mayapan near Mérida, itself destroyed around 1441. When the Spanish invaders landed in Central America, Maya civilization was in decline. During the spring of 1517, when the giant black galleons of an unknown power drew closer to the shore, the inhabitants of Yucatán must have thought of the prophecies of the return of Tezcatlipoca: "That day things will fall asunder. . . . "

A few scattered groups escaped forced acculturation. The last among them were found after World War II in the jungle of Chiapas, living around extraordinary abandoned temples. Today over two million descendants of the ancient Maya live in Central America: the Yucatec, the Chol, the Chontal, the Lacandón, the Tzotzol, the Tzeltal, the Tojolabal, the Quichés, the Cakchiquel, the Tzutuhil, and so forth, speaking some thirty different dialects. They remain the keepers of ancient sacred rituals, which they, although good Catholics for four hundred years, have never ceased to practice.

6.2.1 Religion. Only three books in Maya hieroglyphs survived the general destruction ordered by a zealous Spanish friar, Diego de Landa. Later Maya priests used their dialects and the Latin alphabet to write down their ancient mythology. The most important documents pertaining to this category are the *Popol Vuh* of the Quiché and the *Books of Chilam Balam* of the Yucatecs.

The supreme Maya priesthood was in the hands of the *halach uinic* (true man), among whose functions was the teaching of hieroglyphic writing, calendrical computations, and divination.

Sacrifice was the central moment of the cult. In Yucatec it was called *p'a chi* (opening of the mouth), from the practice of rubbing the mouth of the god's statue with blood. Only seldom were the victims animals. Human sacrifices were preferred, and the gods had further personal preferences: the rain gods Chacs, for example, loved the precious blood of children. Blood, a substance so noble that the reliefs represent it in the shape of *quetzal* feathers, was extracted in many ways: using the spectacular technique of heart removal, by perforation, by flaying, and so forth. During penitential rites, all people would bleed themselves, and in order to make the wounds more memorable they would use the spine of a stingray.

Without being an actual monotheism, the cult of the heavenly god Itzam Na (Iguana House), represented as an edifice whose entrance was the mouth of the god, was close to that, for the other deities of the

Maya pantheon (the Chacs, the Sun, the Moon, etc.) were his servants. Itzam Na was also god of hell, of fire, and of medicine.

Human existence continued after death either in the heavenly paradise, in the underground world, or in the celestial place of rest for warriors.

Maya myths, of which the *Popul Vuh* is a collection of paramount importance, contained familiar themes: the periodic destruction of the world by water and by fire, the creation of a man soluble in water and incapable of movement, or of a wooden man whose rigidity was the opposite of the other's fluidity, and so forth. The mythical origin of corn was a combination of two forms of myth that the German ethnologist Ad. E. Jensen (1899–1965) called *dema* and *promethean. Dema* myth presented the appearance of certain edible plants, especially tuberous, as a consequence of the killing of a divinity called *dema* in New Guinea, whereas Prometheus myths applied to the theft of cereals in heaven. Often the two were combined. The cut-off head of the sacrificed corn god figured as the origin of the ball game, whose ritual importance in Central America was extraordinary. The game was played in all earnest. The players of the winning team were all beheaded.

6.3 THE AZTECS OR MÉXICA, who like the Toltecs were speakers of the Nahuatl language, settled around 1325 on the island of Tenochtitlán in the lake that at the time covered part of the Mexico Valley. They came from the north, where they had not been dominators, but dominated. They had left in search of the Promised Land, guided by their great priest Huitzilopochtli, who was set in motion by the god Smoked Mirror (Tezcatlipoca) and born again from the Mother Goddess Coatlicue. Having settled on the Mexican Plateau, they soon became a people of conquerors, whose principal activity has been defined as "mystical imperialism." Indeed, obsessed with the necessity to sacrifice new victims so that their blood would allow the continuation of the movement of the sun, the Aztecs had no other choice but to procure them among the neighboring peoples.

When Hernán Cortés (1485–1547) landed at the Yucatán in 1519, with 508 soldiers and 10 cannons, the Aztec Empire of Moctezuma II, like the Inca Empire under Atahuallpa (29.3), showed none of the signs of decadence of the Maya civilization. Cleverly exploiting the belief in the return of Quetzalcóatl and the end of the world as well as the rivalries among Aztec cities, Cortés in two years defeated a great empire, making thus an end to two centuries of bloody and triumphant Aztec history.

6.3.1 Religion. The Aztecs built on the mythical prestige of Teotihuacán (Place of Deification), seat of an advanced culture that had disappeared around 700 C.E., shifting into that of the Toltecs of Tula. From the latter, the Aztecs inherited several gods such as Quetzalcóatl and Tezcatlipoca, writing, the calendar, and divination. In one of the Aztec myths, the richest in ritual consequences, Teotihuacán was the mythical plain where the sacrifice of the gods gave way to the Fifth Age (or Sun) of the world. The first four Suns had been removed by violent destruction. There, in the Teotihuacán plain, the gods came together in order to make a new Sun and a new human race. Tezcatlipoca and Quetzalcóatl shaped the first couple of humans and give them corn for sustenance. To create the Sun, a god had to be immolated. Yet the new Sun and the new Moon born from the sacrifice of two gods in the fire were immobile. To make them move, all the other gods shed their blood under the sacrificial knife, and the Sun finally started its course. Only Xolotl shamefully fleed to escape death and became god of the Monsters and of all things double, such as twins.

The primordial sacrifice had to be periodically renewed to allow the Sun to keep its pace. This was why the Aztecs, People of the Sun, were obsessed with blood and with the duty of obtaining it in order to make the Fifth Sun last. Hecatombs of victims, women and war prisoners, were ritually immolated in front of the shrine of Huitzilopochtli on the top of the Templo Mayor of Tenochtitlán, the symbolic center of Aztec power. Although the Aztecs knew at least as many ways to slaughter as the Mayas, they gave definite preference to the removal of the heart. In a mystical atmosphere punctuated by the sound of wind and percussion instruments (the Mesoamericans did not have stringed instruments), the sacrificing priest would quickly extract the heart and dispatch it into a vase containing the bloody food of the gods; he would sprinkle with blood the huge image of Huitzilopochtli and then, after having beheaded the dead victim, would set the head on a special rack together with many others. The body thrown down from the top of the sacrificial platform was the object of a cannibalistic repast in which the multitude took part.

Like the Mayas, the Aztecs had a rather elaborate cosmology, based on the existence of thirteen heavens—thirteen being the basic number of the divinatory calendar of 260 days (not to be confused with the normal solar calendar) and of Aztec numerology. Based on the two calendars were numerous festivals, fixed or mobile, to which many other ceremonies were added: of propitiation, of grace, of consecration, and so forth. The use of fermented beer (*pulque*) in quantities as large as those consumed by other Mesoamerican peoples marked the development of the major feasts; preparation for them was accompanied by deprivations and mortifications. During the Sun festival on 4 Ollin, the entire community bled in ritual penitence.

6.4 MODERN RELIGIONS. With a few exceptions, the peoples of Central America today have assimilated the languages and the religion of their Christian conquerors, which resulted in the drastic change or simply in the deletion of their own traditions. Unintelligible debris of mythologies, cosmologies, and references to divination or ritual still emerge out of the Mesoamerican imagination, like the ruins of vast, archaic religious complexes swallowed by the jungle.

The Supreme Being of the Mesoamericans is today either God the Father or Jesus Christ, preached by those who came in the tracks of Cortés and Pizarro. He is identified with the Sun by such tribes as the Quichés or the Tepehua. Yet it is Mary, the Virgin of Guadalupe, who received a central position in the natives' pantheon. In December 1531, the Indian Virgin appeared on the sacred hill of the Aztec goddess Tonantzin, the immaculate mother of Huitzilopochtli, and spoke to the natives in Nahuatl language. Celebrated ever since, she takes care of them and complies with their modest requests more than any past or present power in place has done.

6.5 BIBLIOGRAPHY. M. León-Portilla, "Mesoamerican Religions: Pre-Columbian Religions," in *ER* 9, 290–406; H. von Winning, "Preclassic Cultures," in *ER* 9, 406–9; D, Heyden, "Classic Cultures," in *ER* 9, 409–19; H. B. Nicholson, "Postclassic Cultures," in *ER* 9, 419–28; K. A. Wipf, "Contemporary Cultures," in *ER* 9, 428–38; D. Heyden, "Mythic Themes," in *ER* 9, 436–42; Y. González Torres, "History of Study," in *ER* 9, 442–46; J. M. Watanabe, "Maya Religion," in *ER* 9, 298–301, D. Carrasco, "Aztec Religion," in *ER* 2, 23–29; D. Carrasco, "Human Sacrifice: Aztec Rites," in ER 6, 518–22.

On the Mayas, see especially J. E. S. Thompson, *Maya History and Religion* (1972); Charles Gallenkamp, *Maya: The Riddle and Rediscovery of a Lost Civilization* (1987).

On the Aztecs, see Jacques Soustelle, *Les Aztèques* (1970), and especially the recent work by David Carrasco, *Quetzalcóatl and the Irony of the Empire: Myths and Prophecies in Aztec Tradition* (1982).

7

Christian Religion

7.1 CANON. In the fourth century C.E., the Christian canon was finalized. It consisted of twenty-seven writings called the "New Testament," as opposed to the Hebrew Bible (*Tanakh*), or "Old Testament," also canonized by the Christians. The New Testament included the four Gospels (of Matthew, Mark, Luke, and John), the Acts of the Apostles (a continuation by the writer of the Gospel according to Luke, supposed to be a disciple of the apostle Paul), the epistles of the apostles (fourteen attributed to Paul, one to James, two to Peter, three to John, one to Jude), and finally the Apocalypse (Revelation) attributed to John. In all this literature, the Old Testament was usually interpreted typologically as containing prophecies about the coming of the Messiah Jesus Christ. Actually, the inclusion of the Old Testament in the Christian canon met early with resistance from the theologian Marcion of Sinope (ca. 80–155 C.E.). The question was raised again by Martin Luther (1527 and 1537 C.E.) and by German evangelism into the twentieth century (Adolf von Harnack).

The authenticity of the New Testament writings has been debated for hundreds of years. Every now and then, some theologian comes up with a shocking new theory; yet, despite the proliferation of hypotheses, some certainties have been reached: the authentic letters of Paul (generally accepted to be: Romans, 1 and 2 Corinthians, Galatians, Philippians, 1 Thessalonians, and Philemon, often in composite form, often with post-Pauline insertions) form the most ancient part of the Christian canon (ca. 50–60 C.E.). Several among the other canonical epistles were composed during the first half of the second century, when their alleged authors had long been dead. The Gospels date from the second half of the first century, based on several earlier traditions and undergoing accretions and deletions. The first three (Matthew,

Mark, and Luke) are called *synoptic* because of their resemblances, which can be seized at a glance when we put them in three parallel columns. The Gospel according to Mark, dated to around 70 C.E., is the oldest, with verses 16:9–20 being a later addition. Matthew and Luke (about 80 C.E.) follow Mark, and a source called Q (*Quelle,* a sayings source). Probably written shortly before 100 C.E., the Gospel attributed to John is more esoteric and contains prominent Platonic features, especially in the identification of Christ with the Logos of God, which is the divine word and plan immanent in the material world. John's Gospel contains a very negative opinion of the social world (called "*this* world"), dominated by the devil, who appears as an opponent rather than a servant of God. This conception has only too often been compared with both Gnosticism and the Essene literature from Qumran, which proves nothing more than that certain writings of the New Testament are vague enough to be the object of many contradictory hypotheses at the same time. It is beyond doubt that the Essenes and even the Gnostics belonged to the religious spectrum of that period.

7.2 JESUS CHRIST, a Jewish prophet from Nazareth in Galilee born toward the commencement of the Common Era and crucified, according to tradition, during the spring of 33 C.E., is the center of the Christian religion. His life and short career as a teacher and healer and his self-sacrificial death are described by the Gospels. The historical sources of the time contain almost no reference to Jesus; a radical theological trend still regards his existence as fiction, whereas the mainstream commonly treats it as a fact, although elusive.

The Jesus of the Gospels was the son of Mary, wife of the carpenter Joseph. After being baptized by John the Baptist, a prophet later beheaded by the Roman puppet king Herod, Jesus began preaching and performing miraculous healings. Attempts to reconstruct his original message assert that he taught in parables—a rabbinical custom—and that he announced the impending establishment of God's reign on earth, vindicating the good and oppressed. Although Christianity, which postdates Jesus' lifetime, was advertised as a religion of peace, it is beyond doubt that Jesus himself had links with the Zealots, Jewish fundamentalist terrorists whose aim was to bring an end to the Roman occupation of Palestine. S. G. F. Brandon gives evidence that Jesus' relation to this organization was extremely close. Be that as it may, Jesus' attitude was not fit to attract the sympathy of the Jewish religious (or civil) authorities, who put him under arrest and subjected him to

Roman justice. The accusation against Jesus is far from clear; it appears, however, that he was considered blasphemous by some and seditious by the others. After a summary judgment during which the Roman representative Pilate (at least according to the cautious authors of the Gospels, who did their best to ingratiate themselves with Roman power) took care to leave the sentence up to local mobs, Jesus was crucified by Roman soldiers under the probable accusation of being a false Messiah, which in order to become relevant in the eyes of Roman justice must have been accompanied by evidence of seditious activity. Despite Jesus' ties with the Zealots, evidence of such was not explicit in the Gospels, nor in any contemporary source. On the cross, Jesus soon expired and was buried the same Friday.

One of the problems modern biblical criticism debated for some years was the nature of Jesus' own beliefs concerning his identity and function. Did he really believe himself to be God's Son? The Messiah (and *what* Messiah)? A prophet? The Jesus of the Gospels seemed to act as the messenger of an authority higher than the Torah, whose aim was to bring sinners back to God and to announce the coming of the Kingdom of God. It is evident that Jesus called God by the intimate appellation *Abba,* more familiar in tone than "Father"; but it is certainly legitimate to doubt that this filiality was more than metaphorical, as the next generation surmised, under the influence of current Platonism, which was ready to accept that the archetypal world contained in the divine mind could be incarnated in a human body. The synoptic Gospels several times gave Jesus the title of Son of Man (used by the prophet Daniel), of which the contextual meaning is unclear (in Aramaic idiom it simply means "man"). His followers called him *mashiah,* Messiah (anointed), that is, consecrated—in Greek, *christos.* If he truly was crucified under the inscription "Jesus of Nazareth, King of the Jews," it is possible that to him was attributed the claim of belonging to the Davidic lineage. Yet he never seemed to proclaim his messianic identity in public. After this enigmatic character dies, his disciples maintained that he revived in three days and stayed among them forty days (Acts 1, 3; the Gnostic apocryphal traditions give much higher alternative figures). Yet at the time when Christianity was only a Jewish sect, a splinter group such as that of the Ebionites held Jesus for a mere prophet and did not believe in his resurrection from the dead. It was Paul who made the Resurrection into the central episode of the Christian message.

7.3 PAUL OF TARSUS, the genius who fashioned the ideology of Christianity, was a complex personality. His true name was Saul and he came from a Jewish family of the diaspora, rich enough to give him a classical education aside from solid instruction in the Torah. He was a Roman citizen and a Pharisee. He began by persecuting the Christians but converted as a result of his experience of the resurrected Christ on the road to Damascus. His missionary activity began shortly thereafter, consisting of the revolutionary propagation of Christianity outside Judaism, among the Gentiles. About 48 C.E., Paul and his colleagues, after having spent two years in Asia Minor, embarked for Europe. They founded the churches of Philippi, Thessalonika, and Corinth. Whereas the Jerusalem group still conceived of Christianity as a branch of Judaism that required circumcision and respect for the normative prescriptions of the Torah, Paul took the bold stand of liberating Christianity from Judaism by opposing what he called the slavery of the Law to the freedom enjoyed by the Christian under the blessing of Faith. This moment of crisis and tension between Paul and the Jerusalem mother-church led by James, Jesus' brother, and by Peter, was the topic of the Epistle of Paul to the Galatians of Asia Minor (about 53 C.E.). Paul's activity in Ephesus ended with his imprisonment. Later in Corinth he prepared his mission to Rome. He made a stop in Caesarea, where he was imprisoned for two years. Using the rights he enjoyed as a Roman citizen, he required a hearing from the emperor himself. Thus, he arrived in Rome about 60 C.E.; two years later he was executed under Nero.

7.4 CHRISTIAN ORTHODOXY. The establishment of a basic Christian orthodoxy required four centuries and the process continues today. Early Christian doctrinal development appears as a system with multiple interconnected subsystems, whose functioning depends either on the internal dialectic of two major trends of Christian theology (the Judaic trend and the Platonic trend) or on the interaction of a main subsystem and other subsystems that gravitate around it (its "heresies").

7.4.1 Marcion. One early intellectual who helped orthodoxy to define itself against alternatives is Marcion of Sinope (ca. 80–155 C.E.), a rich ship owner and navigator of Sinope, whose doctrine as well as gifts were rejected by the church of Rome. Justin Martyr (ca. 100–165), the first Christian apologist, saw in Marcion (about 150–155) the number-one enemy of the Christian religion and a disciple of the accursed Gnostics. The first biblical theologian in history, Marcion came to the conclusion that the New and the Old Testaments could not possibly be speaking of the same God. With this, he further emphasized the gap between Christianity and Judaism already affirmed by Paul. By the defeat of Marcion and the Marcionite church, developing orthodoxy showed that it did not intend to give up the Old Testament, on account of its prefiguration of the redemption instigated by the sacrifice of Jesus Christ as well as its establishment of traditional legitimacy for Jesus' historical mission. Indeed, Jesus was only meaningful against the background of his own tradition.

7.4.2 Gnostic thinkers (9.4), along with Marcion and his opposite, the Jewish Christians, were among the early groups to be singled out as deviating from the mainstream of Christianity. The preserved heresiological tradition began with Irenaeus of Lyon (ca. 130–200 C.E.), followed by Hippolytus of Rome (d. 235). There is a whole range of contradictory positions toward Judaism and Christianity that are called Gnostic (see I. P. Couliano, *The Tree of Gnosis* [1992]). It is, however, possible to assert that Gnosticism went beyond Platonism in emphasizing the inferiority of the world and of its creator. This is one of the reasons the church fathers, who often exalted virginity and sometimes even condemned procreation and marriage, could not resolve to accept the idea of the negativity of the world. Some of them, such as Tertullian of Carthage (ca. 160–220), adopted double standards, accusing their Gnostic opponents of the same tenets that they themselves would not hesitate to preach in other contexts. Others, such as Clement of Alexandria (d. ca. 215), asserted the radical superiority of the Mosaic revelation over Greek philosophy, admitting however the existence of a "gnostic" elite among Christians, an elite that had access to a truth inaccessible to the rest of the community. Nevertheless, an unsurmountable barrier ended up separating Christianity from Gnosticism: the former recognized the truth of the biblical Genesis and the God of the Torah, whereas the latter changed the Old Testament God into the demiurge of *this* world, in contrast with the true God, first and foremost, isolated in his inaccessible transcendence. By accepting the terms of Genesis, Christians held the world to be good, but again they came close to the Gnostics as far as the doctrine of the Fall of the primordial couple of human beings was concerned, especially in the interpretation of the Fall proposed by the converted Manichaean, Augustine of Hippo (7.4.7).

7.4.3 Origen. Before the Council of Nicaea (325 C.E.), the most brilliant and influential, if not embarrassing, church father was doubtless Origen of Alexandria (ca. 185–254). A Christian and son of a Christian martyr (203), he probably studied philosophy under Ammonius Saccas and, like Plotinus (205–270), he fought as a Platonist those lost brethren who were the Gnostics, at the same time undergoing their influence. He began to write about 215 with the aim of bringing back into the church his rich friend Ambrose of Alexandria, who had been seduced by the subtleties of Valentinian gnosis. Among those endlessly depressing ecclesiastical debates that would only gain in intensity after Christianity was accepted and finally promoted to state religion of the Roman Empire, Origen was ordained a priest in Caesarea but defrocked by the bishop of Egypt amid intrigues over promotion. This must be the origin of the legend of his excommunication. The Origenist doctrine condemned in the environment of solidifying dogma of the fifth and sixth centuries made reference to his name, yet did not reflect personally on a man who had been dead for two hundred years.

Origen wrote before the great trinitarian and christological conflicts of the fourth century. His theology was therefore not explicit, for which it was more easily defensible or condemnable, whichever the case. His allegorical exegesis of the Bible, while virtuosic, was not more courageous than that which Ambrose or Augustine would later use. As a Platonist, Origen believed in the preexistence of the soul, yet his doctrine was not identical with Platonic or Hindu metensomatosis (reincarnation). During that period, Tertullian's traducianism still prevailed, according to which each new soul was conceived by the psychic copulation of the parents. The narrowing and galvanization of orthodox doctrine on this as well as on christological trinitarian matters, which, when enforced politically would eventually break the Byzantine Empire, and the recalcitrance of the Origenist monks were key factors in Origen's *post factum* anathematization.

7.4.4 Adoptionism. The importance of the dialectic of two major trends in primitive Christian theology, the Judaizing trend and the Platonizing trend, has been highlighted by R. M. Grant with particular emphasis on the christological debates in Antioch, where a "low" christology was contrasted to a "high" christology of Platonic origin, developed especially by Origen in Alexandria. "Low" christology seemed to go back as far as the apostle Peter himself (Acts 2:22, 36; 10:38). Among its proponents were the Ebionites, Judaizers who escaped the influence of Paul's theology; and Bishop Theophilus of Alexandria, author of the three books *For Autolycus,* who laid the bases of what later would be called "adoptionism," according to which Jesus Christ was born a human being and was adopted by God as His Son during baptism in the Jordan. On the contrary, the "high," Platonic, christology, represented by Ignatius of Antioch and by his disciple Tatian, emphasized the divinity of the Christ. An extreme form of this, especially meaningful in a Platonist context and characteristic of several Gnostic groups, was docetism (Gk. *dokein,* to seem) in which a lofty, transcendent being such as the Christ (Logos) could not possibly have taken on flesh, suffered, or died, but only seemed to. The rich christology, connected with the Alexandrian philosophy of the Logos, prevailed over adoptionism, which was condemned (264–268 C.E.) in the person of the heresiarch Paul of Samosata, bishop of Antioch. The debates increased in intensity once Christianity gained first the status of tolerated religion (313 C.E.), then was encouraged and possibly adopted on his deathbed by the emperor Constantine (d. 337) and eventually became the state religion (391), with the exclusion of all pagan cults.

7.4.5 The Cappadocian Fathers. During the fourth century C.E., the formation of orthodoxy received the fundamental contribution of the Cappadocian fathers, Basil of Caesarea (ca. 329–379 C.E.), his friend Gregory of Nazianzus (ca. 329–391) and the former's brother Gregory of Nyssa (ca. 335–395), who consolidated the trinitarian dogma, definitively formulated at the Council of Constantinople in 381. The three Cappadocians were Origenists and Neoplatonists.

7.4.6 Ambrose. First Latin father born in the Christian religion, Ambrose of Milan (ca. 339–397 C.E.) came from a family of the imperial aristocracy. His theology was modeled on Origen and the philosophy of Philo of Alexandria as interpreted by other Latin authors.

7.4.7 Augustine. During the golden age of Christian theology, the second half of the fourth century, unfortunately marked by internal debates in which another Latin father, Jerome (ca. 347–420 C.E.), the translator of the Bible into Latin (the *Vulgate*), stood out not only through his learning but also through his aggressiveness, a special place was occupied by the Latin father Augustine (354–430), bishop of Hippo. After joining the Manichaean auditors for nine years, the young and ambitious African rhetorician who settled in Milan (384) felt that the future belonged to Christianity. He abandoned the Manichaeans and received baptism from Ambrose in 387. Ordained as a priest in Hippo Regia, today Annaba in Algeria, in 391, he became bishop in 395. Two years later, he wrote the *Confessions,* addressed to all those who were not satisfied with the finitude of mundane existence. And yet the repentant bishop dwelled upon his bittersweet mundane experience: while mitigating the exaggerations of certain ascetics and moral rigorists, at the same time he understood that the sin of concupiscence is too much a part of ourselves to be dealt with lightly. His fight against Manichaean world rejection lacked elegance: slander and the pressure of the threatening mob were more persuasive than any argument. Against the dominant church in North Africa, that of the Donatists, who required from their sacerdotes moral purity, Augustine did not hesitate to summon state authorities. (In Christian heresiology, "Donatism" would end up as a genre designation, to which belong such sects as the Waldenses, which refuse to recognize the validity of the sacrifice *ex opere operato,* by virtue of the performance only, maintaining that the moral quality of the priest influences the oblation, which takes place *ex opere operantis.*) Today we cannot but be dismayed by Augustine's authoritarian doctrine and by his lack of moral concern for his victims, whom only one thing separated from a contingent truth that the shrewd bishop possessed: power. Yet Manichaeism was preserved in him and to a certain extent became through him official church doctrine.

It all began with the doctrine of grace of the monk Pelagius (d. 418 C.E.), who firmly believed in free will. According to him and perhaps to a majority of Western bishops, human nature was fundamentally good and could perform good deeds even without the aid of grace. Augustine's past experience of the world with its sensuality and frivolity, which on the one hand he strongly condemned and on the other showed nostalgia for, did not fit the clarity and simplicity of Pelagius' position. It was not for a church of saints, but for a church of sinners like himself, that Augustine eventually formulated his anti-Pelagian doctrine of free will, maintaining that all human beings inherit Original Sin and thus only grace can restore to them the faculty of choice, giving back the very same freedom that, wrongly used, had brought about the Fall of the first human beings. This is tantamount to saying that only Adam and Eve had actually been free to choose, and they had chosen evil. This Original Sin is inherited: upon birth, each and every one of us is thus free to choose—the evil (that is, one scarcely has freedom of choice). Only by the intervention of divine grace can one choose the good again. Yet grace is not bestowed upon just anyone, nor for computable reasons. It is only allotted to certain predestined ones (*praedestinati*), according to a mysterious reason of God. Moreover, the number of the predestined is limited to the number of fallen angels whose places remain free in heaven. The rest of humankind belongs to the masses cut off from redemption, the *massa perditionis*.

Confronted with the decline of the Roman Empire, Augustine maintained in *The City of God* (413–427 C.E.) the total independence of the church from any political system. The same position was shared by his follower Orosius (418): the empire will disappear, the church will subsist under its conquerors.

7.4.8 The Middle Ages. This forecast that the empire would disappear was an easy one, for it was obvious to anyone that the days of the empire were numbered. If at the end of the fourth century C.E. the Egyptian monks, dirty and bearded, dared to show up in Rome, the mob threw stones at them. The situation changed radically when the thick walls of monasteries became the only barriers protecting order from the anarchy that followed the fall of the Roman Empire (476). The Benedictine order and the monastery of Montecassino (ca. 529) were founded by Benedict of Nursia (ca. 480–547). The monastic spirit did not have much in common with the spirit that animated the solitary ascetics of the desert such as Anthony (ca. 300); his ideal was too difficult and the occasions for failure too numerous. The cenobitic movement, started in Egypt by Pachomius (292–346), offered an alternative that the East hastened to adopt and to propagate: collective solitude. By making it available in the West, Benedict created relatively protected centers that actually—as the far-seeing monk Cassiodorus (d. 575) very well recognized—served as greenhouses for a new intellectual elite ready to emerge as soon as external conditions were more favorable.

The first occasion arose with the creation of the Carolingian Empire (800 C.E.). Charlemagne (768–814) attracted to his court the most knowledgeable religious and lay personalities of the West, such as Alcuin of York (ca. 730–804), who became abbot of Saint-Denis (796), the historian Paul the Deacon (ca. 720–795), and so forth. This intellectual movement reestablished in Europe the teaching of the *artes liberales* (the *trivium* and the *quadrivium*) and transformed the monasteries into centers for the preservation and propagation of culture. The papacy, whose solid foundations had been laid by Gregory the Great (590–604), by legitimizing the empire that it exhumed in 800 in order to obtain a temporal sword against external menaces (the Muslim Arabs and Berbers had conquered Spain in 711), created by the same move its greatest enemy. Medieval political life until after the Ghibellin (partisan of the empire) Dante Alighieri was dominated by the painful, dialectical opposition of church and state. The pope-reformer Gregory VII (1073–85) proclaimed himself superior to any temporal authority and denied the empire (now German) the right of conferring ecclesiastical investitures. Emperor Henry IV deposed the pope in 1076; the pope in turn deposed and excommunicated the emperor, who was obliged by his princes to beg the pope's pardon at Canossa (1077). Yet the conflict was far from over. Henry IV named his own pope (Clement III), occupied Rome (1083), and was crowned by Clement (1084). The quest for European supremacy continued for centuries, in a political climate of increasing complexity. History manuals follow every vicissitude of this irresolvable debate between spiritual and temporal power. Only marginally does it belong to the *religious* history of the West, which was to show spectacular developments from the twelfth century.

7.4.9 The twelfth-century renaissance. The so-called "twelfth-century renaissance," as Charles Homer Haskins called this period, was to a large extent the result of events in the precedent century: in 1085 C.E. the reunited kingdoms of Castille and León had won Toledo, the former capital of the Visigothic kingdom, from the Muslims; in 1099 the crusaders in the Holy Land had conquered Jerusalem from the Muslim Seljuk Turks, proclaiming in 1100 the Kingdom of Jerusalem under Balduin. Bernard of Clairvaux (1091–1153) gave a new reading to the history of his time and formulated new religious ideals among the reformed religious orders as well as among laypeople in quest for spiritual achievements.

The consequences of the conquest of Toledo were of paramount importance in Western history. Attracted by the exoticism, the mystery, and the progressiveness of Arabic culture much more than by the overt purpose of the College of Translators set up in Toledo by Archbishop Raymundo, which refuted the principles of Muslim religion, monks from all parts of Europe and Britain met in this new center of learning. Theologians such as Peter the Venerable, abbot of the Cluny monastery, and Rodrigo Ximénez de Rada engaged in the dirty work of religious debate, yet even they failed to conceal their interest in Islamic civilization. Under their cover, excellent translators under the direction of the archdeacon Dominicus Gundisalinus effected the slow and monumental work of transposing Arabic culture, and, through it, Hellenic antiquity, into Latin. The master translator, to whom the Latin versions of no less than seventy different works of medicine, science, and philosophy are attributed, was Gerardus of Cremona (1114–1187 C.E.). Through the activity of the College of Translators, Christian Europe discovered and adopted Aristotle's philosophy, which would become the base of the new scholastic philosophy, whose chief representatives were Albert the Great (1193–1280) and Thomas Aquinas (1225–1274). Their precursors had been important yet less known thinkers such as Anselm of Aosta (1033–1109), Peter Lombard (d. 1160), author of the famous *Sentences,* and Peter Abelard (1079–1142), interesting for his conceptions concerning the superiority of women over men, probably borrowed from the theories of courtly love.

The new age was also characterized by special devotion to the Virgin Mary, Mother of God, who became if not *de jure* then at least *de facto* equal with the Trinitarian persons, the true *Regina coeli,* the star of redemption who intercedes with God for the human beings. The cathedrals, mainly dedicated to Our Lady, which rose in northern France around 1150 C.E., were the visible symbol of the new spirituality. Little by little, the schools functioning alongside these cathedrals moved into autonomous universities. Among the Provençal troubadours, the equivalent of the devotion to Mary was the devotion to a Lady. This phenomenon called "courtly love," the existence of which is doubted by many scholars who reason that it, was never practiced, consisted of an intellectual tension in the lover who, by exasperating his desire for the Lady without ever fulfilling it, was supposed to undergo a special experience that had much in common with a mystical experience, if it was not one. In Italy courtly love would produce the poetical genre called *Dolce Stil Novo,* to which belong many of the compositions of the Florentine exile Dante Alighieri (1265–1321), author of the *Divine Comedy.* For those engaged in the practice of courtly love, many must have been the occasions of stumblings and relapse; yet the documents are clear to the point that only historians who operate by projecting a simplified worldview of their own time onto the past could doubt it: unfulfilled desire was indeed the key to this trend of sublimated eroticism, whose ideal was the opposite of the medical lore of that period, according to which unconsummated love was a dangerous and even lethal syndrome. It is equally clear that the novels of the Arthurian cycle, whose ideology must have originated in some monastic central intelligence agency of northern France (probably Cistercian), made unflinching devotion to the Lady the ultimate test of a knight's inner quality. This quality was mystical, for the Arthurian cycle worked from the idea that struggle against infidels and solid virtue were sufficient to bring about holiness. A profound relation linked the Arthurian cycle, with its sanctification of moral purity and service to the Lady, to the formation of the religious military orders. The idea of founding the Templar Order came to Hugues de Payens in Jerusalem, possibly inspired by the order of the Assassins or Isma^cili Nizaris founded by Hasan-i Sabah in the Elburz mountains of Iran (17.6.3). Known under the name of *muhamar,* "the Red ones," the *fedawa* of the Isma^cili Caliphate wore red caps, belts, and boots with a white tunic. The Templars wore a red cross on a white cloak and the knights of the Hospital of Saint John of Jerusalem (known as Knights of Malta between 1530 and 1798), who oftentimes reversed the symbolism of the Templars, eventually adopted as their coat of arms a white cross on red background. In 1118, with the support of young Bernard of Clairvaux, who adapted for them the strict Rule of Saint Benedict to the conditions of military life, the Templars received official recognition and the right to bear arms to defend the pilgrims to the Holy Land. Actually, they would become specialists in the defense of Jerusalem. After the pope granted the Templars and the Hospitalers the privilege of direct dependence from the papal see, cutting through the endless ranks of church bureaucracy, they became virtually the true masters of the Holy Land. Recklessly courageous in battle, this Christian elite corps won an extraordinarily important role in the West as well. First the Templars were entrusted with the transfer of the pilgrims' money to the Holy Land; then, through a tight network of fortresses from Scotland to Spain, they transported money within Europe; eventually becoming bankers and issuing certificates of exchange redeemable from another Templar agency. Bankers to kings, accountable to no one but the pope, the Templars inevitably ended up, by their riches and their independence, being the object of envy, jealousy, hatred, and anxiety among the emerging powers of the state.

The loss of Jerusalem in 1187 C.E. did not yet cast any doubt on the usefulness of the Templars; on the contrary, in 1198 a new military order appeared in Germany, the Teutonic knights, who would remain faithful to the excommunicated emperor Frederic II (1210–1250). The situation changed for the Templars when the last Christian bastions in the Holy Land fell in 1291 to the Mameluke Turks. In 1307, wishing to make an end to their financial power, the French king Philip the Fair put the Templars of France under arrest and pressed the pope (Clement V, exiled in Poitiers and then in Avignon, outside French jurisdiction yet dangerously close to French territory) to withdraw his protection from them. The Templar order was dissolved in 1312; its great master Jacques de Molay became, in 1314, the last victim of the bloody staging devised by Philip the Fair and by his counselor William of Nogaret.

The formation of military religious orders and the phenomenon of courtly love can be understood against the background of the chivalrous ideal propagated in the twelfth century, for example, through the novels of Chrétien of Troyes. It is more difficult to show the organic links that tied the Cathars to the entire twelfth-century renaissance. A popular author connected them with courtly love, but the supporting evidence is meager. They were believers of two different religions coming from the Byzantine Empire, whose church had cut off all relations with the West after the "Eastern Schism" of 1054 C.E. One of the two religions, Bogomilism, had appeared in Bulgaria and reached Constantinople by the beginning of the eleventh century. It was treated as a heresy and persecuted by sword and fire, yet in reality it was fairly close to orthodoxy. One can find in it ancient docetic doctrines, according to which the physical body of Jesus Christ (and probably of Mary as well) was a deceiving, ghostly apparition. The Bogomils were anti-Judaic: for them the God of the Old Testament was Satan (9.8).

The second Cathar doctrine, which completely replaced the first in Provençe after 1167 (date of the Cathar council of Saint-Félix-de-Lauragais, with the participation of the Byzantine bishop Nicetas), was the revitalization of an ancient heresy, the Origenism of the fathers of the Nitrian desert in the fourth century C.E. The Origenist Cathars (or the Albigenses), who professed a form of radical dualism in contrast with the moderate dualism of the Bogomils (9.9), had a doctrine that, for all its gloom, was not deprived of a certain grandness, especially in the poorly known thinker Jean of Lugio (perhaps Lugano), a Lombard heresiarch of Bergamo about 1250.

In 1209 C.E. a Crusade was launched against the Albigenses, led at the onset by a professional military man, Simon of Monfrot, who leveled entire towns and villages without making any distinction between heretics and good Catholics. More moderate afterward, the Crusade became a war of conquest of the southern independent feudal territories by the Crown of France, ending with the victory of the latter after the fall of the last and foremost Cathar stronghold in Montségur (1244). However, the Cathar supreme hierarchy seemed to have had time to flee to Lombardy, where shortly afterward the famous Lombard bankers and merchants made their appearance. The Albigenses had been the bankers of the south, and it is not impossible that they took their treasury with them, as the eminent specialist Jean Duvernoy believes.

The instrument of papal Inquisition appeared during the same Albigensian Crusade in 1231 C.E., being staffed by the Order of Preachers, better known as Dominicans after their founder (1216) Dominic Guzman. The Dominicans were followed shortly thereafter by the Franciscans or Minor Friars, a religious organization professing strict asceticism, founded by Francis of Assisi (1182–1226), who in his youth had devoured French chivalrous novels and sought to emulate the moral perfection of Percival and Galahad in a field of peace. Knight of Christ and Lady Poverty, Francis relinquished all earthly goods in order to serve the truly disinherited of the earth: the poor, the sick, the miserable. Through the channel of the two mendicant orders, the Christian message penetrated to the heart of the masses, where it often inflamed millennial dreams and apocalyptic visions of the end. The Fraticelli or Spiritual Franciscans pursued the millenarian ideas of the Calabrian Abbott Joachim of Flora (ca. 1135–1202), whose work prophesying the coming of a new World Age was proclaimed "Eternal Gospel" by a Franciscan in 1254.

7.4.10 Nominalism. The edifice of scholasticism, based on the Aristotelian scientific and philosophical system, seemed to have found a solution to every question in the world, when a whole series of first-rate thinkers systematically began attacking its too-narrow premises. The leader of the new trend was the Franciscan John Duns Scotus (d. 1308 C.E.), followed by the famous William of Ockham (ca. 1285–1349), with whom the "way of the moderns" took the name of nominalism and reached the University of Paris, where it was taught by professors such as John Buridan (d. 1358) and Nicole of Oresme (d. 1382). The extraordinary merit of nominalism was to shake the theological premises of scholasticism, rejecting Aristotelian and Ptolemaic conceptions of a finite universe. It was within nominalist circles and under church persecution that ideas such as the infinity of the universe, the plurality of the worlds, and the arbitrary (that is, noncentral) position of the earth in the universe emerged in Europe. These doctrines were later expounded by the German nominalist, Cardinal Nicholas of Cusa (1401–1464).

7.4.11 Humanism. Scholasticism was not the only thirteenth-century product that failed to satisfy the intellectual demands of the fourteenth century. Having discovered that behind the science of the

Arabs lay the lost Greco-Roman civilization, the intellectuals of this age hoped to quench their thirst for knowledge directly from the sources. Less inhibited by the strictness of thirteenth-century religious ideals, they uncovered lost sensuality and gave it an expression of frankness unparalleled in Western history. Francesco Petrarca (1304–1374 C.E.) and Giovanni Boccaccio (1313–1375) were the precursors of the fifteenth-century humanists, who invented the concept of the Middle Ages as an epoch of darkness and fanaticism interposed between modern times and Greco-Roman Antiquity, the latter being viewed not only as an epoch of superlative intellectual splendor, but also of *scientific truth*. The humanist search is a search in reverse: *the future lies in the past and can only be discovered by mastery of Latin and Greek.*

7.4.12 The Italian Renaissance. Since Aristotle had already been discovered and had contributed to the emergence of a product—scholasticism—which modern times had begun to critique, certain influential minds in Florence were persuaded that only Plato's revelation would be able to reestablish the whole truth. This is why the banker and industrialist Cosimo de' Medici (d. 1464 C.E.) decided to confer upon Marsilio Ficino (1433–1499) the task of translating into Latin Plato's complete work, which was followed by Plotinus's *Enneads* and by many tractates by Neoplatonic philosophers. This epoch, commonly known under the name of "Italian Renaissance," was characterized by Platonic syncretism, that is, by the idea (present in Augustine of Hippo) that God had already been the object of a "primordial revelation" made to all pristine human beings in the world, a revelation whose traces are to be found in all ancient religions and whose code can be broken with the aid of Platonic hermeneutics. For Ficino and for his disciple Giovanni Pico della Mirandola (1463–1494), this amounts to saying that Hermes Trismegistus, Zoroaster, Moses, and Orpheus were in equal proportion depositaries of a unique occult truth. This truth found expression in Neoplatonic and Arabic magic and in the Kabbalah of the Jews, discovered by Pico della Mirandola, who, having an interest in sources that went beyond Greek, tried to learn some Hebrew, some Aramaic, and perhaps some rudiments of Arabic. It is important to note that modern education adopted Greek and Latin under the pressure of humanism, and it was likewise under the influence of the latter that the distinction was made between the "specialist" who had access to the sources and the "dilettante" who had not. Enforced in the early nineteenth century by the reformer of education Wilhelm von Humboldt (1767–1835), these principles managed to survive to the present day, though completely deprived of what made them attractive in the fifteenth century, that is, the belief that our bright future is to be sought in the past, and that the knowledge of other cultures serves to discover hidden truths, important for the salvation of humankind.

7.4.13 Reform movements. The first organized reform movements, whose purpose was to return to apostolic poverty, emerged in the twelfth century. Among them, the Waldenses of Lyon (1173 C.E.) were the most important. If the Franciscans were able to absorb part of the legitimate complaints of the population, they were also the inspirers of pauperistic and millenarian movements. John Wycliff (d. 1384), professor at Oxford, was the creator of the movement of the Lollards, who rejected the eucharist, priestly celibacy, and the church hierarchy. The Prague preacher John Hus (burnt at Constance in 1415) was accused of being a disciple of Wycliff, despite his protests. He started a popular movement that was not as much a war of religion as a war of Bohemian independence from the Germans.

On the positive side of the balance, the ecumenical overtures of the time seemed to meet with success, and the Western and Eastern churches were briefly reunited. Unfortunately, the fall of Constantinople to the Turks (1453 C.E.) marked an end to the idyll. The conflict that opposed Constantinople to Rome, albeit disguised as an absurd debate concerning the word *filioque* introduced (abusively) by the Iberian Christians in the credo of Nicea-Constantinople, was a conflict of power. The Greek Patriarchate annulled the reunification treaty signed in 1439 in Florence by the Byzantine emperor John VIII Palaeologus. At the beginning of the sixteenth century, a far more dramatic religious schism opposed the German north to the rest of Europe.

This schism was the work of the Augustinian monk Martin Luther (1483–1546 C.E.), theology professor at the University of Wittenberg, led by his reflections on Paul and Augustine to the conclusion that the intercession of the church for the faithful is useless, that the sacraments are not effective, that humankind is sinful by nature whence celibacy is impossible and marriage abominable yet necessary, that individuals are predestined and their fate is not to be changed by human endeavor, and finally that one is justified by faith alone, without the works. After having hung his ninety-five theses on October 31, 1517, to the door of the Wittenberg cathedral, Luther bravely defended his viewpoint before the cardinal legate Caetano. Under the influence of his younger friend the humanist Philip Schwartzerd-Melanchthon (1497–1560), Luther ended up compromising on many points of religious doctrine and practice, whereas his French disciple Calvin, who reigned in Geneva starting in 1541, professed a far more rigid, dogmatic, and gloomy form of Protestantism. The Protestant movement won many adepts among the particularist princes of Germany and Switzerland. The secularization of monasteries was acclaimed by bands of armed knights and by peasants as well who, led by the radical Protestant Thomas Münzer, began a revolt, disavowed by Luther and ferociously repressed by the League of the Reformed princes in 1525.

The Protestant movement itself was not uniform: fundamentalist in its essence, it contained nevertheless an important libertine component (Anabaptists, Enthusiasts, Mennonites, etc.). The situation grew more complex as Luther himself in his later years disclaimed much of what he had stood for in his youth, whereas his old students and followers, among them the radicals Ulrich Zwingli (1484–1531) and Calvin, would stick to Luther's primitive views. In its turn, the Catholic church started its own Reformation (usually known as Counter-Reformation, somewhat misleadingly), incorporating many of the tenets defended by the Protestants during the long proceedings of the Council of Trent (1545–1563). The heroes of the Catholic Reformation were the members of the Company of Jesus, or Jesuits, a religious order founded in 1534 by the Spaniard Ignatius of Loyola (1491–1556). Like the Protestant Reformation, the Catholic one was a fundamentalist movement, whose austere morality and numerous prohibitions (e.g., the reading of forbidden books listed in the *Index librorum prohibitorum*) marked the coming of modern times. In 1534 another national church, the Church of England, separated from the Roman church, following the pattern of secularization seen in Germany. As a result, Catholics in England became an oppressed minority. Religious conflicts and the Calvinist Puritans' quest for power would lead to the English Revolution (1642).

7.5 THE HISTORY OF THE EXPANSION OF CHRISTENDOM is difficult to summarize. The Germans were evangelized by Boniface-Ulfila (680–754 C.E.), after which they sent Christian missions to the Slavicized Bulgars, whose Khan Boris, however, preferred the baptism of the Greek Church (860). The Greeks met with less success among the Moraves, but the "Cyrillic" alphabet created by the missionary Cyril (ca. 826–869) and his brother Methodius (ca. 815–885) was adopted by the Slavs. In 988, Vladimir, the Scandinavian prince of Kiev, opted for Eastern Christianity, which became the religion of Russia.

European territorial expansion led to the evangelization of numerous peoples. The concordat between the pope and the kings of Spain and Portugal allowed Christianity to plant solid roots in South America. Together with the Franciscans and the Dominicans, the Jesuits spent the best of their energies in missionary activities. This new and dynamic order aimed at copying the European social model among the natives, by creating a local educated elite. In Brazil the Jesuits began a mass experiment that saved hundreds of thousands of South American natives from certain death by giving them food and shelter in reservations ruled by rigorous communalist discipline. From the viewpoint of the European settlers, the Jesuit experiment had gone too far. The order was expelled from Latin America in 1767. Shortly thereafter (1808), the colonial church came to an end with the liberation of the South American states from European tutelage.

Missions in Africa, both Protestant and Catholic, did not become successful on a large scale before the first half of the nineteenth century. The expansion of Christendom in Asia proved to be more difficult. In China, missionaries landed at different periods (635; 1294; ca. 1600), but were unable to put down roots before the Opium War of 1840–1842. The mission of Francis Xavier to Japan (1549) met with more success: at the end of the sixteenth century, Japan had 300,000 Christians. This period was followed by persecution lasting until 1858, when many crypto-Christians were discovered, communities that had kept their Christian faith hidden.

In Southeast Asia, Catholicism set foot in the Philippines at the time of the Spanish conquest (1538); in Buddhist countries, the Christian expansion met with serious opposition. Korea has seen a vast expansion of Christianity in the twentieth century.

In spite of the very early foundation of the first Christian churches on the western (Malabar) coast of India, Christianity remained a very limited phenomenon in the Indian subcontinent. Christians were a majority only in the small Portuguese colony of Goa (1510). After the British conquest of India (1858), all sorts of missions were active; yet in 1980 no more than three percent of the Indian population was Christian.

Australia and New Zealand were subject to missions during the nineteenth century by Anglicans (1788), Catholics (1838), and Protestants (1840).

7.6 COUNCILS. Problematic issues of the church, both of a doctrinal and of a practical nature, are discussed in its councils.

The first ecumenical council was summoned by Emperor Constantine in Nicaea (Asia Minor) from June 19 to August 25, 325 C.E. The 318 bishops present condemned the Arian heresy (7.7.2). The Nicaean credo affirmed the full divinity of Christ. The long version of the credo, adopted by the Council of Chalcedon in 451, is the profession of faith of most Christians to the present day.

The second ecumenical council was summoned by Theodosius I at Constantinople in 381. It dealt with the Pneumatomachians, who believed that the Holy Ghost was inferior to the Father and the Son.

The third ecumenical council was summoned by Theodosius II in 431 at Ephesus (Asia Minor) to make an end to the christological debate that opposed Nestorius, patriarch of Constantinople, to Cyril, bishop of Alexandria in Egypt. The two parties excommunicated each other, yet Cyril succeeded (433) in making the moderate Nestorians accept both the title of *Theotokos* (Mother of God), which he gave the Virgin, and his views concerning the union of the two natures of Christ in one person.

In 451 the Council of Chalcedon took a firm christological position, leading to a declaration distinguishing the two natures of Christ that unfortunately did not make an end to the debate, but alienated Monophysites. Justinian I summoned in 553 the Second Council of Constantinople in order to reformulate the Chalcedonian definition in such a way as to emphasize more consistently the divinity of Christ. The same council formally condemned Origenism.

During the eighth century the iconoclast controversy (730–843) carried the day. Worship and access to divine power through the icons revered by the populace and monks was condemned—in a time of natural disasters, depopulation of the cities, and the rise of Islam—as idolatry deserving of God's punishment. The fate of images, accepted and then again rejected, was contested by the synods of 754 and 787.

The Western authorities took positions on these Eastern controversies a number of times. The tension between the East and the West (which repudiated iconoclasm) became intolerable when the Western church denied its recognition to the anti-iconoclastic (or "iconodoule") Photius as patriarch of Constantinople. In turn, the Byzantine church condemned the use of the word *filioque* in the profession of faith (867). Deposed from the patriarchate in 877, Photius came back, with the pope's consent, in 879–880. The Eastern Schism (1054) marked a new and irreversible point of decline for Byzantium, concluded with the

Ottoman conquest (1453), and the rise of the West, which came to stand as self-sufficient in ecclesiastical matters. The Latran synods in 1123, 1139, 1179, and 1215 had the ambition of being ecumenical councils. The last of them was especially known for having put into circulation the word *transubstantiation*. A council summoned in Lyon in 1274 tried to reestablish the unity of the two churches, but its results were sabotaged by a synod in Constantinople (1283).

The Council of Vienna (1311–1312) dealt with several thorny questions such as the alleged sacrilegious practices of the Knights Templars and the interpretation of the poverty of Christ advanced by the Spiritual Franciscans. The proceedings of the Council of Constance, summoned in order to make an end to the Western Schism (1378), that is, to that particular historical situation in which several popes were competing for the general recognition of the church, were held between 1414 and 1418.

A new attempt to reinstate church unity was at the center of an ecumenical council that, between 1430 and 1442, moved several times from place to place. In 1439 the Latin and Greek churches signed a treaty in Florence, followed by other treaties with the Armenian (1439), the Coptic, and the Ethiopic (1442) churches. After the occupation of what was left of the Byzantine Empire (Constantinople) by the Turks in 1453, a 1484 Greek synod revoked the 1439 treaty.

In the sixteenth century the Catholic Council of Trent (December 13, 1545, to December 4, 1563) answered by a series of reforms the climate of moral rigorism installed by the Protestants.

In the nineteenth century the First Vatican Council (1865–1869) affirmed the primacy and infallibility of the pope, thus increasing the distance that separated the Roman church both from the other Christian confessions and from the modern secular states that were emancipated from the values of religion.

More recently the Catholic council known as Vatican II (October 11, 1962, to December 8, 1965) took place under the sign of conciliation and ecumenical unity. Summoned by Pope John XXIII, with the participation of over two thousand bishops and generals of religious orders, the council decreased pontifical centralism, replaced the Latin mass with mass in vernacular languages, turned the celebrant to face the people for the eucharistic sacrifice, and recognized the value of historical methods in the study of religion.

7.7 **CHRISTIAN THEOLOGY** forms a system that can be described in synchronic terms. The history of this system forms another system, which entertains very complex relations of interdependence with the first. Having outlined in general the history of Christianity, we will now concentrate on the synchronic system of possibilities in Christian thought.

7.7.1 Trinitarian doctrines. One of the peculiarities of Christianity is that it plays with three traditionally male divine persons engaged in complex trinitarian relationships (the Father, the Son, and the Holy Spirit) and also in a relationship with a female entity (the Virgin Mary), whose connection with each person of the Trinity is not easy to describe.

On the other hand, the persons of the Trinity are part of a multidimensional scenario. To give an example, some of the dimensions characterizing Christ are his divinity, his humanity, the composition of the aggregate called Christ, his nature, his substance, his hierarchical position, his relation to his Father, his relation to his Mother, and so forth. We can say that Jesus Christ is part of a multidimensional *fractal* that evolves according to certain rules. To simplify the matter rather drastically, we might treat these rules as binary. As a result, we can envisage Christ as only divine, only human, divine and human, neither divine nor human (of a third nature). Christ's double nature can further be described as mixed or separated, and in the mixture the two natures can be either distinct or merged. Additionally, the mixture may contain more of the divine than of the human nature, or vice versa. (Any analogue model can be used to achieve a representation of mixture: water and wine, water and oil, flour and water, and so forth; in this case we can say that a theology has a technomorphic model. It is legitimate to think that natural models may have played a role in christology, that is, in the minds of those who have devoted their attention to the christological system.)

Hierarchically, the trinitarian persons can be described as equal or unequal, and the distinctions among them can follow many patterns.

These simple genetic rules reveal the huge number of possibilities present in the christological network. Let us have a look at the *actual* filling of these possibilities.

7.7.2 "Low" christology. The great christological debates are in part the result of the existence of two trends mentioned above, a theologically "low" trend of Jewish background and a theologically "high" trend of Platonic background. "Low" christology emphasized Christ's humanity. Its earliest representatives were the Ebionites (the "Poor"), a Jewish-Christian sect that went back to the historical phase in which Christianity was nothing but a Jewish sect. The Ebionites followed the Torah, practiced circumcision, kept the Sabbath and the Jewish festivals, and rejected Paul because of his hostility toward the Law. For them, Jesus was only a prophet, a human being with nothing divine in him. The story of his immaculate conception and virgin birth was meaningless.

"Low" christology counts adoptionism among its outcomes (7.4.4). Arius (ca. 250–336) was excommunicated in 318 by Bishop Alexander of Alexandria for having stated that Christ was substantially inferior to the Father. The first ecumenical council of Nicaea was summoned in 325 against Arian subordinationism. The word *homoousios* (consubstantial), already used by Origen, was adopted to describe the relation between Father and Son.

A more elaborate version of "low" christology is part of Nestorianism. Nestorianism was rooted in the Antiochene theology of Diodore of Tarsus and Theodore of Mopsuestia. Nestorius, who became patriarch of Constantinople in 428, asserted the complete separation of the two natures of Christ, divine and human. He was condemned at the Council of Ephesus (431). After the Muslim conquests, the Nestorians were protected by the Abbassid caliphs (750–1258), and their leader, or Catholicos, settled in Baghdad in 762. After the Mongol conquest (1258), the patriarchal see moved to the north of Iraq. The Nestorian missions to the Far East ceased after this date. Later on, while the Nestorian Church of Iraq was under constant attack from the Kurds and the Ottoman Turks, many Nestorians from Cyprus and India converted to Catholicism. The Catholicoi of the church called "Assyrian" have lived in exile in the United States since 1933.

The consequence of the separation of the two natures of Christ led the Nestorians to the Antiochene christology (God descends in the human being Jesus as He descended in the prophets) and to a "poor" mariology, for they believe that Mary did not give birth to God, but only to the human being Jesus. Consequently, they deny her the title of Theotokos (Dei genitrix), opting for the more sober Christotokos (That Who Bore Christ), which would be acceptable by all standards (for Christ *can* be God) if Theotokos had not been pressed upon the church in 431 by the Alexandrian school.

7.7.3 "High" christology is usually associated with Alexandrian theology and especially with the patriarch Cyril of Alexandria (d. 444). It had several schools, such as that of Apollinaris of Laodicaea (ca. 310–390), who did not believe in the full humanity of Christ and whose views were condemned by the Council of Constantinople (381). Apollinaris built his christology from anthropology, according to which Christ must have a soul and a body. Apollinaris denied Christ a *human* soul: this had been entirely replaced by the divine Logos. The council decided to the contrary: Christ had a human soul.

Later on, Eutyches of Constantinople (ca. 378–454) maintained that the divine nature of Christ deleted his humanity. His views were refuted by the Council of Chalcedon (451), which declared that Christ had two natures: divine and human. Even after this council, Nestorianism still maintained the *separation* of the two natures, leading to an adoptionist christology and to a "poor" mariology. The trend that is the opposite of Nestorianism is generally called Monophysitism (Of One Nature Solely), although it adhered to the Chalcedonian formula of the two natures. Its contrast with orthodoxy is subtler, introducing the notion of mixture: Christ's two natures were mixed, and "God-in-Christ" was a *tertium genus,* a being of a new species, neither divine nor human.

The Nicaean profession of faith maintained that Christ was of the same substance as the Father. If this was true, argued the Monophysites, then he could not possibly have been of the same substance as humanity.

After 451 the Christians of Egypt and Syria showed their preference for the "rich" christology of the Monophysites. Emperor Heraclius (610–641) sought compromise between them and the orthodox by introducing the formula of *Monoenergetism* and *Monothelitism,* according to which the Son has two natures, but one power and one will, stemming from the Father. Against this position, the Council of Constantinople (680) decided that Jesus Christ had two wills. When Egypt and Syria were conquered by the Arabs, the persecuted Monophysite inhabitants showed little resistance to being thus liberated from the doctrinal yoke of Constantinople. Monophysite beliefs, combined with docetic ideas, became the ethnic confession of the Copts and prospered in Syria as Jacobitism. It is necessary to emphasize once again that Monophysitism was different from both Nestorianism (two separate natures) and from the orthodox formula (two natures, not separate but distinct). Monophysitism offered a "high" mariology that became orthodox. Against the Nestorians, whose christology was, in the last instance, adoptionist, the patriarch Cyril of Alexandria asserted that Mary was *Theotokos, Dei genitrix,* a position that the church further radicalized in conferring upon her the title of *Mater Dei.*

A few mariological explanations are required. The position that prevailed was expressed during the second century by the proto-Gospel of James: Mary had stayed *virgo in partu* and *post partum,* i.e., *semper virgo.* Among the characters of the Christian cosmology, she assumed more and more supernatural features. The Second Council of Nicaea (787) set her above the saints, to whom reverence (*douleia*) was due, whereas Mary must be the object of "superreverence" (*hyperdouleia*). Slowly she became a member of the divine family, Mother of God. The *dormitio Virginis* became *Maria in caelis adsumpta,* the Franciscans excluded her from Original Sin, she was given the title of *Mater ecclesiae,* and she became *mediatrix* and *intercessor* for human beings with God. This was how Christianity gradually installed in heaven a familial pattern that is far less strict and inexorable than the solitary patriarchalism of the biblical God.

7.7.4 Summary. This brief christological sketch admits a synchronic interpretation, all its possibilities being latently present in the system:

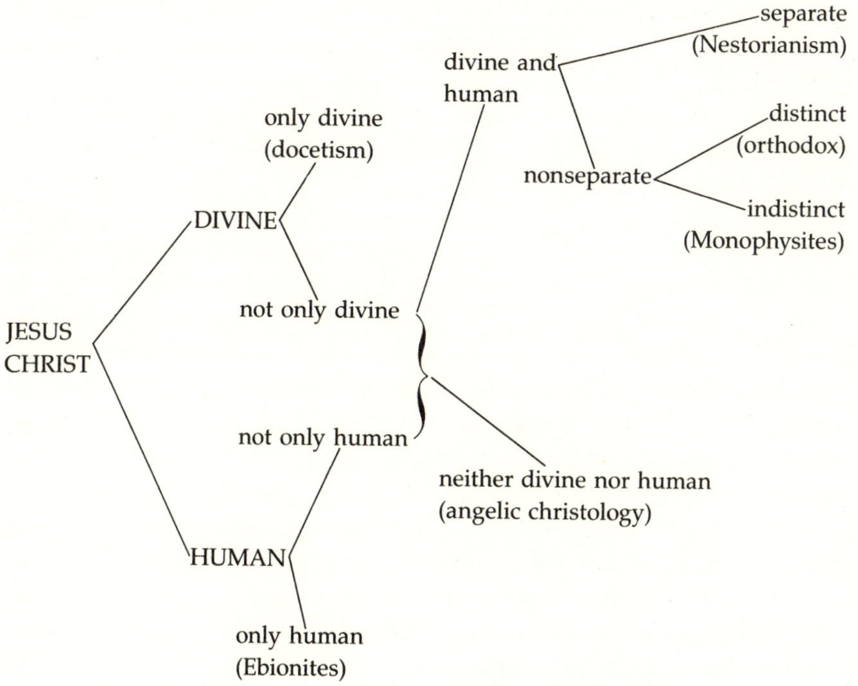

7.7.5 The divine persons. Another dimension of christology consists of the hierarchical relations within the Trinity. The orthodox position asserts that the Father, the Son, and the Holy Spirit are three hypostases that share the same substance (*ousia*) and the same energy (*energeia*). Among the positions not included by orthodoxy are subordinationism, according to which Christ is inferior to the Father; pneumatomachism, a trend fought by Basil the Great in the fourth century, which claimed that the Holy Spirit was inferior to both the Father and the Son; modalism, according to which the Father, the Son, and the Holy Spirit are one person with three different names, etc. Modalism has patripassianism as a consequence, according to which Christ being God, God the Father has suffered and died on the cross with him. It is easy to note that the trinitarian hierarchy can be studied in an entirely systematic, synchronic perspective, according to such dimensions as identity/nonidentity, superiority/inferiority, and so forth.

7.7.6 Psychology. The great psychological debates may be deduced from the following scheme:

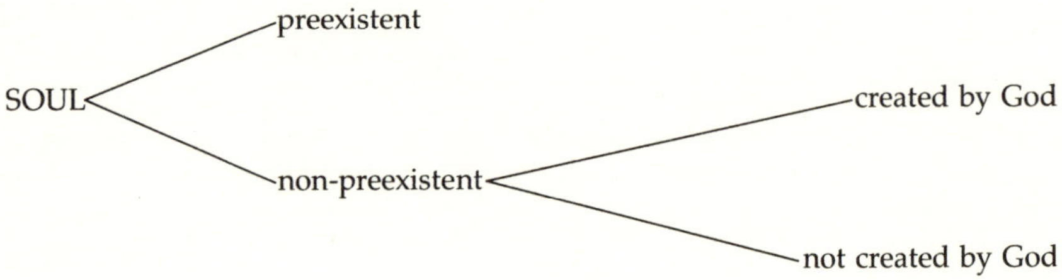

The conception of the preexistence of the soul entails either the classic, Platonic view of metensomatosis (reincarnation), or the more refined Origenist view, implying embodiment of the soul in a rather wide range of subtle bodies, according to its merits.

If the soul is not preexistent, then it is either newly created by God together with the body (creationism, a view that would end up becoming orthodox), or produced by the souls of the parents through psychic copulation (traducianism, a view defended by Tertullian and widely accepted in early Christianity).

7.7.7 Free will. Finally, a synchronic perspective applies equally to the great debates on free will, in Augustine's as well as in Luther's time.

Augustine opposed Pelagius, according to whom original sin was unable to obstruct free will. On the contrary, asserted Augustine, God created human beings able to choose between good and evil; yet, having already chosen the evil, they lost the faculty of conforming completely to the divine will. This is why grace is indispensable in order that human beings may be saved. As Luther said against Erasmus of Rotterdam, under these circumstances man's will is *servum arbitrium* (subservient will) rather than *liberum arbitrium* (free will).

Moreover, declared Augustine, God decided for all eternity who was going to be saved and who was not and He dispenses grace by his sempiternal decision. The number of predestined (*numerus praedestinatorum*) is limited and equal to the number of places freed in heaven by the fall of the angels; the rest of humanity is negatively predestined to form the *massa perditionis,* the mass of the damned. The Council of Orange (529) accepted Augustine's view as orthodox, but the Council of Quiercy (853) rejected the idea of double predestination (positive *and* negative), because the *massa perditionis* is not really predestined by God, but simply delivered unto the everlasting punishment of hell because of their bad choice.

The Reformation resumes the whole debate on predestination, which has a central place in the doctrinal question raised by Luther. Under the pressure of Luther's friend Melanchthon, orthodox Evangelism abandoned the discussion on predestination, taken over by the Calvinists. The synod of Dort (Netherlands, November 13, 1618, to May 9, 1619), made up of representatives of all Protestant confessions, confirmed the double character—positive and negative—of predestination.

7.8 CHRISTIAN LIFE has several dimensions. For certain confessions (Catholic, Orthodox, Nestorian, Monophysite, and Anglican), the liturgical year is especially important. Two main events, whose emphasis is rather different in the East and in the West, dominate the Christian calendar: the birth of Christ, or Christmas, traditionally celebrated on 6 January then transferred to 25 December—which happened to be the festival of the pagan god Mithra, *Sol invictus* (Unconquerable Sun)—and Christ's death on the cross (Good Friday) and resurrection (the following Sunday, Easter), traditionally preceded by forty days of fasting. The eucharist, that is, the administration of the holy host and of consecrated wine, is a sacrament, a rite instituted by Christ himself. Catholics recognize seven sacraments: baptism, confirmation, eucharist, extreme unction, marriage, entry into holy orders, and penance. The frequency of the eucharistic communion varies according to the confession and the time period: in Catholicism after the Second Vatican Council it became a daily practice; in Orthodoxy it is a practice accomplished at rather long intervals and not by all of the faithful.

The moral life of the Christian is important in all denominations. One would perhaps tend to emphasize the importance of morality among the antisacramental Protestant churches such as the Calvinist church, yet this would mean ignoring its role elsewhere. Although having traditionally favored patriarchal values, from its early centuries the Christian churches have opened monastic orders for numerous women, who in this way won access to education and culture and could enjoy a certain independence impossible to find elsewhere in their society. Many scholars such as Ida Magli, Rudolph Bell, Dagmar Lorentz, and others have noted that the only two establishments in which women, during the Middle Ages and the Renaissance, could salvage some independence were the nunnery and the brothel. Consequently, the institution of women's monastic orders has recently undergone a very positive reinterpretation. On the contrary, the dismantling of women's monastic orders by the Protestants in the sixteenth century and the obligation of marriage are today held responsible for the degrading opposition, which still exists in certain countries with a Christian tradition, between married and unmarried women. In Germany during the great persecutions by the authorities against witches and even much later, women's celibacy was regarded with a suspicion that could easily become repression and that did not apply to male celibacy. As Prudence Allen noted, it was the triumph of Aristotelianism in the thirteenth century that generalized Christian denigration of womanhood for the modern period. Aristotle was indeed the author of a theory among whose variants is the Freudian myth of "penis envy": woman is but an incomplete male, defective to the extent that her seed does not contribute to the generation of a new being. This theory, combined with common and groundless prejudgments such as that of the sexual insatiability of women, which would lead to the destruction of man, or that of the "irrationality" of women, the two offering an explanation for the privileged relationship between woman and the devil, must be held responsible for the savage persecution of womanhood begun in Germany at the time of the papal bull *Summis desiderantes affectibus* (1484) and the treatise *Malleus maleficarum* (1486) of the Inquisitors Institoris and Sprenger. A century later the enforcement of patriarchal values took the shape of the witch hunt, much more intense—as J. B. Russell observed—in the regions affected by Protestantism.

Traditionally, the liveliest Christian hope was survival after death and heavenly reward for the merits accumulated during one's lifetime. Symmetrically, negative merits were exchanged for punishment in hell. The Last Judgment was supposed to make these temporary joys or torments everlasting. The idea of a purgatory to expiate for venial sins only appeared—as was brillantly shown by Jacques Le Goff in his monumental *La Naissance du Purgatoire* (1981)—between 1024 and 1254 C.E., a period that roughly coincided with the proliferation of medieval apocalypses describing a visit to paradise and hell. The most ancient among them was a Latin *Visio Beati Esdrae*, probably of the tenth century; there followed an Irish *Vision of Adhamhnàn* (eleventh century), the *Vision of Alberic of Montecassino* (1111–1127), the *Vision of Tundal* (1149), the *Tractate of the Purgatory of Saint Patrick* (1189), etc. Dante's *Divine Comedy* belongs in this category of apocalypses.

7.9 MYSTICAL TRADITION. It would be impossible to conclude these pages without a brief survey of the rich mystical tradition of Christianity, which can be envisaged as a form of Platonic contemplative asceticism integrated with devotional and often liturgical activities. In its multifarious historical occurrences, Christian mysticism embraces almost all available mystical phenomenology, emphasizing to almost the same extent both ecstasy and introspection. The mystical experience tends toward the union with God in the complete surrender of the body and the world. This experience was given its first interpretive framework by Origen (7.4.3), later by Neoplatonism, from which it is, however, distinct through its emphasis on the dimension of *love.*

The unknown author, an admirer of the Athenian Neoplatonist Proclus (410/412–485 C.E.), who wrote under the name of Paul's disciple Dionysius the Areopagite, inaugurated a form of mysticism that, in its insistance on the unknowability of God (negative or apophatic theology), started a whole tradition that, albeit favoring ecstasy, is strikingly similar to the Buddhist "mysticism of emptiness." The state of *fanā'* in Sufism; the God of Meister Eckhart (1260–1327), Jan van Ruusbroec (1293–1381), and John Tauler (1300–1361); the *noche obscura* of the Carmelite friar John of the Cross (1542–1591), disciple of the great ecstatic mystic Teresa of Avila (1515–1582); the discovery of the unfathomable and therefore almost diabolical character of God the Father made by the Sylesian Protestant Jacob Boehme—all this belongs to the negative mode of theology, magnificently represented by Nominalist theology (twelfth to fifteenth centuries) as well. Yet, as many scholars have noted, it is impossible to separate love mysticism from the mysticism of emptiness, for the latter is often nothing but a stage (the desert, the night) on the mystical path. At this point speculative mysticism steps in, to delineate the stages of mystical experience. The model for this mysticism is again Dionysius the Areopagite. His tradition spread eastward and westward, from John Climacus (d. ca. 650), author of *The Ladder (klimax) to Paradise,* which proposes a hierarchy of mystical experiences in thirty stages, to the Franciscan Bonaventura of Bagnoreggio (1221–1274), author of *The Mind's Journey to God* (modern translators often prefer "Soul" to "Mind," although the Latin title is *Itinerarium mentis in Deum*).

All love mysticism seems to rest, according to the famous expression of Thomas à Kempis (1379/1380–1471 C.E.), on the imitation of Christ. Another form of mysticism, the mysticism of the eucharist, seemed to be more frequent in women mystics. This was in part a variety of the feminine love mysticism, remarkably represented by the Benedictine Mother Julian of Norwich (1342–ca. 1416), by Teresa of Avila, by Thérèse de Lisieux (1873–1897), and by many others. On the other hand, not all women mystics can be ranged under the heading of love mysticism: a visionary such as Hildegard of Bingen (1098–1179) explored all modalities of mysticism.

The historian Rudolph Bell diagnosed symptoms of anorexia nervosa among many Italian mystics from the thirteenth to the seventeenth century: Claire of Assisi (ca. 1194–1253 C.E.), Francis of Assisi's (1181–1226) mystical companion; Umiliana de' Cerchi (1219–1246); Margareta of Cortona (1247–1297); Catherine of Siena (1347–1380); Benvenuta Bojani (b. 1384); Eustachia of Messina (d. 1485); Colomba of Rieti (b. 1466); and Orsola Veronica Giuliani (1660–1727). Caroline Walker Bynum added to these several other cases from other parts of Europe, giving the whole phenomenon a suggestive interpretation. Bynum rejected the analogy with anorexia nervosa emphasized by Bell, interpreting fasting and other extremely severe mortifications that these mystics adopted by their own choice as an instance of *positive worldview.* For these women mystics, the eucharist, in which Christ was changed into nourishing bread, becames the symbol of their own transformation: giving up food, these mystics *were changed into food themselves.* Bynum's refreshing interpretation completely contradicts the hermeneutical tradition according to which all mortification of the body is a symptom of dualism. Yet several scholars strongly disagree with Bynum's view of the two main periods of spirituality: late antique and early medieval spirituality, dominated by the male concern with sex, and late medieval spirituality, dominated by the female concern with food. It has also been suggested that anorexic mystics are so out of the desire to efface gender in themselves, for it is well known that anorexic women do not menstruate and are not fertile.

If Western mysticism evolved in four different yet indistinctly mixed ways (negative theology, love, speculative mysticism, and eucharistic mysticism), Eastern mysticism took on special techniques with the Hesychastic movement defended by Gregory Palamas (ca. 1296–1359). Hesychasm evolved in the direction of visualization, breath and posture control, wakefulness, and meditational practices ("the prayer of the heart"), possibly reminiscent of yoga or Sufi spiritual techniques. Practiced by the monks of Mount Athos, Hesychasm spread all over the Orthodox world, and especially in Russia, through the writings collected at the end of the eighteenth century under the title of *Philokalia.* The typically Russian institution of the *starets,* an Orthodox guru or Sufi shaykh (17.10), was a local interpretation of Hesychasm. Another form of Russian Hesychasm, formulated in monastic establishments for use by the masses, was the so-called "perpetual prayer," which consisted of repeating mentally and incessantly, like a mantra, the name of Jesus Christ.

7.10 BIBLIOGRAPHY. A short popular introduction to the general history of Christianity is *Eerdmans' Handbook to the History of Christianity* (1987). Many Church histories exist; as a work of reference one can use the twenty-one volumes of the French *Histoire de l'Église des origines à nos jours* (Fliche-Martin) (1964–1984) and the *Dictionnaire de théologie catholique* (1909–1950). A good general survey of Christian doctrine through the ages is offered by Jaroslav Pelikan in his four volumes of *The Christian Tradition: A History of the Development of Doctrine* (1971–1984). A remarkable history of the spread of Christianity is Kenneth S. Latourette's *A History of the Expansion of Christianity,* 7 vols. (1937–1945). For the ancient period, a good historical and doctrinal survey is offered by W. H. C. Frend in the 1,022 pages of his *The Rise of Christianity* (1984), to be completed with Johannes Quasten's *Patrology,* 4 vols. (1950–1960). On the early apologists, see R. M. Grant, *The Greek Apologists of the Second Century* (1988), and A. J. Droge, *Homer or Moses? Early*

Christian Interpretations of the History of Culture (1989). Among the best books on the formative period of Christianity are R. M. Grant's *Augustus to Constantine* (1970), and *The Gods and the One God* (1986).

A good introduction to medieval civilization is contained in the works of Jacques Le Goff, *La Civilisation de l'Occident médiéval* (1967), and *Pour un autre Moyen Age* (1977). Le Goff has also devoted a capital work to the appearance of the doctrine of the Purgatory, *La Naissance du Purgatoire* (1981) and has edited the volume *Hérésies et société dans l'Europe préindustrielle XIe-XVIIIe siècle* (1968). On medieval heresy, see also J. B. Russell, *Dissent and Reform in the Early Middle Ages* (1965), and R. I. Moore, *The Origins of European Dissent* (1977); a complete bibliography can be found in I. P. Couliano, *Les gnoses dualistes d'Occident* (1978). On medieval rituals of investiture and their religious meaning, see Michel Stanesco, *Jeux d'errance du chevalier médiéval* (1988).

On the medieval apocalyptic tradition, see especially the capital work of Bernard McGinn, *Visions of the End: Apocalyptic Traditions in the Middle Ages* (1979), to be supplemented with the volume edited by McGinn and containing a good Introduction and translation of texts from Adso of Montier-en-Der, Joachim of Flora, the Franciscan Spirituals and Savonarola, *Apocalyptic Spirituality* (1979). On medieval otherworldly journeys, see I. P. Couliano, *Expériences de l'extase* (1984), and the book *Out of this World: A History of Otherworldly Journeys and Visions* (1991).

On comparative mysticism, see Samuel Umen, *The World of the Mystic* (1988); Moshe Idel and Bernard McGinn (eds.), *Mystical Union and Monotheistic Faith: An Ecumenical Dialogue* (1989). On Christian spirituality, see André Vauchez, *La spiritualité du Moyen Age* (1975), and *La sainteté en Occident aux derniers siècles du Moyen Age* (1981); Bernard McGinn, John Meyendorff, and Jean Leclercq (eds.), *Christian Spirituality: Origins to the Twelfth Century* (1987).

On late antique views on the human body, see especially the magisterial work of Peter Brown, *The Body and Society: Men, Women, and Sexual Renunciation in Early Christianity* (1988); on late medieval views on the body, see Rudolph Bell, *Holy Anorexia* (1985); Caroline Walker Bynum, *Holy Feast and Holy Fast* (1987). On the concept of woman in Christianity, see Prudence Allen, *The Concept of Woman: The Aristotelian Revolution, 750 B.C.–A.D. 1250* (1985); Pierre Darmon, *Mythologie de la femme dans l'Ancienne France* (1983); Barbara Becker-Cantarino (ed.), *Die Frau von der Reformation zur Romantik,* (1987). On the European witch craze, see I. P. Couliano, "Sacrilege," in *ER* 12, 557–63.

On the different aspects of the twelfth-century Renaissance (which bear fruit in the thirteenth century), see Michel Pastoureau, *Vie quotidienne en France et en Angleterre au temps des chevaliers de la Table ronde* (1976); Jean Richard, *Le Royaume latin de Jérusalem* (1953); *Les Croisades*, with an Introduction by Robert Delort (1988); Roger Boase, *The Origin and Meaning of Courtly Love* (1977).

On the late Middle Ages to the Reformation, see Steven Ozment, *The Age of Reform, 1250–1550: An Intellectual and Religious History of Late Medieval and Reformation Europe* (1980).

On magic in general and especially Renaissance magic, see I. P. Couliano, *Eros and Magic in the Renaissance* (1984), also containing a select bibliography on the Renaissance.

On Protestantism, a balanced synthesis has been written by Martin Marty, *Protestantism* (1972); on Luther, see especially Brian Gerrish, *Grace and Reason: A Study in the Theology of Luther* (1962); on Calvin, see A. M. Schmidt, *Jean Calvin et la tradition calvinienne* (1956). On the metamorphoses of biblical interpretation, particularly in England and Germany, see H. Frei, *The Eclipse of Biblical Narrative* (1974).

8

Confucianism

8.1 THE CONFUCIAN CANON rests on a collection of "classics" (*ching*) whose number varies, but the six classics are: the Book of Changes (*I Ching*), the Book of Odes (*Shih Ching*), the Book of History (*Shu Ching*), the Book of Rites (*Li Chi*), the Book of Music (*Yüeh Ching*) and the Spring and Autumn Annals (*Ch'un-ch'iu*). Confucius himself is held to be the author of the last. Familiar with the oracles of the *I Ching,* he probably wrote a commentary on them. During the twelfth century C.E., the thirteen classics included three ritual texts, *Li Chi, Chou Li,* and *Yi Li.* Confucius's sentences are known under the title of Analects (*Lun Yü*). A second-century B.C.E. version thereof is extant.

8.2 CONFUCIUS is the Latin name of K'ung Fu-tzu (master K'ung). The founder of Confucianism, Confucius was probably born K'ung Ch'iu in the second half of the sixth century B.C.E. in the family of a low-ranking officer. His beginnings and his education were modest. He enjoyed rituals and music, yet these enjoyments were not enough to pave his way to a public function. He did not become a civil servant before the age of fifty, and he quit his job after one year. This was repeated several times in other states. Finally K'ung Ch'iu went back to his native state to fill a modest public position and dedicate himself to his teaching among a select group of disciples, of equally modest means, whom he tried to transform into *jen,* or accomplished human beings. The analogue model we might use to understand the notion of *jen* is not the medieval knight, but the gentleman who excels in formal correctness in all the circumstances of life, from the most common to the most unexpected. Characteristic for Confucianism is the role of *ritual:* it keeps up the propriety (*li*) of all things, the continuity of social situations, the immutable position of individuals within society as a whole.

The Confucian ethos, which would eventually become the base of the Chinese Empire until 1911, was not aristocratic but bourgeois. It did not enforce the privileges of birth, but of education and formal behavior. It did not favor military furor, but clerical patience.

8.3 THE DOCTRINE. Although Confucianism is part of the three religions that form the traditional heritage of China (with Taoism and Buddhism), it is legitimate to question its being a religion in the common, however inadequate, sense of the term. Superficially, it does not seem to be one, for its enterprise appears to be the *demythologization* of Chinese beliefs: supernatural beings are made into virtues, heaven stops being a god, being made into a mere principle that warrants order, and so forth. In a certain sense, Confucius's criticism of traditional religion had much in common with the Buddha's critique of Hindu beliefs and practices (3); yet in sharp contrast with the latter it did not at all concern the "salvation" of human beings, for the simple and basic reason that it in no way occurs to Confucius *that there is anything in social life to be saved from, nor consequently anyone to be saved.* "When one is unable to serve human beings, how can one serve spiritual beings?" says one aphorism, clearly meaning that one is to abandon any pursuit of an invisible reality. "When you do not know life, how would you know death?" is meant to discourage whoever has any inclination toward the mysteries of afterlife.

In contrast to Buddhism, which developed a powerful organization based on a hierarchy of monks and laypeople, Confucianism did not have priests. The performers of rituals were the same *ju*, or bureaucrats, who filled, by state examination, the openings in the imperial administration, both central and provincial. Our term "religion" does not immediately seem to apply to this formal cult mechanically performed by nonpriests for divinities toward which they do not aspire.

If it is not a religion in our received meaning of the word, Confucianism is not a philosophical system either. Its cosmology, formulated by Tung Chung-shu (176–104 B.C.E.), prime minister of the emperor Wu-ti (140–87 B.C.E.) of the Han dynasty, is rudimental and borrowed from Taoism (30). Logic did not interest Confucius any more than mythology. His main concern was to discover the Middle Way (*Tao*) in human society and in individual actions, the Way that would guarantee the balance between the will of the earth and the will of heaven.

"Heaven" here, it should be carefully stated, was not a divinity, but a universal and omnipresent principle, hidden and undefinable, whose operations "are noiseless and odorless."

If Confucianism pursues some form of "salvation," this is not religious soteriology. Confucians do not have a negative worldview, like Buddhists or Christians; they do not understand immortality, like Taoists, as something one may individually acquire, but as a goal naturally attained by the succession of many generations; they do not have a direct, however painful and problematic, relation with God like Jews, and do not tremble before the will of heaven like Muslims before Allah. Confucianism does not assign human beings any other objective than the pursuit of the excellency of their humanness (*jen yi*) by the correct and proper accomplishment of their social duties (*li*). The foundation of Confucianism is summarized in the aphorism: *The father must be a father, and the son a son.*

Human society is supposed to be regulated by a movement, educational in intent, that goes from the top to the bottom and corresponds to paternal love (for a *son*) and by an opposite movement of reverence that goes from the bottom to the top and is tantamount to filial piety. This is the only Confucian duty whose absoluteness nearly shows a trace of passion, for otherwise gentlemen indiscriminately abhor passions. A breach of the rule of piety (toward one's family, one's superior, one's homeland, one's chief of state, etc.) is the only Confucian definition of sacrilege. Historians of the Far East had a tendency to emphasize, after World War II, that such a paternalistic ideology could perhaps degenerate more readily than others into blind obedience to the interests of a totalitarian state.

8.4 THE HISTORY OF CONFUCIANISM in China is especially marked, at its inception, by the doctrines of the philosophers Meng-tzu (Mencius, fourth to third century B.C.E.) and Hsün-tzu (third century B.C.E.). The former believed in the intrinsic goodness of human nature, the latter in its basic malignity; the former believed that rules and rituals are internalized and sincerely express individual will, the latter that they are only unwilling submission to social constraints; the former believed that the feelings of the ruler toward his subjects are paternal, the latter that the ruler has no feelings. Between the two, there was the same distance that separates Augustine from Pelagius (7.4.7) or Immanuel Kant from Jean-Jacques Rousseau. The impersonal mechanics of Hsün-tzu began by prevailing under the legalistic scool of the Ch'in dynasty (221–207 B.C.E.) and under the Han dynasty (206 B.C.E.–220 C.E.). Yet later on, starting with the Sung (960–1279 C.E.), Mencius's thought became as influential as to turn him into a "Second Sage" and sole legitimate heir to Confucius's spiritual legacy. It is thus striking that, in complete opposition to the West, where pessimistic doctrines of the human nature would be constantly resumed through the ages by the most influential popular and trend-making thinkers such as Augustine, Luther, or Kant, in China the doctrine of the goodness of human nature triumphed definitively with the Confucianism of Han Yü (768–829 C.E.), the philosopher who first rehabilitated Mencius during the T'ang epoch (618–907).

The movement known as Neo-Confucianism began during the Sung era. It reinterpreted the notion of *li* (here meaning "principle") in ontological terms and developed cosmological speculations. The most important representatives of Neo-Confucianism were the Five Northern Sung Masters (Shao Yung, 1011–1077 C.E.; Chou Tun-yi, 1017–1073 C.E.; Chang Tsai, 1020–1077 C.E.; and the brothers Ch'eng Hao, 1032–1085 C.E., and Ch'eng Yi, 1033–1107 C.E.), followed by Chu Hsi (1130–1200), the creator of an original metaphysical synthesis based on the works of his predecessors. During his lifetime, Chu Hsi had to defeat the opposition of his southern colleague Lu Hsiang-shan (1139–1193). The two met twice in 1175, yet continued to critique each other without coming to terms. Their debates strangely resembled those that affected western nominalism roughly during the same period of time (7.4.10). Chu Hsi has no equal as a master of the Confucian tradition. From the beginning of the fourteenth century until 1912, the Confucian canon, also used in the Chinese bureaucratic system for the preparation of the awesome state examinations, was the one established by Chu Hsi, and the orthodox line of transmission of Confucianism was also determined by him. His school knew only two important rivals: Wang Yang-ming (1472–1529) during the Ming epoch (1368–1644) and Tai Chen (1723–1777) during the Manchu period. In 1912 the proclamation of the Republic of China temporarily marked an end to the official sacrifices to heaven and to Confucius, which were, however, resumed as early as 1914. At first scarcely favorable to Confucianism, the Republican intelligentsia did not fail soon to recognize its role in the history of China. Persecuted in communist China, Neo-Confucianists have maintained an important status in Hong Kong and in Taiwan, as well as in the Chinese communities of the United States. Today Neo-Confucianist thinking has not lost its vigor, as is shown by the works of Tu Wei-ming and other philosophers and scholars.

8.5 OUTSIDE CHINA. Confucianism first spread to Korea before the Common Era, but it was not until the fourteenth century C.E. that Neo-Confucianism, with its canon of the Four Books and the Five Classics, was solidly installed in Korea as the philosophy of the Yi state (1392–1910) and as a system of public education and examination.

From Korea, Confucianism reached Japan about the close of the third century C.E. and became influential by the mid-seventh century, declining shortly thereafter. Neo-Confucianism was introduced to Japan from China after the death of Chu Hsi (Japanese Shushi) and was combined with Zen Buddhism, actually living in its shadow. About 1,600 new Confucian texts were brought from Korea. They attracted the attention of Fujiwara Seika (1561–1619) and of his disciple Hayashi Razan (1583–1657), who created a modest place for the teachings of Chu Hsi in Tokugawa, Japan. Many other Confucian schools functioned simultaneously.

At the beginning of the twentieth century, Confucianism became the ideology of Japanese imperialism and kept up this role during all of World War II.

8.6 BIBLIOGRAPHY. J. Ching, "Confucius," in *ER* 4, 38–42; Wing-tsit Chan, "Confucian Thought: Foundation of the Tradition," in *ER* 4, 15–24; "Neo-Confucianism," in *ER* 4, 24–36; L. G. Thompson, "The State Cult," in *ER* 4, 36–38; J. Kim Haboush, "Confucianism in Korea," in *ER* 4, 10–15; P. Nosco, "Confucianism in Japan," in *ER* 4, 7–10.

About the association between Confucianism and militarism in Japan during World War II, see Warren W. Smith, Jr., *Confucianism in Modern Japan: A Study of Conservatism in Japanese Intellectual History* (1959).

On contemporary Neo-Confucianism, see the book by Tu Wei-Ming, *Confucian Thought: Selfhood as Creative Transformation* (1985).

9

Dualistic Religions

9.1 THE WORD "DUALISM" was coined in 1700 C.E. to describe the Iranian doctrine of the two spirits (33). Later on, scholars discovered that dualistic myths have universal extension and show innumerable transformations at all levels of culture and in a large number of religions, from those of illiterate societies to the so-called "higher religions" such as Buddhism, Greek religion, Christianity, Hinduism, Judaism, Islam, and so forth. The simplest definition of dualism is: *opposition of two principles.* This implies a judgment of value (good *versus* bad) and the establishment of a polarity at all levels of reality: cosmological, anthropological, ethical, and so on.

The recognition of two types of religious dualism is traditional: *radical* dualism, which posits the existence of two coeternal principles, both responsible for the creation of what is; and *mitigated* or monarchian (i.e., based on the monarchy of a Supreme Creator) dualism, in which the second principle appears only later and generally stems from an error in the system set in motion by the First Principle.

9.2 DUALISTIC MYTHS. Ugo Bianchi, the author of the monograph *Il dualismo religioso* (1958; reprint, 1983), ascertained that myths with a Trickster as protagonist are often dualistic. A Trickster is a character, human or animal, that plays dubious jokes and tricks, loves to make fun and is made fun of, can change shape and gender, appears on all continents at every stage of civilization and is often camouflaged as one of the gods or demigods of the great religions, such as Seth in Egyptian religion, Prometheus in Greek religion, or Loki in Scandinavian religion. In most cases, the Trickster is male, but a number of myths all over the world feature a female Trickster.

In one category of myths, the Trickster of both sexes acts as a second creator of the world or part thereof and plays the role of spoiler of the supreme god's creation, such as introducing into the world all afflictions present in it today: the mortal condition of humans, birth pangs, pain, etc. In the biblical myth of Genesis, one can recognize the discrete presence of a Trickster *ex machina,* the serpent who reveals sexuality to the primordial couple of humans, thus effecting their expulsion from paradise, marked by labor pains, the domination of male over female, the curse of work, and death. Radical dualism is here maintained in a moderate form: the serpent is said to be created by God. But as soon as one starts asking questions about its intelligent and malignant nature, one can already foresee the manifold interpretive transformations this myth may spawn. Everywhere—in the Americas as well as in Eurasia, Africa, or Oceania—the Trickster may be an imperfect demiurge, author of a countercreation whose consequences are often catastrophic.

9.3 DUALISTIC RELIGIONS. Not only dualistic myths, but whole dualistic religions exist, whose attitude toward the world is not necessarily the same. It actually varies from anticosmism (the world is evil) and antisomatism (the body is evil) to procosmism (the world is good) and prosomatism (the body is good). Zoroastrianism, for example (33), is a dualistic religion, procosmic and prosomatic; Orphism is a dualistic religious trend, anticosmic and antisomatic; Platonism, a philosophical trend whose religious import was enormous for millennia, is dualistic and strongly antisomatic but not anticosmic; and, finally, other religions such as Gnosticism, Manichaeism, Paulicianism, Bogomilism, and Catharism deserve here special treatment insofar as they always have been analyzed by scholars as a particular group, depending on Christianity, of which they had been viewed as "heresies."

9.4 GNOSTICISM was an outlook contemporary with early Christianity, which freely manifests itself in the form of a large number of divergent trends. The common denominator that inclines some to speak of Gnosticism as a religion with its own essence is the presence of a particular set of myths. These are variants of two basic myths, inserted in most cases into a structure that belongs to mitigated or monarchian dualism: the myth of a female Trickster, the heavenly goddess Sophia (Wisdom) who produces the catastrophe or at least the unpleasant situation that leads to the creation of the visible world; and the myth of a male Trickster, the miscarried son of Sophia, who makes the world starting either from an ignominious substance called "Water" (from Genesis 1:6), or from litter or fragmented dreams fallen from on high, from the true God. This demiurge or fashioner of this world is usually identified with the Old Testament God. He is not unequivocally evil, except in a few testimonies; he is said to be ignorant, proud, and "mad" in a number of Coptic texts that are part of the collections of Gnostic codices, the largest of which was dug up in Nag Hammadi in Upper Egypt in 1945. In testimonies pertaining to the gnosis of Valentinus (fl. 140–150), the ignorant demiurge repents and is pardoned for having created the world.

Within the spectrum of ideas of the epoch, Gnosticism is revolutionary insofar as it contradicts the two principles asserted both by the Bible and by Plato: the principle of an *ecosystemic intelligence,* according to which the world has been created by a benevolent and intelligent cause, and the *anthropic principle,* according to which this world has been purposefully created for this human species and this human species has been created for this world. On the contrary, Gnosticism asserts that the demiurge of the world is bumbling and ignorant, so that consequently the world is bad and human beings are superior to both the world and its creator for being endowed with a spark of Spirit stemming from the distant and good Father of the divine emanations. The goal of the Gnostic is thus to escape from the prison of the world.

Gnosticism most often used Christian materials and its Redeemer is usually called Jesus Christ. His function is to reveal to adepts the existence of the spark of Spirit enclosed in their souls, which is at the same time the eternal gnosis that would allow them to ascend beyond the cosmos to the realm of divine plenitude. This Jesus Christ does not generally have a physical body (docetic christology), and consequently he could not have suffered and died on the cross. Interpretations of his passion and death are extremely varied. In some cases someone else (Simon of Cyrene) is crucified in his stead, while the true Savior stands laughing in the shadow of the cross. This mocking smile of Jesus directed toward the blind demiurge and his henchmen has certainly no correspondent whatsoever in the gospels.

9.5 MARCION. Most of the writings of the New Testament already existed in some form at the time of Marcion of Sinope (ca. 80–155 C.E.), the first important heresiarch who obliged the Christian church to define its attitude toward its scriptural canon, its christology, and so forth. Marcion was not a Gnostic, but only a critical rationalist. He noticed that the God of the Old Testament hardly matched the criteria of omnipotence, omniscience, and perfect goodness that were obligatory during his own period but had scarcely been so during that uncertain past when the various and often contradictory mythical materials forming the Bible had been put together. Yet obviously one can excuse the inconsistencies of the Bible on historical grounds only if one does not believe in its truth. This was not Marcion's case. As a believer, he stumbled upon contradictions and sought to eliminate them by positing a radical dualism between a good and entirely unknown God living in his third heaven, and a demiurge who is not good but inferior and just, who is the God of the Old Testament and has created this world, made of matter corrupted by the devil, and human beings. There is no communication between these two worlds before the moment when the good God grants to the system of the demiurge's world the gift of Christ. Although Christ's body is a deceiving phantasm (a variety of docetism called phantasiasm), his suffering and death have their reality, to which the willing and liberating martyrdom of the Marcionite adept is deemed to correspond.

Opposite to Gnosticism, which in its conception of human beings superior to their creator constitutes a case of optimism unique in the history of ideas, Marcionism entails a pessimistic worldview, for it negates the principle of ecosystemic intelligence but not so the anthropic principle: the world is qualitatively inferior (and, in this sense, "bad"), but humans do not transcend it in any way, being no better than the place where they were born. Human beings do not deserve, as in Gnosticism, salvation by virtue of their consubstantial relationship with the good God. Their selective salvation is a free and undeserved gift coming from a complete stranger.

Marcionism evolved into a well-constituted church, whose vocation of martyrdom was so strong within the Roman world that the church was soon extinct. A good number of Marcionites, champions of asceticism, survived to the fifth century in Syriac-speaking regions, where Theodoret of Cyprus converted eight Marcionite villages to what he thought orthodoxy was.

9.6 MANICHAEISM is the most influential among the Gnostic-dualistic religions. It was founded by Mani (216–276 C.E.), the prophet born in a Mesopotamian Baptist community and active in Persia until his martyrdom under the Sassanian ruler Bahram II. Manichaeism spread westward to Rome, where it braved persecutions until the fifth century, and eastward to China (694), becoming for some time the state religion of the empire of the Uigur Turks (763–840). Like the Marcionites, once expelled from cities, the Manichaeans settled in the country, especially in Asia Minor. A universal, missionary religion based on direct and written revelations, Manichaeism translated its scriptures into various languages, adapting some of its fundamental notions or terminology to those of local religions such as Zoroastrianism or Buddhism. It actually did not rest on an Iranian background at all, as many scholars have argued, but built its original doctrine upon preexisting Gnostic systems. It was characterized by radical dualism, by its peculiar idea of the world as "mixture" of Darkness and Light, by its anticosmic optimism, and by its strict asceticism. The innovation of Manichaeism in comparison with precedent Gnostic systems (which, by the way, do not always exclude radical dualism in favor of a mitigated form of dualism) was to have ascribed the act of world creation to a good demiurge called Living Spirit. The fact that the material out of which this was made consisted of the corpses of the Rulers of Darkness has led many scholars to the conclusion that Manichaeism was strongly pessimistic. However, the carcasses of the demons were mixed with particles of Light swallowed by them. No matter how painful this embrace of Darkness, Light nevertheless shone in every blade of grass. And the immediate experience the Manichaean had of the world was not traumatic. In it, that reverence for the world was certainly not missing as it was missing for certain Gnostics. That part of nature that is an epiphany of Light constitutes for the Manichaean a mystery and the object of constant religious astonishment. Manichaeism established a line of prophets concluded with Mani himself and ascribed to Jesus a cosmic function.

9.7 PAULICIANISM, known to us from the late report of a ninth-century C.E. Byzantine writer, a certain Peter of Sicily who was sent in 869 by Emperor Basil I on a mission to the chiefs of a threatening Paulician state that was soon to disappear (872), was a popular form of Marcionism that evolved for centuries in the absence of a written tradition, in an environment certainly not favorable to intellectual speculations. Most of the Paulicians of the Euphrates valley were deported in the tenth century to Thrace (today Bulgaria). They left no other trace in history, although many modern scholars have mistaken them for an Armenian sect of adoptionist Paulinianists, adepts of Paul of Samosata.

According to Peter of Sicily, the sect had been founded in the seventh century by a certain Constantine from the town of Mananali on the upper Euphrates.

Among the ethical consequences of the radical dualism professed by the Paulicians was the rejection of sacraments, which probably served to express their contempt for the relaxed institutions of the Orthodox.

9.8 THE BOGOMILS have often and wrongly been associated with the Paulicians because of their Bulgarian background. In reality, even if they shared the Paulicians's attitude toward the Orthodox, the Bogomils were not dualistic to the same degree, for they asserted that Satan was not the creator but only the organizer or architect of the world. One can find among them ancient Christian doctrines that were not considered heretical during the early period, such as traducianism (a new soul is born through the psychic copulation of the souls of the parents), the auricular conception and birth of Jesus Christ, and others such as docetic phantasiasm, which, without ever having prevailed, were nevertheless ancient as well. Bogomilism was not a new outburst of long-forgotten gnosis. It was a new concoction made of old ingredients in ultraconservative Byzantine circles of encratites and vegetarians.

Bogomilism, which made its appearance in Bulgaria in the tenth century C.E., soon arrived at Byzantium, from whence it spread westward through Dalmatia and Italy, reaching France during the first part of the twelfth century and disappearing from Provence in 1167, when the French bishops were converted by a Byzantine Bogomil bishop to a new heresy professing radical dualism. This was Bogomil Catharism, which continued to exist in Lombardy (northern Italy), until the beginning of the fifteenth century and revisited Provence during the first decades of the fourteenth century through a few new Provençal converts initiated into Catharism in Italy after the fall of the Albigenses by the mid-thirteenth century.

9.9 THE CATHARS were, as we have seen, the adepts of two different doctrines, both coming from Byzantium. One was Bogomil and the other, which was professed by the Provençal Albigenses from 1167 to the fall of the stronghold of Montségur in 1244, was a mixture of Origenism with a few Manichaean elements originated in Byzantine ascetic intellectual circles. In Northern Italy the doctrinal differences between the two Cathar churches found expression in the polemic between the monarchianist Cathars of Concorezzo in Lombardy (who were called "Bulgars" and were nothing but Bogomils) and the radical cathars of Desenzano on the Garda Lake, called "Albanese," probably from "Albigenses."

All extant documents concerning radical Catharism, among them seven original tractates in Latin collected under the title *Liber de duobus principiis*, originated among Italian Cathars. They show that Origenism, which was professed in the fourth and fifth centuries by the ascetics and intellectuals of the Egyptian desert and was condemned in the sixth century, formed the largest part of their beliefs, which included metensomatosis (preexistence of the soul), corporeality of the angels, double creation, the existence of parallel worlds, the idea of multiple judgments of the soul, the existence of resurrection bodies that are not physical bodies, and the denial of the omnipotence and free will of God.

In the fifteenth century C.E. a heretical Church of Bosnia apparently founded in the twelfth century seemed to have professed radical dualism.

9.10 BIBLIOGRAPHY. An exhaustive commentary of the sources and the doctrines of dualistic religions is furnished in I. P. Couliano, *The Tree of Gnosis* (1992).

10

Egyptian Religion

10.1 INTRODUCTION. Despite the familiarity of its images today, Egyptian religion remains conceptually distant from us. Pluralities at such a distance appear as contradictions: the regional theologies and cosmogonies, the multiple structurings of the pantheon, varying myths and merging gods are compacted by retrospection and riddled with lacunae. Even the most common elements are now disputed: the divinity of the pharaoh, the substance of the afterlife, not to mention the precise nature of entities such as the *ba* and *ka* (usually rendered "soul" and "spirit"). But this most conservative of religious traditions, resisting change in every aspect and shaping its heroes and history into archetypal patterns, looked with pleasure toward an afterlife of similarly static perfection with a vision that has provoked the imagination of its witnesses for centuries.

10.2 EARLY PERIOD. The unique iconographic style of the Egyptians emerged along with hieroglyphic writing with the advent of the first dynasty and the unification of the northern and southern Nile Valley about 3000 B.C.E. Before this time was a period of Mesopotamian influence, during which cylinder seals, Mesopotamian mud-brick construction, and other eastern imports broke the relative isolation of the land. Still earlier, prehistoric populations in the region buried their dead facing west and supplied with grave goods for an expected afterlife.

The beginning of history in Egypt is the beginning of kingship, seen first in the Narmer palette in which the king wears the crowns of Upper and Lower Egypt. The earliest kings identified themselves with the god Horus, a second-dynasty party with Seth, or a Horus and Seth title. In mythology, Horus and Seth contended for kingship; the king's elevation to superhuman status was early and proved an enduring political tool. Menes, as the first king and unifier of Egypt was later called, traditionally founded the capital of Memphis. The kings of the first few dynasties, the Old Kingdom, built the greatest pyramids and funerary complexes, and the texts and spells inscribed in them tell us of their early theologies.

10.3 COSMOGONIES AND THEOLOGIES. An Old Kingdom cosmogony told of Re/Atum's creation of Shu (Air) and Tefnut (Moisture), who produced Geb (Earth) and Nut (Sky). They in turn produced Osiris and Seth and Isis and Nephthys. The rightful king of earth, Osiris, was murdered by his brother Seth. Isis managed to become pregnant by the dead Osiris and bore Horus, the son who would avenge him and who was also identified with the pharaoh.

As in Mesopotamia, temples in cities that were seats of power created their own composite cosmogonies featuring their local god at the top of the hierarchy. From the lake at Hermopolis, the egg from which the creator god came was said to have emerged. It came from the watery chaos expressed in four pairs of beings: hiddenness, darkness, formlessness, and the watery abyss. At Heliopolis one could point to a primordial hill of sand still visible as the starting point of the world. The coarsest cosmogonic acts such as the expectoration of the creator god seem to have had a wide appeal, but more refined theories were developed in the major religous centers, such as the later tradition of Ptah's conceiving Atum in his heart and creating him by speaking his name. By this myth, Ptah was made to supersede Atum; similarly, Re could be placed above Atum by inserting him one place before him in the cosmogony.

The Egyptians believed that the world was flat and supported the sky, which was an inverted bowl or the underside of Hathor the cow or of the goddess Nut who swallowed the sun each evening. Their depiction of their gods with attributes of various animals did not imply a worship of animals, but perhaps an expression of otherness or appreciation of the archetypal patterns of living things; the ever-shifting natures of the gods remain a puzzle to us. Human nature was derived from the divine, spoken by Ptah or fashioned on a potter's wheel. Preservation of the spirit was linked to physical preservation, and proper burial was valued above a comfortable earthly life; tombs were more important than elaborate houses, and mortuary priests should be employed at whatever cost to the family.

10.4 THE FIRST INTERMEDIATE PERIOD. About 2200 B.C.E., political breakdowns and civil war brought a divided Egypt for some 150 years. Literary works arising in this period show an increasing individualization or "democratization" of religious life in the face of anarchic social change. Formerly royal tomb spells found their way into the coffins of those who could afford them. The *Harper's Song* enjoined one to live in the present, recognizing a doubtful future in which tombs were despoiled and innocents wronged. Doubts were expressed about the self, the afterlife, the gods, and the pharaoh. In works of prophetic discourse such as the *Admonitions of Ipuwer,* an ancient sage was depicted railing against the lies and violence of the king and his reign. The *Instruction for Merikare* also decried the vicissitudes of this existence while reasserting the traditional Egyptian moral values of justice and generosity, especially toward the poor. An especially striking piece of the period is what we call the *Dialogue of a Man with His Ba,* in which a man despairing of the wickedness of the world argued for suicide against his soul, which encouraged the continuation and enjoyment of life. The soul, as the securer of future life, promised not to leave the man, yet attainment of an afterlife was perhaps no more appealing than this flawed existence. Outraged laments against ascendant social chaos (children rise up against their parents, people against their king, etc.) became standardized literary motifs that persisted for centuries.

10.5 RELIGIOUS PRACTICE. As elsewhere in the Near East, the gods had their capital cities in which their temples served as their houses. These were ordinarily restricted to ritually clean priests. A staff of priests cared for the image of the deity, making offerings and bringing it out for festivals. The large temples were elongated for processional rituals, events immortalized in the wall paintings that stood as graphic liturgies. Some deities gave oracles when manipulated by their attendant priests, rendering judgment in disputes. A temple could have a scriptorium and special libraries where scrolls might be preserved for generations. Positions of chief priest or priestess were politically powerful footholds in which a king might place his children or supporters. Temples and wealthy citizens held income-generating land in widely spread regions of the Nile Valley, and so had a stake in the stability and unity of the country as a whole.

Among common people, we seem to find an expectation of justice in society and the cosmos. The pharaoh ought to be the incarnation of *ma'at,* right order and truth. Egyptian wisdom literature, collections of moral aphorisms such as the fifth-dynasty *Wisdom of Ptahhotep* and the New Kingdom *Wisdom of Amenemopet* have the appeal of Old Testament Proverbs and many similar messages. Of popular piety among all classes we have evidence of amulets for protection and medical cures, scarabs, and figurines. Magic was said to be given by the gods to human beings as a weapon of self-defense. Spells were collected on papyrus and ostraca for both temple use and private use. These manipulated names and sounds and invoked the aid of the gods, who themselves could ultimately be magically coerced.

Osiris as the undying god and the judge of the dead had a place in popular piety. He was a symbol of rebirth and the god in whose eyes all sought approval. His traditional burial place at Abydos was the chief Egyptian pilgrimage site. Votive offerings of figurines, stelae with inscribed petitions, and perishable items were manifold at such cult centers. Festivals such as the carrying of the god's ceremonial boat or statue took place amid music, dance, and crowds of onlookers. The popular Min festival was a harvest festival that came to be part of the royal cult. A sacred white bull participated in this event.

10.6 THE REFORM OF AKHENATON. In the fourteenth century B.C.E., after the expulsion of the Hyksos rulers, a period of conquests in the east and the rise of international diplomacy, the young king Amenhotep IV effected a radical political and religious reform. He declared that the sole great god was the Aton, the solar disk. He changed his name (Amon-Is-Satisfied) to Akhenaton (He-Who-Serves-Aton), moved his royal capital from Thebes to the new site of Akhetaton (modern Tell al-Amarna), and embarked on a campaign of erasing the name of Amon and even the word *gods* where it appeared. The movement has been called henotheism, monolatry, even monotheism, but its political dimension was clear: the powerful Amon priesthood and temple officials were disempowered. The new Aton temples were to be unroofed, and a new, naturalistic style of art came about. The solar disk was represented with rays ending in hands, sometimes offering the *ankh* to his people. The king placed himself in a special intermediary position, divine above humankind. The Aton was hailed as the one source of all life.

After the death of Akhenaton, his wife Nefertiti may have reigned for a short time under the name of Smenkhare, after which the name of the son Tutankhaton was changed to Tutankhamen and he was brought back into line with the powerful Amon priesthood. With the close of their dynasty (the eighteenth), the Aton movement was execrated as heresy.

10.7 DEATH: VOYAGE AND REMEMBRANCE. The afterlife seems originally to have been located in the sky, and associated with the West. The equipment for physical preservation of the dead is well known, including a solid tomb with a false door, *ka* figurines, and a model of the head for the revivifying "opening of the mouth" rite, food offerings and household goods, models of servants, and mummification. Tombs were provided with curses to discourage pillaging and reuse, and passersby were enjoined to speak an offering to the deceased that would provide him sustenance. Also critically important was the voyage itself: secure passage into a comfortable position in the otherworld was engineered by spells placed within the tomb.

The first generation of these were a royal prerogative, the Pyramid Texts: some 760 spells inscribed in royal tomb chambers beginning in the twenty-fourth century B.C.E. with the pyramid of Unas, the last king of the fifth dynasty. In the pyramid texts, we follow the divine king's burial rites and ascent, which ended with the sun god's embracing of the king for eternity, in accordance with the theology of the temple of Re of Heliopolis. The king, because of his divine status unable to die, flew as a bird, scarab, or grasshopper toward his celestial destination in the East, the Field of Offerings. He had to complete several purifications to pass the judgment of the ferryman who was to take him across the lake, and answer by magic, passwords, or persuasion the initiatory interrogation for advancement to the next level. The king was kept out of the hands of Osiris the judge, even as the king was likened to Osiris the undying. At last he was enthroned above his people, like the sun god to rule eternally.

A later diffusion and reinterpretation of this system is found in the popular Coffin Texts of the ninth to thirteenth dynasties (twenty-second to seventeenth centuries B.C.E.). These spells for justifying the deceased in the netherworld were written inside wooden coffins. In them, Osiris and the judgment of the dead figure prominently. From the sixth dynasty onward, political decentralization and the rise of local "nomarchs" brought elaborate tombs within the reach of nobles and wealthy families; themes found in the royal Pyramid Texts are found in the Coffin Texts in later stages of development and popularization.

A third phase of efficacious mortuary literature is seen in the *Book of Going Forth by Day,* usually today called the *Book of the Dead.* From the eighteenth dynasty (sixteenth century B.C.E.) to the Roman period, this book was placed beside the body in the coffin and provided spells for the journey and judgment drawn primarily from the Coffin Texts with some expansion and reinterpretation. The magical content is now explicit: these spells will bend the gods to beneficence.

10.8 BIBLIOGRAPHY. Eliade, *H* 1, 25–33; L. H. Lesko, "Egyptian Religion: An Overview," in *ER* 5, 37–54; D. B. Redford, "Egyptian Religion: The Literature," in *ER* 5, 54–65.

General works on Egyptian religion include Eric Hornung's *Conceptions of God in Ancient Egypt* (1982) and Siegfried Morenz's *Egyptian Religion* (1973). A good reference work is Hans Bonnet's *Reallexikon der ägypotischen Religionsgeschichte* (1952). For a selection of texts in translation, we find Miriam Lichtheim, *Ancient Egyptian Literature: A Book of Readings,* 3 vols. (1973–1980); J. B. Pritchard (ed.), *Ancient Near Eastern Texts Relating to the Old Testament* (1967); and Raymond O. Faulkner's translations of the funerary texts, *Pyramid Texts (1969), Coffin Texts,* 3 vols. (1973–1978), *The Egyptian Book of the Dead* (1972).

11

Germanic Religion

11.1 THE GERMANIC TRIBES are a group of ancient Indo-European tribes whose presence is archeologically attested in Northern Europe about 600 B.C.E. Their neighbors during that early period were the Lapps and Finns in the north, the Balts and the Iranian tribes of the Scythians and Sarmathians in the east, and the Gauls in the south. During the Roman conquests (first century B.C.E.), they practiced herding, agriculture, and hunting.

11.2 SOURCES. The most important direct sources for the religion of the Germans go back to the age of the Vikings. The poetical *Edda* in the Icelandic language contains ten poems about the gods and eighteen poems about the heroes. The prose *Edda,* the work of the Icelandic historian Snorri Sturluson (1179–1241 C.E.), is a manual of Scaldic poetry in three parts, whose Preface, called *Gylfaginning,* is an introduction to Norwegian mythology. The first part of the history of the Norwegian kings by Snorri (*Heimskringla*), called *Ynglingasaga,* is devoted to the mythical origin of northern kingship.

11.3 COSMOGONY-COSMOLOGY, THEOGONY-THEOLOGY.

11.3.1 Cosmogony in the *Gylfaginning* is introduced according to three Eddic poems (*Vafthrúdnismál, Grimnismál,* and *Voluspá,* or Prophecy of the Seeress). In the beginning there was nothing but a great emptiness called Ginnungagap. Before the earth, Niflheimr, or the world of the dead, came into being. From the great pit Hvergelmir eleven rivers came out; in the south was located the glowing hot world Múspell, belonging to the Black Giant Surtr. The water of the rivers turned into ice as soon as it met Ginnungagap. Through the action of the fire of Múspell on the ice, an anthropomorphic giant, Ymir, appeared. From the sweat of his right armpit originated a couple of giants, and his legs had intercourse and produced a son.

From the melting ice emerged the cow Audhumla, who fed Ymir on her milk, feeding in her turn on salty ice, from which another being was born, called Búri, whose son Borr married Bestla, the daughter of the giant Bolthorn. Three sons were born to this couple: Odhinn, Vili, and Vé. The three divine brothers killed the giant Ymir, whose blood drowned the race of giants, with the exception of Bergelmir and his family. The gods took Ymir's body to the middle of the Ginnungagap, where his flesh formed the earth, his blood the waters, his skull the sky, his bones the mountains, his hair the trees, and so forth. The stars, whose movement is controlled by the gods, were sparks from the fire of Múspell.

In the middle of the circular earth, surrounded by a great ocean, the gods built a fence from the eyebrows of Ymir, thus establishing the borders of Midhgardhr, the dwelling of the human beings, created shortly thereafter. Creation was concluded by the gods with the building of Asgardhr, their own dwelling.

The primordial human couple was created by Odhinn from two trees, Askr and Embla, found on the shore of the ocean. He gave them life, Hoenir gave them the senses, and Lódhurr gave them human shape and the gift of language.

11.3.2 The Cosmic Tree. The world exists in the shadow of the cosmic tree Yggdrasill, the *axis mundi* supporting the heavenly vaults. According to the western Scandinavians, Yggdrasill is an ash tree in which the council of the gods meets daily. Yggdrasill has three roots, diving into the three worlds: the world of the dead (Hel), the world of the giants, and the world of the human beings. Several springs originate at its foot, which originally were probably one: Urdhr, the source of destiny; Mímir, the source of wisdom; and Hvergelmir, the source of all earthly rivers. From the bark of the cosmic tree drips the vivifying liquid *aurr.*

11.3.3 Theology. The gods are divided into two classes: the Ases and the Vanes. Asgardhr is the city of the Ases, among whom the most important are Odhinn and Thórr. At the beginning of time, the Ases were at war with the Vanes; then they made peace by exchanging hostages: the Vane Njordhr and his son Freyr settled among the Ases, whereas the Ases Mímir and Hoenir went to live among the Vanes. The role of the Vane goddess Freya during the war is not clear, but she probably planted in Asgardhr something of which the Ases would never be able to rid themselves—lust. She also taught Odhinn the magical arts (*seidhr*).

11.3.4 Gods. Julius Caesar and especially Tacitus (*Germania*) gave us important information on the gods of the Germans. Tacitus equated the god Odhinn-Wódhan with Mercury, an interpretation still common in the fourth century, when the day of Mercury (*Mercurii dies:* see the French *mercredi* or the Italian *mercoledì*) was called by the Germans "day of Wódhan," Wednesday. Human sacrifices were offered to this god "who reigned over all things" (*regnator omnium deus*). Other divinities were identified with Mars, Hercules, or Jupiter, the thunder god. Tacitus also mentioned a mysterious goddess, the equivalent of Nerthus, and the cult of divine twins, introduced as Castor and Pollux.

During the Viking period, Odhinn was the sovereign god, but Thorr received most of the cultic honors.

11.4 ESCHATOLOGY.

11.4.1 The end of the world was connected with the activity of an extremely important character in Germanic mythology, the giant Loki, who was nevertheless at home among the Ases. Son of the giantess Laufey, he had intercourse with the giantess Angrbodha, who gave birth to the wolf Fenrir and to the serpent Midhard, who surrounded the universe—two threatening, utterly destructive beings. Loki can be described as a Trickster, a being more ancient than the gods, who in many world mythologies appears as jocular and oftentimes mischievous, sometimes bisexual or transsexual, bizarre and ridiculous. In his female mode, Loki was fecundated by the stallion Svadhilfari and gave birth to the eight-legged horse Sleipnir; he was likewise the mother of the race of beings called *flagdh.* In the poetical *Edda,* Loki showed no inclination for evil. Only the later poem *Lokasenna* made him the author of a great number of mischiefs.

11.4.2 The murder of Baldr. One of Loki's mischievous stunts, which had a direct relation to the end of the world, was the murder of

Baldr, the glowing son of Odhinn. Baldr's mother Frigg had asked all things in the world to take an oath that they would never harm Baldr, but she forgot to ask the little mistletoe plant. Jealous of Baldr, Loki disguised himself as an old woman and learned this secret from Frigg, after which he armed Hodhr, Baldr's blind brother, with a sprout of mistletoe and directed him to Baldr, telling him to throw it toward him as an expression of joy. Baldr was killed on the spot, but the goddess Hel agreed to release him if everything in the world would shed tears for his death. Everything, including the stones, cried over Baldr's disappearance except the giantess Thokk, who was again Loki in disguise. Her condition not having been fulfilled, Hel detained Baldr.

In punishment for the murder of Baldr, the gods tied Loki to a rock with the entrails of his own sons. Above him was a venomous serpent whose poison fell on Loki's head, causing him renewed pain. But he was to escape before the end of the world.

11.4.3 The Ragnarok (the destiny of the gods) or world's end was a long process. Destruction was already part of the Yggdrasill tree itself, whose leaves were devoured by a deer, whose bark was rotting, and whose root was eaten by the serpent Nidhoggr. After an idyllic beginning, the gods engaged in a blind war, during which lust crept into Asgardhr. The penultimate act of the tragedy was the murder of Baldr, and the last was the unleashing of all those terrifying forces that the Ases had temporarily chained: Loki and his descendants, the wolf Fenrir, and the Great Cosmic Serpent. Preceded by awesome portents, the forces of destruction threw themselves upon Asgardhr: the untamed giants headed by Loki and the fiery demons who would set the universe aflame headed by Surtr, the ruler of Múspell. The Ases and their enemies were mutually annihilated: the wolf Fenrir killed Odhinn, Vidharr son of Odhinn killed Fenrir, Thorr and the Great Serpent killed each other, Freyr was killed by Surtr, all heavenly lights were extinguished, and the glowing earth was drowned by the water of the ocean. It will reemerge some day, and be ruled by the good and innocent Baldr, home to a sinless human race that will live under a golden cupola.

11.5 SHAMANISM AND BROTHERHOODS OF WARRIORS.

11.5.1 Odhinn. The existence of shamanistic aspects in Germanic religion concerns Odhinn, the sovereign Ase god, who possessed the magical power *seidhr.* Like the shamans, Odhinn had a miraculous eight-legged horse (Sleipnir) and two omniscient ravens; he could change shape, talk with the dead, and so forth.

11.5.2 The Berserkr. Odhinn was likewise a war god, and warriors had a special destiny: after death, they went to the heavenly palace Valholl, not to the underworld of the goddess Hel. The death of a warrior was the equivalent of a supreme ecstatic experience.

The warrior entered the state of *berserkr* (literally "bear-skinned"), which is a state of murderous furor and invulnerability in imitation of the behavior of a predator, especially a wolf.

11.5.3 The Jarl. In Germanic society, Odhinn was the god of the *jarl* (noblemen) and did not enjoy popularity among the *karl,* or freemen, whose god was Thorr. The armed bands of Odhinn terrorized the villages. The god required human sacrifices. Its victims were hung on trees, perhaps in memory of the fact that Odhinn himself, hung for nine months on the tree Yggdrasill and wounded by a spear, had obtained at this stage the magical wisdom of runes and the precious gift of poetry.

11.6 BIBLIOGRAPHY. Eliade, *H* 1, 173–77; E. C. Polomé, "Germanic Religion," in *ER* 5, 520–36.

The sources of Germanic mythology are translated in F. Wagner, *Les poémes héroiques de l'Edda* (1929), and *Les poémes mythologiques de l'Edda* (1936). On Loki, see Georges Dumézil, *Loki* (1986).

12

Greek Religion

12.1 MINOAN RELIGION. The civilization of second-millennium B.C.E. Crete takes its appellation from the legendary King Minos. Stories of his labyrinth are conjectured to be distorted reflections of the sprawling Knossos palace or perhaps of the cave sanctuaries characteristic of Crete from the Neolithic period onward. This was a civilization remembered for its palace complexes, artistic motifs celebrating nature, and its hieroglyphic and Linear A scripts (the former deriving from Luwian hieroglyphic, the latter a Semitic language according to J. Best and F. Woudhuizen, *Ancient Scripts from Crete and Cyprus* (1988). In decline after the great explosion of Thera, Minoan civilization was both supplanted by and partially preserved within the robust and advancing Mycenean culture (ca. fifteenth century B.C.E.)

Themes of Minoan religion are best conveyed by its iconography, seen in colorful palace frescoes, decorative metalwork, vases, and figurines. Such depictions show us that a great goddess of nature ruled the island, appearing in epiphanies to her priests and worshipers, sometimes in company of her undersized male consort—an adolescent god conceivably of the dying/reconstituted variety. Snakes and panthers are attributes of the goddess, as are her bell-shaped, flounced skirt and open-breasted bodice. She is a mistress of animals, but also of mountains and sea, agriculture and war, reigning over the living and the dead. Dominant symbols of Minoan sacrality are the goddess's double ax and the "horns of consecration," both of Anatolian/Near Eastern origin. The dove and the bull also served to represent the goddess and god respectively.

Worshipers depicted in votive figurines and goldwork stand rigidly straight facing a divine epiphany, right hand raised to the forehead. The goddess may be depicted enthroned or hovering in the air above a ritual dance of worshipers. The goddess typically stands with both arms raised when she reveals herself.

Minoan cult was characterized by sacrifices and offerings at cave (e.g., Kamares, Psychro) and mountain peak sanctuaries (for example, the so-called Grave of Zeus, unthinkable for Greek religion but evidence of the dying god motif for Crete) and at small sacred buildings that might be rural (centered around a sacred tree) or rooms within a palace complex. Slaughter of bulls and smaller animals, burnt offerings, food gifts, and libations have left traces for archaeologists to uncover throughout the twentieth century, led by the master Sir Arthur Evans. Also offered to the goddess were small votive figurines (often in human or animal shape) and double axes, swords, and knives, and even miniature sanctuary models. Remains bear witness to mountaintop fire rituals, festive processions led by priests and (more prominently) priestesses, and acrobatic bull-dancing competitions—an ordeal perhaps echoed by the mythical minotaur's activities, although human sacrifice in early Cretan and perhaps Mycenaean cultures is a viable possibility.

A Minoan necropolis was equipped with facilities for sacrificial offerings, libations, and ritual dancing. Burials were outfitted with fine grave goods; circular stone tombs, *tholoi*, originate in early Minoan Crete and reach their peak with the beehive tombs of Mycenae, the most celebrated being the fourteenth-century B.C.E. "Treasury of Atreus."

12.2 MYCENAEAN RELIGION. Mycenaean culture, Greek speaking but related to Minoan, has often been interpreted as the triumph of male qualities in both society and religion. Admitting the naïveté of this theory, it may be noted that Mycenaean cities, unlike Minoan, are walled fortresses (such as Tiryns, Gla, and Thebes), patriarchy and battle are dominant themes, and the great goddess (Potnia: "Lady," "Mistress") is displaced in her preeminence by the sky god of Indo-European origins, Zeus the father. This was the civilization that brought us the Trojan War, or the misty historical precedent for the Homeric poem, and then burnt itself out in princely adventurism, falling with the Sea Peoples' invasions into a four-century dark age (twelfth to ninth century B.C.E.) after its flourishing trade network had stretched across the Mediterranean from Asia Minor perhaps to Sicily.

Linear B records reveal local pantheons, in which numerous gods may be identified with gods of later Greek history. At Pylos, for example, Poseidon and Zeus-Hera sanctuaries are mentioned, and gods such as the Divine Mother, Artemis, and Dionysus, but who are the deities Manasa or Drimios the son of Zeus? Tablets from Knossos record offerings also to Potnia of Athana and Potnia of the Labyrinth, Enyalios, Paiawon (Apollo), Erinys, and the Priestess of the Winds. Dedications to these gods are like those of later times, including grain, wine, oil, honey, rams and fleece and oxen, but men and women are also occasionally listed as dedications to a god.

Minoan artistic styles and luxury goods pervade Mycenaean sites, making it hard to delineate religious distinctions. Deposits of votive figurines include a goddess with raised arms, and a grain goddess is also in evidence. We also find cult idols, some quite difficult to interpret. In general, it appears to have been a palace-centered cult, its sacrifices and the roasting of meat accomplished at the circular hearth of the megaron, a large court central to Mycenaean palace architecture.

12.3 GREEK RELIGION: ARCHAIC AND CLASSICAL. Greek religion was the dynamic interplay of myth and ritual, both rich and variegated traditions in Greek culture. Ritual enacted myth, and both were localized; all statements of myth were variants, as were local cult practices. The gods were localized, too, their attributes and legends varying in different regions and cult contexts; Apollo was the Pythian at his Delphic Oracle, the Delian at his island birthplace, Phoebus in the Iliad, shooting from afar. The Homeric poems were pan-Hellenic, deliberately emphasizing shared and general attributes of the gods. Greek religion was extraordinarily complex and moving on many levels. Psychological, sociological, historical, artistic, and linguistic investigations reveal level after level, many still resonant with modern sentiments, but others impenetrably alien, obscure, or troubling.

12.3.1 Civic religion. Whereas Greek popular religion affirmed community cohesion and stratification, civic religion (the sacred calendar, offices, and precincts of the polis, which developed from the eleventh to eighth centuries B.C.E.) was characterized by, among the elements listed below, animal sacrifice and common banqueting on the carefully apportioned meat. Pythagorean and Orphic nonconformism from the sixth century B.C.E. was a marked disavowal of the community sacrifices, for they included a rarefied vegetarianism among their abstentions. Individualism and internalization similarly at odds with popular piety increased with the evolution of the Eleusinian mysteries into the narrower, exclusive societies of the Hellenistic era (21).

12.3.2 Shamanism. The tendency toward individualism had already been present in an ancient and rather strange character, a seer and healer technically known as *iatromantes* (from *iatros*, healer, and *mantis*, seer), who shows striking similarities to the Central Asian shaman (26). Among the Greek *iatromantes* who do not seem to be merely mythical were Epimenides of Crete, Hermotimus of Clazomenae, Aristeas of Proconnesus, Empedocles of Agrigentum, and Pythagoras of Samos. Their deeds included abstinence, forecasting the future, performing miracles of various kinds, bilocation, memory of their precedent lives, ecstatic trips, and rapid journeys through space. There was a whole Pythagorean and Platonic tradition that continued to exalt the superhuman qualities of these characters, trying to match them by using different theurgical methods, especially fashionable in the late Roman Empire.

12.3.3. Early philosophy. This tendency to exalt such superhuman attributes manifested itself in ancient Greek philosophy. According to F. M. Cornford and other scholars, the first philosophers were the *iatromantes* themselves. Philosophy as it developed in Greece was to be a reversal of popular religion's underpinnings: it bridged the institutionalized discontinuity between human and divine (by exalting the human or rationalizing divinity) and ransomed an immortalized soul from gloomy Hades. The classical scholar Walter Burkert linked philosophy's impact to the rise of the book—communication from one thinking individual to others. And as the gods gradually receded through the centuries from vivid anthropomorphism into exalted abstraction, skepticism, voiced early by pre-Socratics, blossomed into rationalism, that peculiarly Greek legacy. All this was harmonious with what scholars today recognize as the changing meaning of the Delphic maxim "Know Thyself"; originally, it counseled recognition of one's human finitude: pretentions to divinity were *hubris*. Later, in a Platonic light, it was recast to imply that a human's truest nature is divinity, recognition of which would be a spiritual panacea.

Any time Plato had to enounce a truth, which by definition was external to any dialectical process, he had recourse to myth. One of the fundamental principles of Plato's thought was the vertical hierarchy of being: we are inferior beings, living in the clefts of the earth like worms;

to us, even the surface of the earth, called by him True Earth, is like a paradise. People living there use the almost weightless element air as we use water and their air is the ether. This vision of the earth surface, sketched in the dialogue *Phaedo*, takes more precise shape in *Gorgias* (523a ff.), where the inhabitants of the True Earth are said to live in the Isles of the Blessed, surrounded by the ocean of air. Plato's great eschatological and cosmological myths (*Phaedo, Phaedrus, Timaeus,* the myth of Er in Book X of *The Republic*) stem from the shamanistic beliefs of the *iatromantes*. They tell us the story of the soul, which fell in the prison of the body (*Cratylus* 400b) and would only be able to break free if practicing the philosopher's way of life, which implies systematic separation from bodily desires; according to the degree of separation achieved during one's lifetime, the soul will be rewarded or punished in afterlife.

Like certain *iatromantes* and the Orphic puritans before him, Plato made *metensomatosis* (and *not* metempsychosis, as the misguided believe; metempsychosis means multiple animation of the same body by several souls) into a central tenet of his doctrine. The soul of the accomplished philosopher would be dispatched for a few thousands of years to the higher regions of the cosmos, where she would contemplate the immortal Ideas, after which she would be again sent into a mortal body. If for a number of consecutive cycles, the soul successfully defeated the body, then she would remain in permanent contemplation of the incorruptible world of Ideas. On the contrary, if she did not resist the temptations of the body, she would end up being born again and again in increasingly lower kinds of human beings, coming right to the end of the scale, where, after the tyrant, the worst incarnation is to be born as a woman. (Strangely enough, although in the *Republic* Plato is in favor of political equality between men and women, in his other dialogues he strongly asserts the woman's ontological inferiority to man.) With Er the Pamphylian, Socrates the narrator of *Phaedo* and *Phaedrus,* and Timaeus of Locri, all the corners of this vast cosmos become known to us, except for the inaccessible regions of the astral gods, which introduce the even more extraordinary world of ideal essences. The later Platonist Plutarch of Chaeronea (first to second century C.E.), who would create cosmological and eschatological myths that rivaled the master's own work, was equally reluctant to disclose any information about things beyond the sphere of the Moon, the lowest among the ancient planets.

According to Platonic tradition, philosophy is religion and religion is philosophy. It is only a matter of emphasis if a branch of Platonism would end up in a more abstract and speculative direction, or would open itself up to religious cults and mysteries. Christianity kept up the dualism between soul and body, together with a simplified Platonic cosmos. The Christian Logos is a compendium of the world of Ideas, who became man in order to take upon himself the sins of humankind. Neoplatonism, starting in the third century C.E., went through two main phases: after Plotinus' austere philosophy, it became more and more permeated with magic and theurgy. Even in Christian garb, Neoplatonic magic continued to exist, with Michael Psellus in the Byzantine Empire and with Marsilio Ficino and his Platonic Academy in late fifteenth-century Florence.

12.3.4 Early theology. Literature fixes myth, but oral poetry such as the Homeric epics (eventually written down between the eighth and sixth centuries B.C.E.) was fluid, maleable, and continuously created through recitation. Homer, Hesiod, and their fellow poets were incalculably influential as theologians. Hesiod's *Theogony* narrates the sprouting of the natural forces and gods from primordial Chaos, Earth and Tartaros, and Eros, followed by Kronos' castration of his father Uranos and Zeus' triumph over Kronos, while the generations of gods fruitfully multiply. He set forth the Generations of Men in the Works and Days, from golden perfection to the arrested silver generation to the Bronze Age to the heroes to our own Iron Age. Later didactic wisdom poetry (for example, Theognis of Megara) and lyric poetry including the shatteringly beautiful poet of Aphrodite, Sappho, voiced new developments in the evolution of the gods.

Anatolian and Near Eastern influences were evident in the configuration of the Greek pantheon as well as in the names and qualities of certain individual gods. Zeus the sky father and storm god had the clearest Indo-European inspiration. As king of the Olympian gods, his symbols were his thunderbolt, eagle, and libidinous virility. His wife was Hera, who oversaw matters of seasonality, including marriage. Zeus' children were many; the least favored was his only child with Hera, Ares. From Zeus' head like a thought emerged Athena, the armored virgin who taught women their crafts and men their battle intrigues. Leto bore Artemis and Apollo, the twins. Artemis, a Mistress of Animals (*potnia theron*), was the virginal huntress with a cruel edge and a role in coming-of-age rites for girls (as at Brauron); for the Greeks, hunting and athletic competition require sexual abstinence. Apollo was a shining but distant god of lyre and bow, healing and plague, companion of the Muses. Also to Zeus, Maia bore Hermes, the mercurial divine messenger, psychopomp, and trickster with origins in the phallic boundary stones called herms. Demeter bore Persephone to her brother Zeus, and Semele bore Dionysus. Aphrodite, probably a reflection of Ishtar/Astarte come via Cyprus, was awkwardly married to Hephaestus, the lame smith of the gods. Poseidon and Hades were the brothers of Zeus, presiding respectively over sea (and the waters that irrigate the earth) and underworld. The gods, especially Zeus, determined and enforced ethical standards that included piety, generosity, and balanced, polytheistic worship. Their capriciousness waned after the Iliad, but they continued to embody forces clearly at play in the world.

12.3.5 Dionysus was an exceptional god. He was the son of Zeus and the Theban princess Semele, but at the same time a god coming from the east, with Anatolian or Phrygian-Thracian roots. Superficially, we might list his links to wine, phalloi, masks, and theater, but he was more deeply a god of divine madness, representing the Other within each individual and overturning behavioral norms. In Euripides' *Bacchae,* Dionysus sent his maenads, his frenzied female devotees, running to the mountains to tear wild animals apart and feast on raw flesh. Raw meat, properly offered to Dionysus only, was imagined as the next step to cannibalism, the antithesis of humanity. Dionysus's festivals were lewd, nocturnal revels at which sexual freedom reigned, quite the opposite of ordinary life in the polis.

12.3.6 Other deities. A step down from these personalized divinities, daimones were forces or beings that were cited as the causes of inexplicable events or psychological processes, such as unusual recognition or memory. Socrates' "demon" voice of conscience is well known. E. R. Dodds noted the increase of causal daimones in the Odyssey, accompanying the retreat of Zeus, who appeared less as a character and more as a reference. In daily life an extraordinary or incomprehensible person might be called a daimon, including after death; ordinarily a person was reduced to a *psyche* after death.

Euhemerism was the rationalizing of divinities as people from the historical past who grew larger and larger in memory until they became mythical, godly. This scenario was probably true for Orpheus, a reformer of Dionysiac religion in Thrace. Orphism, or rather the *orphikos bios,* or "Orphic kind of life," was a semantic inversion of Dionysism, which was submitted to a radical change of course. Indeed, Orphism was not content to mitigate the excesses of Dionysism; rather, it transformed them in opposite excesses: abstinence became the norm, both from food and sex. Setting aside the myths about Orpheus' journey to Hades in search of his wife Euridice and his dismemberment by Thracian maenads, Orphic texts won a following in the sixth and fifth centuries B.C.E. A contractive and negative anticosmogony was one of these myths; it thus proceeded in a direction rather the opposite of Hesiod's theogony. The creation of humanity from remains of the Titans who slew and consumed the baby Dionysus was central to Orphism. But most visible were Orphic ascetics and wandering holy men whose way of life included special clothing, bathing, and restricted diet. In civic religion, in which priesthood was an office, not necessarily a different way of life or a different class of people, the Orphic *bios* was a break with the past and with society, promising separateness and election. Orphic puritanism, which must have played a considerable role in Plato's own antisomatic doctrine, was the expression of a worldview that was the opposite of that embodied in Dionysism.

12.3.7 The cult of heroes apparently began by the eighth century B.C.E., when Mycenaean funerary buildings began receiving offerings and when famous names of the past, such as Helen and Menelaos, were linked to these sites. The tomb evolved into the heroon, the cult center and locus of power for the hero, whose very bones acted as a talisman of invincibility for the community possessing them, even if relocated in a new polis; notable examples are the Spartans' acquisition of the seven-cubit long skeleton of Orestes and the return of Theseus' bones to Athens. Heroizing accomplishments were extraordinary and not necessarily admirable acts, usually capped by a glorious death; the dying Oedipus of Sophocles' *Oedipus at Colonus* is sought after for his talismanic body much as medieval saints were pursued for their potential relics. A hero might be claimed as a city founder or ancestor of a noble line, or, like Helen and Herakles and Achilles, might have one divine parent but were at odds with some god during life and became godlike only after death. Herakles, the only hero to become divine in myth, was relentlessly persecuted by his stepmother Hera. Libations and chthonic sacrifice (12.4) were performed for the dead hero. The *agon* of yearly athletic competitions glorified the hero and drew together the community seasonally.

12.4 SACRIFICES. Hesiod's *Theogony* describes Prometheus' division of a slaughtered ox between himself and Zeus. He made two piles, one of meat covered with the animal's stomach, the other all bones under a layer of fat. When Zeus chose the latter, more appetizing pile, he unwittingly established a precedent: "And thenceforth the tribes of earthly humans burn to the immortals white bones on fragrant altars" (*Theogony* 556). Sacrifice to the Olympian gods was indeed a smoke offering; humans, eating corruptible flesh, were consigned to corruptibility themselves. The gods, for their part, needed the meat savor; they grew desperate without it. In practice, after a festive procession of garlanded worshipers, the animal was slaughtered at a raised altar and ceremoniously butchered, after which fat and bones were dispatched to the heavens and the meat was roasted, then boiled and distributed. Stone inscriptions record sacred laws concerning the division of labor and of meat in festival sacrifices, alluding to titles and duties of officiants. Divination, much influenced by the Mesopotamian sources that systematized it beyond any sophistication the Greeks were to reach, might take place at a sacrifice in the form of reading the animal's organs. But divination by bird observation, dream interpretation, meteorological portents, and so forth was widespread, as seen in the Homeric poems and later literature.

For chthonic deities, heroes, or, as mythologist Vernant notes, to ward off sinister forces threatening the city's well-being, the procedure was different. A low altar with a hole to channel blood into the earth was employed. The ceremony was more likely to take place in the evening and rather than providing a feast the whole animal was burned. Drinking blood gives the dead awareness and voice in Odyssey Book XI. The ordinary dead, although they were not worshiped, received grain cakes, libations, and commemorative picnics, especially at anniversaries and festivals such as the Genesia. Pollution from murder, disease, broken social taboos, profanation of a sanctuary, or the ill will of a god needed treatment. The ritual compensation received by heroes could transform them from sources of pollution to loci of power and protection. The Greeks did have the institution of the scapegoat (*pharmakos*), who could be a human being burdened with the city's guilt, beaten and banished.

12.5 THE FESTIVAL CALENDAR varied from polis to polis, but there are a number of standard celebrations, such as New Year's ceremonies. The climax of Athens' New Year's proceedings, which stretched over months of purifications and preparations, was the Panathenaia, celebrated in midsummer. The climax of a procession from the city gate to the Acropolis (a procession depicted on the Parthenon frieze) came when a new robe was presented to the old cult statue of Athena Polias. Sacrifices and chariot racing, as well as nocturnal festivities, mark the Panathenaia. A very ancient and widespread festival was the spring Anthesteria, a three-day festival of Dionysus when the year's wine was unsealed. The entire city celebrated with wine mixing and drinking, even a drinking competition. At night in a sacred marriage ritual, the wife of the *archon basileus* was given to Dionysus. Wandering spirits of dead visitors were at large during this festival, to be chased out at its close. An example of a festival in which only women participated was Demeter's Thesmophoria. Women left their homes and camped in huts at some remove, sacrificing pigs and undergoing certain chthonic mysteries of fertility.

12.6 THE ELEUSINIAN MYSTERIES, the most famous in the ancient world, were associated not only with Demeter and her lost daughter Kore (Persephone) but had Bacchic elements as well. The Homeric Hymn to Demeter is an early and important source providing mythic counterparts to the ritual. Initiates were purified through fasting and in a sea bath near Athens with a piglet to be sacrificed to mark both the death and new life of the initiate and the descent of Kore to Hades. A cheerful, ribald procession to Eleusis ended with a solemn visitation at Pluto's cave, the entrance to the underworld. Initiates were veiled as the mourning Demeter once veiled herself, and a special barley drink was imbibed. Inside the *telesterion,* more like a roofed theater than a temple, a sacred drama unfolded, accompanied by sacrifices. Kore was reunited with her mother, meaning rebirth for the initiate and abundance for the earth, symbolized by an ear of corn. The lasting effect of initiation was to assure smooth passage through death into a favored status in the afterlife.

12.7 TEMPLE. A sacred precinct was a *temenos,* usually a walled enclosure; sacred spots commonly persisted for hundreds, even thousands of years, many being translated into Christian holy sites. A temple was the home of the god, represented by a cult statue, which in the fifth century B.C.E. could be a shining masterpiece of ivory and gold upon a wooden core. Plentiful deposits of votive figurines are commonly excavated at sanctuaries, and offerings of coins; worshipers with more resources might fund buildings or set up stelae and statues as dedications in both sacred and public places. The home was also a religious unit, with a hearth for sacrifices and remembrance of dead ancestors. In the fifth century B.C.E., there was some move to suppress independent household cults in favor of state-controlled religious functions.

Another type of sacred precinct was the oracle, the most famous being Apollo's at Delphi, called the *omphalos*, or navel of the world. In response to an inquiry, a priestess called a Pythia would sit on a tripod (a cauldron used for boiling meat in sacrifices) and speak under the influence of burning or chewed leaves and the fumes anciently believed to rise from a cleft in the rock. Her utterances were transformed into metrical verses by priests of the oracle, providing often deceptive answers to questions ranging from military strategy to personal problems. The oracle served other functions difficult to enumerate here. It was a place of sacred oaths, ritual purification, sanctuary, manumission of slaves, and periodic festivals.

12.8 BIBLIOGRAPHY. The best introduction to both general themes and important details is Walter Burkert's *Greek Religion* (1985); see also M. P. Nilsson's classic *Geschichte der griechischen Religion*, 2 vols. (1941–1957), 3rd revised ed. (1967–1974); J. -P. Vernant's *Myth and Thought Among the Greeks* (1983); Ugo Bianchi's *La religione greca* (1975); B. C. Dietrich's *Origins of Greek Religion* (1974).

On Minoan and Mycenaean religion, see Ch. Picard, *Les religions préhelléniques: Crète et Mycènes* (1948); B. Rutkowski, *Frühgriechische Kultdarstellungen* (1981); E. T. Vermeule, *Gotterkult. Archaeologia Homerica* (1974); E. T. Vermeule, *Greece in the Bronze Age* (1964). On the epics of the Homeric age, see G. Nagy's *The Best of the Achaeans* (1979).

On Orphism, see I. M. Linforth, *The Arts of Orpheus* (1973; 1941); W. K. C. Guthrie, *Orpheus and Greek Religion: A Study of the Orphic Movement* (1952); on Dionysus, see H. Jeanmaire, *Dionysos: histoire du culte de Bacchus* (1951).

13

Hellenistic Religions

13.1 HELLENISM is the culture that arose subsequent to the conquests of Alexander the Great (362–331 B.C.E.), leaving on the conquered territories a durable imprint of Greek language and culture. While classicists may close what they call the Hellenistic period with the Roman Imperial (first century B.C.E.), historians of the Middle East and Byzantium trace the ebbing and flowing of Hellenism into the Islamic period and even into the second millennium C.E.

13.2 HELLENISTIC RELIGION in its inception underwent the powerful influence of the philosophy of Aristotle (384–322 B.C.E.), of the Stoic philosophical synthesis (around 300 B.C.E.), and of the general development of Greek science. The result of the latter was a wave of astral mysticism culminating with the appearance, in the third century B.C.E., of Hellenistic astrology, combining Mesopotamian and Egyptian astral divination and astral deities with Greek astronomy.

The Hellenistic ruler cult adopted by Alexander and particularly by the Seleucids of Syria and by the dynasty of the Ptolemies of Egypt (322–30 B.C.E.) had a Middle Eastern background; in Roman times, it would evolve into the Roman imperial cult.

13.2.1 Hades in the air. One of the general tendencies in Hellenistic religion, supported by the Stoic tenet of the lightness of the fiery human soul, was the disappearance of the underground hell for the punishment of the wicked. In the religious geography of Platonism, the subterranean Hades, with its caves in the interior of the earth and its infernal rivers Acheron, Pyriphlegeton, and Cocytus, had played an important role. Some scholars claim that Plato's disciple Heraclides Ponticus (born between 388 and 373 B.C.E., died after 322 B.C.E.) transferred Plato's Hades to heaven. Yet even much later a Platonist like Plutarch of Chaeronea (ca. 45–125 C.E.) had not completely given up the Platonic subterranean Hades. However, for Plutarch the place of punishment of the soul was positively situated in sublunar space. A similar tendency was visible in Jewish visionary literature (1 Enoch: early third century B.C.E.; *The Testament of Levi*: second century B.C.E.) and in the Jewish Platonist Philo of Alexandria (ca. 15 B.C.E.–50 C.E.). In the second century C.E., Gnosticism and Hermeticism had already adopted a doctrine that would remain very influential in Platonism, from Macrobius (ca. 400 C.E.) to Marsilio Ficino (1433–1499 C.E.). According to it, every individual soul would descend into the world through the spheres of the planets and would ascend again to the starry heaven following the same path. Journeys to heaven are very frequent during the first few centuries C.E. in all three great religious traditions of the time: Platonism, Judaism, and Christianity.

13.2.2 Astrology is based on a principle that goes back to Mesopotamia and Egypt: that there is a connection between the system of astral movements and the system of human life, with its waning and waxing, its highs and its lows. Yet the Hellenistic synthesis is unique, in so far as it combines Eastern divination with Greek astronomy. Attributed to the Egyptian god Hermes-Thoth, astrology appears toward the end of the third century B.C.E. and deals from the onset with universal (*geniká, thema mundi*) as well as individual forecasts, concerning either future events or medical etiology, prescriptions, or posology (*iatromathematika*). The new astrological synthesis, still in use today, although after the Protestant Reformation it lost the status of hard science that it had during the Renaissance, is the work of Ptolemy (Claudius Ptolemaeus, ca. 100–178 C.E.). Hellenistic astrology reached India from the first to the second century C.E. and Persia in the sixth century C.E., when several astrological tractates were first translated into Pahlavi or Middle Persian then into Arabic by Abu Ma'shar (Albumasar, 787–886 C.E.).

13.2.3 Hellenistic-Roman magic consisted of large collections of conjurations, signs, incantations, amulets, curses, and hymns whose formulae and recipes were preserved in handbooks written in Greek or

Demotic Egyptian: the famous "magical papyri." Tales and narratives concerning magical arts were very frequent during that epoch. The most important among them, which was also connected with another institution influential during this period, i.e., mystery religions (21), was the novel *Metamorphoses* (or *The Golden Ass*) by the Latin African writer Apuleius of Madaurus (ca. 125–170 C.E.).

The study of Hellenistic magic is still in its beginnings. Numerous papyri have survived, from which one day a sociology of magic may be attempted. The abundance of love philters seems to show that the magician's most common customer was a man seeking a mate or trying to make sure that his mistress would not betray him; the number of women consulting the magician was quite lower than the number of men. Often the customer's wish was to be rid of an enemy or to damage someone's property or health. Sometimes an auxiliary spirit was conjured up, who would help the client obtain all sorts of supernatural qualities.

13.2.4 The miracle workers, without being a creation of Hellenism, were especially influential at the turn of the Christian era. Some view Jesus himself as a magician. Miracles were, during the whole period, a part of daily existence. Magicians promised their clients invisibility, the gift of speaking in unknown tongues, and instantaneous travel through space; they believed that everything could be influenced at a distance, not only human subjects but also inanimate objects. A typical portrait of the Hellenistic "divine man" (*theios anêr*) was drawn by Philostratus (ca. 217) in his *Life* of the miracle-working philosopher Apollonius of Tyana (first century C.E.). Apollonius, initiated in Pythagorean wisdom, was a student of the pious Brahmans of India and of the Egyptian priests. Later on, Neoplatonists like Porphyry (ca. 234–301/305 C.E.) and Iamblichus (ca. 250–330 C.E.) could write versions of the *Life of Pythagoras,* based on circulating traditions, in which the ancient philosopher was made into the prototype of every "divine man."

The discipline of *theurgy,* already manifest in the influential *Chaldaean Oracles* composed at the end of the second century C.E. by Julian the Chaldaean and by his son Julian the Theurgist, and highly appreciated by the late Neoplatonists from Porphyry to Michael Psellus (eleventh century), provided techniques for conjuring the gods and elevating one's spiritual condition. The Neoplatonist Synesius of Cyrene (ca. 370–414 C.E.), before converting to Christianity and becoming a bishop, wrote a tractate *On Dreams,* in which he asserted that the gods can be encountered in dreams. Even the stricter philosopher Plotinus (205–270 C.E.), the first Neoplatonist, made ecstatic union of the soul with the universal Intellect into the supreme goal of existence; his followers insisted on the many categories of intermediary beings (souls, daimones, heroes, angels, archangels, etc.) visibly and invisibly inhabiting the intervening layers of the cosmos.

13.2.5 Alchemy was equally a Hellenistic discipline and culminated between the second and the fourth centuries C.E. with the writings of Zosimus and his commentators. The ideology of alchemy was part of the Hellenistic religious context. It emphasized initiation and change of state: the qualitative "transmutation" of the individual. In Aristotelian terms, it may be expressed as the separation of form from matter and the imposition of a new form in its place.

13.2.6 Hermetism was another creation of Hellenism. Astrological books attributed to the immemorial wisdom of the Egyptian god Hermes-Thoth were already in circulation at the end of the second century B.C.E.; yet the so-called *Corpus Hermeticum*, a collection of various writings used in Gnostic circles, appeared between 100–300 C.E. "Hermetism" was but a label put on astrological, magical, and alchemical knowledge, borrowed from the cultural environment and presented as revealed or esoteric. The only original feature of the *Corpus Hermeticum* occurred in the cosmogony of the tractate *Poimandres*. The existence of a hermetic community during the first century C.E. is controversial; its existence during the Middle Ages is just a scholarly fiction.

13.3 BIBLIOGRAPHY. Eliade, *H* 2, 209–11; I. P. Couliano, "Astrology," in *ER* 1, 472–75; by the same author, see *Psychanodia I* (1983), *Expériences de l'extase* (1984), and especially *Out of this World* (1991). See also, in this guide, Chapters 9 and 21. On Hellenistic magic, see Hans-Dieter Betz (ed.), *The Greek Magical Papyri* (1985).

14

Hinduism

14.1 THE INDUS VALLEY, covering the territory of present-day Pakistan and northwestern India, was the location of a great culture (roughly contemporary with the cultures of the "Fertile Crescent"), whose centers were the cities of Mohenjo Daro and Harappa. Already by about 1600 B.C.E., i.e., *before* the Aryan conquest, this culture decayed. Lacking temples, its cult places were probably the ablution pools: indeed, the two cities had an impressive system of running water and sewage. Statuettes representing a female divinity seemed to dominate in private cult, whereas the public cult was probably centered on male animal divinities. An ithyphallic (with erect penis) god surrounded by animals has been identified as a proto-Śiva Paśupati, the Hindu god whose pre-Aryan origin seems probable.

About 1500 B.C.E. the Aryans, Indo-European nomadic warriors, opposed their ideology of conquerors to that of the peaceful sedentary farmers of the Indus Valley. In the Aryan literature, the only one that has survived, the image of the aborigines was far from flattering: they were either black-skinned demons or slaves (*dāsas*), primitive worshipers of the phallus. The Aryans were carnivorous and practiced animal sacrifices. Later on, the Vedic priests adopted a vegetarian diet.

14.2 VEDIC TRADITION, originally oral (*śruti*), consists of several categories of writings whose formation took place between 1400 and 400 B.C.E.

The four collections (*saṃhitās*) of the Vedas, to be dated about 1000 B.C.E., contained the Ṛg-, the Sāma-, the Yajur-, and the Atharva-veda. The Ṛgveda consisted of hymns used by the *hotṛ* priest, who performed oblations and invocations of the gods. The other collections were initially the cult handbooks of the secondary priests: the *udgātṛ*, or hymnodist, who wrote down the music in the *Sāmaveda;* the *adhvaryu*, or master of ceremonies, specialist in the sacrificial formulae gathered in the *Yajurveda;* and finally the brahman, who controlled the ritual activity of the former three priestly classes, silently reciting the verses of the *Atharvaveda*. The four Vedic priests, surrounded by assistants, had to perform faultlessly the minute details of the ritual, which began with the ceremonial kindling of the three fires on the altar that symbolized the cosmos and ended with the sacrifice (*yajña*). In the *agnihotra*, or fire oblation, the *adhvaryu* and the customer offered milk to Agni the fire god. This was the simplest sacrifice of a long series, of which one of the most important rituals was the sacrifice of the intoxicating juice of the plant called *soma*. Some rites required the presence of specialized priests; others, like the seasonal, monthly, votive, expiatory, or propitiatory offerings, were performed by the head of a family on the domestic altar.

The *saṃskāras*, or consecrations, were nonperiodical ceremonies that pinpointed the four most important moments of life: birth, initiation (*upanayana*, the introduction of a young boy to his brahman *guru*), marriage, and death.

Vedic mythology is extremely complex and cannot be seriously dealt with here. The Ṛgveda hymns attributed the same qualities to different divinities whose functions were at variance; it is therefore difficult to establish the primary nature of these divinities. Sūrya, Savitar, and Viṣṇu were solar gods, Vāyu was connected with wind, Uṣas with dawn, Agni with fire, Soma with the homonymous plant. Varuṇa and Mitra were the warrants of cosmic order, of which moral and social order were a part. Rudra-Śiva was a disturbing god, frightening even in his role as healer. Indra was a warlike god whose traits were often attributed in other religions to the Trickster (9), a supernatural joker, binge eater, and hypersexual and often tragic buffoon.

The evolution of the *asuras* and *devas* in India was parallel and contrary to that of the Iranian *ahuras* and *daivas* (33.3.2): the *devas*, like the Iranian *ahuras*, were beneficent, whereas the *asuras*, like the *daivas*, were demons.

The cosmologies present in the Ṛgveda were no less complex than its mythology. They were notoriously contradictory, for being the result of speculations that took place at epochs separated by centuries from each other. Next to a world creation through the sacrifice of a primordial *anthropos* (Puruṣa: see *Puruṣasūkta*, X 90) more abstract ideas were present, among them that of an original *big bang* (X 129).

14.3 THE BRĀMAṆAS, composed by Vedic priests between 1000 and 800 B.C.E., translated the Vedic *Puruṣasūkta* cosmogony in biological terms. Prajāpati, the brahmanic equivalent of the primordial Puruṣa (*Śatapatha brāhmaṇa* VI 1.1.5), created through burning asceticism (*tapas*) and emanation (*visṛj*). Every single sacrifice referred to this original creation and guaranteed the continuity of the world through repetition of the founding action. Brahmanic sacrifice has multiple dimensions: it is cosmogonical, eschatological, and also reintegrative, insofar as the sacrificer interiorizes the process of reintegration (*samdha, saṃskri*) of Prajāpati, applying it to his own person, thus obtaining a unified Self (*ātman*).

Once started in the *Brahmanas,* this interiorization process is continued throughout the *Āraṇyakas* (Forest Books) and especially through the *Upaniṣads,* or spiritual teachings of the masters. Thirteen *Upaniṣads* are counted as *śruti,* or revealed; the first among them—the *Bṛhadāraṇyakopaniṣad* and the *Chāndogyopaniṣad*—were composed between 700 and 500 B.C.E. In the Upanishads, the Vedic external sacrifice is completely devaluated for being an "action" (*karman*), and every action—even if ritual—bears negative "fruits" that contributes toward submerging human beings in the cycles of metensomatosis (*saṃsāra*). Like Platonism, the Upanishads envision metensomatosis as an entirely negative process, as the result of ignorance (*avidyā*) that creates the structures of the universe and the dynamics of every existence. Freedom is brought about by gnosis (*jñāna*), which is the opposite of ignorance and reveals the intricacies of cosmic deception. According to this worldview, creation is the staging of nonbeing, whereas gnosis—ontological wholeness—delivers us from the deceptive bonds of creation. Such a worldview occurred again in the Gnostic texts of the early centuries C.E. (9.4). In both cases, we meet with acosmic doctrines, which seek for human identity in those unfathomable depths of being that have not been contaminated by nature or emotion. In both cases, human psychomental activity, like physical activity, suffers a loss in status through being broken from its divine roots.

14.4 THE HINDU SYNTHESIS, which formulated those basic concepts that have maintained their validity to the present day, took place after the Upanishadic epoch, from 500 B.C.E. to 500 C.E. During this period, the six traditional *darśanas* (literally, "views"), or philosophical schools, took shape, together with the system of castes (*varṇas*), the four stages (*āśramas*) of life, traditional law (*dharma*), the difference between revelation (*śruti*) and tradition (*smṛti*), and so forth.

14.4.1 Śruti. Even before the composition of the *Laws of Manu* (*Mānavadharmaśāstra*, second century B.C.E. to first century C.E.) the corpus of the *śruti* literature—a word literally meaning "heard" and thus "oral," yet technically indicating texts that had been "revealed" to the sages and saints (*ṛṣis*) of old—was closed. The *śruti* contained all ancient Hindu texts, from the *Vedasaṃhitās* to the thirteen revealed Upaniṣads. Everything that came later belonged to *smṛti*, or "tradition": the six "limbs of Veda" (*Vedāṅgas*), i.e., phonetics, grammar, metrics, etymology, astronomy, and ritual, legal works such as the *Mānavadharmaśāstra*, and so forth.

14.4.2 The six darśanas, or traditional philosophical schools, formed three couples: Mīmāṃsā/Vedānta, Nyāya/Vaiśeṣika, and Sāṃkhya/Yoga. Nyāya dealt with logic, Vaiśeṣika with an atomistic cosmology; these two schools did not belong to the *smārta*, or corpus, of the Vedic tradition. Yoga and Sāṃkhya were closer to *smārta*. Sāṃkhya, the origin of which is difficult to place in time, was an emanationistic philosophy featuring twenty-four principles, or *tattvas*, forming a vertical hierarchy from the top dominated by the primordial pair Puruṣa/Prakṛti to the bottom, where we meet the five material qualities (*tanmātra*) and the five elements (*bhūta*). The Sāṃkhya system was a Hindu variant of what scholars would call "Alexandrian scheme," present in late Platonic philosophies, among Middle and Neoplatonists, Gnostics, and Christians. According to both Sāṃkhya and Alexandrian Platonism, the visible world, which was partially illusory, was the outcome of the descent of principles that moved farther and farther down from the essences above. The five organs of senses (*jñānendrīya*) and the five organs of action (*karmendrīya*) produced the five material projections (*tanmātra*) that formed the external world when filled up with *bhūtas*, or material elements. Our interior was made before our exterior, which depended on the former. Throughout the twenty-four principles circulate three "states" or *guṇas* of all things: *sattva* (luminosity and lightness), *rajas* (emotion, action), and *tamas* (darkness, heaviness).

Yoga was a system of mystical techniques, codified for the first time by a certain Patañjali in the *Yogasūtra* (second century B.C.E. to fifth century C.E.), which allowed the practitioner to climb up the ladder of internal principles, transcending the Ego (*ahaṃkāra*) and thus acquiring the qualities of the Absolute. Yoga had eight "limbs" (*aṣṭāṅga*) or stages: abstention (*yāma*), observance (*niyāma*), bodily postures (*āsana*), breathing techniques (*prāṇāyāma*), internalization (*pratyāhāra*), concentration (*dhāraṇā*), meditation (*dhyāna*), and unitive contemplation (*samādhi*). The bodily yoga techniques aimed to channel the energies (*prāṇas*) and make them circulate rhythmically through the principal channels (*nāḍis*) of the subtle organism, in order to awaken the formidable serpentlike energy Kundalini, coiled in the center (*cakra*, "wheel") of the base of the backbone (*mūlādhara*) and make it climb through the other *cakras* to the "thousand-petaled lotus" (*sahasrāra*) at the top of the head.

Among the six *darśanas* only Mīmāmsā and Vedānta ("End of Veda") were *smārta*, for they were focused on the Vedas. Vedānta in particular relied on the wisdom of the Upanishads. Its founder was Bādarayaṇa (ca. 300–100 B.C.E.), author of the *Brahma-* or *Vedānta-sūtra*.

14.4.3 The theory of castes (*varṇas*) was formulated in the legal corpus of the *smārta:* there were four impermeable levels of Hindu society, the brahmans, the warriors (*kṣatriya*), the merchants-bankers (*vaiśya*), and the servants (*śūdra*). Men belonging to the first three castes were *dvija*, or twice born, for they had received *upanayana*, or initiation, from a brahman. They had thus the possibility to fill all four stages (*āśrama*) of life of a Hindu male, although they would usually stop at the second: *brahmacāryā* (study), *gṛhastha* (head of a family), *vānaprastha* (withdrawal in the forest), and *sannyāsa* (renouncing the world). Another fourfold series explained the goals (*arthas*) worthy to be pursued in life. The first three (*trivarga*) were human goals: *artha*, or material goods; *kāma*, or eros; and *dharma*, or law. The fourth was freedom from the pursuit of any material goal (*mokṣa*). *Trivarga* was the opposite of *mokṣa* in the same way as the first three *āśramas* were the opposite of *sannyāsa*.

14.5 HINDU EPIC LITERATURE appeared when the main trends of Hinduism—Vaiṣṇavism, Śaivism, and the cult of the Goddess—were taking shape. The great epics *Mahābhārata* (fifth century B.C.E. to fourth century C.E.) and *Rāmāyaṇa* (fourth to third century B.C.E.) were better known than *Harivaṃśa* (Genealogy of Kṛṣṇa, fourth century C.E.) or the vast body of the *Purāṇas* (300–1200 C.E.).

Valmiki's *Rāmāyaṇa* (Deeds of Rāma) went back to a period when Rāma was not yet envisaged as an incarnation, or *avatāra*, of the god

Viṣṇu. It is, however, impossible to determine all sucessive textual layers: the oldest manuscript of the epic went only as far as 1020 C.E. The story tells the 1,001 adventures of Rāma, who, helped by the monkey god Hanuman, succeeded in releasing his wife Sītā from her abductor, the demon Rāvaṇa from Laṅkā.

Mahābhārata (yuddha) or "The Great (battle) of the Bhāratas" (descendants of Bhārata, the ancestors of the North Indian rulers) was an epic in 100,000 *ślokas,* stanzas of two or four verses, eight times longer than the Iliad and the Odyssey together. It was the story of the terrible battle between the five Pāṇḍava brothers and their cousins, the one hundred Kauravas, for the kingdom of Bhārata. Kṛṣṇa, an avatar of the god Viṣṇu, took the part of the Pāṇḍavas and gave to one of them, Arjuna, a lesson in philosophy that was to become one of the most important religious texts of humankind: "The Song of the Blessed," *Bhagavadgītā,* a second century C.E. poem inserted in the structure of the *Mahābhārata* (VI 25–42). Like an Indian Hamlet, Arjuna refused to enter a battle against his own relatives. To change his mind, Kṛṣṇa presented him with the three alternatives of yoga: yoga of action (*karma yoga*), yoga of gnosis (*jñāna yoga*), and devotional yoga (*bhakti yoga*). The way of *karma yoga,* detached action that did not entail solitude and renunciation (*sannyāsa*), has impressed the Western mind accustomed to the Protestant (especially Calvinist) tenets of intramundane asceticism. This rather fortuitous circumstance explains the fashion of the *Bhagavadgītā* in the West since the nineteenth century.

The theory of Viṣṇu's avatars was expounded in the epics; in the *Harivaṃśa,* or Genealogy of Viṣṇu (fourth century C.E.); and in the eighteen Greater and eighteen Lesser Purāṇas, encyclopedic writings composed between 300 and 1200 C.E. The ten generally accepted avatars were Matsya (Fish), Kūrma (Turtle), Vāraha (Boar), Narasiṃha (Lion Man), Vāmana (Dwarf), Paraśurāma (Rāma-with-the Ax), Rāma, Kṛṣṇa, Buddha, and the avatar Kalki, who would appear at the end of time. In the Purāṇas and other philosophical collections such as the *Yogavasiṣṭha* (tenth to twelfth century C.E.) complex theories of cosmic cycles occurred. Wendy Doniger analyzed their mind-boggling implications in her books *Dreams, Illusion and Other Realities* (1985) and *Other Peoples' Myths* (1988). Traditionally, a cosmic cycle (*mahāyuga*) contained four epochs (*caturyuga*): *kṛta-, tretā-, dvāpara-,* and *kali-yuga,* which correspond more or less to our golden, silver, copper, and iron ages, the last of which is our present age. One thousand *mahāyugas* formed a cosmic period, or *kalpa,* also called "one day of Brahmā." The god Brahmā lived one hundred years, each formed of 360 cosmic days and nights, that is, more than 300 billion terrestrial years (*mahākalpa*), yet his life did not last any longer than the blink of an eye of the supreme god Viṣṇu. The end of the life of a Brahmā was the dissolution of a universe (*mahāpralāya*).

14.6 NONDUALISM. Thanks to the genius of Śaṅkara (eighth century C.E.), commentator of Bādarayaṇa's *Brahmāsūtra*, of nine Upanishads, and of the *Bhagavadgītā*, the Vedānta system was rejuvenated with the help of Sāṃkhya. Śaṅkara's philosophy was called "nondualism" (*advaitavāda*), for it implied the absolute monism of the impersonal principle *brahman* and the illusory (*māyā*) character of the world, created by transcendental ignorance (*avidyā*).

A qualified nondualist was Rāmānuja (d. 1137 C.E.), who belonged to the devotional (*bhakti*) Vaiṣṇava trend. Contrary to Sankara, who asserted the basic simplicity of *brahman*, Rāmānuja believed in the internal diversity (*viśiṣṭa*) of this principle. Rāmānuja achieved a more complete integration of Sāṃkhya into Vedānta.

Madhva (1199–1278 C.E.), although brought up in the teachings of Śaṅkara, he soon opposed to them his own dualistic (*dvaita*) worldview. Following in the steps of Rāmānuja, with whose work he actually did not seem to be acquainted, he rejected the idea of the unity of human beings, of the cosmos, and of the divinity.

14.7 DEVOTIONAL HINDUISM (*bhakti*) had ancient roots. No matter if the object of *bhakti* was Viṣṇu, Śiva, or the Goddess, *bhakti* created its own cult *pūjā*, to replace Vedic sacrifice (*yajña*), and its own literature, consisting of texts such as the *āgamas* and the *tantras*.

14.7.1 Viṣṇu. Already introduced in the *Bhagavadgītā* as one of the three ways of freedom, *bhakti yoga* was the focus of a huge Vaisnava writing in eighteen thousand *ślokas*, the *Bhāgavata purāṇa*, according to which Viṣṇu-Kṛṣṇa "only delights in pure *bhakti*, all the rest being superfluous [*anyad vidambanaṃ*]" (VII 7.52). One of the central stories of Vaisnava devotion concerned the love that the *gopis*, or "cowgirls," had for young Kṛṣṇa and the *rāsa-līlā*, the dance of love he danced with them, multiplying himself in such a way that each *gopi* could dance with her own Kṛṣṇa and caress him. This symbolic episode of the *Bhāgavata purāṇa* gave rise to the most important Vaiṣṇava festival.

Devotion to Viṣṇu had its own heroes and saints. The poet Kabīr, born according to tradition in the fifteenth-century Banaras in the house of a poor Muslim, was worshiped by both Hindus and Muslims. Actually, if Kabīr truly fostered religious unity, he did so in rejecting both Hinduism and Islam, both the teachings of the *paṇḍits* and those of the mullas. Neither a sufi nor a yogin, Kabīr speaks the ageless yet so personal language of the great mystics.

Caitanya, born Viśvambhara Miśra in Muslim Bengal (1486–1533), knew the rapture of devotion at twenty-two, was initiated by the sage Keśava Bhāratī and then settled in Puri (Orissa), where he experienced frequent ecstasies and instructed his disciples concerning Kṛṣṇa's projects for the *kaliyuga.* To obtain freedom from ignorance (*avidyā*), gnosis was no longer necessary; love suffices. Caitanya taught that everyone should choose to impersonate a character of Kṛṣṇa's legend and live out the character's love for Kṛṣṇa. He himself cherished Kṛṣṇa as Kṛṣṇa's lover Rādhā: therefore, Caitanya's disciples held him to be an incarnation of both divine spouses, Kṛṣṇa *and* Rādhā. Caitanya wrote very little, but inspired others to write. His influence in Bengal was overwhelming. In the nineteenth century, the cult of Kṛṣṇa-Caitanya was revitalized and became international under the name of Krishna Consciousness (1966).

A worshiper of Rāma, the poet Tulsīdās (ca. 1532–1623) rewrote the *Rāmāyaṇa,* making it into a very popular *bhakti* romance.

14.7.2 The cult of Śiva-Pāśupata goes back to the Mahābhārata. Its actual founder was Lakulīśa (second century C.E.) Śaivism became influential in south India toward the seventh century C.E. A wealth of Śaivite sects exist, many of them professing yogic and tantric doctrines and practices. The Kālamukas and Kāpālikas excelled in antinomian asceticism. Starting with the seventh century C.E., a whole Śaiva literature appeared, consisting of twenty-eight orthodox *āgamas* and about two hundred auxiliary tractates, or *upāgamas.* Besides tantric Śaivism, a devotional and poetic Śaivism exists, especially in the line of the sixty-three Nāyanmārs, the mystics of Tamilnadu.

14.7.3 The Goddess. A third devotional divinity was the Goddess (*devī*), often called Great Goddess (*mahādevī*) or *śakti.* Worshiped as early as the sixth century C.E., the goddesses Durgā and Kālī, as well as their cult, had frightening aspects. The *śakti* was central in Tantrism.

14.7.4 Hindu Tantrism probably preceded Buddhist Tantrism (3.6); it had solid roots in India in the seventh century C.E. and flourished between the ninth and the fourteenth centuries. Its deities have been adopted by popular Hinduism.

Although a Vaiṣṇava Tantrism existed, the main gods of Tantrism were Śiva and his Śakti (female energy), or simply the Śakti. The various doctrines contained in the tantric *āgamas, tantras,* or *saṃhitās* were not original. They borrowed many elements from the Sāṃkhya-Yoga. Tantric practices were very elaborate and were based on a subtle physiology that ultimately stemmed from yoga. Their description was expressed in a "double language" containing sexual allusions. These practices insisted on *mantras* or meditational formulas communicated to the disciple by his guru during *dīkṣā,* or initiation; on *mudrās,* or symbolic gestures; on *maṇḍalas,* or symbolic images of which the *yantra* is the simplest and most widespread; on *pūjās,* or offering ceremonies; and on sexual techniques that often but by no means always entailed ritual intercourse (*maithuna*) with semen retention.

14.8 THE SIKHS. The word *sikh* stems from the Pali *sikkha* (Sanskrit, *śiṣya*) for "disciple." Sikhism can be envisaged as a branch of *bhakti* devotional mysticism.

14.8.1 Bābā Nānak (1469–1538 C.E.), the founder of Sikhism, showed indications of a precocious mystical vocation. Son of *kṣatriyas* from Lahore (Punjab, today Pakistan), he soon conceived the project of harmonizing Hinduism and Islam and chose to preach to this effect through song, accompanied at the *rabab* (a stringed instrument of Arabic origin) by a Muslim musician. After a mystical experience he had at twenty-nine, Nānak declared, "There are no Hindus, there are no Muslims."

Nānak's doctrine can be interpreted as a reform of Hinduism, especially as far as polytheism, rigid separation of castes, and asceticism as a warranty for religious life were concerned. He had disciples among both Hindus and Muslims.

Against polytheism, Nānak proposed an uncompromising monotheism inspired by Islam. Ecstatic union with God was possible, and the gurus of the Sikhs had all obtained it. From Hinduism, the Sikhs inherited the doctrines of *māyā* (the cosmic illusion), of reincarnation, and of *nirvāṇa* as cessation of the painful cycle of transmigration. Brahmā, Viṣṇu, and Śiva were the divine trinity (*trimurti*) created by *māyā*. To attain salvation, it was indispensable to have a guru, to repeat mentally the Divine Name, to sing the hymns, and to become associated with holy people. Women benefited from the teaching of the gurus to the same extent as men; and, even if some gurus practiced polygamy, this was not the rule. Asceticism and mortifications were contrary to the spirit of Sikhism. Before God all were equal, and therefore castes were unnecessary.

14.8.2 The gurus. Guru Nānak was followed by a line of nine gurus, or religious chiefs; the rank became hereditary starting with the second, Angad (1538–1552 C.E.), who was followed by Amar Dās (1532–1574), Rām Dās (1574–1581), Arjan (1581–1606), Har Gobind (1606–1644), Har Rāi (1644–1661), Har Krishan (1661–1664), Teg Bahādur (1664–1675), and Gobind Singh (1675–1708). Angad drew the sacred alphabet of the Sikhs from the Punjabi alphabet. Arjan began the construction of Har Mandar, the Golden Temple in the middle of the Amritsar Lake, and established the Sikh canon, the Granth Sāhib, or Noble Book (known later as Adī Granth, or First Book), a sacred scripture containing Arjan's own hymns, the Japjī, or sacred prayer, composed by Nānak, the songs of the first gurus and the fifteen precursors—Hindu and Muslim saints among whom Kabīr (1380–1460), the Banaras saint, was supposed to be Nānak's direct forerunner. Persecuted by the Mongol Muslim rulers, the Mughals, who had conquered northern India (1526–1658), Arjan instructed his son Har Gobind to bear arms. Averse to alcoholic beverages, tobacco, and mortifications of the body, the Sikhs cultivated military virtues that transformed them in a true army, especially after the execution of Guru Teg Bahādur in 1675. His son, Gobind Rāi, called Singh (Lion) after his baptism as a warrior, established the Khanda-di-Pahul, or Sword Baptism, which makes the adept under oath into a Lion until death. He also made the rules of the Sikh community. A Sikh was supposed to bear on his or her person the 5 Ks: *kes* (long hair), *kangha* (comb), *kripan* (sword), *kach* (shorts), and *kara* (steel band). By abolishing all caste differences, Gobind Singh became the chief of a powerful army of pariahs changed into Lions. Before death, he also abolished the institution of the guru. A new *Granth*, the "*Granth* of the Tenth Guru," was compiled in his honor, containing the Japjī of Gobind Singh, the *Akal Ustat*, or "Praise of the Creator," hymns dedicated to the Holy Sword, symbol of God's beneficent power, and the "Wonderful Drama," a verse history of the ten gurus.

14.9 NEO-HINDUISM is an Indian national movement that attempted to integrate Western values into Hindu life and propagate Indian wisdom in the West. The Bengali reformer Rammohan Roy (1774–1833 C.E.) founded the Brāhmo Samāj in 1828 in order to facilitate India's westernization. His efforts were continued by the two consecutive leaders of the Brāhmo Samāj, Devendranath Tagore (1817–1905) and Keshab Candra Sen (1838–1884). In 1875 Swāmī Dayānanda (1824–1883) founded the Ārya Samāj, an organization whose main goal was to preserve Indian religious traditions and to make them available to the whole world.

From the consequential encounter between Keshab Candra Sen and the Bengali mystic Ramakrishna (1836–1886 C.E.), the Neo-Vedānta synthesis was born, which continues to represent the image of traditional India in the West as it was expounded by Ramakrishna's disciple Vivekananda (1863–1902) starting at the 1893 Parliament of Religions in Chicago, Illinois.

This religious climate was the setting for the political figure Mohandas Gandhi (1869–1948) and the mystic and yogin Aurobindo Ghose (1872–1950) of Pondicherry.

14.10 POPULAR HINDUISM is a network of rituals and festivals, seasonal or punctuating the major events of life, which is the religious inheritance of every Hindu. The most important festivals of the gods are dedicated to Indra (Rākhī-Bandana), Kṛṣṇa (Kṛṣṇa-Jayantī), Ganeśa the Elephant god (Ganeśa Caturthī), the Goddess (Navarātra), Śiva (Mahāśivarātri), and so forth. Among the most common religious practices should be mentioned pilgrimage to holy places (*tīrtha*), that is, the springs of the great rivers, holy cities such as Varanasi, Vṛndavan, or Allahabad, or great religious festivals such as the Jagannath in Puri.

Domestic religious cult varies according to caste, region, and the local evolution of beliefs. In general, a brahman is supposed to salute the rising sun with a recitation of the *gāyatrī mantra*, to perform the morning oblation and libations to gods and ancestors and the *devapūjana*, or worship of the divine images held in a special room, starting with the *iṣṭadevatā*, or personal deity.

The major events in life are marked by special ceremonies or *saṃskāras:* the *saisava saṃskāras* at birth; the *upanayana,* or religious initiation of a boy; the *vivāha,* or marriage rites; and the *śraddha,* or funeral rites.

14.11 BIBLIOGRAPHY. See in general Eliade *H* 1, 64–82, and 2, 135–46 and 191–95; A. Hiltebeitel, "Hinduism," in *ER* 6, 336–60; Th. J. Hopkins and A. Hiltebeitel, "Indus Valley Religion," in *ER* 7, 215–23; D. N. Lorenzen, "Saivism: An Overview," in *ER* 13, 6–11; A. Padoux, "Hindu Tantrism," in *ER* 14, 274–80; J. T. O'Connell, "Caitanya," in *ER* 3, 3–4; K. Singh, "Sikhism," in *ER* 13, 315–20.

Useful introductory works are Louis Renou, *The Nature of Hinduism* (1962); Thomas J. Hopkins, *The Hindu Religious Tradition* (1971); David R. Kinsley, *Hinduism: A Cultural Perspective* (1982).

15

Hittite Religion

15.1 THE HITTITE EMPIRE covered most of Anatolia (modern Turkey) from the mid-second millennium until the invasions of the early twelfth century B.C.E. Ethnic diversity (Hattic, Hurrian, Semitic, and the Indo-European Hittite peoples) led to linguistic and religious diversity: the majority of gods and myths discussed here are not Hittite in origin but were incorporated interpretively into the Hittite language and cult. During most of the empire's height, its capital was Hattusas (Bogazköy) on the central Anatolian plateau, and it is there that archaeological finds including cuneiform tablets, statuary, many temples, and the carved rock sanctuary (or tomb) of Yazilikaya present our clearest picture of Hittite culture.

The divine pantheon of the Hittites was very large, but certain gods were most prominent and they were each headquartered in a chief temple in a particular city. As everywhere in the ancient Near East, the divinities dwelled as images in the temples and were bathed, dressed, fed, and entertained by the priests. On special holidays—and the calendar was filled with festivals and feasts—images came forth from their cellae. Temples were economic establishments as well, with rich storerooms and endowments of land, farmers, and artisans. Chief among the gods were the storm and weather god designated by the Hurrian name Teshub, his son Telepinu, and the great goddess of many guises, much worshiped as the sun goddess of Arinna. Just as the queen played an especially important role in the Hittite state, so that a ruling pair was set above the people, gods, too, had their consorts and often came in pairs.

Hittite kingship and queenship were religious roles, and kings were known to leave off war making to return home for cultic ceremonies. The king acted as high priest, often with the queen, and epitomized his people while serving the gods on earth. For a king, to die was to "become a god," and his statue would receive offerings from his posterity.

Divination was a prominent part of the official cult, and it ranged from interpretation of royal dreams to extispicy (prognostication by animal entrails) in the Mesopotamian fashion. Other practices of which we have written records included bird and snake observation and watching the successive relocations of an animal before its sacrifice. Most divinatory techniques worked by the posing of a series of yes or no questions to compile a picture of the issue at hand; others imposed a grid with a certain topic in each square, such as the king's future, the weather, or war, upon which the moving object or creature situated itself significantly. Such inquiries were undertaken on a regular basis and especially when it was perceived, by some negative event, that the god or goddess was angry and required appeasement.

15.2 MYTHOLOGY. A recurring myth connected to the anger and ritual appeasement of divinities was the story of the disappearing god. In the myth, a god, in this instance Telepinu, vanished and natural disasters ensued. In such an actual situation, it was the role of the priests to determine the cause of his anger and pacify him. In the myth, a bee sent by the goddess found Telepinu sleeping in a grove, stung and awakened him to his fury. By ceremonies and formulas performed by the goddess Kamrushepa, Telepinu was pacified and returned to beneficence.

Another myth of the subsidence and return of a god included the theme of the battle of a god and a dragon well known in the Near East and Greece. The serpent Illuyanka ("snake") had defeated the storm god, and a human, Hupashiya, was recruited by the goddess Inara to help in defeating the snake, to which he consented in return for sleeping with the goddess. Inara prepared a banquet at which Illuyanka and his family ate and drank so much that they could not afterward descend into their hole. Hupashiya then tied them with a rope and the storm god came and killed them. The same tablet gives another version in which Illuyanka had defeated the storm god and taken his heart and eyes. The storm god had a son with a mortal woman and the son married the daughter of Illuyanka. In requesting a present from his father-in-law according to custom, the son followed his father's orders and obtained the heart and eyes. With his forces returned to him, the storm god battled the serpent beside a sea and defeated him. But the son had to remain loyal to his father-in-law as well, and, asking not to be spared, was killed along with Illuyanka by his father. The festival contexts of Hittite myths are explicit in the tablets, and that of the defeat of Illuyanka comes from one that may well be a New Year festival.

The myth told in the cycle of *Kingship in Heaven* recounts the struggles for succession among the first gods. The first king of the gods was Alalu, who after a nine-year reign was overthrown and driven into the netherworld by his cupbearer Anu. Alalu's son Kumarbi served Anu for nine years, then in turn overthrew him, chasing him up to the sky and biting off his genitals. The seed of Anu was not so easily foiled but took root, and Kumarbi bore three gods, one of whom was Teshub, the storm god, who succeeded Kumarbi.

Kumarbi went to great lengths to take kingship for himself in the succeeding episode of this cycle, the *Song of Ullikummi.* Through intercourse with a large rock, he produced the tremendous stone giant Ullikummi, who grew dramatically until he reached the sky. From his place on the right shoulder of the Hurrian Atlas, Ubelluri, the stone monster defeated Teshub and threatened all humanity. The gods assembled in fear and appealed to Ea, who at last secured from the old gods the ancient knife with which heaven and earth had been cleaved apart. After the stone god's feet had been cut off, Teshub was able to defeat him.

15.3 BIBLIOGRAPHY. See H. Hoffner, Jr., "Hittite Religion," in *ER* 6, 408–14; Eliade, *H* 1, 43–47.

An introduction to Hittite civilization is O. R. Gurney, *The Hittites* (1952; recent impression 1972). Text translations are in J. B. Pritchard, *Ancient Near Eastern Texts Relating to the Old Testament* (1955). A short presentation is found in M. Vieyra, "La religion de l'Anatolie antique," in *Histoire des Religions, I* (1970), 258–306.

16

Indo-European Religion

16.1 A FAMILY OF LANGUAGES. The idea of a linguistic relationship among languages such as Sanskrit, Greek, and Latin is fairly recent (1786). The expression "Indo-European" has been in use since 1816; the word "Aryan," of sad memory, since 1819; and the German nationalistic concept of "Indo-Germanic" languages was coined in 1823—needless to say, it does not have more meaning than, for example, "Indo-Slavic" or "Indo-Greek." The first Indo-European linguist was the German Franz Bopp (1791–1867).

Nineteenth-century philologists took seriously the reconstruction of a common Indo-European language, called "Proto-Indo-European" (P.I.E.), as if it had actually existed. Most scholars today treat Proto-Indo-European as a construct.

16.2 THE HOMELAND. If they never had a common language, the Indo-Europeans seem to come from a single geographic area, which archaeologists have often identified with the lower Volga basin, from whence seminomadic tribes of patriarchal warriors expanded in several waves starting from the mid-fifth millennium B.C.E., forming the so-called Kurgan, or tumulus, culture. About 3000 B.C.E., a second Kurgan wave began from a second center of expansion that corresponded more or less to what most linguists would designate as the "homeland of the Indo-Europeans." About 2500 B.C.E., this zone stretched between the Ural Mountains and the Loire River and from the North Sea to the Balkans. According to the theory of Marija A. Gimbutas, the patriarchal Indo-European culture destroyed a previous culture, matriarchal and peaceful, that had covered the whole continent of Europe for approximately twenty thousand years, from the Paleolithic to the Neolithic. The principal feature of this culture was worship of a goddess with several attributes. During the Bronze Age (1600–1200 B.C.E.) the majority among European peoples were of Indo-European origin, with the exception of the Finns, a Finno-Ugrian people from the Ural mountains.

16.3 THE RELIGIONS of Indo-European peoples had common traits, which were pointed out by the school of comparative mythology of the nineteenth century, whose most prominent representatives were Adalbert Kuhn (1812–1881) and Friedrich Max Müller (1823–1900). A new dimension was added to the comparative approach by Georges Dumézil (1899–1986), a student of the linguist Antoine Meillet (1866–1936) and of the sociologist Émile Durkheim (1858–1917). In 1938 Dumézil formulated the first sketch of his theory of the "three functions" in early Indo-European society, having as representatives the priests, the warriors, and the producers. In the classical statement of his doctrine (1958), Dumézil asserted that these three functions made Indo-European society distinct from any other. Dumézil's tripartite schema based on the classes of priests, warriors, and producers was seen as permeating all levels of the culture as well as the psychology of Indo-European peoples. Dumézil claimed to have discovered the tripartite scheme in the religions of India, Iran, the Romans, and the Germans, from which he inferred that it should also exist among the Celts, Greeks, and Slavs; nevertheless, documentation would be too scarce to corroborate his interpretation.

16.4 BIBLIOGRAPHY. See in general I. P. Couliano, "Ancient European Religion," in *Encyclopaedia Britannica.* On the matriarchal religion of Old Europe, see Marija Gimbutas, *The Goddesses and Gods of Old Europe, 6500–3500 B.C.: Myths and Cult Images* (1982); on the Indo-European expansions, see Edgar C. Polomé (ed.), *The Indo-Europeans in the Fourth and Third Millennia* (1982).

17

Islam

17.1 ARABIA BEFORE ISLAM. The word *Islām* stems from the fourth verbal form of the root *slm: aslama,* "to submit," and means "submission" (to God); *muslim* is an active participle, meaning "one who submits" (to God).

One of the most important religions of humankind, Islam is present today on all continents. It is dominant in the Middle East, Asia Minor, Caucasus, northern India, Southeast Asia, Indonesia, and North and East Africa.

Ancient Semitic polytheism met Arabized Judaism and Byzantine Christianity in pre-Islamic Arabia. The northern and eastern regions had known substantial Hellenistic and Roman influence along the important trade routes. Timelessly old worship of three astral deities—sun, moon, and Venus—was by Muhammad's time overshadowed by the cults of the tribal gods. The chief god or goddess of each tribe was worshiped in the form of a stone, perhaps meteoric, or a tree or grove of trees. These were honored with shrines, offerings, and animal sacrifices. The existence of sometimes mischievous spirits, the *jinn,* was universally recognized and would continue to be so in Islam. Allāh ("God") was revered along with the important Arabian goddesses, and feasts, fasts, and pilgrimages were standard practice. Some henotheists and monotheists existed, as in the cult of al-Raḥmān, and large and influential Jewish tribes were found in cities such as the oasis town of Yathrib, which would come to be called Medina. Proselytizing missions by the Christians made some converts (we know of one in the family of Muhammad's first wife), but as a foreign revelation and a foreign scripture Christianity was not readily embraced. In the sixth-century C.E., Mecca, with its Kaʿbah shrine enclosing the famous black meteorite, was the religious center of central Arabia and a small but important trading city as well. The great disparity between its rich traders and the destitute street dwellers, its harsh social structures and decadent morality, were pondered and lamented by Muhammad all of his life.

17.2 MUHAMMAD. Muhammad was born into a trading family in Mecca about 570 C.E. Left without an inheritance because of the death of his parents and grandfather, he worked on trading ventures and at age twenty-five married an older widow who had employed him as a trading agent. In about 610, during one of his periodic meditative retreats in the caves near Mecca, he began to experience visions and auditory revelations. According to tradition, the angel Gabriel appeared to him with a book, commanding Muhammad, "Read!" In the pattern of the Hebrew prophets, Muhammad took up messages of God's all-surpassing greatness and of the doomed avarice and immortality of humans generally and of the Meccan community specifically. For a time he spoke of his revelations, which included his prophetic commissioning, only to his family and closest friends, but the circle widened and began to meet daily. After three years Muhammad began to preach his monotheistic message publically, meeting with some acceptance but much angry and contemptuous opposition, such that he had to be protected by members of his clan.

The following years brought more revelations that would shape the theology of the Qurʾān, and some that would not. That is, he received a revelation later annulled and attributed to Satan, which advocated three local and popular goddesses as intercessors for humans with Allāh. As time passed, the ranks of Muslims grew, but opposition, which included insulting requests for miracles and accusations of falsehood, continued, and the prophet's life was threatened. Looking about for a new headquarters for his movement, he received friendly invitations from some clans of Yathrib (Medina), a town some 250 miles to the north with a considerable Jewish population. His followers began relocating there, and in 622 Muhammad and his adviser Abū Bakr left secretly for Medina. This event, the Hijrah (emigration), marks the beginning of the Islamic era and its dating.

In the ten years Muhammad was to live in Medina, he continued writing down revealed messages, which, together with his long-remembered sayings and actions (preserved as traditional material, *ḥadīth*) outlined the total Muslim way of life. Along with leadership in prayer and ritual, he was occupied with dozens of raiding expeditions against enemies of Medina and his opponents in Mecca. Caravan raids escalated into something of a war between Mecca and Medina, accompanied by negotiations toward the conversion of the Meccans. Eventually Muhammad and his men occupied Mecca, and the city's sacred precinct became the focal point for Muslim prayer (*qibla*) and pilgrimage (*ḥajj*). Muhammad's military and economic might ensured his eventual political domination of most of the Arabian peninsula. At his death in 632, he left no male heir.

17.3 THE QUR᾿ĀN. The Qur᾿ān (*qara᾿a*, "read, recite") is for Muslims the word of God transmitted by Gabriel through the prophet Muhammad, the last of the line of biblical prophets. In a way it is the "Newest Testament," not contradicting but corroborating and surpassing the Jewish and Christian bibles. Yet in another way it more approximates the role of Jesus, the Logos, as the eternal and divine Word of the creator God; for Muhammad, while spotless and elect, is entirely human. Muhammad and some amanuenses probably wrote down many of his intermittent revelations, and after his death there remained many written fragments and many who remembered his recitations. The comprehensive text was compiled under the first few caliphs and variants were suppressed.

The Qur᾿ān as we have it today is divided into 114 chapters called *sūrahs* that contain varying numbers of verses called "signs" (*āyāt*). The chapters are not arranged chronologically or topically, but roughly from longest to shortest; thus many of the pithy and poetic early Meccan revelations are at the end and the longer, more narrative Medinan *sūrahs* are toward the front. Along with short titles, all but one *sūrah* begin with the Basmallah: "In the name of God, the merciful, the compassionate." Many begin as well with a few symbolic letters, perhaps originally signifying blocks of written material. The book is written in poetic, rhyming prose with vivid and beautiful imagery.

As was the original intention, the advent of the Qur᾿ān brought the Arabs into the community of peoples of the book, even as the Jews and Christians who received the Torah and Gospels. The two largest themes of the Qur᾿ān are the uniqueness and might of God and the nature and destiny of humans in relation to God. God is the sole creator of the universe, humans, and spirits, benificent and just. He is given descriptive names such as the Omniscient and the Almighty. Human beings are God's privileged slaves and with their free will often ignore God's commands, as they may be tempted by the fallen angel Iblīs (Satan), who incurred his own demise by refusing to bow down before

Adam (2:31–33). On the coming day of judgment, all will rise from the dead, be weighed, and sent to paradise or hell for eternity. The Qurʾān also includes interpretive recountings of some stories from the Hebrew Bible, such as Adam and Eve, Joseph's adventures, and Abraham's monotheism.

The moral exortations of the Qurʾān were many and with the traditions of the prophet's life formed the basis of Islamic law (*sharīʿah*). Generosity and fairness were paramount, and the selfish merchants of Mecca were harshly condemned. Basic requirements of Muslim life, such as daily prayers, almsgiving, fasting in the month of Ramadan, and the Meccan pilgrimage appeared. Social reforms were set out, such as inheritance law, criminal law, as is the conduct of husbands and wives, parents and children, slave owners, merchants, and Muslims toward non-Muslims. Usury was banned, and food laws instituted. Women were allowed half the inheritance of men (instead of nothing) and a limit of four wives was set, although more than one was discouraged.

17.4 SUCCESSION AND SECESSION. Upon Muhammad's death (632 C.E.), when his cousin and son-in-law ʿAlī ibn Abī Ṭālib and his uncle al-ʿAbbas piously guarded the lifeless body of the Prophet, the other followers came together to choose a successor or caliph (*khalīfah*, from *khalafa-*, "to follow"). This title accumulated significances through the centuries: the caliph became one who united in himself two separate functions, the function of *amīr al-muʾminīn* or Commander of the Faithful, and the function of *imām al-muslimīn* or Imam of the Moslems. At dawn, after a long deliberation, the assembly decided that the first successor of the Prophet would be Abū Bakr, his father-in-law and a companion of the *hijra* to Medina, delegated by Muhammad himself to lead the communal prayers. During the two years of his caliphate, Abū Bakr definitively established Muslim domination in Arabia, appeased the seditious Bedouin tribes, and fought against Byzantine Syria. Abū Bakr's successor and second caliph according to the Sunna was ʿUmar (634–644), who conquered Syria and part of Egypt and Mesopotamia. After ʿUmar's death, the great religious schisms that would characterize Islam in the classical period began. The followers of ʿAlī, the Prophet's cousin and the husband of the Prophet's daughter Fāṭimah, expected him to become the new caliph, but the aristocrat ʿUthmān (644–656) of the family of the Meccan Umayyads, former enemies of the Prophet, was elected in his stead. The ideology of the *rawāfiḍ* (those who repudiate [the first caliphs]), members of the *shīʿat ʿAlī* or "party of ʿAlī," claimed that succession had to be established according to closer kinship relations: the caliph must be not only of the tribe of the Quraysh, but also of the Hashemite family and legitimately born from the marriage of Fāṭimah, the Prophet's daughter, with ʿAlī ibn Abī Ṭālib. This would have meant an Alid dynasty; yet history decided for an Umayyad dynasty.

In 656 C.E. the Umayyad ʿUthmān was murdered by a group of followers of ʿAlī, who did not disavow their action. Elected caliph (fourth in the Sunni line), ʿAlī had to face a formidable duo: the rich and powerful Umayyad governor of Syria, Muʿāwiyah, and his shrewd general ʿAmr ibn al-ʿĀs, the conqueror of Egypt. When ʿAlī's troops were definitely at an advantage in the battle of Ṣiffīn on the Euphrates, ʿAmr ibn al-ʿĀs attached pages from the Qurʾān to the spears of his soldiers, and ʿAlī's army ceased fighting. ʿAmr ibn al-ʿĀs asked for a mediation between ʿAlī and Muʿāwiyah, and represented the latter so successfully that ʿAlī's representatives recognized Muʿāwiyah's claim to the caliphate. A new complication occurred, which divided ʿAlī's supporters among themselves, thereby weakening even further ʿAlī's position. A large group from ʿAlī's army, the Kharijites or "schismatics" *par excellence* (from *kharaja-*, "to leave, go out"), did not recognize the arbitration of human beings, for *lā hukmatu illā Allāh*, "there is no other judgment except for God's." The Kharijites, Islam's puritans, were not interested in the establishment of dynasties. They wanted a caliph elected by his peers, the most pious Muslim of his time, regardless of tribe or race: an Ethiopian slave should become caliph rather than a Qurayshite, if the former had more merits. Kharijite doctrine mandates the expulsion of a sinner from the Islamic community (the Ummah). Contrary to the later Christian Puritans, the Muslim puritans claimed that faith was not sufficient to maintain one's status as a Muslim; pious and proper action was required. Moral rigorism went hand in hand with concern for historical veracity. As a matter of fact, the Kharijites maintained that not all the Qurʾān has the status of revelation. Instead of fighting Muʿāwiyah, ʿAlī moved against the Kharijites, thus becoming their mortal enemy. And in 661 a Kharijite assassinated him. Muʿāwiyah the caliph founded the Umayyad dynasty of Damascus (661–750).

17.5 TERRITORIAL EXPANSION. Under the first four caliphs (632–661 C.E.), Syria, Palestine, and Mesopotamia were conquered: Damascus in 635; Jerusalem, Antioch, and Basra in 638. Persia was won between 637 and 650, and Egypt between 639 and 642. The conquests of 661–750 under the Damascus Umayyads included Afghanistan, much of North Africa, and Spain.

The Berber tribes of North Africa were converted by persuasion, although they would for centuries manifest their ethnic particularism by adopting heresies such as the Kharijite. In 711 C.E. the Muslim army crossed Ifriqīya (North Africa) to the Maghrib al-aqṣā, the extreme west. Helped by the Byzantine governor of Ceuta and urban Jews persecuted by the Visigothic Christians, the Muslims moved to the conquest of al-Andalus (unknown etymology, perhaps from Vandalicia), the Iberian peninsula. With the fall of the Visigothic capital, Toledo, the Muslims became masters of the whole territory west of the Pyrenees. The mountains were the limit of their expansion, especially after Charles Martel made an end at Poitiers (732) to their advance into Provençe. Dethroned in 750 by the Baghdad Abbasids, the last Umayyads found refuge in water-rich Andalusia. The caliphate of Córdoba became a capital of world civilization from 756 until 1031, when it fell prey to the anarchy of the *reyes de taifas,* the "party kings," during whose reigns the Christian northern kingdoms made spectacular progress in the Reconquista of Spain, reaching a sort of climax with the conquest, in 1085, of the city of Toledo. The occupation by two Berber dynasties—the Almoravids (1090–1145) and the Almohads (1157–1223)—did not make an end to this process; on the contrary, the Muslims would slowly withdraw to a narrowing southern zone (the Nasrid emirate of Granada), conquered in 1492 by the "Catholic kings."

In 827 C.E., the Aghlabids of Ifriqīya began the conquest of Sicily and South Italy. The Byzantine army expelled them from the latter, but the island was conquered in 902, became Fatimid in 909, and almost independent in 948. The Normans took it in 1091.

Starting with the eleventh century C.E., the strongmen of Islam were the Turks, converted to Islam in the tenth century, and especially the Seljuks, who controlled the Abbasid caliphate after the Buyids (1058). They were expelled in 1258 by the Mongols (converted to Islam around 1300), who occupied Iraq but were stopped by the Mamluk Turks, who controlled Egypt until the Ottoman conquest of 1517. From the fifteenth to the nineteenth century, the interests of Islam were mainly represented by the powerful Ottoman Empire, founded in 1301 in Asia Minor. In 1453 the Ottomans took Constantinople, which became their capital (Istanbul). In the East, the Mamluk Turks founded the Delhi sultanate (1206–1526). Between 1526 and 1658 all northern India would submit to the Islamic empire of the Great Mughals, descendants of the Mongols. Indonesia and Malaysia were mainly converted through the commercial routes that linked them to Muslim countries. The same occurred in certain regions of sub-Saharan Africa.

17.6 THE SCHISMS of Islam seem always to have at least three inextricable dimensions: genealogical, theological, and political. In spite of their differences, the major religious groups would not deny their opponents the right of belonging to Islam; they would only question their orthodoxy. The rather imprecise borderline of Islam would only exclude certain sects of *ghulat*, or extremists, who proclaimed the divinity of the imams and the belief in metensomatosis, or the transmigration of souls (*tanāsukh al-arwāḥ*).

Fāṭimah had two sons with ᶜAlī: al-Ḥasan and al-Ḥusain. Upon ᶜAlī's death the Shiᶜites of Kufa in Iraq urged Ḥasan to take the caliphate upon himself, but apparently Ḥasan ceded his rights and withdrew to Medina. Upon Muᶜāwiyah's death in 680 C.E., Huṣain and his retinue were planning to join their partisans in Kufa. Intercepted by the force sent by Yazid, the son and successor of Muᶜāwiah, Ḥusain fell on 10 Muḥarram (October) 680 in a skirmish at Karbalā. ᶜĀshūrāʾ ("Tenth" of October) became a day of mourning for Shiᶜite Muslims. With Ḥusain dead, the hopes of the Kufite Shiᶜites were focused on ᶜAlī's natural son Muḥammad ibn al-Hanafiya (son of the Hanafite), who was unwittingly proclaimed Mahdī (God-guided bringer of just rule) by the adventurer al-Mukhtār with the support of local "clients" (*mawālī*)—converts to Islam and the social system it had brought. But Muḥammad ibn al-Hanafīya did not acquiesce to Al-Mukhtār's religiopolitical zeal and continued to live peacefully in Medina well after Al-Mukhtār's bloody end. One of the latter's followers, Kaisān, was the author of the first Shiᶜite doctrine, according to which the only legitimate caliphs had been ᶜAlī, Ḥasan, Ḥusain, and Muḥammad ibn al-Hanafiya. Some refused to believe in the latter's death; thus, the title Mahdī came to designate the caliph hidden in the mountain, whose coming would be announced by eschatological signs.

17.6.1 Shiᶜites. The most influential Shiᶜite doctrine was based on the descendants of Ḥusain, the martyr of Karbalā, who had a son and a grandson, neither of whom fulfilled the hopes of the Shīᶜa: ᶜAlī, nicknamed Zain al-ᶜAbidīn and his son Muḥammad al-Bāqir. Far more interested in the anti-Umayyad campaign was Zaid ibn ᶜAlī, the half-brother of Muḥammad al-Bāqir. Zaid recognized the first two caliphs but denied the Umayyads the right to rule, for according to his adherents the caliphate belonged to whichever meritorious Hashemite should fight for its claim. Zaid died in 740 C.E., shortly after he had started his fight.

Shortly thereafter, with Shiʿite support, the family of the Hashemite al-ʿAbbas, uncle of the Prophet, claimed the caliphate. In 749 C.E. the black flags of the Abbasids replaced the white flags of the Umayyads in Kufa. The Abbasids, who settled in the new capital of Baghdad, cut their bonds with the Shiʿites who had helped them to come into power, keeping ʿAlī's descendants under surveillance. Among the later, the most important character in Shiʿite history is undoubtedly Jaʿfar al-Ṣādiq (the Righteous), who distanced himself both from the Shiʿites who proposed him the caliphate and from the extremists who divinized him. Jaʿfar had three sons, ʿAbdallah al-Afṭaḥ, Ismāʿīl, and Mūsā al-Kāẓim. Ismāʿīl's death (755) preceded his father's (766); ʿAbdallah's followed after a few months. The Shiʿites called *Ithnāʿasharīya,* or Twelvers (who recognize twelve imams), the most numerous and powerful in Persia to this day, trace the line from Jaʿfar to Mūsā (prisoner in Baghdad of the Abbasid caliph Harūn al-Rashīd) and from the latter to his descendants ʿAlī al-Riḍā (designated as heir to the caliph al-Maʾ-mūn as a conciliating gesture in 817), Muḥammad al-Jawād, ʿAlī al-Hādī and Ḥasan al-ʿAskarī, who died in 873 without male offspring. The death of the eleventh imam brought confusion (*al-ḥaira*) upon the Shiʿite community. Twelvers claimed that Ḥasan had a son, Muḥammad, the hidden imam who would come back as Mahdī and would be Master of the World (*Ṣāḥib al-zamān*). Twelver Shiʿism was protected by the dynasty of the Buyids (945–1055). The greatest theologian of the imami tradition was Muḥammad ibn Bābōye al-Qummī (918–991).

17.6.2 The extremists, or *ghulāt,* would generally make the imams into divine beings and would believe in metensomatosis of the soul. Many elements of Shiʿite, Sufi, and extremist beliefs are called "gnostic" by a number of scholars. They are distinct from second to third century Gnosticism. The first extremist was probably ʿAbdallāh ibn Sabaʾ of Kufa, who worshiped ʿAlī as God. Only two groups of *ghulāt* have survived into our time: the *ʿAlī-ilāhī* Kurds ("Those who divinize ʿAlī"), who call themselves Ahl-i Ḥaqq ("Truthful"), and the Nuṣairī, whose doctrine would be based on the revelations of the eleventh imam Ḥasan al-ʿAskarī to his disciple Ibn Nuṣair. Most of the

Nuṣairis (600,000) live today in Syria, where they have occupied a prominent political position since 1970.

17.6.3 The Ismāʿīlīs, or Sevener Shiʿites, a branch of whom leads to the present day Aga Khans, derive their name from Ismāʿ-īl, the son who predeceased his father Jaʿfar al-Ṣādiq in 755 C.E. According to the Sevener sequence of imams, Ismāʿīl was the sixth caliph after Ḥasan (the first); the seventh was his son Muḥammad, who originally was a hidden or "silent" (*ṣāmit*) imam, expected to make his reappearance (*qiyām*) as a Mahdī or Qāʾim al-Zamān. But in the ninth century, a certain ʿAbdallāh, who claimed to be a descendant of ʿAlī, began missionary activity (*daʿwa*) preaching the return of the Mahdī. Persecuted, he withdrew to Salamya in Syria. Among the first missionaries (*duʿāt*, singular *dāʿī*) was a certain Ḥamdān Qarmaṭ, who gave his name to the Iraqi Ismāʿīlī or Qaramiṭa. In Iran, and especially in Reyy, the Ismāʿīlī converted many imamis during the period of "confusion" that followed the death of their eleventh imam. The missions of Yemen and Algeria were equally successful. The Qarmaṭian doctrine during the period of concealment of the imams posited two double series of Prophets, composed of one who talks (*nāṭiq*), revealing the exoteric (*ẓāhir*) aspect of the revelation, and an "executor" (*waṣī*), who reveals esoteric religion (*bāṭin*). Each couple of Prophets is in charge of a world epoch (*daur*). The first Prophets were Adam, Noah, Abraham, Moses, and Jesus. Muhammad and his esoteric counterpart, or *waṣi*, ʿAlī ended this series. They were followed by six imams. The seventh, Muḥammad ibn Ismāʿīl ibn Jaʿ-fār is the expected Mahdī, whose epoch will be marked by the abolishment of all laws (*rafʿ al-sharāʾī*) and the return of humankind to the state of Adam and Eve in paradise before the Fall. The fourth *ḥujja* ("witness, warrant") of Salamya proclaimed himself Mahdī (899 C.E./286 H.). In his name, the missionaries with the support of the powerful Kutāma Berber tribe started the conquest of North Africa. In 910/297 the Mahdī proclaimed himself caliph, the first of the dynasty of the Fatimids, which would last until 1171. His successor, al-Muʿizz, established the Fatimid capital in the new city of Cairo, called *al-Qāhira*, or the Victorious (a name of the planet Mars). The third caliph, al-Ḥākim, was divinized by a sect of *ghulāt*, the Druzes. Upon the death of the fourth Fatimid caliph, al-Mustanṣir (1094), the Iranian *dāʿī* Ḥasan-i Ṣabbāḥ took the side of a presumable descendant of Nizār, the murdered son of al-Mustanṣir, whom he held in the impregnable stronghold of Alamūt ("Eagle's Nest") in the Elburz mountains. This is the origin of the Nizari Ismāʿīlīah, also known as Assassins (from the word hashish), the ancestors of the Aga Khans. In 1164 the Nizari imam Ḥasan II announced the *giyāma* and the end of the Law, and proclaimed himself caliph. After the fall of Alamut in 1256, the Nizaris of different provinces disappeared, with the exception of the Hojas of northwestern India, who since 1866 have recognized the Aga Khans as their imams. In 1978 the Hojas numbered about twenty million people.

Upon his death, the sixth Fatimid caliph, al-Āmir, who fell victim to the Assassins in 1130, left a male successor, al-Ṭayyib, eight months of age. When al-Ṭayib disappeared, the dāʿī of Yemen proclaimed him the hidden imam. This was the origin of the Yemenite Ṭayyibis and of the Indian Bohoras, who exist to the present day.

17.7 THE SHARĪʿAH is the the divine law of Islam, and the understanding of that law is *fiqh,* or jurisprudence. Muhammad did not impose a distinction between religious and secular law; the extent to which the Sharīʿah prevails in today's Muslim countries depends on each country's degree of secularization. The Sharīʿah applies to every dimension of life, including family relations, inheritance law, taxation, purification of pollutions, and prayer; the activity of its scholars includes the ranking of human actions on a spectrum ranging in shadings from mandatory to encouraged, discouraged, and prohibited. The four generally accepted sources for legal scholars are the Qurʾān, *sunnah* (traditions of the Prophet), *ijmāʿ* (consensus), and *qiyās* (reasoning by analogy). The science of ḥadīth criticism produced such great collections as those of al-Bukhārī and Muslim. Shiʿite jurisprudence differs somewhat, as their ḥadīth traditions emphasize the imams and their conception of consensus and independent reasoning differs.

The classical schools of law are the Ḥanafi, Māliki, Shāfiʿī, and Ḥanbali. In each of them lies a tension: to what extent is independent reasoning permissible for a jurist, when cases lack a clear precedent from Muhammad's lifetime? Abū Ḥanīfah (d. 767 C.E.) was a Kufan merchant and legal systematizer, whose influential school was to prevail in Iraq. Mālik ibn Anas (d. 795) was a Medinan legist, whose aim was to codify the practices of the community that had been the prophet's own, with an emphasis on communal harmony through individual responsibilities; his school, considered strict almost to the point of literalism, prevailed in North Africa and Spain. Reports of the sayings and actions of the Prophet served a guiding purpose in the tradition of Muḥammad ibn Idrīs al-Shāfiʿī (d. 820), who supplemented the instructions of the Qur'ān with carefully selected accounts of the Prophet's sayings, limited reasoning by analogy, and reference to collective opinion; according to prophetic tradition, Muhammad's community would never agree upon an error. Aḥmad ibn Ḥanbal (d. 855), orthodox vanquisher of the Baghdad Muʿtazila, was not alone in emphasizing the weight of a recorded word of the Prophet over any jurist's reasoning.

17.8 KALĀM is a word meaning speech. The Qur'ān is the *kalām Allāh*. The *ʿilm al-kalām* was the dialectical theology of Islam that grew from origins in apologetics and heresiology. Its aim was the establishment of orthodoxy, and it incorporated Hellenic logic and rationalism.

Dialogue with Christians in such cities as Damascus and Baghdad, who viewed Islam (which they called Hagarism or Ishmaelism) as a heretical innovation, raised new questions for Muslim theologians even as it exposed them to the Aristotelian and Neoplatonic traditions of their interlocutors. For Christians, Jesus Christ was the Divine Logos; for Muslims the Qur'ān took this position. Yet for Christians Christ was eternally coexistent with the Father; for Muslims, this would be *shirk*, polytheistic association of other things with God. Related questions were the reality of God's attributes, such as the anthropomorphic images of the Qur'ān, their createdness or changeability, the much-debated status of the sinning Muslim, and of course free will. John of Damascus (d. ca. 750 C.E.) described a debate on the origin of evil: Christians placed it with free will to preserve God's justice; Muslims originated good and evil with God, to preserve his omnipotence. The tension regarding predestination also arose early on: Qadarites and Muʿtazilites compromised Qur'ānic affirmations of predestination for the sake of free will, that God might conform to their sense of justice.

From 827 to 848 the rationalistic doctrines of the Muʿtazilites were violently enforced by the Abbasid Caliphate, a period called the Mihna, or inquisition. A backlash followed this period, and a leading figure to arise as a mediating voice was Abū al-Ḥasan al-Ashʿarī (874–935 C.E.), whose theology triumphed as Sunni orthodoxy. He accepted predestination, the eternal Qur'ān, the mercy of God with even sinful believers, and the reality and incomprehensibility of God and his attributes.

17.9 THE ISLAMIC RELIGIOUS CALENDAR is a lunar one (354 days); thus, the holy days that punctuate it shift through the seasons. The month of Ramadan is especially sacred; complete fasting is practiced during daylight hours, and particularly pious behavior prevails throughout. Near the end of Ramadan is the Night of Power (Laylat al-Qadr), the night in which Muhammad received his first revelation, and a night on which the boundary between the angelic world and the world below may open. The ʿĪd al-Fiṭr is the fast-breaking celebration.

Dhū al-Ḥijjah is the month of the Meccan pilgrimage. There, having entered a state of physical and ritual purity (*iḥrām*), pilgrims circumambulate the Kaʿbah, visit the graves of Hagar and Ishmael and the well of Zamzam, run between two small hills in memory of Hagar's search for water, stand for an afternoon at the Mount of Mercy on the Arafat plain, and cast stones at the pillar of Aqaba in Mīna (which represents Satan's temptation of Abraham to forego the sacrifice of his son (here, Ishmael). The great sacrifice and distribution of meat that ends the ḥajj is performed throughout the Muslim world (the ʿĪd al-Aḍḥā), in memory of Abraham's sacrifice.

A festival more representative of Shiʿite Islam is ʿĀshūrāʾ (10 Muḥarram), the commemoration of the martyrdom of Ḥusain ibn ʿAlī, grandson of the Prophet. The days of mourning for Ḥusain may include songs, poems, and dramatization of the conflict and street processions of wooden "tombs" accompanied by popular self-flagellation. Muhammad's birthday (Mawlid al-Nabī: 12 Rabīʿ al-Awwal), in fact the anniversary of his death, is celebrated by all, and the night of his *miʿrāj* is remembered in the month of Rajab.

17.10 SUFISM, the interior or mystical aspect of Islam, is a way of life directed toward the realization of God's unity and presence through love, experiential knowledge, asceticism, and ecstatic union with the beloved Creator.

Ascetic and devotional activities of Orthodox Christian monks and circulating Neoplatonic and Hermetic ideas were influences at various points in the history of Sufism, as is apparent in Sufi texts themselves, but the origins and impulse of the Sufi quest can be found in the Qurʾān, ḥadīth, and early pious and ascetic movements within Islam. Among the many scholars recently reacting against earlier inclinations to attribute Sufism (and other elements of Islam) to outside sources, S. H. Nasr pointedly remarks, "as if the yearning of man's soul for God could ever be due to historical borrowing" (S. H. Nasr, *Sufi Essays* [1972], p. 39). The terms Sufi (*ṣūfī*) and Sufism (*taṣawwuf*) probably derive from the garments of wool (*ṣūf*) worn by Muslim ascetics, who were commonly called by the names *faqīr* and *dervish,* meaning "poor."

Sufism began with Muhammad, for by virtue of his close relationship to God, his revelation and mystical ascent through the heavens (*miʿrāj*) and his exalted cosmic status, he was claimed by the Sufis as one of their own. Evidence of this was found both in traditions of the Prophet's deeds and sayings (*ḥadīth*) and in the Qurʾān, which proved a limitless and multilayered source of insight and edification. For the Qurʾān communicated the original testimony of the seed of Adam and Eve recognizing God as their eternal Lord, establishing a covenant of faithfulness (Sura 7:172). And in another verse dear to the Sufis God stated: "We created man and surely know what anxieties stir in his soul, for We are closer to him than his jugular vein" (Sura 50:16).

Another seed of Sufism within the Qurʾān was the instruction to practice *dhikr,* which was recollection, contemplation, or invocation of God (e.g., 13:28, 33:14). In Sufi practice, this might be accompanied by use of prayer beads, breath control, music, or the whirling dance by which we know the Mawlawīya "dervishes" in the tradition of Jalāl al-Dīn Rūmī (1207–1273), the mystical poet of Konya.

In traditions relating to Muhammad's own community, we hear of especially pious and stern believers who were to remain a conservative, antiworldly influence on the developing faith. Even under the first caliphs to follow Muhammad, during the years of the conquests, reservations about the transformations happening in the community and its practices were voiced. Should emphasis be placed more on ritual observance and law or on inner faith and love? Is God a distant and wholly other Master or is He loving and accessible, even internal? When the caliphate passed to the Umayyads in Damascus, culturally a world away from the harsh Arabian peninsula, many balked at the secularization, if not decadence, of princely rulers who should rather be stewards of God on earth.

Ḥasan al-Baṣrī (d. 728) was one of the early Muslim ascetics who always kept before his eyes the impending judgment of God. He criticized the materialistic goals of the conquests and all things worldly. His outlook surpassed mere sobriety for outright gloom and lachrymosity, drawing on a saying of the Prophet, "If you knew what I know you would laugh little and weep much."

An important transitional figure in Sufism is Rābiʿah al-ʿAdawīyah (d. 801), a renunciant who lifted the ascetic tradition that she inherited into a new dimension through her paradoxes and passionate love mysticism. As in the case of certain other Sufis, Rābiʿah's influence was magnified through popular and inspirational anecdotes about her life that circulated and were written down. Her love of God was absolute and exclusive of all else, allowing room neither for fear of hell nor desire for paradise nor hatred of Satan. Sufi piety often seemed to rest on a pivot, by which love of and reliance on God comes at the expense of love and reliance on God's creation. Many were set against friendship, family ties, providing for food and shelter, even rejecting the beauties of nature.

The master-pupil relationship was at the heart of Sufi practice. A master (*shaykh* or *pīr*) was to be carefully chosen and given complete power over the initiate. A great master might come to be considered a saint (*walī allāh*, "friend of God") in which case he would continue to exert beneficent power even after death and his tomb would become a pilgrimage site.

Groups of disciples began to collect around great masters, and communal dwellings evolved into convents (*ribāṭ, zawiyah, khāniqāh*) by the late eighth century. At first casual and transient, in the twelfth century these were often endowed and flourishing establishments with political power, hierarchical stratification, monastic rules, and institutionalized chains of initiation reaching back to famous early mystics. The twelfth century saw the rise of Sufi orders or brotherhoods perpetuating the teachings of certain great masters and their disciples. Prominent among the orders were the Bektāshīyah (from the mid-fourteenth century), the Suhrawardīyah (from ca. 1200; came to be influential in India), the Rifaᶜīyah, or Howling Dervishes (from the mid-twelfth century, known for their outrageous stunts), the Egyptian Shādhilīyah, the Qādirīyah, and the Naqshbandīyah. On the borders of Islamic civilization, the orders were instrumental in conversion, and certain pirs degenerated into local power brokers and petty warlords. Indian pirs might be charismatic gurus or inheritors of their title and position through hereditary lines.

Shiᶜite doctrines of the imams and their succession shared certain features with Sufism such as the status of the *wali*, the *quṭbs* and their succession, the chain of prophets and stages of spiritual progress. The first eight imams seemed to have moved in and out of Sufi circles, and both Sufism and Shiᶜism developed esoteric, hidden dimensions of Islam.

Sufi theology and practices often chafed the orthodox establishment, provoking accusations of pantheism, antinomian libertinism, and neglect of ritual duties such as prayer, fasting, and pilgrimage. Sufis were banned or persecuted by some regimes. Mendicant Sufis were often suspected as charlatans or heretics, and certain of these did indeed make light of standard Islamic traditions. The great Sufi Ḥusayn ibn Manṣūr al-Ḥallāj (857–922 C.E.) was tortured and executed in Baghdad both for his extreme religious stance and his political ties. He remains famous for his praise of the Qurʾānic Satan (Iblīs) refusing to bow down before Adam when God commanded all his creatures to do so (2:28–34). Rather than evil insubordination, this refusal was interpreted as monotheistic fidelity. Al-Ḥallāj was also known for his ecstatic statement, "anāʾl-Ḥaqq" (I am the Truth). In Sufi parlance, this may be taken as a declaration of merging with God, who was called by them the Truth, but to the orthodox ear it is the highest form of blasphemy, not to mention that Sufis were generally bound to silence before the uninitiated in spiritual matters. Al-Ḥallāj's indiscreet pronouncements may be compared with Abū Yazīd al Bisṭāmī (d. 874) declaring, "Glory be to me! How great is my majesty!" or "I saw the Kaʿba walking round me."

Abū Ḥāmid Muḥammad ibn Muḥammad al-Ghazālī (1058–1111) was a master of jurisprudence, *kalām* (dilectical theology), and philosophy, but a breakdown in midlife transformed him into a Sufi, and he is best remembered as a champion of experiential knowledge over philosophical knowledge and revelation over reasoning. Aside from his famous *Tahāfut al-Falāsifah* (*Incoherence of the Philosophers*), his autobiography and his *Revivification of the Religious Sciences* (*Ihyāʾ ʿulūm al-dīn*) persuasively argue for the orthodoxy, legitimacy, and even necessity of mysticism.

Mystical poetry such as the mathnavīs of Mawlānā Jalāl al-Dīn Rūmī and Farīd al-Dīn ʿAṭṭar's *Conference of the Birds* (*Manṭiq al-ṭayr*) has brought the beauties of Sufism to wider circles than another literary form of the mystics, the Sufi manuals. These guides were at once both utterly practical and inaccessibly abstruse. The spiritual path was variously diagrammed by the manual writers, who fell into schools or orders. Stations (*maqāmāt*) that ascetics reach along the way, and God-given states (*aḥwāl*) appeared in differing numbers. From the *Kitāb al-lumaʿ* of Abū Naṣr al-Sarrāj (d. 988), a good introduction to Sufism, we take these seven stations:

1 tawbah	repentance
2 waraʿ	abstinence
3 zuhd	asceticism

4 faqr	poverty
5 ṣabr	patience
6 tawakkul	trust in God
7 riḍaʾ	satisfaction

Other stations often reckoned (even one hundred or more) include conversion (*inābah*), invocation (*dhikr*), surrender (*taslīm*), worship (*ʿibādah*), knowledge (*maʿrifah*), unveiling (*kashf*), annihilation (*fanāʾ*), and subsistence in God (*baqāʾ*).

The states are more personalized and elusive than the stations. Here is al-Sarrāj's list of ten:

1 murāqabah	constant attention
2 qurb	proximity
3 maḥabbah	love
4 khawf	fear
5 rajāʾ	hope
6 shawq	desire
7 uns	familiarity
8 iṭmiʾnān	tranquility
9 mushāndah	contemplation
10 yaqīn	certainty

This gives some idea of the Sufi way; grace, initiation, a skilled spiritual guide, inner purification, and intuition of Divine presence (*dhawq* or "taste") could lead to realization of *al-tawḥīd*, the absolute unity of God.

Two principal Sufi doctrines are explicit in the writings of the extraordinary man often considered the greatest Muslim mystic: Abū Bakr Muḥammad ibn al-ʿArabī, called Muḥyī al-Dīn ibn ʿArabī (1165–1240). This Andalusian-born systematizer, traveler, poet, and *shaykh* was a prolific writer whose productions were often the result of some revelatory communication or inspiration. His most famous works are the *Interpreter of Desires* (*Tarjumān al-ashwāq*), which contains love poetry; *Bezels of Wisdom* (*Fuṣūṣ al-ḥikam*); and the gigantic *Meccan Revelations* (*Al-futūḥāt al-makkīya*).

Fundamental to Ibn ʿArabī's system was the doctrine called *waḥdat al-wujūd*, "unity of being." All that really exists is God, utterly ineffable and transcendent. He needs his creation to know himself, to be his mirror; we are the attributes of God. This was not quite pantheism, although its expressions may well sound pantheistic, nor was it simple monism.

A second of Ibn ʿArabī's theories was the Perfect Human Being (*al-insān al-kāmil*), the culmination of God's creation. This being had many dimensions: he may be a cosmological hypostasis acting as the keystone of the creation; he may be a spiritual pole or *quṭb* guiding and sustaining his age; he may be the essence of the Prophet—from Adam to Muhammad. The human is the microcosm of the universal macrocosm; this connection can be exploited for the utter transformation of the mystic. As the peak of creation, the human being is the polish on God's mirror, the sharpest image of the Divine, piercing the veil of illusion that makes the creation appear as real as its creator.

17.11 BIBLIOGRAPHY. See in general Fazlur Rahman, "Islam: An Overview," in *ER* 7, 303–22; A. Schimmel, "Islamic Religious Year," in *ER* 7, 454–57. Highly useful is *The Encyclopedia of Islam,* 2nd ed. (1954–), and *The Shorter Encyclopedia of Islam,* H. A. R. Gibb and J. H. Kramers (eds.) (1953). An excellent historical introduction is Marshall G. S. Hodgson's three-volume *The Venture of Islam* (1975). On Muhammad, see W. M. Watt, *Muhammad: Prophet and Statesman* (1961), and the best source, Ibn Ishaq's *Life of Muhammad,* translated by A. Guillaume (1955).

On Muslim sects, see especially Shahrastani, *Muslim Sects and Divisions,* translated by A. K. Kazi and J. G. Fly (1984) (incomplete translation); Henri Laoust, *Les sectes de l'Islam* (1983), and the three books by Heinz Halm: *Kosmologie und Heilslehre der frühen Isma'iliya* (1978), *Die islamische Gnosis* (1982), and *Die Schia* (1988). Halm believes in "gnostic" influence on Islam, which is debatable. On Ismaili history and doctrine, see S. H. Nasr (ed.), *Isma'ili Contributions to Islamic Culture* (1977); Bernard Lewis, *The Origins of Isma'ilism* (1940); W. Ivanov, *Brief Survey of the Evolution of Ismailism* (1952); M. G. S. Hodgson, *The Order of the Assassins* (1955); Bernard Lewis, *The Assassins* (1967).

On community practice, see M. Gaudefroy-Demombynes, *Muslim Institutions,* translated by S. MacGregor (1950). Another careful introduction is W. M. Watt's *Islamic Philosophy and Theology* (1962), or his *The Formative Period of Islamic Thought* (1973).

A sensitive, scholarly introduction to Sufism is Annemarie Schimmel, *Mystical Dimensions of Islam* (1975). Other important works on Sufism are R. A. Nicholson, *Studies in Islamic Mysticism* (1980; 1921); S. H. Nasr, *Sufi Essays* (1972); J. Spencer Trimingham, *The Sufi Orders in Islam* (1971); Tor Andrae, *In the Garden of Myrtles* (first published, 1947), translated from Swedish by Birgitta Sharpe (1987); Louis Massignon, *La Passion d'al-Hosayn ibn Mansur al-Hallaj* (1975; 1922), translated into English by H. Mason, Bollingen Series (1982); Louis Massignon, *Essai sur les origines du lexique technique de la mystique musulmane* (1922); R. A. Nicholson, *The Mathnawi of Jalalu'ddin Rumi,* 8 vols. (1925–1971); Ibn al-Arabi, *La sagesse des prophètes,* partial translation and notes by Titus Burckardt (1955), English translation by A. Colme-Seymour (1975); Ibn al-ʿArabī, *Sufis of Andalusia,* translated by R. W. J. Austin (1972).

18

Jainism

18.1 SOURCES. The name Jainism comes from the title *jina,* or "conqueror," given to the founder of the religion. Jaina literature is vast. It is divided in two branches, according to the two traditions, or "sects," that produced it: the Dighambaras (Sky-clad; i.e., naked) and Śvetāmbaras (White-clad). The writings of the Śvetāmbaras are reunited in a doctrinal canon comprising dozens of tractates divided in six sections; the language of the oldest writings is Prakrit, spoken by the founder himself, whereas the rest of the tractates are in Sanskrit. The Dighambaras excel in systematic works (*prakaraṇas*), the most ancient of which go back to the first century C.E.

18.2 MAHĀVĪRA (Great Hero) was the founder of Jainism. His true name was Vardhtmāna (prosperous), and he was a contemporary of the Buddha (sixth century B.C.E.). His mythical biography is the focus of the Śvetāmbara tradition. It features a rather impersonal type of Indian divine character, the Mahāpuruṣa. Conceived in Bihar in a family of brahmans, his embryo was allegedly transferred by the god Indra to the womb of the princess Triśala, so that the child would be born in a royal family. Fourteen or sixteen premonitory dreams warned the mother about the prodigious birth. The royal infant, who would not wait to leave his mother's womb to begin performing miracles, was brought up according to the religious teachings of a certain Pārśva, on whom Jaina tradition confers the title of twenty-third *tīrthaṃkara,* literally "ford maker [in order that the others could cross the water]," comparable perhaps to the Latin word *pontifex,* meaning "bridge maker." Mahāvīra himself was the twenty-fourth *tīrthaṃkara.*

Much of Mahāvīra's biography resembles that of the Buddha. Certain sources attributed to Mahāvīra a wife and a daughter whose husband would be the cause of the Jaina schism. Be that as it may, at the age of thirty, after the death of his parents, Vardhtmāna left the world to join the eccentric *śrāmaṇas,* whose feats of asceticism were often spectacular. Among them, Vardhtmāna practiced nudity and the five commandments that were to become the Great Vows (*mahāvrata*) of the Jaina monk: renunciation of killing, lying, stealing, having sex, and accumulating transient goods. Mahāvīra spent twelve years on the thorny path of asceticism. Enlightenment came upon him under a *sal* tree, during a summer night on a river shore. He reached complete omniscience, or Perfect Gnosis (*kevala-jñāna*), of everything that is, was, and will be in all the worlds. This state of "the Perfected One" (*kevalin*) is the equivalent of the Buddhist *arhat.* As in the latter's case, two Jaina traditions exist: one that asserts that the *kevalin* is free from all constraints of human nature, and another one that makes him or her free not of the constraints themselves (ingestion, excretion, etc.), but of the state of impurity that accompanies them. After the attainment of Perfect Gnosis, the Jina (Conqueror) began to spread the truth and founded the Jaina community made up of religious and laypeople of both sexes. According to tradition, he entered *nirvāṇa* at the age of seventy-two (mystical numerology: $2^3 \times 3^2$) in 527 B.C.E., a date that might be corrected to 467 B.C.E. As the teaching of the Buddha is epitomized in the Eightfold Path, whose formulae all begin with the word *samyak-* ("proper"), so the teaching of the Jina is summarized in the Three Jewels (*triratna*): Proper Worldview (*samyagdarśana*), Proper Gnosis (*samyagjñāna*), and Proper Conduct (*samyakcaritra*).

18.3 HISTORY. According to the Jaina legend, Mahāvīra passed the leadership of the community onto eleven disciples (*gaṇadharas*) whose chief was Gautama Indrabhūti. In 79 C.E., the community split in two: the liberals, or Śvetāmbaras, and the conservatives, followers of the heroic tradition of antiquity, the Dighambaras or integral nudists. From northeastern India (Magadha, today Bihar), the movement spread south and east, knowing periods of efflorescence. Today Jainism does not seem to have more than three million believers. An economic ethic that tends toward commercial success grants them a certain prosperity. Intellectually, the Jainas have an outstanding place in Indian social life that far exceeds the percentage of population they represent. Their contribution to the movement of Mohandas Gandhi was significant.

18.4 THE WORLDVIEW (*darśana*) of the Jainas is condensed in the above-mentioned religious Great Vows, as well as in the Lesser Vows (*aṇuvrata*) of laypeople: *ahiṃsā* (noninjury), *satya* (honesty), *asteya* (correctness), *brahma* (continence, i.e., abstention from illicit sexual intercourse), and *aparigraha* (giving up accumulation of riches).

Jainism shared with traditional Hinduism and certain Buddhist schools the idea of reincarnation of the living part (*jīva*) of the human being in all animated beings, under the influence of the "karmic body," which is the outcome of past actions. The Jaina tried to reverse this natural process by constant reaction (*saṃvara*), consisting of long lists of mental, verbal, and bodily renouncements and of submission to the severe rules of religious life. Such was the ethical dualism of Jaina doctrine that suicide by fasting (*Saṃlekhanā*) was recommended. Yet this extreme carelessness for one's own life was only equaled by the excess of care for any other life. Life should be respected, be it the life of a flea or an ant; and therefore Jainas not only practiced the strictest vegetarian diet, which went so far that they would filter water in order not to kill minute organisms, but they would try by all possible means never to harm any animate being. Those who had taken orders, for instance, would abstain from eating at nighttime out of concern for the insects they might unwittingly swallow.

Only complex asceticism (*tapas*), as it was practiced in the community of monks (*nirgrantha*), could bring about deliverance from the bonds of *saṃsāra*. When the monk's *saṃvara* prevailed over his *karman*, or accumulation of actions, he reached the goal of perfection (*siddhi*).

Although very organized, Jaina cosmology does not go far beyond traditional brahmanic cosmology, in the same way that the biography of the Mahāvīra resembles the biography of most of the other Mahāpuruṣas, the Great Men of India.

18.5 CAVES were the favorite dwellings of Jaina monks in ancient times. They were transformed into places of worship, which the later sanctuaries of Badani and Ellora, sculpted in rock, endeavored to imitate. Without always respecting the following structure, a Jaina temple often consisted of a central image of the *Tīrthaṃkara catur-mukha* (Four-faced Ford maker), to which led ways of access. The most famous Jaina temples are in western India, at Mount Abu, and in the Aravalli hills.

18.6 BIBLIOGRAPHY. Eliade, *H* 2, 152–53; C. Caillat, "Jainism," in *ER* 7, 507–14, and "Mahavira," in *ER* 9, 128–31. See also Walther Schubring, *The Doctrine of the Jainas* (1962); Collette Caillat, *La cosmologie jaïna* (1981).

19

Judaism

19.1 THE JEWISH PEOPLE made their appearance in history after 2000 B.C.E. They were in part the descendants of the Amorites or "Westerners" who settled in Mesopotamia at the end of the third millennium B.C.E.; in part, they possibly can be identified as the *khabiru* mentioned by sources of the mid-second millennium B.C.E. According to the Bible, the ancestors of the Israelites reached Egypt as free people but were later on made into slaves. Thousands of them left Egypt about 1260 B.C.E., following their prophet Moses, whose name was Egyptian. They settled down in Canaan, forming there twelve tribes.

About 1050 B.C.E., the *shofet* (judge) and seer Samuel named Saul king of Israel in order to lead the battle against the Philistines. After Saul's death, David was designated as a king by the southern tribe of Judah. He pacified the region and made Jerusalem into a religious center where the Ark of the Covenant was kept. David was followed by his son Solomon (ca. 961–922 B.C.E.), a king of legendary wisdom, who had the Jerusalem Temple built and installed the Ark. After Solomon's death, the state split into a northern and a southern kingdom, Israel and Judah. In 722 B.C.E. Israel was conquered by the Assyrian Empire. In 587 B.C.E. the Babylonian emperor Nebukhadnezzar (Nabu-kudurri-usur) destroyed the first Jerusalem Temple. Most of the population of Judah was deported to Babylon at this time. They were freed from the Babylonian captivity by the Persan emperor Cyrus, who occupied Mesopotamia in 539 B.C.E.

Most of the Jews returned to Jerusalem and rebuilt the Temple with Cyrus' support. After the death of Alexander (323 B.C.E.), Judah fell within the territory of the Ptolemies, who ruled Egypt from their capital Alexandria, a city with an important number of Jews. In 198 B.C.E. Judah passed under the Seleucid Empire. In 167 B.C.E. Antiochus IV abolished Jewish law and profaned the Temple by installing in it a statue of Zeus. This situation catalyzed the Maccabean revolt. The Temple was occupied and purified by the rebels in 164 B.C.E.; in memory of this event the eight-day festival of the Hanukkah or new dedication was established. In 140 B.C.E. Simon, the last among the brothers Maccabee, was proclaimed high priest and ethnarch or chief of the people. Thus began the Hasmonean dynasty, which still retained a religious function under Roman protectorate (60 B.C.E.).

In 40 B.C.E. Herod, the son of Antipater, who was superintendent of Judah for the Romans, was proclaimed in Rome king of the Jews. After 6 B.C.E. Judah was directly administered by a Roman prefect, then by a procurator. In 66 C.E., in response to the provocations of procurator Florus, a revolt broke out, with the support of the Zealots (*sicarii*), Jewish nationalists who resorted to terrorism against Romans and Romanized Jews. The Roman general Vespasian, proclaimed emperor in 69 C.E., left his son Titus in charge of the campaign begun in Judah. On 28 August 70 C.E. the Second Temple of Jerusalem was destroyed by fire; and in September the imperial army razed Jerusalem to the ground. The last resisters met their end in 74 C.E. in the stronghold of Masada.

Even if it is not true that thereafter Jewish religion was no longer recognized by the Romans, the Fall of the Temple certainly was a pivotal moment of the diaspora, which was already an ancient phenomenon. In 133 C.E. a revolt broke out under the Messiah Bar Kokhba, or "Son of the Star," encouraged by the religious authority of Rabbi Aqiva (ca. 50–135). In ferocious retaliation, Judah was devastated by the Romans, which led to further depopulation. For a few years Jewish religious practices were banned, yet at the beginning of the third century the general situation of the Jews and local administration—which now fell to an indigenous *nasi*, or prince—were notably improved. Only much later (end of the fourth century), when Christianity became the official religion of the Roman Empire, were the Jews excluded from most previous privileges and denied official public functions.

This situation lasted in general up to the eighteenth century in all Christian states as well as in Muslim states (despite a difference in juridical status) after the coming of Islam; the few and much exaggerated exceptions in Muslim Spain unfortunately confirmed the rule rather than breaking it. First hunted down by Muslim fundamentalists and then expelled by the Christian conquerors in 1492, the Jews of Sefarad (Spain and Portugal) sought refuge in North Africa, in Asia Minor and

Greece, in Holland, and wherever else the authorities would allow them to settle.

This extremely short sketch of the history of the Jewish people is indispensable in order to understand the historical dimension of Judaism. Other data will be supplied as we will move toward the major tragedy of the Jewish people, the Holocaust (*ha-shoa*) that took the lives of some six millions Jews between 1937 and 1944. Yet we should make clear from the outset that if on the one hand ancient Judaism seems indeed to interpret in a historical key the seasonal cults of Canaan, on the other hand—as outstanding students of Judaism such as R. J. Zwi Werblowski, Moshe Idel, and others have emphasized—it is one of the religions whose enduring core transcends history, being based on intemporal structures.

19.2 SCRIPTURE. Thanks to recent archaeological finds, the common religious substratum of Canaan has begun to yield some of its secrets. Some scholars assert that the historical value of the Bible has been widely exaggerated in the past. Yet it is reasonable to believe that a good part of the biblical stories have a historical background.

The Jewish sacred scripture is called *Torah nebi'im we ketuvim,* in acronymic abbreviation *Tanakh:* "The Law, Prophets, and Writings." It has accordingly three basic sections: the Torah, or the Pentateuch (five writings); the Prophets (which in reality also contain historical books); and the other writings (which in reality contain a few prophetic texts). The most ancient part of the Pentateuch is dated to the tenth century B.C.E.; the most recent parts of the *Ketuvim* belong to the second century C.E.

The Pentateuch consists of Genesis (*Bereshit*), Exodus (*Shemot*), Leviticus (*Vayikra*), Numbers (*Be-Midbar*), and Deuteronomy (*Devarim*). The Torah was assembled from four texts of various epochs: J, or Jahwist, using for God the name YHWH (tenth century B.C.E.); E, or Elohist, using for God the (plural) Elohim (eighth century B.C.E.); D, on which part of Deuteronomy is based (622 B.C.E.); and P, redacted by a group of priests, on which Leviticus and certain parts of other writings are based. The variety of sources provide for a multiplicity of conceptions of God and myths about the origination of the universe and of human beings. The ancient figure of the sky god YHWH, the focus of Judaic monotheism, was certainly not conceived to stand the rationalistic exigencies of Hellenism. Contradictions therefore arise when we try to make him omnipotent, omniscient, etc.; yet his divine monarchy is safe.

The Prophets are divided into "ancient" and "new." The ancient prophetic writings actually consist of six historical books: Joshua, Judges, 1 and 2 Samuel, and 1 and 2 Kings, whose heroes are Joshua (Moses' successor), Samuel, Saul, David, the prophets Elijah and Elisha, up to the Babylonian conquest of 587 B.C.E.. The new prophetic writings consist of the omens and visions of Isaiah, Jeremiah, Ezekiel, and the "twelve" (Hosea, Joel, Amos, Jonas, Zachariah, etc.). The *Ketuvim* are a series of various writings belonging to different periods such as the Psalms (150 hymns and prayers), the Proverbs, Job, the five *megillot* (Song of Songs, Ruth, Lamentations, Ecclesiastes, Esther), Daniel, Esdras, Nehemiah, and 1 and 2 Chronicles.

The first collection of all of the biblical texts is the Greek version called the Septuagint or "of the LXX" (which stands for the traditional number of sages who allegedly made the translation), completed in the second century B.C.E. The Septuagint contains certain materials (called the Old Testament apocrypha) not included in the Hebrew canon. The constitution of the latter was the result of the patient work of the Masoretes.

Starting with the third century B.C.E., Jewish religion added to its extracanonical writings a number of apocalyptic texts that describe either heavenly journeys (like the cycle of Enoch) or the coming of a new aeon (like 4 Esdras and 2 Baruch), or again a combination of vertical ascent to heaven and horizontal eschatological prophecy. Toward the end of the first century C.E., two types of Jewish mysticism appeared: one was a mystical interpretation of the Book of Genesis (*ma'aseh bereshit*); the other one—called *ma'aseh merkabah* or "Work of the Chariot"—of the description of the chariot (*merkabah*) that transported God's throne in the vision of the prophet Ezekiel. A branch of *merkabah* mysticism, the so-called hekhalotic literature, described the heavenly palaces (*hekhalot*) crossed by the mystic in his journey to the throne of God.

Hellenistic Judaism produced the major Platonic philosopher Philo of Alexandria (ca. 20 B.C.E.–45 C.E.), who attempted a harmonization of Plato (or Middle Platonism) and the Bible. The enterprise seems more haphazard than it actually was, for the spirit of part of the Pentateuch and especially of the Book of Genesis was very "Platonic." Indeed, like Plato himself, the Bible proclaimed that the world had been created by a good demiurge and was therefore good, as God himself asserted (Gen. 1:10, 18, 25, 31, etc.). As far as the fall is concerned, Plato made it into the fall of the soul in the body; yet Genesis did not contradict him, for it talked about the Fall of the essential part of the primordial couple, before they were clad in the "garments of skin" (Gen. 3:21). Philo therefore could easily interpret the biblical passage as an allusion to the material body that held the soul like a prison (Plato, *Cratylus* 400c).

A Jewish ascetic sect professing dualistic beliefs, the Essenes, lived in the desert of Judah near the Dead Sea from about 150 B.C.E. to their destruction by the Roman soldiers in 68 C.E. Part of their literature—the so-called Dead Sea Scrolls—has been found in eleven caves at Qumran since 1947.

Yet the largest body of Jewish literature consists of the Mishnah and its successors, the two Talmuds (the Jerusalem and the Babylonian).

The Mishnah is almost entirely a work of *halakhah*, or legal matters, not of *haggadah* (theology and legends). Completed around 200 C.E., it contains sixty-three tractates grouped in six sections, or *sedarim:* Zeraim (Seeds), Moed (Festivals), Nashim (Women), Nezikim (Damages), Kodashim (Holy Matters), Teharot (Purifications). Traditions not included in the Mishnah (the *beraitot*) were collected in a supplement (the Tosefta). The masters quoted in the Mishnah are called *tannaim*, whereas the later Palestinian and Babylonian rabbis, five times more numerous than the former, quoted in the Talmud are called *amoraim*. Both *tanna* and *amora* mean "master."

The Palestinian Talmud, more ancient and one-third the length of the other, yet less polished, was completed at the beginning of the fifth century, the Babylonian Talmud about 500 C.E. The two were compiled by the Amoraim and contain mishnaic texts with a long commentary called *gemara*.

The halakhic corpus of the Talmud is only one part of the rabbinical writings. The other part consists of the commentaries called *midrashim*, which can be both halakhic and haggadic. The halakhic *midrashim* deal with Exodus (*Mekhilta*), Leviticus (*Sifra*), Numbers, and Deuteronomy (*Sifrei*). The haggadic *midrashim* were brought together in numerous collections at different periods up to the eighth century C.E. Among these collections the most important are the Midrash Rabbah (the Great Midrash, containing the *Bereshit Rabbah*, a commentary of Genesis compiled ca. fourth century C.E.), the *Pesikta de Rav Kahana* (containing liturgical and homiletic texts), the Midrash Tanhuma (after the name of a Palestinian rabbi of the fourth century), and so forth.

19.3 MONOTHEISM. In the Book of Genesis one can follow a process that started as YHWH monolatry and ended up in monotheism.

Scholars such as F. M. Cross and Jon Levenson distinguish several conceptions of creation in Genesis, which are understandable only in the context of dialectical opposition of the biblical writers toward Babylonian and Canaanite myth. Elsewhere, in Psalm 82 and in several passages of the Prophets, one can still recognize traces of myths also found in the Babylonian *Enuma Elish* and at Ugarit.

Opposition to the Canaanite environment is one of the major keys of interpretation that allowed numerous scholars to assess the originality of Judaism. Starting from the observation that the Jews kept up most Canaanite festivals while changing their meaning, relating them to events the Bible defines as "historical," scholars have defined Judaism as a "religion of history."

19.4 FEASTS. Let us briefly examine the Jewish feasts, of which the most important are the New Year (Rosh Hashanah), the Atonement (Yom Kippur), the Feast of the Tabernacles (Sukkot), the Consecration (Hanukkah), Purim, Passover, and the Pentecost (Shevuot).

Rosh Hashanah, celebrated on the first day of the autumn month of Tishri, is the first of a series of festivals that include Kippur (tenth of Tishri), Sukkot (fifteenth to twenty-second of Tishri), and the more recent feast of the Torah on the twenty-third of Tishri, at the end of the agricultural season.

The participants gather at the sound of the *shofar,* a wind instrument made from a ram's horn, supposed to expel the demons. The rite of *tashlik* (he will cast out), which delivers from sin, is celebrated near a watercourse; sin is "cast out" at the bottom of the water. The evening meal is based on the double meanings of such food names as beets (*silga',* "to chase away"), leeks (*karate,* "cut off"), dates (*temarim,* "finish off"), and so forth. The eaten message is thus the following: "May God have our enemies *chased away, cut off, finished off,*" and so on.

The Yom Kippur consists of a number of ceremonies of atonement that begin with a nocturnal fasting and with mourning. In ancient times, they were concluded by the transfer of sins onto a scapegoat who was released in the desert. Many of these customs are reminiscent of the Babylonian New Year's festival (Akitu).

An example of the transformation of a seasonal festival into the commemoration of a biblical event is the Tabernacles feast (Sukkot), which initially concluded the gathering of the crops with a ceremony of gratitude toward God. Leviticus 23:43 shows its transformation into a celebration of the Exodus from Egypt and the erection of tents in the desert.

Another transformation was undergone by the Purim feast, whose name alludes to the lots drawn during the annual divination ceremonies performed by all Near Eastern peoples. Yet the Jewish Purim celebrates the biblical heroine Esther who on the thirteenth of Adar saved the Jewish people from a massacre (Esther 13:6).

One can also follow to some extent the transformations of Passover and the feast of unleavened bread, originally separated but later on unified to commemorate the Exodus from Egypt. The paschal lamb indicates that initially this festival celebrated on the full moon of the fourteenth of Nisan was a spring festival. Its symbolism was modified to remember the tenth plague sent by God upon the Egyptians (Exodus 11) and the salvation of firstborn Jewish children, who were spared because the doors of their houses were marked with blood from the sacrifice of the firstborn lambs. Exodus 12 prescribes that Passover should be observed by one whole week during which the consumption of leavened bread is forbidden; the lack of leaven is related to the haste of the departure from Egypt. All this seems to indicate that Jewish religious symbolism is often the product of a particular kind of exegesis that most of the time referred to events narrated in biblical writings and constituting the sacred history of the Jewish people. This history may be "linear," i.e., noncyclical; yet it took place in the archetypal past and codifies the mythical past of the Jews. It is therefore very difficult to accept the distinction between the "biblical religions" and the other religions as based on the fact that the latter envision time as the repetition of a cycle of creation and the periodical rejuvenation of the world, whereas the former (Judaism and Christianity) are "religions of history," of a nonrepetitive, linear time. Actually, the cycle of Jewish festivals shows close relationship to the biblical myth of the foundation of God's covenant (*berit*) with the Chosen People and of the renewal of the covenant in the primordial history of the Jews. This observation also applies to Christianity: that Jesus Christ lived "under Pontius Pilate" may be a historical indication, but its meaning is transformed for those who celebrate his resurrection.

19.5 JEWISH PROPHECY probably represents the outcome of the merger of two institutions: the *ro'ehim* (seers) and the Palestinian *nabi'im*. The word *nabi* indicates the classical biblical prophets such as Amos, Hosea, Isaiah, Jeremiah, Ezekiel, and so forth, preceded in the ninth century B.C.E. by Elijah and his disciple Elisha, two miracle workers who demonstrated the superiority of the biblical YHWH over Baal, the Canaanite god. The central message of prophecy is moral. Canaanite cultic practices such as sacred prostitution and bloody sacrifice were condemned. Confronted with the general corruption of the people, the prophets preached atonement and threatened that otherwise God would severely punish his unfaithful servants.

19.6 JEWISH APOCALYPTIC LITERATURE is in general extrabiblical, with the exception of the Book of Daniel. *Apocalypse* is a Greek word meaning uncovering or revelation. Apocalyptic literature therefore consists of stories of revelations obtained in different ways, of which the most important are, according to J. J. Collins, otherworldly journey, vision, dialogue, and "heavenly book." Apocalypses have a historical, "horizontal" dimension insofar as they are concerned with the end of time; and a visionary, "vertical" dimension, concerning the structure of the universe and the heavenly abode of God. The most ancient Jewish apocalypses, whose fragments have been found among the Essene manuscripts of Qumran, are chapters 1–36 and 72–82 of the Book of Enoch or *1 Enoch,* also known as the Ethiopic Enoch, since its only complete version is an Ethiopic translation from Greek. The *Book of the Jubilees* (second century B.C.E.) was influenced by *1 Enoch.* The *Book of Daniel* consists of several independent stories put together in a common narrative framework during the second century B.C.E. revolt of the Maccabees. The *Sybilline Oracles* are Jewish and Christian texts of various periods. Among the other apocalyptic writings worth mentioning are the *Testaments of the Twelve Patriarchs* (second century B.C.E.), the *Life of Adam and Eve,* the *Apocalypse of Abraham,* the *Testament of Abraham, 2 Enoch,* or the Slavonic Enoch, *4 Esdras, 2 Baruch* (Syriac Baruch), all composed between 70 and 135 C.E. Most of these narratives share the Hellenistic Jewish belief in "two aeons": the aeon of world history and the eschatological aeon, the first containing the vicissitudes of earthly Jerusalem, continuously threatened by sin and enemies, the second the coming of heavenly Jerusalem, where the Righteous will find the crowns, the thrones, and the garments of glory waiting for them since the world's creation.

19.6.1 Merkabah mysticism consists of a special kind of visionary literature, whose first elements already appeared in the second century

B.C.E. In general, the chariot and the throne of God were contemplated at the end of a voyage through seven palaces, or *hekhalot,* populated with heavenly beings. Here the visionary would sometimes meet the famous angel Metatron, who was none other than the biblical character Enoch (Gen. 5:18–24) promoted to the rank of angel. However, this Enoch had retained some human attributes, like that of having joints (the angels have not). This is why the Babylonian Talmud (Hagigah 15a) affirms that Metatron-Enoch, by not standing in his presence like the other angels, misled the ecstatic Elisha ben Avuya, who mistook him for God himself and became therefore a heretic called *Aher,* "Other." Typical of hekhalot literature is the Hebrew Book of Enoch, or *3 Enoch.*

19.6.2 The Dead Sea Scrolls, found between 1947 and 1977 in eleven caves near the Dead Sea, probably belonged to the ascetic sect of the Essenes, although a few scholars contend against this commonly shared attribution. The Essene community had settled in the Judean desert during the second century B.C.E. and continued there until its destruction by a Roman unit, probably in 68 C.E. Two kinds of documents have been found at Qumran: more or less extensive fragments of biblical or para-biblical writings (such as *1 Enoch*), and writings belonging to the sect itself, to which the *Damascus Document,* found at the beginning of the century in Cairo, should be added. Among the Essene texts, the most important are the *Rule of the Community* (1Q Serek); the *pesharim,* or biblical commentaries, of which the most well known is the commentary of the prophet Habakuk; and the *War Scroll* (1Q Milhamah). Essene doctrine was dominated by the figure, possibly historical, called the Master of Justice, and by his archenemy, the Impious Priest.

The documents portray the Essenes as dualists, believing in the existence of two spirits—good and evil—who had divided between themselves the generations of the living. The Essenes fostered the conviction that the Good would eventually prevail over the Evil through a conflict between the Sons of Light and the Sons of Darkness. This battle does not seem to have occurred in the past; many believe that it concerns the conviction of the Essenes that their spiritual power would easily defeat the heavy weapons of the Roman contingents. If that was indeed the case, the Essenes must have been terribly disappointed with the outcome of the invasion by Vespasian's troops.

19.7 RABBINIC JUDAISM arose after 70 C.E. from a branch of the Pharisees, the traditional opponents of the conservative party of the

Sadducees, namely from the school of Rabbi Hillel, which became more popular than the more legalistic school of Shammai. Hillel's outlook could be expressed in a "golden rule": "Do not do to your neighbour what you do not want him to do to yourself." After 70 C.E., the Rabban (that is, the Nasi or chief of the assembly) Yohannan ben Zakkai, followed by Rabban Gamaliel II, organized the Sanhedrin, or rabbinic assembly, of Yavneh in Judah. The generation of the Fall of the Temple produced many illustrious *tannaim* such as Eliezer ben Hyrcanus, Eleazar ben Azariah, Joshua ben Hananiah, Ishmael ben Elisha, Aqiva ben Yosef, and others. After the bloody repression of Bar Kokhba's revolt and Akiva's martyrdom, the Sanhedrin was transferred to Galilee. The great masters Simeon bar Yohai and Meir are associated with this period. Under Rabban Judas ha-Nasi, the Mishnah was compiled.

Later on, the main centers of rabbinic Judaism would become the *yeshivot,* or academias, of Sura and Pumbedita in Mesopotamia, where an important Jewish community under the authority of a Jewish exilarch lived under Persian rule. After the Muslim conquest, the Jews became *dhimmis,* or "subjects," of the new power, in return for whose "protection" they were supposed to pay tax on religion and recognize the authority of the Islamic state. According to the collection of rules and regulations redacted around 800 C.E., and known under the name of the "Pact of Umar," Jews as well as Christians were excluded from Muslim administration, did not have the right to proselytize or to build new synagogues or churches, and so forth. In the tenth century, the Babylonian yeshivot, whose president was called a Gaon, were definitively transferred to Baghdad, the capital of the Abbasid caliphate. The most prestigious Gaon of the Iraqi yeshivot was Saadia ben Joseph (882–942), known as a champion of the struggle against the fundamentalist Jewish sectarians called Karaites.

When the Arabs conquered Spain in 711 C.E., they found precious allies in the Sefardi Jews; for a short period, the Jews were rewarded with some tax exemptions. Yet the Pact of Umar was not revoked in Sefarad. During the Umayyad caliphate of Córdoba (756–1031), the capital of Andalusia became a brilliant center of Jewish intellectual life, even if the Lucena yeshiva did not surpass in splendor the yeshivot of Baghdad, Jerusalem, and Cairo. While his grandness was not recognized by his Jewish contemporaries, one Andalusian luminary was the Platonist Solomon ibn Gabirol (ca. 1020–1057), author of the tractate *Mekor hayyim,* or Fount of Life, of which only a complete Latin translation (*Fons Vitae*) has survived. Ibn Gabirol, like most of the great Jewish thinkers of that period, wrote mainly in Arabic; yet he also wrote fine

Hebrew verses such as the poem *Keter malkhut* (The Royal Crown), whose title has Kabbalistic echoes. Another important Platonist was Bahya ibn Paquda (eleventh century). Abraham ibn Daud (ca. 1110–1180) was an Aristotelian, Judah Halevy (ca. 1075–1144) an anti-Aristotelian.

The Almoravid domination of Spain (1086–1147 C.E.) and especially the oppressive Almohad rule (ca. 1150–1250) led to a complete deterioration of the status of Andalusian Jews and Christians. Many Jews chose to move to more hospitable places. This was the case of the greatest Jewish intellectual of that period, Moses ben Maimun, or Maimonides (1135–1204), born in Córdoba, who would eventually settle in Cairo as a court physician to the last Fatimids of Egypt. Maimonides, an Aristotelian philosopher, was the author of a fundamental halakhic work. His best-known writing was *More nebohim,* or "Guide of the Perplexed."

Some of the other foremost Jewish intellectuals lived in Christian territory: Levi ben Gerson or Gersonides (1288–1344 C.E.) in Provençe, Hasdai Crescas (ca. 1340–1412) in Saragossa. Yet the Jews were always under the threat of persecution, and eventually those who refused conversion to Christianity were expelled from Spain in 1492 and from Portugal in 1497, whereas those who converted were periodically accused of being *marranos,* a contemptuous word for people suspected of practicing their own religion (Judaism or Islam) in secret. Many of these (9.8 percent) underwent the humiliation of inquisitorial trials and *auto-da-fés,* a number of which ended up in the death of the convicted (1.8 percent). Accusations were usually based on misunderstanding: although genuinely converted, many Jews would still celebrate Jewish feasts, which belonged to their popular culture and had lost religious meaning.

A wave of Sefardi immigrants settled in the Ottoman Empire, in Asia Minor, in the Balkans (e.g., Joseph Caro, 1488–1575, a great halakhic author) or at Safed in Palestine, which would become the intellectual center of the Jews during the second half of the sixteenth century. There the Sefardi kabbalist Moshe Cordovero (1522–1570) would met the Ashkenazi kabbalist Isaac Luria (1534–1572) and his disciples. It was likewise in the Ottoman Empire that the messianic movement of Shabbetai Tsewi (1626–1676) was started, whose prophet was the kabbalist Nathan of Gaza. Shabbatianism entered Poland through the activity of Jacob Frank (1726–1791). In the eighteenth century the vital centers of Judaism moved north. They were Vilna with the yeshiva of Gaon Solomon Zalman (1720–1797); Podolia (Polish Ukraine), where the Baal Shem Tov ("Master of the Good Name [of God]") Israel ben Eleazar (1700–1760) gave rise to the powerful Hasidic movement, and central Poland, where the Hasidim would settle.

Persecuted and dispersed according to the whims of rulers, the oppressed European Jews won many supporters during the Enlightenment. At the end of the eighteenth century, the assimilation of Jews became possible in Germany (1781–1787) and in France (1790), yet their situation remained precarious in Russia and in the neighboring countries until the end of the nineteenth century. During that same period, in Great Britain, Benjamin Disraeli would become prime minister. The Enlightenment had a profound influence on Judaism itself. Moses Mendelssohn (1729–1786) fathered the *maskilim* (singular *maskil,* representative of the Enlightenment) and the *haskalah,* or modernization of Jewish literature. Like all Western people, Jews rediscovered the depth of their own traditions at the beginning of the nineteenth century; with Samuel David Luzzato (1800–1865) and with Nahman Krochmal (1785–1840), they would produce a philosophy of history in which monotheism would become the foremost symbol of Israel. And conservative Judaism redefined itself by contrast with reform Judaism.

The end of the nineteenth century witnessed a massive return of anti-Semitism in all European countries and especially in Russia; yet at the same time the Zionist movement appeared, whose founding fathers were Leon Pinkster (1821–1891) and Theodor Herzl (1860–1905). Haven of freedom for many oppressed Jewish immigrants, the United States would practically become the first modern Jewish homeland, before the tragic events that led to the formation of the state of Israel after a world war during which six million Jews were murdered in Nazi concentration camps. At the turn of the century, the United States had become the center of Judaism and of the eternal debate between reformed, neo-orthodox, and conservative Jews such as Solomon Schechter (1848–1915), the head of the New York Jewish Theological Seminary.

19.8 KABBALAH is a form of Jewish mysticism rooted on the one hand in the grammatological and numerological speculations that led to the *Sefer Yetsirah,* or "Book of Creation" (fourth century C.E.?) and on the other in hekhalot literature. Moshe Idel made a distinction between two Kabbalistic trends throughout history: a "theosophic-theurgic" and an "ecstatic" Kabbalah.

The *Sefer Yetsirah* was already acquainted with the cosmological system that would become classic in Kabbalah: the ten *sephirot*—which probably corresponded to the ten commandments—and the twenty-two paths that connected them, corresponding to the twenty-two letters of the Jewish alphabet. Creation occurred through these thirty-two primordial elements. The *Sefer Yetsirah* and hekhalot literature were the intellectual focus of the Hasidei Ashkenaz, or German Pietist (Jews), among whom the Kalonymus family is especially illustrious: Samuel ben Kalonymus of Speyer (twelfth century C.E.), his son Judah ben Samuel (ca. 1150–1217), and the latter's disciple, the famous Eleazar of Worms (1165–1230). Yet actual Kabbalah did not arise among the Ashkenazim, but among the Provençal Sefardim, who authored the *Sefer ha-Bahir,* or Book of Splendor, in which the *sefirot* were for the first time designated as divine attributes. The first Provençal mystic who studied the *Bahir* was Isaac the Blind (ca. 1160–1235), son of Rabbi Abraham ben David of Posquières (ca. 1120–1198). From Provençe, Kabbalah spread to Catalunya, flourishing in the Gerona circle of the rabbis Ezra ben Solomon, Azriel, and the famous Moses ben Nahman or Nahmanides (1195–1270). In Castilla the immediate precursors of the author of the *Zohar* were the brothers Jacob and Isaac Cohen. The kabbalists of this period devised various techniques of permutation and combination of the letters of the alphabet and of numerology (*temurah, gematria, notarikon*); although their prototypes seemed to be Hellenistic, they were in use in Mesopotamia from time immemorial.

Abraham ben Samuel Abulafia, the great thirteenth-century C.E. Sefardi mystic, was the most outstanding representative of ecstatic Kabbalah, whose goal was *devekut,* or *unio mystica* with God. Abulafia's generation also counted some of the major figures of classical Kabbalah: Joseph ben Abraham Gikatilla (1248–1305) and Moses of Leon (1250–1305), author of the pseudepigraphic *Sefer ha-Zohar* (Book of Splendor), which he attributed to the Tannaite master Simeon bar Yohai (second century C.E.).

Classical Kabbalah integrated hekhalot cosmology in one of the four spiritual universes that prolong each other, from above: *atsilut, beriyah, yetzirah,* and *asiyah.* The universe *atsilut* (Emanation) contained the ten *sefirot* (Keter, Hokhmah, Binah, Gedullah/Hesed, Geburah/Din, Tiferet/Rahamim, Netsah, Hod, Yesod/Tsaddik, Malkhut/Shekinah) that made up Adam Kadmon, the primordial anthropos. The *beriyah* (Creation) universe contained the seven hekhalot and the merkabah. The universe *yetsirah* (Formation) contained the angelic armies. The universe *asiyah* (Making) was the archetype of the visible world. In *asiyah* the presence of the ten sefirot was manifested in the rainbow, the sea waves, the dawn, grasses, and trees.

Kabbalah would develop many mystical techniques—such as visualization of colors and the like—in order to make possible access to the universe *atsilut*. This operation was difficult because of the presence of evil (*sitra ahra*, "the other side") in *asiyah*. Yet it is important to understand that the Kabbalah did not systematically share the Platonic dualism of soul and body or its contempt for this world. Sexuality, for instance, was good to the extent that it effected the merger of entities that had been separated at the descent of the souls in bodies.

All actions of the kabbalist had three goals in view: *tikkun*, or restoration of primordial unity and harmony, both within the individual and in the world; *kavvanah*, or contemplative meditation; and *devekut*, or ecstatic union with God.

Given that scholars such as Moshe Idel believed in the intemporal character of the central doctrines of Kabbalah, synthesis of Isaac Luria, *Ari ha-Kadosh*, the Holy Lion of Safed (*Ari*, Lion, is the acronym of "Ashkenazi Rabbi Ishaq") and his disciples (of whom the most important was Hayyim Vital, 1543–1620) was revolutionary insofar as it envisioned creation as a process of contraction (*tsimtsum*) of God into himself and evil as the active presence of spiritual refuse ("shells," or *qelippot*), fallen due to the "breaking of the vessels" (*shevirat ha-kelim*) supposed to contain them. This cosmic drama resembled the event known as the "fall of Sophia" in Gnosticism; no historical link has been traced, however, between Luria and the Gnostics of early Christianity. Luria simply walked on the same intellectual paths as the Gnostics. And, like certain groups of Gnostics, he also valued positively the reincarnation of the soul, or metensomatosis, which allowed the sage to gain an additional number of souls or "sparks of soul" belonging to illustrious masters.

19.9 SHABBETAI TSEVI. The identification of Shabbetai Tsevi (1626–1676 C.E.) as the expected Messiah was the work of the Lurian kabbalist Nathan of Gaza (Abraham Nathan ben Elisha Hayyim Ashkenazi, 1643/1644–1680), who discovered in the mystic of Smyrna all the signs of divine election, including weaknesses and temptations stemming from the *qelippot*. In his monumental work *Sabbatai Sevi: The Mystical Messiah* (1973), Gershom Scholem minutely reconstructed the history of Shabbatianism. When in 1665 the Messiah was revealed, Nathan took an antinomian attitude, replacing mourning ceremonies with joyful feasts in honor of Shabbetai. He also predicted that the Messiah would take upon himself the crown of the Turkish sultan.

Unfortunately, when Shabbetai set foot in Istanbul in February 1666 the sultan had him arrested, and on 6 September gave him the choice between the gallows and conversion to Islam. To the dismay of his followers, Shabbetai chose the latter. Yet Nathan and many Shabbatianists of the Ottoman Empire understood his choice and decided to convert *pro forma* to Islam, yet continue their antinomian practices. Messianic rejection of the Torah was preached in Poland by the radical Shabbatianist Jacob Frank (1726–1791), who believed himself to be the reincarnation of Shabbetai.

19.10 POLISH HASIDISM is one of the most recent and richest religious syntheses, which contains elements from all historical trends of Jewish mysticism. The founder of Hasidism was the performer of miracles Israel ben Eliezer, called the Baal Shem Tov (acronym Besht), followed by the *maggid,* or itinerant preacher, Dov Baer (1710–1772 C.E.). The movement won many adepts, exasperating the Jewish authorities (the *kehillah*), who opposed to it the ideology of the Enlightenment represented by the *mitnagdim.* After a century of conflict between the two factions, the differences were smoothed down: the Hasidim lost much of their revolutionary impetus, and the *mitnagdim* learned a lesson in ethics. Contrary to traditional Ashkenazi pietism, which consisted of a relentless and inhuman asceticism, the Hasidism of the Besht and his followers—whose leadership would take dynastic shape over time—emphasized the joy of divine omnipresence. The Hasidim would experience *devekut,* which is *aliyat ha-neshamah,* or ascent of the soul in the divine Light. The Hasidim recognized the presence of God in the humblest activities of their bodies and practiced "physical worship" (*avodah ba-gashmiyut*), that is, they would praise God not only in prayer or sacred ceremonies, but also in the middle of the most profane activities such as sexual intercourse, eating, or sleeping. Only intention matters, and if an action is fulfilled with *devekut* in mind then ecstasy will ensue. Dances, songs, and even rotatory movements such as those of the whirling dervishes have *devekut* in view. The accomplished Hasid would descend from contemplative heights to rescue his community, practicing what is called *yeridah le-tsorekh aliyah,* "descent in view of the ascent." The literary legacy of the Hasidim, who have thriving communities in Israel and the United States today, includes stirring legends and collected sayings of spiritual masters.

19.11 BIBLIOGRAPHY. See in general Robert M. Seltzer, *Jewish People, Jewish Thought: The Jewish Experience in History* (1980); Geoffrey Wigoder (ed.), *The Encyclopedia of Judaism* (1989); R. J. Zwi Werblowski and Geoffrey Wigoder (eds.), *The Encyclopedia of the Jewish Religion* (1966); Isidore Epstein, *Judaism* (1959); Julius Guttmann, *Philosophies of Judaism* (1964); Michael Fishbane, *Judaism: Revelation and Traditions* (1987). The best collection of texts relating to Judaism translated in a European language is Samuel Avisar, *Tremila anni di letteratura ebraica*, 2 vols. (1980–1982). An excellent introduction to Jewish scriptures is the volume under editorship of Barry W. Holtz, *Back to the Sources: Reading the Classic Jewish Texts* (1984).

On Ancient Palestine, see W. F. Albright, *Archaeology and the Religion of Israel* (1946), and current works by L. Stager and Gösta Ȧhlstrom, "An Archaeological Picture of Iron Age Religions in Ancient Palestine," in *Studia Orientalia* 55 (1984), 1-31; in general, see Roland de Vaux, *Histoire ancienne d'Israël, des origines à l'installation en Canaan* (1971).

On creation in the Torah, a ground-breaking work was F. M. Cross's *Canaanite Myth and Hebrew Epic* (1973); see also Jon D. Levenson, *Creation and the Persistence of Evil* (1988).

On the prophets, see Joseph Blenkinsopp, *A History of Prophecy in Israel: From the Settlement in the Land to the Hellenistic Period* (1983).

On Jewish festivals, see Julius H. Greenstone, *Jewish Feasts and Fasts* (1945).

On Jewish apocalyptic literature, see John J. Collins, *The Apocalyptic Imagination: An Introduction to the Jewish Matrix of Christianity* (1984); Michael E. Stone, *Scriptures, Sects, and Visiona* (1980); Michael E. Stone (ed.), *Jewish Writings of the Second Temple* (1984); David Hellholm (ed.), *Apocalypticism in the Mediterranean World and the Near East* (1983).

Several translations of the Dead Sea Scrolls are available in English. One of the best introductions to the literature of the Essenes of Qumran is Mathias Delcor and Florentino García Martínez, *Introduccion a la literatura esenia de Qumran* (1982), with good bibliography. The hypothesis of a non-Essene origin of the Qumran manuscripts has its advocate in Norman Golb, "The Problem of Origin and Identification of the Dead Sea Scrolls," in *Proceedings of the American Philosophical Society* 124, 1–24.

Next to the magnificent expositions of the major stages of Jewish mysticism contained in the books of Gershom Scholem, the reader should consult more specialized works such as Ithamar Gruenwald's *Apocalyptic and Merkavah Mysticism* (1980) and *From Apocalypticism to Gnosticism* (1988).

On early Kabbalah, see *The Early Kabbalah,* edited and introduced by Joseph Dan, texts translated by Ronald C. Kiener, preface by Moshe Idel (1986). The best recent synthesis on Kabbalah is by Moshe Idel: *Kabbalah: New Perspectives* (1988). On Safed, see especially R. J. Zwi Werblowski's *Joseph Caro, Lawyer and Mystic* (1977; 1962).

The best work on Shabbetai Tsevi remains Gershom Scholem's *Sabbatai Sevi, The Mystical Messiah: 1626–1676* (1973).

20

Mesopotamian Religion

20.1 THE LAND surrounding the Euphrates and Tigris rivers, modern Iraq, was populated by farmers and herders by the seventh millennium B.C.E., but the development of writing that initiated the prehistoric into history occurred around 3500 B.C.E. Artifacts from the early Ubaid (fifth to fourth millennium B.C.E.) and later Uruk (fourth millennium B.C.E.) periods include fine painted pottery and figurines and increasingly complex and decorative architecture. The people spoke a language that had enduringly named many places and tools by the time the Sumerians appeared in the south, bringing their unique language and eventually a system of tallying and accounting for flocks that would advance into the first writing system. The rise of the Semitic-speaking Akkadians preserved and reinterpreted Sumerian traditions and divinities through centuries of warring city-states and invasions from every direction. From about the eighteenth century B.C.E. we begin to speak of two ebbing and flowing entities, Assyria in the north and Babylonia in the south, and royal archives from these later periods, especially the seventh and sixth centuries B.C.E., supply us with myths and epics already centuries old when they were edited and copied.

20.2 THE GODS. Looking far back into Mesopotamian religion, a picture of the land emerges, for natural forces were the earliest divine forces. Every Sumerian god had a locus, a territory, possession of which was intrinsic to the nature of godhood. In the early collective temple communities, the land was the god's estate, the people his servants, and the priests his stewards and attendants. Rivers and fields had their local gods, whose essence at this early time was not readily severed from the natural phenomena they manifested. Other divine territories were the dynamic forces of nature, both caused and embodied by the gods, such as the thunderstorm (Ishkur/Adad), the swelling bud of the date-palm tree (Amaushumgalna-Dumuzi), and the date storehouse filled with fruit (Inanna).

These primal deities gradually took on human form and social roles at the hands of priests and scribes. Formally at the head of the developing pantheon was An, the sky and father of the gods, whose name was also the sign for sky and divinity. An was already a *deus otiosus* (inactive deity) when written history began in the second half of the fourth millennium B.C.E. More active as leader of the assembly of gods was Enlil, whose chief temple was in the religious center of Nippur. While almost all of the gods eventually acquired a spouse or consort, the great goddess of Mesopotamia was Inanna, assimilated to the Akkadian Ishtar. She was the planet Venus and her domains were fertility, love, and war; her role is prominent in many myths. Her father was the moon god Nanna (Sin), and her brother the sun god Utu (Shamash). Enki (Ea) was the clever god of fresh, irrigating waters who helped humans develop crafts and survive the great flood that was meant to eliminate them. Dumuzi (Tammuz) was a god of fertility and growth in certain animals and plants; in some myths, he was the tragic figure of the dying youth. Nergal was the king of the underworld.

Gods were assimilated into each other and had fluid and multiple natures in all periods. Even with the anthropomorphization of the gods, the land retained its hierophanic nature for centuries, such that the name of a river was likely to be written with the sign for *god* in front of it. Individuals often had personal gods as patrons and protectors, seen on cylinder seals ushering them into the presence of one of the great gods.

20.3 POLITICAL USE OF RELIGION. The Sumerian temple communities were economic, state, and religious institutions: bank, temple, administration of land and labor. Towns had assemblies of elders arbitrating and electing leaders and generals in times of war. These grew in wealth and power into kings and dynasties. As may be expected, kings positioned themselves in favorable relation to the gods, as special favorites or appointed shepherds. The first king to appropriate divine iconography was Naram Sin (ca. 2254–2218 B.C.E.), grandson of the great Akkadian king and conqueror Sargon, who appears on a victory stela wearing the horns of divinity and towering over his men on the field of battle.

Later records show that portents were consulted before military campaigns, and many rulers saw a particular god as the cause and the beneficiary of their successes. The rise of the holy city of Babylon was the rise of its local god Marduk, and indeed Marduk rose to the top of the pantheon, displacing Enlil in the Babylonian *Enuma Elish.* In the Assyrianized version, the eponymous city god Assur was substituted for Marduk's name wherever it occurred.

Royal religion included an elaborate divination system. Astronomical observations, precisely calculated and spreading eventually throughout the world, signaled the sentiments of the gods and portended drought, war, or personal crises of the king. Rituals of prayer, purification, and appeasement were carried out in response to omens gleaned from extispicy (prognostication through examination of animal entrails) or interpreted dreams. The New Year's festival required the participation of the king, as did the early Sacred Marriage rite seen at Uruk, in which the king wed the goddess Inanna to ensure the year's fertility.

20.4 POPULAR PRACTICE. A bureaucracy of professional priests, scribes, astrologers, and craftsmen served the large temple complexes. The daily services for the temple image—feeding, bathing, clothing, entertainment—were performed by select priests. Individual worshipers could leave food offerings or votive statues to stand before the god's altar, and they could participate in the processions and watch the mythic reenactments at festival time. Also for popular consumption we find numerous spells for a couple's fertility, curses, and apotropaics (toward off evil), and incantations to cure specific illnesses and mishaps—such as the spell for a woman to impress onto the face of her adulterously conceived child the features of her husband. These often called on a god or a large number of gods, asked for the reparation of offenses and defilements known and unknown, and in their written versions they had blanks for the insertion of the petitioner's name. Very popular were small terra-cotta figurines of gods and spirits that could be activated by professional magicians and kept in the home or buried under earth floors for protection. As may be seen in a survey of personal names, most of which are theophoric, Mesopotamians of all periods relied on their personal gods for prosperity and health.

20.5 ENUMA ELISH. The Babylonian creation epic *Enuma Elish* (When on High) was associated with the New Year's festival (Akitu) celebrated each spring in the city of Babylon. The story exalted Marduk as the greatest of the gods, and so may have taken the shape in which it is best known in the twelfth century B.C.E., when the kidnapped statue of Marduk was returned to Babylon and the city's preeminence was celebrated through their city god's mythological triumph.

As the first of its seven tablets begins, nothing existed but the two primordial waters, the fresh and the salt sea (Apsu and Tiamat). Gods emerged, and the younger generation of gods disturbed the older with their incessant noise. When Apsu went to battle the younger gods, he was killed by Ea, who then produced a son, Marduk. Tiamat was persuaded to avenge his death, and only the young Marduk dared to face her. He was given kingship over the gods, and he took his winds and lightning to battle. The winds rushed into Tiamat's consuming mouth, and an arrow killed her. Her allies were surrounded and captured, along with the tablets of destiny that her consort Kingu had unrightfully taken.

Marduk then split Tiamat's body in two like a fish, and created the world from it. From the blood of Kingu, he made humans to do the work of the gods. Marduk's reward was supreme sovereignity and a great temple at Babylon. Several elements of this tale have counterparts in Genesis and as images of Yahweh in the Psalms and in Job.

20.6 GILGAMESH. Gilgamesh, king of Uruk, may well have been a king of the early dynastic period, and some of his legendary adventures are preserved in Sumerian. The Akkadian epic as we have it was edited and expanded by a scribe in perhaps the Middle Babylonian period who inserted the flood story of Atrahasis. This most complete version of the epic begins with praise of the monumental building projects of Uruk, a city famed for its Inanna temple and circled with mud-brick walls. Gilgamesh, two-thirds divine and one-third human, tyrannized his people with excessive corvée labor and his rule of sleeping with brides for one night at their marriage. The gods created Enkidu, a wild man of the plains who lived at peace with the animals. A prostitute was sent to humanize Enkidu, and she led him to Uruk, where he and Gilgamesh fought a dramatic battle for superiority in the street. Thus turned into best friends, they went on an expedition to the cedar mountains to kill the monstrous Huwawa. Afterward, Ishtar invited Gilgamesh to marry her, but he insulted her, recalling that all her former lovers ended up in the netherworld. When she revenged herself with the onslaught of the deadly bull of heaven, Gilgamesh and Enkidu killed it. For their offenses, the gods took the life of Enkidu, and Gilgamesh confronted his inevitable destiny—death.

Gilgamesh began a long journey to the source of the rivers to find the one man who attained immortality, the distant Utnapishtim. He journeyed to the mountains and the gate through which the sun passed daily. The fearsome Scorpion man who guarded the gate and his wife allowed Gilgamesh to pass through the tunnel. By the sea at the end of the world, he met Siduri the barmaid, who told him, "When the gods made men, they saw death for men; they kept life for themselves. Thou, Gilgamesh, fill thy belly and make merry by day and night." But Gilgamesh was ferried across the waters of death, met Utnapishtim, and questioned him as to how he obtained immortality.

Here the later editor inserted Utnapishtim's history: how he was warned by Ea of the coming flood, built an ark and filled it, was made one of the gods along with his wife and taken to live in this distant place. This was an abridged variant of the flood stories such as that of the Sumerian tale of King Ziusudra, who was warned by Enki to build an ark to escape the watery erradication of the noisy and irksome human race. Similarly, the composite story of Atrahasis ("the very wise") was an Akkadian language version of the story. In the earlier Gilgamesh text, Utnapishtim challenged Gilgamesh to keep away Death's younger brother Sleep for seven days. But he fell asleep immediately. Utnapishtim sent him home to Uruk; in the later version, Gilgamesh lost to a serpent the rejuvenating thorn plant that made one young in old age. The monuments of Uruk would be his only immortality.

20.7 BIBLIOGRAPHY. Eliade, *H* 1, 16–24; T. Jacobsen, "Mesopotamian Religions: An Overview," in *ER* 9, 447–66.

A comprehensive collection of texts in translation is J. B. Pritchard (ed.), *Ancient Near Eastern Texts Relating to the Old Testament*, 3rd ed. (1969). Good introductions are S. N. Kramer, *The Sumerians* (1963); Jean Bottéro, *La religion babylonienne* (1952). Thorkild Jacobsen's *The Treasures of Darkness: A History of Mesopotamian Religion* (1976) is thorough and sensitively analyzed.

21

Mystery Religions

21.1 THE WORD "MYSTERY" has a rather precise technical meaning and refers to an institution capable of conferring initiation. The ideology of mysteries has two sources: archaic initiations and secret societies on the one hand, and on the other ancient Mediterranean agrarian religiosity. The anthropologist Ad. E. Jensen recorded two early agrarian versions of the myth of origins. Among the Marind-Anim of New Guinea the divinities connected with the epoch of creation were called *dema*. One of the two above-mentioned myths dealt with the death of a *dema* at the hand of the other *demas*. The slain divinity marked the passage from primordial time into historical time, whose traits were death, necessity of sustaining oneself, and procreation by sexual means. The sacrificed divinity was the "first dead"; she turned into all useful plants and into the Moon. The religious cult was a dramatic rendering of the killing of the *dema*, commemorated by the ritual chewing of food items. Jensen gave this mythologeme the name of Hainuwele, the murdered deity of the Wemale of the Ceram island, and related it to the cultivation of vegetables and especially tuberous plants such as potatoes. The other mythologeme, which Jensen related to the cultivation of cereals, consisted of the theft of cereals from heaven and therefore has received the name of Prometheus. Actually, the two myths occur in various geographical areas to account for the appearance of both types of foodstuffs.

21.2 GREEK MYSTERIES. There were no Iranian, Babylonian, or Egyptian mysteries, as some scholars of the past have claimed. The phenomenon of mystery religions was Hellenic. In Greece during the classical period, the most typical mysteries were those of Eleusis, around which Dionysus already appeared in ancient times, yet without having his own mysteries. The Orphics and the Pythagoreans did not have initiatory institutions either. Mysteries accompanied the Cabiri and Cybele and Attis. The Phrygian Attis was the only one among the "dying gods" of the Near East (Tammuz, Adonis, Osiris) who functioned within an organized initiatory cult of Greek origin.

The complex of the mysteries of Demeter and her daughter Kore-Persephone was based on an agrarian ideology and on a mythological scenario that closely resembles the myth of Hainuwele, the Kore of the Moluccans. Like Hainuwele, Persephone disappeared in the depth of the earth, was a lunar deity and presided over the destiny of plants (especially cereals); again like Hainuwele, her sacrificial animal was a piglet.

The Eleusis mysteries belonged to the Athenian state and granted collective initiations. Their secret has been well guarded; yet even without complete data about their sea bath, processions, sacred drama, and symbols of rebirth, one can surmise that the climax of initiation revealed to the citizens of Athens that they shared in a privileged afterlife.

21.3 THE ROMAN EMPIRE. During the Roman imperial period, new divinities were associated with the institution of mysteries: Dionysus, Isis, Mithra, Sarapis, Sabazios, Jupiter Dolichenus, and the Dacian Rider. All these mysteries gave secret initiations and were not mutually exclusive; one could accumulate initiations according to sex, rank, and financial means. Moreover, some mystery gods (Zeus, Jupiter, Helios, Sol, Sol Invictus) showed common traits: they had solar attributes and even shared the same names. This phenomenon is often called "solar syncretism."

During the fourth century C.E., all mystery gods and goddesses were heavenly, often had solar features, and each of them was proclaimed supreme without incurring any contradiction. The hermeneutics that prevailed during that period emphasized that the different names of the mystery gods actually masked their essential identity.

21.3.1 Dionysus. The institutional structures that turned Dionysus into an independent mystery god appeared toward the end of the first century C.E. His cult during this period was particularly rich in eschatological symbols. The afterlife hopes of the Dionysiac initiates were masterfully described by the Platonist Plutarch of Chaeronea (ca. 45–125 C.E.) and were illustrated on many monuments. The soul was supposed to enjoy in afterlife a permanent state of bliss and heavenly drunkenness.

21.3.2 Isis. The stages of initiation into the mysteries of the Egyptian goddess Isis, which seemed to contain authentically Egyptian traits, were mentioned by the Latin writer Apuleius of Madaurus (ca. 125–170 C.E.) in his fantastic novel *Metamorphoses* (or *The Golden Ass*). Unfortunately, Apuleius' description was incomplete and mysterious itself. After a nightly initiation of which he was forbidden to reveal the secret, Lucius, the main character of the novel, received the twelve *stolae* of the initiate, was installed on a wooden platform in front of a statue of Isis, held a torch in his right hand, and was crowned with palm leaves. This ritual symbolized divinization. Lucius was entitled to it after a rite of passage, which he described in these enigmatic terms: "I crossed the border of death and, after having been beyond the threshold of Persephone, I came back being carried through all the elements; in the middle of the night I saw the bright sun shining; I was led before the gods, inferior and superior, and I worshiped them closely." Scholars have interpreted this passage in three different ways: as referring to an expensive staging with machines simulating a journey in Hades; as an ordeal conferring invulnerability; or as a heavenly ascent.

21.3.3 Mithra. Very important among the soldiers of the empire and endowed with a hierarchy steeped in the secrets of astrology, the mysteries of the god Mithra, Iranian by name and Hellenistic by content, took place in special underground temples called *mithraea,* built during certain favorable astral conditions in the shape of a grotto. Initiation had seven degrees, each under the auspices of a different planet:

Korax (Raven)	Mercury
Nymphus	Venus
Miles (Soldier)	Mars
Leo (lion)	Jupiter
Perses (Persian)	Moon
Heliodromus	Sun
Pater (Father)	Saturn

Among Mithraic monuments one of the most frequent was the taurobolium, for example, Mithra killing the bull and surrounded by symbolic animals: a snake, a dog, a scorpion, and so forth. The interpretation of all these symbols was astrological.

A symbolic object called "the seven-gate ladder" (*klimax heptapylos*) was ascribed to the mysteries of Mithra by the second-century C.E. pagan philosopher Celsus in his *True Discourse,* summarized by the Christian apologist Origen. According to Celsus, the ladder was supposed to represent the passage of the soul through the spheres of the planets.

21.3.4 The Dacian Rider. The mysteries of the Dacian Rider, in which a goddess with a fish was prominent and a ram was probably sarificed, were a simplification of Mithraism with the integration of certain religious elements from the Danubian provinces of the empire. Initiation was reduced to three degrees: Aries (Ram), Miles (Soldier), and Leo (Lion), the former two under Mars, the latter under the auspices of the Sun.

21.3.5 Sabazios was an ancient god of the Thracians and the Phrygians; he became a mystery god in the second century C.E. According to the Christian writer Clement of Alexandria (d. before 215 C.E.), the central moment in Sabazios' initiation consisted of the contact of the adept with a golden serpent pulled downward over his breast.

21.3.6 Sarapis, or Serapis, was an artificial god, a synthesis of Osiris and Apis, whose theology was coined in Memphis and developed in Alexandria under the Ptolemies. The main Serapeum, or temple of Sarapis, was at Alexandria, but the god was worshiped in numerous Greek cities by brotherhoods of *Sarapiastai.*

21.3.7 Jupiter Optimus Maximus Dolichenus was an imperial mystery god who received the name of the chief Greek god, also present among the epithets of other mystery gods such as Sabazios or Sarapis. He was originally the sky god of Doliche in Asia Minor, whom the Greeks worshiped as the syncretic Zeus-Oromasdes, and was imported to Rome by the soldiers of the province of Commagene.

21.4 BIBLIOGRAPHY. On mystery religions, see especially the volumes edited by Ugo Bianchi: *Mysteria Mithrae* (1979), and *La soteriol-*

ogia dei culti orientali nell'impero romano (with M. J. Vermaseren) (1982). See also I. P. Couliano, *Expériences de l'extase* (1984); I. P. Culianu and C. Poghirc, "Dacian Rider," in *ER* 4, 195-96, and "Sabazios," in *ER* 12, 499–500.

22

North American Religions

22.1 NATIVE AMERICANS, called Indians because of a 500-year-old misunderstanding, as shown in Elémire Zolla's *The Writers and the Shaman* (1969; 3rd ed., 1989), have been the object of fluctuating hermeneutics imposed by the invaders and their descendants who destroyed their culture. Most of these interpretations, Zolla emphasized, had nothing to say about the Indians themselves: they live in the eye of the beholder, and reflect the dominant conceptions of Euro-Americans at different epochs, such as Puritanism, Enlightenment, Romanticism, and unconditional exaltation of Progress—the latter essentially ambivalent, for it regards the native now with sympathy and now with contempt and suspicion. Yet at all times the colonists ascertained that the Indian showed little interest in his or her advanced civilization, in both its religious and technological aspects. One exception was noteworthy: some Plains Indians who in our imagination, formed by Hollywood Westerns, are inseparable from their horses, had not seen a horse before the eighteenth century, when horses reached the northern continent via Mexico.

State authorities of the eighteenth and nineteenth centuries C.E. were harsh, and genocide needed few supporting arguments. Dutch Calvinists, whose notorious exploits in South Africa were by no means more atrocious than their North American accomplishments, treated Indians like wild beasts and Governor Kieft set a price for any Indian scalp collected in New Holland. Before changing hands, southern New York State and New Jersey had been cleared of Indians. The British kept up the system, raising the bounty: in 1703 in Massachusetts the scalp of an Indian was worth $60, in Pennsylvania a male's scalp earned $134 and a female's $50, in accord with a narrow patriarchal logic, for it is obvious that population growth depends less on males than on females.

The East Coast Indians who were not killed were deported west of the Mississippi River by President Andrew Jackson as a consequence of the 1830 Removal Act, which expelled from their territories even the "good" Cherokees, duly baptized and proud of having access to the "superior" civilization of the colonists.

The explorer Jedediah Smith contemptuously dubbed the Grand Basin Shoshones "diggers" in 1827, noting their deplorable state of poverty and hygiene, symbolic of the Indians in general, who were "barbarous" if not "savage." The Romantic writer Washington Irving, rediscoverer of Muslim Spain, mentioned that even the French trappers, much more favorable to racial integration than the Puritans, found nothing good among the Shoshones, whom they called *les dignes de pitié*, the pitiful. No one was exempt from hideous suppositions. Mark Twain in 1861 corrected Darwin's theories as far as the Indians were concerned: they did not descend from primates, but either from gorillas or from kangaroos or from Norway rats. And in 1867 the Topeka *Weekly Leader*, a worthy heir to the pious Dutchmen, described the natives as "a set of miserable, dirty, lousy, blanketed, thieving, faithless, gut-eating skunks as the Lord ever permitted to infect the earth and whose immediate and final extermination all men, save Indian agents and traders, should pray for." This prayer, which General William Sherman was saying during the same period, was unfortunately answered to a large extent, in spite of the great native revival movements at the close of the nineteenth century. General Phil Sheridan devised a peaceful solution for the extermination of the Indians: the destruction of the buffalo would deprive them of sustenance. However, this attitude was not shared by those early heroes of anthropology, from James Mooney to Franz Boas, who were relentlessly describing the wealth of native beliefs, customs, and societies. Today this strange world is not less exciting or better known than one hundred years ago, for the discovery of new depths and complexities continues to stir the mind of the researcher and the audience, although facts seem sometimes to be mixed up with fiction, as in the stories of the novelist Carlos Castaneda.

22.2 THE ORIGIN OF NORTH AMERICAN INDIANS has been the object of a long debate. That they were the ten lost tribes of Israel was among the most tenacious hypotheses; yet occasionally their background was considered Egyptian, Trojan, or Carthaginian.

The truth is slightly less unexpected. The ancestors of the Indians came from Siberia, crossing an icy Bering Strait in pursuit of game. By eleven thousand years ago, they had reached the tip of South America. North of Mexico there are only a few traces of monumental civilization; North American Indians did not build empires; they defended their ethnic particularism and at the arrival of the first colonists they spoke over five hundred languages.

The far north and the islands are populated with Eskimo; what is Canada was the territory of Indians belonging to two linguistic families: the eastern Algonquins (like the Ojibwa and the Penobscot) and the central and western Athapascans (Yellowknife, Chippewan, Kaska, Slaves, and Beavers).

East and south of the Great Lakes were the territories of the Iroquois and Sioux. Southward the Muskogeans lived together with Algonquins, Sioux, Iroquois, and Caddoans.

The central plains were especially inhabited by Sioux tribes (Assiniboins, Crow, Deghiga, Gros Ventre, Chiwere, Mandan, Arikara, Hidatsa, etc.). The pejorative word "Sioux" originally designated the related tribes of the Dakota, Lakota, and Nakota. Six other linguistic families were present in the Plains: Algonquin (Cree, Cheyennes, Blackfoot), Athapascan (Apaches), Caddoan (Pawnee, Arikaras), Kiowa-Tanoan, Tonkawan, and Uto-Aztec (Comanches, Ute).

The northwest coast consisted of three units: northern (Tlingit, Haida, Tsimshian), central (Bella Coola, Nootka, Kwakiutl), and southern (Salish, Chinook).

The great basin was populated by Indians belonging to a single linguistic family, such as the Shoshones and the Paiute. The plateau and California gave shelter to a great variety of peoples.

Farthest south, six linguistic families were represented: Uto-Aztec, Hokan, Athapascan, Tanoan, Zuñi, and Keres. Their economic classification cut through language grouping. The Indians of the Pueblos or villages for instance, who were all sedentary farmers, spoke languages of the Tanoan (Tiwa, Tewa, Towa), Keres, Zuñi, and Uto-Aztec (Hopi) families. Some of these Pueblos have been uninterruptedly inhabited since the twelfth century.

The Navajos and Apaches are Athapascan Indians who left Canada before the arrival of the colonists.

22.3 THE ESKIMO people, who call themselves *inuit* ("humans"), live along the Arctic coasts of northeastern Asia, Alaska, Canada, and Greenland. The Aleutian islands were inhabited by a people related to the Eskimo. Like the North Siberian peoples, the Eskimo had a shamanistic religion (26). Their livelihood being based on fishing and hunting, they had ceremonies of atonement and propitiation for the spirits of killed game.

22.4 THE NORTHERN INDIANS had complex mythologies about different world ages, each of them with its own mythical beings, such as the culture hero, whose deeds receive particular emphasis. In Alaska, this hero was an animal; elsewhere he was a human being. His stories were often combined or contaminated with Trickster tales.

Rituals played a relatively minor part in the collective life of Canadian natives. The shaman, whose knowledge was revealed in dreams, was the only religious specialist of the region.

22.5 THE NORTHEASTERN INDIANS shared the concept of a sacred power, good or evil, dwelling in certain beings and objects. It was called *manitu* by the Algonquins, *oki* by the Huron, *orenda* by the Iroquois. The power delegated spirits to speak to human beings.

The peoples of the northeast coast have a rich ritual life, with ceremonies of atonement and propitiation for animals slain and edible plants as well as sometimes complex rites of passage. The individual comes to possess personal spirits conjured up through shamanic rites. Spells, masks, and other objects filled with power receive special cults. Among certain tribes such as the Ojibwa, initiatic brotherhoods of medicine men such as the Midewiwin have a prominent role; in other Indian societies they do not exist at all. The religious personality of the region is the shaman, specializing in divination and healing through the technique known as "shaking tent" and through suction of spiritual pathogens from the body of a sick person.

Belief in witchcraft and counteractive rituals were the distinctive trait of the Indians of the southeast coast, such as the Cherokee. Survival of the group depended on certain daily rituals of immersion in water. Among seasonal festivals the most important was the New Year, which took place at the ripening of corn.

22.6 THE PLAINS INDIANS formed a conglomerate of cultures that appeared in the eighteenth century as a result of the migration of many groups of Indians who followed game on horses freshly imported from Mexico. In this natural crucible, cultures integrated and the religious life of distinct Indian peoples—who use English as a lingua franca—assumed some common traits: the Sun Dance ceremony and warlike brotherhoods. The plains became the stage of incessant conflicts. Warriors in search of visions were easy prey for the colonists, who used cheap alcohol in order to rid themselves of the natives. The introduction of hallucinogenic plants such as peyote around 1850 led to the formation of new cults and brotherhoods whose members shared secret rituals and visions.

During the sweat lodge ritual, a group of males would suffer intense heat, whipping themselves with twigs, dancing, and singing. The sweat lodge purified the warrior or the visionary.

The shamans and the medicine men or women of the plains took on the important and remunerated function of master of ceremonies. They formed a caste that, like our physycians, affected a special jargon. A *kurahus,* or old man, led the *hako* propitiatory ceremony among the Pawnee, during which the symbolic ties among generations became more intense. A medicine man (or a woman among the Blackfoot) led the Sun Dance, which initially belonged to one particular medicinal brotherhood (of the Mandan), later becoming the most important religious ceremony of all the tribes present in the region. During the Sun Dance, males endured incredible physical suffering in order to get closer to the Great Spirit. Forbidden around 1880, the Sun Dance reappeared in 1934 and, since 1959, the Ojibwa and Lakota have resumed severe mortifications.

About 1870 the millenarian cult called Ghost Dance spread among the Plains Indians, being encouraged by the Utah Mormons, according to whom the Indians were the ten lost tribes of Israel. The prophet Wovoka announced that the Indians should cease fighting the colonists; they should instead purify themselves and worship the Great Spirit through dance; the Spirit had decided to make an end to the oppression of the invader. An earthquake was supposed to dispose of the colonists, sparing the natives. The suppression of the Ghost Dance movement was not effective. In 1890, the government sent troops who slaughtered 260 innocent Sioux who were traveling to Wounded Knee Creek in South Dakota to perform their ceremonies.

The cult of the Mexican hallucinogen called peyote (from the Aztec *peyotl,* "membrane" (*Lophophora williamsii*) spread among the Plains Indians as the Ghost Dance was appearing. The cult was not illegal until 1964, and court battles over the use of hallucinogens and the legal status of such cults are still in process at the present time. The first book of the novelist Carlos Castaneda, *The Teachings of Don Juan,* which appeared in 1968 under the pretense of being a work of anthropology, was probably intended to present the peyote cult as a true religion.

22.7 THE INDIANS OF THE NORTHWEST COAST, whom we usually associate with the well-known totem poles that they, however, started making only after the colonists had sold them iron tools, lived in a region where fishing always provided them with a wealth of food resources that the hunter tribes could not attain before the arrival of horses from Mexico. The Tlingit, Haida, Tsimshian, Haisla, Bella Coola, Kwakiutl, Nootka, Salish, Makah, Quileute, Skokomish, Chinook, Tillamook, Coos, Tolowa, Yurok, Hupa, and Karok of British Columbia and of the Pacific Northwest of the United States (Washington, Oregon) share many institutions and rituals. Food surpluses as well as the institution of chieftainship explain the strange *potlach* festivals, where one is supposed to distribute gifts to other members of the tribe and to territorial neighbors. The quantity of goods given away is in proportion to one's rank in society; chieftains or those who wish to modify their social status would give away or simply destroy incredible amounts of food or objects. Social hierarchy was consolidated by a complex system of debts: contrary to Western use, debts owed were *not* supposed to be restituted, unless someone intended to dishonor his creditor. For as long as the latter had been able to do someone else a favor, he had accumulated a capital of social respect based upon the *nonreturnability* of his credit. The advantages of rank were of another nature: aristocrats had the privilege of maintaining contact with the ancestral spirits. In a world in which many tribes believed in the preexistence of the soul and in metensomatosis (reincarnation), and in which the cult of the ancestors was extremely important, this was a mark of distinction equal to the marks that only the descendants of particular ancestors were allowed to display.

The institution of shamanism, rarely hereditary and usually open to any individual claiming visions, was known in the whole area. The shaman of a group could function as sorcerer toward another group. Witchcraft was punishable by death.

The Trickster—for example, Raven among the Tlingit—was important in many of the mythologies of the northwestern coast.

The most important regional festival consisted of the ecstatic dances held at wintertime.

22.8 The Californian Indians had a rich religious life, populated with spirits of the ancestors and animal spirits, mythical beings such as the culture hero and the Trickster, and powerful shamans. They pursued visions like the Indians of the plateau, the great basin, and the plains. They had religious festivals for the firstborn, puberty rituals (especially for young girls), and sweat lodges where men exuded their impurity. Yet what is typical for the Californian area was the widespread use of a psychotropic potion extracted from *toloache* (*Datura stramonium* in Nahuatl language), a toxic plant also known in European witchcraft. In certain regions the *toloach* cult, which produced visions, was only accessible to an elite. *Toloache* was used in several collective ceremonies such as funerary rites. One of them evolved into the northern Californian cult *Kuksu* (from the name of the hero-creator of the Pomo Indians), based on the existence of masked secret brotherhoods.

22.9 THE INDIANS OF THE PUEBLOS—thirty-one villages inhabited by natives belonging to six different linguistic families—shared both a sedentary agricultural economy and many beliefs. With the ancient religions of Central America, they had in common the myth of many periodical world creations and world destructions. All of them dealt with supernatural beings called *kachinas,* a word that also designated the masks that impersonate them in the rituals of the Pueblos.

The Hopi Indians have a complex system of religious brotherhoods, each one in charge of one of the periodical festivals. The Kachinas (here also the name of one such brotherhood) would appear in public from March to June, whereas from January to March they would be seen only in the *kivas,* or ceremonial rooms. In February, during the Powamuy festival, children were initiated into the Kachinas cult. In July the Kachinas cycle was closed by the festival of Niman ("return"), after which ceremonies are held without masks. The most important symbols in Hopi ritual life were two: corn, symbolizing life, and bird feathers, supposed to carry the prayers of the humans to the spirits.

The Zuñi Pueblo also had several religious brotherhoods, among which the Kachinas and the Kachina priests.

The Kachina warriors of all Pueblos rose up in 1680 against the Spanish colonists, killing their priests and forcing them to withdraw south. In 1690 all the territory was reconquered by the Spaniards, with the exception of the isolated Pueblo of the Hopis, which was never submitted to forced acculturation. Syncretic cults appeared in the other Pueblos.

22.10 BIBLIOGRAPHY. On the American Indians in general and the history of the colonization of the United States, see Elémire

Zolla, *I letterati e lo sciamano* (1969), English translation *The Writer and the Shaman* (1971); Peter Farb, *Man's Rise to Civilization* (1968); William T. Hagan, *American Indians* (1979).

See also W. Müller, "North American Indians: Indians of the Far North," in *ER* 10, 469–76; J. A. Grim and D. P. St. John, "Indians of the Northeast Woodlands," in *ER* 10, 476–84; D. P. St. John, "Iroquois Religion," in *ER* 7, 284–87; Ch. Hudson, "Indians of the Southeast Woodlands," in *ER* 10, 485–90; W. K. Powers, "Indians of the Plains," in *ER* 10, 490–99; S. Walens, "Indians of the Northwest Coast," in *ER* 10, 499–505; T. Buckley, "Indians of California and the Intermountain Regions," in *ER* 10, 505–13; P. M. Whiteley, "Indians of the Southwest," in *ER* 10, 513–25; Å. Hultkranz, "North American Religions: An Overview," in *ER* 10, 526–35; S. D. Gill, "Mythic Themes," in *ER* 10, 535–41; J. D. Jorgensen, "Modern Movements," in *ER* 10, 541–45; R. D. Fogelson, "History of Study," in *ER* 10, 545–50.

On North American Indian religions in general, see Åke Hultkranz, *Belief and Worship in Native North America* (1983) and *Native Religions of North America* (1988). On Northern shamanistic societies and initiation rituals, the most beautiful book remains Werner Müller's *Die blaue Hütte: Zum Sinnbild der Perle bei nordamerikanischen Indianern* (1954).

On the Ghost Dance, the classic work is James Mooney's *The Ghost-Dance Religion and the Sioux Outbreak of 1890*, abridged edition (1965; 1896); on the peyote cult from the origins to the early 1960s, see Weston La Barre, *The Peyote Cult* (1964).

23

Oceanic Religions

23.1 THE ISLANDS OF THE PACIFIC OCEAN form three clusters called Micronesia, Melanesia (including New Guinea, the Solomon Islands, the Admirality Islands, Trobriand, Fiji, New Caledonia, Santa Cruz, Tikopia, Vanatu-New Hebrides, etc.), and Polynesia (New Zealand, Samoa, Tonga, Tahiti, Marquesas, Hawaii, Easter Island, etc.). The distinction among these three areas is rather artificial, for only Micronesia has distinct cultural traits, due to Asian influences. Micronesia contains four groups of islands (Marians, Carolines, Marshall, and Gilbert), with a total of only 140,000 inhabitants, speaking Malayo-Polynesian languages. Melanesia is more populous and shows great cultural diversity. Polynesia is unique because of its length and the thousands of islands that compose it. Most languages of Micronesia and Polynesia belong to the Austronesian group; in Melanesia most languages are non-Austronesian, related to those of the Australian aborigines.

Numerous concepts of Western anthropology were based on the erroneous interpretation of Oceanic religions—for example, the fieldwork of the English missionary R. H. Codrington (1830–1922) in the New Hebrides (Vanatu) popularized the notion of *mana*. Codrington and others after him like R. R. Marett defined *mana* as a sort of energy-substance (more or less like electricity) that could be stored and spent in order to obtain benefits of different kinds. In reality, *mana* seems rather to be a property that gods confer upon persons, places, and things. In society, *mana* is associated with status and spectacular achievements.

The same way, taboo, from the Polynesian *tapu*, was borrowed from the Maori of New Zealand and became popular among anthropologists and psychoanalysts. *Tapu* is closely related to *mana* and means a divine influence whose effects are usually negative and make certain places, persons, and objects unapproachable or dangerous. Under certain circumstances, *mana* and *tapu* could have the same meaning; yet, in general, *mana* designated a long-lasting, transmissible influence, whereas *tapu* indicates transitory states of possession and can be contagious. Menstrual blood, for example, was *tapu,* that is, contaminated; a menstruating woman should not cook food for other people, in order not to contaminate them. One of the functions of priesthood was to purify places of *tapu.*

For the Western audience, Oceania is above all associated with the research of the British functionalist anthropologist Bronislav Malinowski (1884–1942) in the Trobriand Islands (1915–1918) or with the fieldwork of the French missionary Maurice Leenhardt in New Caledonia (*Do Kamo,* 1947).

23.2 POLYNESIA. About 1500 B.C.E., the vast extension of Polynesia began to be reached and settled by navigators from Indonesia and the Philippines (Lapita culture), who reached Easter Island before 500 B.C.E. About 1200 C.E. eastern Polynesia was colonized. During the sixteenth century C.E. the religious life in the whole area was dominated by the cult of the god Oro, son of the heavenly god Ta(ng)aroa from the island of Raiatea. It was here that the shamanic brotherhood of the Arioi was founded, especially known for its influence and its excesses on Tahiti, which became a religious center around 1800. Divine worship took place in rectangular courtyards called *marae,* surmounted by a pyramidal platform (*ahu*). On Easter Island, the Marquesas, and the Raivavae Islands huge stone statues were erected. The civilization of Easter Island, completely destroyed by the arrival of slave merchants from Peru in the nineteenth century, is a riddle of history. Its inhabitants had established contacts with the Incas before 1500 C.E. and had a boustrophedon writing system called *rongorongo,* which has not so far been successfully deciphered.

23.3 RELIGION. Oceanic religious unity is questionable, yet the idea that most of the gods are ancestors living in another world and paying frequent visits to the human sphere was widely spread in the region. The heavenly creator god was inaccessible, but his feats were told by myths. Tangaroa embraced his wife Earth with such a force that their progeny had to separate the two by force in order to create inhabitable space. The god Tane of the New Zealand Maoris, made, together with his brothers, a woman of earth. Tane blew life in her, but did not know which orifice was intended for procreation and therefore fecundated all of them. Eventually a daughter was conceived, whom he married. She gave birth to the ancestors of the human race. The culture hero Maui, who was also a Trickster, set the length of day and night and caught fishes in his net that became the islands of Polynesia. Thereafter he decided to obtain eternal life by killing the female monster Hine-nui-te-po. But when he was going to enter her vagina in order to exit through her mouth, his companions the birds could not refrain from laughing. Sleeping death woke up and crushed Maui.

Human affairs depended on the multitude of gods. Their will could be disclosed by divination, which presupposed special knowledge, and by spirit possession. The priests of Tahiti and Hawaii practiced extispicy, or reading of the entrails of a sacrificial victim. Wizards were supposed to manipulate the will of the gods in order to do good or evil. The gods were ritually conjured and installed in different objects, usually rudimental statues made for this purpose, or god-catching sticks. When the gods were present, they were offered sacrifices (often human) to obtain from them that for which they had been called. The presence of the gods was defined as *tapu.* Special rites of aspersion (sprinkling with water), treatment with fire, or the presence of a woman were necessary in order to expel the god and reenter a normal state of *noa.*

Death was surrounded by elaborate ceremonies. During this period, the dead had to find their way to the underground kingdom from which they would continue to visit the living, either to haunt them or to answer their inquiries upon request.

23.4 BIBLIOGRAPHY. J. Guiart, "Oceanic Religions: An Overview" and "Missionary Movements," in *ER* 11, 40–49; D. W. Jorgensen, "History of Study," in *ER* 11, 49–53; W. A. Leesa, "Micronesian Religions: An Overview," in *ER* 9, 499–505; K. Luomala, "Mythic Themes," in *ER* 9, 505–9; A. Chowing, "Melanesian Religions: An Overview," in *ER* 9, 350–59; F. J. Porter Poole, "Mythic Themes," in *ER* 9, 359–65; F. Allan Hanson, "Polynesian Religions: An Overview," in *ER* 11, 423–31; A. L. Kaeppler, "Mythic Themes," in *ER* 11, 432–35.

On the prehistory of Polynesia, see Peter Bellwood, *The Polynesians: Prehistory of an Island People* (1987).

24

Prehistoric Religions

24.1 THE WORD "PREHISTORY" covers the immense period of time between the appearance of the first ancestors of the human race at least six million years ago and the first local occurrences of writing (late Uruk pictographic script: second half of the fourth millennium B.C.E.). Actually, the earliest prehistoric remains that can be interpreted in religious terms do not go beyond 60,000 B.C.E. Two methods of interpreting them have generally been adopted: the use of analogue models belonging to known religions of peoples not familiar with writing, or the rejection of such models. The former method, as imperfect as it may be, is the one on which historians of religions have relied. It tries to reconstruct the mental horizon of prehistoric peoples by linking meanings given by different peoples studied by anthropologists to comparable practices that left artifacts in prehistoric remains studied by archaeologists. The recent discipline of ethnosemiology has added credibility to this approach.

One of the clearest examples concerns burial postures of the dead, often imitating the shape of an embryo. No activity conceived by humans is devoid of meaning. Accordingly, any funerary practice should reflect certain beliefs. There is a whole repertoire of meanings associated with burial of the dead: burial may ensure the growth of another being, it may imply survival in an afterlife, resurrection, and so forth. The presupposition of interpretation based on analogy is that, in all probability, prehistoric human beings would associate with such practices a meaning similar to those known to us. Obviously, the use of analogue models has its limitations and will never allow us direct access to the universe of prehistory.

24.2 RELIGION. The humanoid species known under the name of "Neanderthal" and extinct around 30,000 B.C.E. most certainly believed in some kind of survival of the dead, who were buried on their right side, their head eastward. In Middle Paleolithic burial places, primitive quartz tools and red ochre have been found. Certain skulls were deformed in such a way as to suggest extraction of the brain.

The so-called art of the Upper Palaeolithic period (ca. 30,000 B.C.E.) consists of the famous steatopygic ("fat buttocks") "Venuses," often showing prominent sexual characteristics, and of the cave paintings, mostly zoomorphic and ideomorphic, yet sometimes anthropomorphic as well. References to "shamanic séances" have been read by some scholars in the masked characters of the Franco-Cantabrian caves.

During Mesolithic times (ca. 10,000 B.C.E.), when the principal form of economy seemed to be hunting, animals were domesticated and the food value of wild grains was discovered. Male institutions, in which men imitated the behavioral patterns of predators, were dated to the Mesolithic period as well. Into the early 1970s, sociobiological fictions asserted that such imitative behavior was much more ancient and the most important factor in the appearance of the human species. Certain sociobiologists went so far as to believe that murderous aggressiveness would be the fate of our race. In reality, these are groundless hypotheses, based on the personal beliefs of certain scholars. Recently acquired, the behavioral patterns of hunters could not fatally mark the whole destiny of humankind. The Austrian ethologist Konrad Lorenz, whose Nazi sympathies are well known, ascribed to humans alone among all living creatures the lack of natural inhibitions, which would lead to suppression of their fellow humans. This position has been reversed by other sociobiologists, such as E. O. Wilson, while new controversies about social hierarchy and gender have opened up.

The Mesolithic period is associated with several consequential inventions: the bow, the rope, the net, the boat. If we are to believe, with neo-Darwinian sociobiologists, in the economic specialization of sexes, then the merit of the discovery of agriculture would belong entirely to women. This "Neolithic revolution" took place around 8000 B.C.E.; about 7000 B.C.E. a new economy based on the cultivation of cereals appeared in the Mediterranean basin: in Italy, on the island of Crete, in Greece, in southern Anatolia, and in Syria and Palestine (the Fertile Crescent).

With agriculture, the rhythms of life and religious beliefs underwent radical change. Among hunters, human destiny—actually and symbolically—depended on the existence of game; among agriculturalists, symbols changed: human beings now lived in mystical solidarity with the plants on which their sustenance depended, grains in the Mediterranean basin and in Central America and tuberous plants in Southeast Asia and in South America. The mystery of womanhood was the focus of the new religion. Woman represented the sustaining earth and the secrets of regeneration and life eternal; her monthly cycle corresponded to all universal cycles: the moon, the tides, the plants, the seasons. Religious cults were focused on goddesses descending from the Paleolithic steatopygic "Venuses." Statuettes of the goddess have been found at Hacilar, Çatal Hüyük, Jericho (ca. 7000 B.C.E.); their numbers increased during the period that Marija A. Gimbutas calls "Old European," from 6500 B.C.E. to the Indo-European invasions. Gimbutas believes that in Old Europe a peaceful matrifocal culture existed for twenty thousand years, between the Paleolithic and the Neolithic periods. Goddesses were often represented as bird-women or snake-women, had prominent buttocks (which actually could represent testicles on phallic statuettes), and various animals as companions: the bull, bear, goat, deer, frog, turtle, and so forth. The Indo-Europeans, patriarchal nomadic warriors, reversed the religious values of the conquered regions, without managing to suppress completely the old goddesses, who continued to be worshiped under the names of Artemis, Hekate, or Kubaba/Cybele.

The new Iron Age technology was based on a mythology in which metals were supposed to behave like seeds sown in the ground: they attained ripeness only after a long gestation in the earth womb. This was the basis of the ideology present in alchemy.

24.3 MEGALITHIC MONUMENTS. The matrifocal and possibly gynecocratic Neolithic cultures produced some fifty thousand megalithic monuments found in Portugal, Spain, France, England, northern Germany, Sweden, and other places. Among them are temples, tombs, menhirs, and stelae. Interpreting the structure of the monuments and symbols contained in the petroglyphs, Marija Gimbutas has come to the conclusion that they consistently refer to the Great Goddess, often viewed under the terrifying aspect of Queen of the Dead. This interpretation has not been unanimously accepted.

24.4 BIBLIOGRAPHY. Eliade, *H* 1, 1–15; M. Edwardsen and J. Waller, "Prehistoric Religions: An Overview," in *ER* 11, 505–6; M. Gimbutas, "Old Europe," in *ER* 11, 506–15; B. A. Litvinskii, "The Eurasian Steppes and Inner Asia," in *ER* 11, 516–22; K. J. Nartr, "Paleolithic

Religion," in *ER* 11, 149–59; D. Srejovic, "Neolithic Religion," in *ER* 10, 352–60; M. Gimbutas, "Megalithic Religion: Prehistoric Evidence," in *ER* 9, 336–44; J. S. Lansing, "Historical Cultures," in *ER* 9, 344–46.

Numerous topics related to prehistoric religions are discussed in Emmanuel Anati (ed.), *The Intellectual Expressions of Prehistoric Man: Art and Religion* (1983).

25

Roman Religion

25.1 HISTORY. The Italian peninsula before Roman unification hosted populations of various origins, the most important of which were the Greeks of the southern colonies, the Latins in the middle, and the Etruscans north of the Tiber River. The Etruscans (ca. eighth to fourth century B.C.E.) were probably descended from colonists from Asia. From the end of the republic (early first century B.C.E.), they were famous for their (lost) *libri augurales,* interpretations of omens, especially relating to extispicy, or divination through animal entrails. Later accounts of Etruscan religion attribute to it a revealer, Tages, or prophetess, Begoia. Their gods and goddesses tended to form triads, such as the Tarquin Capitoline triad of Tinia (Jupiter), Uni (Juno), and Minerva (fourth century B.C.E.). Etruscan conceptions of their gods and goddesses were influential in the formative period of Roman religion, as abstract forces and phenomena received divine, and human, faces.

The Indo-European people of the Latins, first settled in the central region called Latium Vetus (Old Latium), founded the city of Rome (*Urbs*), traditionally on 21 April 753 B.C.E. During the sixth century B.C.E., the Romans began their territorial expansion at the expense of the other Latins and of the neighboring tribes. A series of semi-legendary kings, the first four Latin and the last three Etruscan, would reign in Rome. The last king, Tarquinus Superbus, was probably expelled by the Romans in 510 B.C.E.; Rome was soon proclaimed a republic. During the republic, the expansionist policy was continued in the whole Mediterranean basin. Military leaders grew in political power and accumulated the foremost public offices. One of them, Caesar, a particularly gifted general, proclaimed himself *dictator perpetuus* (dictator for life) and *imperator* in 45 B.C.E., before being murdered by a group of republican senators on 15 March 44 B.C.E. His nephew Octavian, who would receive the honorific title of Augustus, became emperor in 27 B.C.E. without abolishing the republican institutions, which were kept up *pro forma*. After his death at seventy-six in 14 C.E., Augustus was divinized. In the second century C.E., the Roman Empire covered the whole Mediterranean basin, western, central, and southeastern Europe, and Asia Minor. In 395, the empire was divided in a western zone, conquered in 476 by the Germans, and an eastern zone, the Byzantine Empire, whose name derived from the city of Byzantium, or Constantinople, founded by Emperor Constantine I in 330. That city was virtually all that remained of the Byzantine Empire when it was conquered by the Ottoman Turks, converted to Islam, in 1453.

25.2 ARCHAIC ROMAN RELIGION was based on a divine pantheon and a mythology both of which underwent decisive Greek influence. The earlier Indo-European heritage of the Romans still showed through a large number of autochthonous deities and enigmatic rituals. According to Georges Dumézil, the Romans would systematically submit religion to historical interpretation. For example, the historian Titus Livius (59 B.C.E.–17 C.E.) would present the war between the Romans and the Sabine people as a historical episode from the Roman past; yet among other Indo-European peoples the same story is purely mythological. Dumézil also emphasized the existence of the Indo-European "tripartite ideology" in the ancient Roman triad of male gods Jupiter (sovereignty), Mars (war), and Quirinus (sustenance and protection). Ancient Roman priesthood was in the hands of the king (*rex sacrorum*, a function whose merely religious aspects would be kept up under the republic), the *flamines* of the three gods, also known as *flamines maiores* (*flamen Dialis*, *flamen Martialis*, and *flamen Quirinalis*), and the *pontifex maximus*, or high priest, a function that, starting with Caesar, would belong to the emperors, well after they became Christian.

Often compared with Judaism (19) and Confucianism (8), Roman religion shares with the former an interest in concrete, historical events, and with the latter religious respect for tradition and for social duty as expressed in the concept of *pietas*.

25.2.1 The foundation of Rome was a religious act. Within the city, the autochthonous divinities were worshiped in a narrow inner circle marked by stones and called the *pomerium*, from which military rule (*imperium militiae*) was excluded. The Martial Field was located outside the *pomerium.* There the city was purified every five years through the sacrifice of a bull, a boar, and a ram. More recent gods and goddesses, even when among the most influential such as Juno Regina, were placed *extra pomerium,* in general on the Aventine hill. The temple of Castor was exceptionally installed within the pomerial zone by the dicator Aulus Postumius in the fifth century B.C.E. The archaic intrapomerial deities often have strange names, features, and feasts: Angerona, goddess of the winter equinox; Matuta, goddess of the matrons; and so forth.

The ancient triad of Jupiter, Mars, and Quirinus, flanked by Janus Bifrons and the chthonian goddess Vesta, was replaced during the period of the Tarquins by the new triad of Jupiter Optimus Maximus, Juno, and Minerva. The three gods, who corresponded to Zeus, Hera, and Athene, were represented by statues in Greek and Etruscan fashion. The dictator Aulus Postumius installed a new divine triad on the Aventine, formed by Ceres (Demeter), Liber (Dionysus), and Libera (Kore) (12.3). Like other empires in expansion, the Romans adopted local gods from the occupied territories. Among the most famous was the lunar goddess Diana of Nemi, patron of fugitive slaves, whose cult was transferred to the Aventine.

25.2.2 The domestic cult, whose center was the hearth, consisted of animal oblations and offerings of food and flowers to the ancestral *lares* and *penates* and to the spirit protecting the place. Marriage was celebrated by the hearth under the propitious influence of female deities such as Tellus or Ceres; later on, Juno became the warrant of marital oaths. Twice every year the city held a festival in honor of the spirits of the dead, the *manes* and *lemures,* who returned to the earth and ate the food left at their tombs.

Starting in 399 B.C.E., the Romans offered increasingly important sacrifices, called *lectisternia,* to three pairs of gods whose statues were displayed in the temples: Apollo/Latona, Hercules/Diana and Mercury/Neptune.

25.2.3 Roman priests belonged to the pontifical college, which included the *rex sacrorum,* the *pontifices* with their chief the *pontifex maximus,* the three *flamines maiores,* and the twelve *flamines minores.* Six vestals were attached to the pontifical college. They were chosen between the ages of six and ten for a period of thirty years, during which they were supposed to retain virginity. If they ignored the oath of virginity, they might be walled up alive. An analogue institution was known among the imperial Incas. The vestals were in charge of the sacred fire.

The augural college used Etruscan books (*libri haruspicini, libri rituales,* and *libri fulgurales*) and Greek texts (the Sibylline Oracles, of which Jewish and Christian imitations exist) in order to determine if an occasion was propitious (*fas*) or not (*nefas*). Other specialized religious groups existed in Rome, such as the Fetiales, the Salian priests, the *Fratres Arvales,* protectors of the fields, or the *Luperci* (young wolves), who celebrated the *Lupercalia* on 15 February by running around the Palatine striking women with lashes made of goatskin in order to make them fertile. The word *lupa,* she-wolf, was a synonym for prostitute and designated unleashed sexuality. Double meanings can be read in the myth of the foundation of Rome: Romulus and his brother Remus had been brought up by a *lupa,* a she-wolf.

25.3 THE EMPIRE. Roman religious fervor increased during the imperial period, as Arnaldo Momigliano so well noted. Caesar and Augustus were divinized after death. And, even if their successors were not automatically changed into gods upon death, this early precedent was exploited later, when the emperor and even his favorites received divine honors during their lifetimes. Caesar was also the first to combine the military function of *imperator* and the religious function of *pontifex maximus.* All other emperors would do likewise. Like the worship of ancient gods, the imperial cult had its priests and ceremonies. Temples were dedicated to emperors in the territories under Roman rule, either individually or in association with some venerable predecessor or with the newly created goddess Roma. During the third century C.E., the emperors identified themselves with patented gods: Septimius Severus and his wife Julia Domna were worshiped as Jupiter and Juno.

25.4 THE IMPERIAL CULT was an innovation that marked the end of traditional Roman religion and the flowering of its decadent, or *kitsch,* period. Yet the epoch is religiously quite lively and productive along other lines: the Hellenistic-Roman synthesis (13) and mystery religions (21). In order to stop the expansion of Christianity, pagan writers would resort to Platonic exegesis of ancient myths, conferring upon them a new and vigorous symbolism. Celsus during the second century

C.E.; Porphyry during the third century; and the emperor Julian (d. 363 C.E.), the "pagan party" of Symmachus, and the Platonists Macrobius and Servius at the end of the fourth century would oppose the Christian totalitarian worldview with a pluralistic religious proposal whose hermeneutical key was Platonic. They strove toward the understanding and acceptance of all religious beliefs of the past, even those that at first sight were most contrary to reason. Philosophers turned to ascetic self-perfection, and philosophy turned to dogma. The Roman elite would choose from this vast pagan synthesis until the fall of the empire, when there was no room left for such subtleties; yet they would continue their underground existence in the Byzantine Empire.

25.5 BIBLIOGRAPHY. Eliade, *H* 2, 161–68; R. Schilling, "Roman Religion: The Early Period," in *ER* 13, 445–61; A. Momigliano, "The Imperial Period," in *ER* 13, 462–71, with good bibliography. See Georges Dumézil, *Archaic Roman Religion,* 2 vols., translated by P. Krapp (1970); Robert Schilling, *Rites, cultes, dieux de Rome* (1979); Ramsey MacMullen, *Paganism in the Roman Empire,* (1981).

26

Shamanism

26.1 SHAMANISM is not a religion per se, but a system of ecstatic and therapeutic methods whose purpose is to obtain contact with the parallel yet invisible universe of the spirits and win its support in dealing with human affairs. Shamanism is present in the religions of all continents and at all levels of culture; yet its center is central and northern Asia.

The word *shaman,* from the Tungus language, means "sorcerer." The common Turkish word that designates the shaman is *kam.* The Yakuts, Kirgizes, Uzbeks, Kazaks, and Mongols use other words. The great shaman during the period of the Mongol invasions was called *beki,* from which derives the Turk word *beg,* "lord," which became *bey.* Muslim historians ascribe to Gengis Khan himself shamanic powers.

The Turks, the Mongols, and the Tungus-Manchus belong to the Altaic family of languages, which succeeded the more ancient Ural-Altaic family to which the Finns, Hungarians, Estonians, and several other Asian peoples also belonged. Several of these peoples would later convert to one or even more than one of the universal religions: Buddhism, Christianity, Islam, Judaism, Manicheism, Zoroastrianism. In such cases, the institution of shamanism has to be sought either in the historical past or in the modern survival of disavowed beliefs and practices from the past.

The recent discipline of ethnosemiotics attributed a shamanic origin to ancient Siberian cave paintings (ca. 1000 B.C.E.), because of common distinctive traits displayed by the painted costumes and by shamanistic rituals as described by anthropology. This research finds confirmation in Greek sources from the sixth century B.C.E., which suggest that a local type of shaman who could bilocate, travel to the underworld and the North, and take animal form, existed in Greece and would still exist in the fifth century. Local shamans may be inferred from the written evidence of other ancient religions (Iranian, Chinese, Tibetan, etc.), as well as from anthropological research among peoples without written records, who lived in conditions of relative isolation, such as the Australian Aborigines. Shamanism needs to be studied in a new perspective that combines history of culture and historical psychology. While such a discipline does not yet exist, it is clear that shamanism flourished among the Turkish, Mongolian, Himalayan, Finno-Ugrian, and Arctic peoples of central and northern Asia and in other areas as well (Korea, Japan, Indochina, and the two Americas).

26.1.1 Siberia. Among the hunters and fishers of northern Siberia, the shaman had different functions, based on the existence of a clan (Yukagirs, Evenki), or neighborhood (Nganasani), or across society (Chukchees, Koriaks). In the agricultural south (Yakuts, Buriats, Tuvin, Khakases, Evenki, etc.), the institution of shamanism was more complex. The status of shamans varied according to their personal powers. Even when they inherited the shamanic vocation from their parent, Siberian shamans were supposed to undergo individual initiation that consisted both of transmission of knowledge and of the acquisition of supernatural aid from the spirits. Visited by the spirits, the shamans first went through a period of deep depression and psychic illness that would only give way when, having crossed the desert of death, they returned to life and learned how to control the spirits in order to perform ecstatic journeys whose purpose was usually curative. During their performances, the shamans used several objects that symbolized their special faculties and helped them to reach the land of the spirits: the drum made from a tree, symbolizing the cosmic tree; the cap; and the costume that associated the wearer with the spirits and at the same time recalled a skeleton—symbol of initiatory death and resurrection. The séance started with shamans calling upon their auxiliary spirits; then, in a state of trance that was not necessarily obtained through the use of hallucinogenic or intoxicating agents, they traveled to spirit land. In central and eastern Siberia—among the Yukagirs, Evenki, Yakuts, Manchus, Nanay, and Orochi—shamans were often possessed by the spirits who spoke through them.

26.1.2 Arctic Shamanism. The system of shamanism existed among all Arctic peoples, who belonged to different linguistic groups:

Uralic (Saami or Lapps, Komi or Zyrians, Samoyeds and the Finno-Ugrians Khantys or Ostiaks, and Mansi or Voguls), Tungus (Evenki, Eveny), Turkish (Yakuts, Dolgans), Yukagir (Yukagirs, related to the Finno-Ugrians), Paleosiberian (Chukchee, Koriaks, Itelmen), and Inuit (Aleuts). Less complex than in southern Siberia, shamanic séances among the Arctic peoples were nevertheless more intense. In some cases shamans, like their North American Algonquin colleagues, would be tied in a closed tent during the "shaking tent ceremony." The tent was indeed violently shaken, allegedly by the spirits; at the end of the performance, the ropes of the shaman were untied.

Most of the Inuit live in Greenland, in Canada, and in Alaska. Before obtaining shamanic powers, they go through the shocking experience of death. They practice healing through suction and the divination technique called *qilaneq,* which consists of variations in the weight of an object held in the hand in response to the answers of the spirits to different questions. *Quamaneq,* or skeleton visualization, is a widespread technique practiced during the period of attainment of shamanic powers.

26.1.3 In Korea and Japan shamanism was usually practiced by women. Being blind was the sign of a sure vocation. In northern Korea the female shaman was recruited by the spirits; in the south she inherited her function from her parents. She was not spared sickness; sometimes she was visited by a spirit lover, in which case marital life might grow intolerable.

26.1.4 Border peoples. Shamanism was also present among the border peoples of Tibet, China, and India (Miau, Na Khi, Naga, Lushei-Kuki, Khasi, etc.), as well as among the peoples of Indochina (Hmong, Khmer, Lao, etc.), Indonesia, and Oceania.

26.1.5 North American shamanism, like Arctic shamanism, was not originally based on the use of hallucinogens. Shamanic powers were obtained in different ways, the most common being solitude and suffering. In some geographic areas, the shamans formed professional associations. The members of the Great Medicine Society (Midewiwin) of the Great Lakes initiated candidates by "killing" them (shooting at them cowries or other symbolic objects supposed to pierce their bodies and "resuscitating" them in the medicinal cabin. The extraction of spirits of sickness through suction was widespread.

26.1.6 South American shamanism was rich in all beliefs and practices already mentioned in connection with other areas: initiatory sickness, visualization of the skeleton, marriage with a spirit, healing by suction, and so forth. Peculiar to South American shamanism were the use of hallucinogens such as the *Banisteriopsis caapi* or *yagé* or intoxicating substances such as tobacco, and the presence of collective ceremonies of initiation. Rattles were used to conjure up spirits more frequently than drums. Spirits were often ornithomorphic. The shaman's transformation into a jaguar was common.

26.2 BIBLIOGRAPHY. Eliade, "Shamanism: An Overview," in *ER* 13, 201–8; A.-L. Siikala, "Siberian and Inner Asian Shamanism," in *ER* 13, 208–15; S. D. Gill, "North American Shamanism," in *ER* 13, 216–19; P. T. Furst, "South American Shamanism," in *ER* 13, 219–23; A. Hultkranz, "Arctic Religions: An Overview," in *ER* 1, 393–400; I. Keivan, "Inuit Religion," in *ER* 7, 271–73.

In general, see Mircea Eliade, *Shamanism and Archaic Techniques of Ecstasy* (1964); Matthias Hermanns, *Schamanen, Pseudoschamanen, Erlöser und Heilbringer,* 2 vols. (1970).

27

Shinto

27.1 THE NATIVE RELIGION OF JAPAN is a vast complex of beliefs, customs, and practices that at a later stage received the name *shinto,* in order to be distinguished from religions coming from China, including Buddhism (*butondo*) (3.9) and Confucianism (8). With Catholic Christianity, which landed in Japan in 1549 C.E., these remain the four main religions of the Japanese archipelago.

The word *shinto* means "Way (*to,* Chinese *tao*) of the *kami*" or tutelary divinities of everything.

27.2 SOURCES. The most ancient source concerning the ethnic traditions of Japan is the *Kojiki* ("Report of Ancient Things"), compiled about 712 C.E. by the officer Ono Yasumaro at the orders of the empress Gemmei, from a singer with an infallible memory. The *Kojiki* contains the history of Japan from the creation of the world to 628 C.E.

The *Nihongi* ("Chronicles of Japan") in thirty-one volumes (of which thirty have survived) is a vast compilation completed in 720 C.E. Other data concerning Japanese primordial beliefs are contained in the *Fudoki* (eighth century C.E.). the *Kogo Shui* (807–808 C.E.), the *Shojiroku* (815 C.E.), and the *Engi-Shiki* (927 C.E.). Chinese documents since the Wei dynasty (220–265 C.E.) constitute a precious source of information on ancient Japan.

Archaeology reveals to us the existence of a neolithic culture (*Jomon*), from which survive female clay statuettes (*dogu*) and (phallic?) cylinders of polished stone (*sekibo*). During a subsequent period (*Yayoi*), the Japanese practiced scapulomancy (divination by shoulder blade or scapula) and turtle-shell divination. The burial of bodies in squatting positions during the Kofun period poses intriguing hermeneutical problems for the discipline of history of religions.

27.3 MYTHOLOGY. These problems are not the only difficulties the student of Japanese religion faces. Ancient Japanese mythology seems like a combinatory variant of other world mythologies, perhaps better known to the Western reader. Yet, despite the attempts of ancient and new authors from Augustine to Claude Lévi-Strauss, there is to date no convincing explanation for the basic unity of all world mythologies. (To say that this unity rests on the uniformity of logical operations is ingenious, yet implausible; for this would imply among other things the existence of a masked system that would direct binary classification, a sort of a myth-making machine in the human brain.)

The first five divinities of Shinto appeared spontaneously from chaos. Following a series of couplings, Izanagi and his sister, Izanami, were born; from the floating heavenly bridge, they created the first Japanese island by stirring the salty sea water. There they settled and discovered sexuality by observing the movements of a wagtail. The product of their intercourse, during which a mistake occurred, was Hiruko (Leech), who did not satisfy his parents, for at the age of three he was still unable to stand (the mythologeme of the defective firstborn is widespread on all continents). Having had intercourse again, Izanagi and Izanami gave birth to the Japanese islands and to the *kami,* until the fire *kami* burned his mother's vagina, killing her. Enraged, Izanagi beheaded his clumsy offspring, from whose blood many other *kami* sprouted. Like Orpheus, Izanagi then went to hell (the Land of the Yellow Spring) in order to recover Izanami, who was being kept prisoner there for having tasted of hellish food (the Persephone myth). However, Izanagi counted on the cooperation of the god of the underworld, who released Izanami on the condition that she abstain from visiting her husband during the night. Yet Izanami did not keep her promise, and Izanagi, in the light of an improvised torch, saw his wife turned into a rotten corpse covered with vermin. Eight Furies, the Awful Hags of Night Land, pursued Izanagi, but he threw back his headgear, which turned into a vine. The Furies stopped to eat the grapes. This episode, which is a common theme in fairy tales the world over, was repeated three times, the consecutive obstacles being bamboo shoots and a river. Izanagi having escaped, Izanami herself now pursued him, together with the eight *kami* of Thunder and the fifteen hundred Warriors of Night Land. But Izanagi blocked with a boulder the narrow passage between the infernal realm and this world; over this boulder resounded the harsh words that marked the definitive separation of the couple. Their arrangement was that Izanami would take one thousand of the living into her kingdom each day, while Izanagi would cause fifteen hundred to be born daily, and thus the world would not be depopulated. Purifying himself from the pollution caused by his contact with death, Izanagi gave birth to the most important *kami* of the Shinto pantheon, the sun goddess Amaterasu (Great Heavenly Light) and to the trickster god Susa-no-o.

Countless successive generations of *kami* filled the gap between the primordial gods and human beings. A number of mythical cycles, of which the most important are those of Izumo and Kyushu, are focused on particular gods. The people of Kyushu are said to come from the (mythical?) land of Yamato; they became the first emperors of Japan.

27.4 THE KAMI. Ancient Shinto shows special reverence to the *kami,* omnipresent manifestations of the sacred. In the beginning, the *kami*—be they natural forces, worshiped ancestors, or simple concepts—did not have sanctuaries of their own. Their territory was only marked during the celebration of rites in their honor. The traditional Japanese economy being agricultural, most rites and festivals were seasonal. Besides participating in collective ceremonies, Shinto believers also communicated individually with sacred realms and entities. The institutions of shamanism (26) and possession cults are ancient and based on a primary cosmology that entails either three vertical layers (heaven, earth, netherworld) or two horizontal layers of the universe (earth and Tokoyo, or "perpetual world").

Early on, every structured social group possessed its own *kami.* Later, imperial unification led to the imperialism of the imperial *kami,* the goddess Amaterasu Omikami. In the seventh century C.E., under the influence of the Chinese political system, a central office registered all gods of the empire, for the central government to build sanctuaries for them and pay them the due worship. By the tenth century C.E., the government was thus overseeing nearly three thousand sanctuaries.

Buddhism, introduced to Japan in 538 C.E. and encouraged by the state during the eighth century, produced interesting syntheses with Shinto. The *kami* were soon identified with Buddhist *devas,* or gods; later on, they were allotted the superior role of avatars of the Bodhisattvas. An active exchange of iconography took place between Buddhas and *kami.* During the Kamakura shogunate (1185–1333 C.E.), a flowering period for Japanese Buddhism, a Tendai Shinto and a Tantric or Shingon Shinto appeared. During the Edo (Tokyo) epoch (1603–1867 C.E.) Shinto merged with Confucianism, forming the Shuiga Shinto. Although the main goal of the Shinto Revival (Fukko) of Motoari

Norinaga (seventeenth century C.E.) was to restore Shinto to its original purity, criticizing every mixture with Buddhism or Confucianism, the movement ended up making an opening to the fourth great Japanese religion, Catholic Christianity, adopting the idea of the Trinity and Jesuit theology. Whereas during the Tokugawa period (Edo period, 1603–1867 C.E.) the synthesis between Shinto and Buddhism had been made into state religion, during the successive Meiji period (after 1868) pure Shinto became the official religion.

27.5 MODERN SHINTO. The Meiji religious reform led to four branches of Shinto: Koshitsu, or imperial Shinto; Jinja, or sanctuary Shinto; Kyoha, or sectarian Shinto; and Minkan, or popular Shinto.

Imperial rites were private, but they exerted a strong influence on sanctuary Shinto, which was the official religion of Japan between 1868 and 1946. Today Shinto is protected by a central association (*Jinja honcho*).

A Shinto sanctuary is the abode of a *kami*, who is connected with a natural site: a mountain, a grove, a waterfall. When it is not set in nature, the Shinto sanctuary must nevertheless contain inside a symbolic landscape. A temple is a simple wooden structure (as in Ise or Izumo), often enriched with elements borrowed from Chinese architecture. According to tradition, every sanctuary must be rebuilt every twenty years.

Purification rites are essential to Shinto. They consist of certain abstentions preceding the great ceremonies or accompanying menstruation or death. Originally they were practiced by all believers; today they are only performed by the Shinto priest. Only the latter can celebrate the *harai* purifying rite with a rod called *haraigushi*. Purifications are followed by an offering of shoots of the sacred *sakaki* tree, symbol of the crops. Rice, sake, and other offerings, accompanied by music, dance, and prayers (*norito*) to the *kami* are at the center of the ceremony.

In his or her sanctuary, the *kami* is represented by a symbol (e.g., a mirror would symbolize Amaterasu) or, under Buddhist influence, by a statuette. During the festival called *shinko*, or circumambulation of the district, the symbol of the *kami* is carried in procession through the neighborhood. A propitiating ceremony called *jichin-sai* takes place on the site of a new building in order to appease potentially dangerous *kami*. Shinto practice, both collective and individual, is called *matsuri*. Traditionally, a Japanese house possessed a *kamidana*, or private altar, in the middle of which stood a miniature temple where the presence of the *kami* was evoked by symbolic objects.

27.6 NEW SECTS. During the State Shinto period (1868–1946 C.E.), when the priests were state clerks depending on the Jingikan or Shinto department, the government was on the other hand obliged to proclaim religious freedom in Japan, which in the first instance meant the cessation of the ban on Christianity. Yet the 1896 Meiji constitution made room at the same time for restrictive political applications, to the extent that a religion could not rightfully exist if it was not officially recognized by the state. The Jingikan therefore had the often-difficult task of classifying the new religions that appeared starting in the second half of the nineteenth century. Although their relation to Shinto was often liminal and problematic, thirteen new cults, twelve of them founded between 1876 and 1908, were classified as Shinto sects: Shinto Taikyo (without a founder, recognized in 1886), Kurozumikyo (founded by Kurozumi Munetada in 1814), Shinto Shuseiha (founded by Nitta Kuniteru in 1873), Izumo Oyashirokyo (founded by Senge Takatomi in 1873), Fusokyo (founded by Shishino Nakaba in 1875), Jikkokyo (founded by Shibata Hanamori, recognized in 1882), Shinto Taiseikyo (founded by Hirayama Shosai, recognized in 1882), Shinshukyo (founded by Yoshimura Masamochi in 1880), Ontakekyo (founded by Shimoyama Osuka, recognized in 1882), Shinrikyo (founded by Sano Tsunehiko, recognized in 1894), Misogikyo (founded by the disciples of Inone Masakane in 1875), Konkokyo (founded by Kawate Bunjiro in 1859), and Tenrikyo (founded by a woman, Nayakama Miki, in 1838, recognized in 1908, separated from Shinto in 1970; it gave rise to the Honmichi sect). Since 1945 many "new sects" have appeared; a 1971 poll counted forty-seven of them.

Japanese shamans were traditionally women. Several recent religions are led by women and attribute certain particular charisms to women.

27.7 JAPANESE "POPULAR RELIGION," or *minkan shinko,* has many points in common with popular Shinto, yet remains distinct from it. It consists of a number of rites—propitiating, seasonal, and special—borrowed from Japan's three main religions. Indeed, it is often said that the Japanese would live as Confucians, marry in Shinto, and die as Buddhists. At home, they might have a Shinto and a Buddhist altar.

They would respect geomantic prescriptions (e.g., the door of a house should never face northeast) and the calendar of lucky and unlucky days. Among the many festivals they celebrate, the most important are the New Year, or *shogatsu;* the Spring Festival, *setsubun,* on 3 February; the Feast of the Puppets, or *hana matsuri,* on 8 April; Boys' Day, *tango no sekku,* on 5 May; the Water Kami festival, *suijin matsuri,* on 15 June; the Star Feast, *tanabata,* on 7 July; the Festival of the Dead *bon* on 13–16 July; the autumn equinox, *aki no higan;* and others.

Rites and festivals are performed either by an extended family group (*dozoku*) or by a neighborhood (*kumi*).

27.8 BIBLIOGRAPHY. J. M. Kitagawa, "Japanese Religion: An Overview," in *ER* 7, 520–38; Hirai Naofusa, "Shinto," in *ER* 13, 280–94; A. L. Miller, "Popular Religion," in *ER* 7, 538–45; Matsumae Takeshi, "Mythical Themes," in *ER* 7, 544–52; H. P. Varley, "Religious Documents," in *ER* 7, 552–57.

Shinto texts are translated and introduced by Post Wheeler, *The Sacred Scriptures of the Japanese* (1952).

The best single work on Japanese religions is by Joseph M. Kitagawa, *Religion in Japanese History* (1966); see also H. Byron Earhart, *Religions of Japan* (1984). The journal *History of Religions* dedicated its third issue in 1988 to Shinto: *Shinto as Religion and as Ideology: Perspectives from the History of Religions,* containing articles by J. M. Kitagawa and others.

On new Japanese religions, see especially the beautiful book by Helen Hardacre, *Kurozumikyô and the New Religions of Japan* (1986).

On religious policy in present day Japan, see *Japanese Religion: A Survey of the Agency for Cultural Affairs* (1972).

28

Slavic and Baltic Religions

28.1 THE SLAVS made their appearance in European history around 800 B.C.E., but their expansion took place some 1,400 years later, when Proto-Slavic languages split in three branches: West, South, and East Slavic. In the tenth century C.E., the Slavs inhabited the territory between Russia and Greece and between the rivers Elba and Volga. West Slavic would give birth to Polish, Czech, Slovak, and Wendic (disappeared); South Slavic to Slovenian, Serbo-Croatian, Macedonian, and Bulgarian; East Slavic to Russian and Ukrainian. The Slavs were Christianized during the eighth and ninth centuries C.E.

The written sources on Slavic religion do not predate the sixth century C.E. (Procopius of Caesarea). The most important among them are the *Kiev Chronicle* (twelfth century C.E.,) about the Christianization of Russia under Vladimir I (988 C.E.), and the chronicles of the antipagan campaigns of the bishops Otto of Bamberg (twelfth century; written by Ebbo, Herbord, and an anonymous monk of Priefling), Thietmar of Merseburg, and Gerard of Oldenburg (Helmond of Bosau), concerning the western Slavs. The only direct sources are archaeological and consist of a few temples and statues. Slavic folklore preserves the memory of certain pre-Christian gods.

28.1.1 Gods. The *Kiev Chronicle* mentions seven Slavic gods: Perun, Volos, Khors, Dazhbog, Stribog, Simarglu, and Mokosh. These gods received sacrifices. Marija Gimbutas believes that Khors, Dazhbog, and Stribog were aspects of a solar deity called White God (Belobog); among western Slavs, this god, whose opponent was the infernal god Veles, received the names Iarovit, Porovit, and Sventovit. In the *Chronica slavorum,* Helmond mentions a sky god, father of the gods, who did not meddle in human affairs. This function befell Perun, god of thunder, whose name derived from the root *per-*, "to hit"; in Polish, *piorun* means "lightning." Among the Balts (Lithuanians), the name of the storm god Perkunas was derived from the Indo-European word for oak, a tree often dedicated to sky gods. The Rurikid dynasty of Kiev, whose origin was Scandinavian, worshiped under the name Perun the Germanic god Thor, whose mother, according to Norwegian mythology, was Fiorgynn (from "oak"). After the Christianization of Russia, the mythology of Perun was transferred to Saint Elias "the thunderer" (*gromovnik*), whose festival on July 20 contained penance ceremonies. As administrator of rain, Saint Elias was held directly responsible for the crops.

The Slavs knew countless supernatural beings, male and especially female. Among the former were the domestic spirits called *ded,* or *dedushka,* (grandfather or little grandfather); the *leshii,* or forest spirits; and the ancestors. Female supernatural beings were dominant: Mat' Syra Zemlia (Mother Wet Earth), Mokysha (see Mokosh in the twelfth-century list of gods; she was a goddess of fate), Baba Yaga (cold, ugly, deadly), Ved'ma the witch, water nymphs (*vilas*), tree nymphs (*rusalkas*), and so forth.

28.2 THE BALTS entered European history by the mid-second millennium B.C.E., yet written sources about them do not exist before the tenth century C.E., when the Germans and Danes began the occupation of their territory. During this conquest, concluded in the fourteenth century with the Christianization of the Balts, the Lithuanians and the Estonians kept their identity, whereas the Old Prussians, or Pruthenes, were completely assimilated by the conquerors.

28.2.1 Gods. Like the Slavic pantheon, the pantheon of the Balts had three main divinities: an inactive sky god (Lithuanian *dievas,* Lettonian *dievs,*) a thunder god (Lithuanian Perkunas, Lettonian Perkuons) and a solar goddess, Saule, whose function was not the same as the function of the Slavic infernal god Veles. Side by side with them were Mother Earth (Lettonian *zemen mate*) and countless female supernatural beings called "Mothers."

28.3 BIBLIOGRAPHY. Eliade, *H* 3, 249–51; M. Gimbutas, "Slavic Religion," in *ER* 13, 353–61; H. Biezais, "Baltic Religion," in *ER* 2, 49–55.

29

South American Religions

29.1 SOUTH AMERICA is a vast continent inhabited by a great variety of peoples, difficult to classify. Probably the following geographical classification is the most common:

1. The Andean region, from Columbia to Chile, where flourished the Peruvian culture of the Incas;
2. The tropical forest, largely covered by the Amazon jungle;
3. The Gran Chaco area;
4. The southern area, up to Tierra del Fuego.

Some cultures survived the European conquest, such as those of the Quechua and Aymara of Peru and Bolivia and the Araucans of Chile; those of the Tupis, Caribes, Arawak, Tukano, and Pano in Guyana; those of the East Brazilian tribes; and those, today extinct, of the Tierra del Fuego natives such as the Selk'nam.

No general synthesis of South American religion existed prior to the publication of Lawrence E. Sullivan's *Icanchu's Drum* (1988). The reader who desires a careful yet comprehensive investigation into this topic can now rely on this unique work, written for a broad, nonspecialist audience.

29.2 THE ANDEAN REGION. The great cultures of the Andes, of which the Inca civilization (fifteenth century C.E.) is the most famous, evolved on remote mountainsides and valleys already populated ten thousand years ago. During the Spanish conquest, the Inca Empire spread over the immense length of the western coast of South America, from Peru to Chile today. It came to an end in 1532 C.E., when its last ruler was beheaded by the conquerors.

29.2.1 Ancient period. Agriculture, which was probably not preceded by a pastoral economy, appeared in primitive form on the Peruvian coast about 7000 B.C.E. About 2500 B.C.E. climatic changes stimulated the development of an economy based on food gathering and sedentary horticulture. Animal proteins were not supplied by hunting, but by fishing. Corn, whose Central American ancestor is over sixty thousand years old, arrived in Peru about 1400 B.C.E.; an improved variety was obtained about 900 B.C.E. During that period, irrigation techniques and the centralized state interacted to advance complex agricultural and social networks. Their development was made possible by a religious cult that, very probably, exalted the mythical origin of a great civilization without precedent in the area. During the same period the cultural complex discovered at Chavín on the northern plateau was built, whereas the southern coast was dominated by a culture that produced a huge necropolis in the Paracas caves. Unfortunately, no other source but the monuments can shed any light on the Chavín culture, whose meaning is lost to us. Its foremost divinity, in the feline form of a jaguar or puma, had remarkable success in the Andean region for five hundred years.

All traces of cultural homogeneity disappeared from the Andes area about 300 B.C.E.; yet agriculture continued to improve, thanks to the domestication of new plants and the technique of terrace cultivation. One Paracas necropolis pertaining to this period and containing 429 mummies of important individuals shows that burial procedures and afterlife beliefs had changed.

About 200 C.E. the cultures of the intermediate period seemed to reach their climax. They were theocratic, they reinstated the feline deity, they practiced human sacrifice, and they showed, like their predecessors, obsessive interest in the human skull, which was systematically deformed at birth and sometimes trephined during life and at death. Enemies' skulls were collected as war trophies.

Without being overpopulated, the coastal valleys had a larger population than they do today, a population enlivened by religious ideals capable of producing an advanced technology. Certain of the projects realized then are still daring in the present day, such as the seventy-mile La Cumbre canal, which is still in operation.

The Moche culture specialized in immense temples, of which the most famous are their Sun Temple and Moon Temple. Painted ceramics show that the Moche practiced circumcision and shamanic healing of illness by suction of the spirit, which appeared as a tangible object. The Moche used a form of writing: their paintings show ideograms inscribed on beans. Moche society was theocratic; the warrior caste was particularly honored, while the function of women was entirely domestic.

The coastal culture of Nazca has produced numerous flattened cranial trophies, painted and hung on a sling for transportation. The Nazca are famed for their huge drawings in ferrous rocks in the Palpa Valley, seemingly to be gazed upon from above by some heavenly deity, and for codifying an astronomical lore, most of which has not been reconstructed.

During the end of the intermediate period, the megalithic civilization of Tiahuanaco in Bolivia exerted a powerful influence on the Andean cultures. The megaliths, built thirteen thousand feet above sea level, make up a unique religious center with terraced pyramids, carved gates, platforms, tanks, and statues. The center was abandoned before all the buildings had been completed.

About 1000 C.E. the political organization of the Andes resembled Western feudalism. The kingdom of Chimú, the most important during this period, took shape in the north and spread over many valleys, each one of them having its own urban center. Its capital, Chanchán, near modern Trujillo reflected an almost utopian urban planning: its over fifty thousand inhabitants lived in ten rectangular neighborhoods, each one of them with its houses, water tanks, and pyramid temples.

29.3 A STRANGE HISTORY. The foundation of the Inca Empire, about 1200 C.E., was attributed to the mythical hero Manco Capac and to his sisters, who settled down in the Cuzco Valley. The Inca state knew no impressive expansion before its eighth emperor, Viracocha Inca, and his son, Pachacuti, who succeeded him on the throne about 1438 C.E.. At the death of Pachacuti's son Topa Inca in 1493, the empire had reached over three thousand miles in length, stretching from Ecuador to Chile. This feat is as spectacular as Alexander's or Napoleon's conquests; it is stranger still that this immense territory would be conquered by a handful of Spanish adventurers.

The death of the emperor Huayna Capac in 1525 was followed by a war between his two rival sons, Huascar from Cuzco and Atahuallpa from Quito in Ecuador. Atahuallpa won and was proclaimed emperor in 1532. Immediately following these events, the Spanish conqueror Pizarro showed up unexpectedly with 180 henchmen, attracted by stories of the fabulous riches of Peru. What followed shows perhaps, as Tzvetan Todorov made clear in a related case, the superior semiotics of the conqueror; yet it also shows that religion is the motor of history. Atahuallpa surmised that Pizarro was the great god Viracocha with his retinue, returning to the earth in order to announce the end time. Pizarro took advantage of the situation and made Atahuallpa his prisoner. The emperor ransomed himself by filling up his cell with gold but his captors did not release him. Sentenced to death, Atahuallpa accepted Christian baptism, which upgraded him from burning to strangulation. He was executed on 29 August 1533. Less fortunate, the last pretender to the Inca throne was beheaded forty years later.

29.4 INCA RELIGION. In the communist Inca Empire, the state supervised the official religion, which was that of the Quechua of Cuzco and was probably similar to all the minor cults that had been absorbed into it. Among the three plots of land farmers were supposed to cultivate, the land of the gods came first, the land of the emperor followed, and eventually the one for the sustenance of the farmer's own family. The sacred objects, or *huacas,* of the conquered populations were carried in procession to Cuzco and installed in sanctuaries where they continued to be visited in pilgrimage by worshipers from distant provinces. Yet the category of *huacas* was not limited to these objects; it contained everything sacred: hills, stones, trees, anything strange or portentous.

The organization of the Inca Empire bears the mark of a rationalistic utopia; and in fact stories about Peru must have influenced utopianists such as the Italian philosopher Tommaso Campanella in about 1600. The church of the Incas was also highly organized. Its center was the emperor, who was the State, the Law, and God himself. He was a *huaca,* equal to the One Without Equal, the god Viracocha, born from the foam of Lake Titicaca and vanished into the foam of the ocean, walking on water toward the northwest—the direction from which Pizarro and his men appeared in 1532.

Viracocha's metaphysical nature was complex. He was the creator of the natural and social world, the most important god of the Inca pantheon, in which the Sun had the central position. The major temple at Cuzco was dedicated to him. Like many of the ancient Near-Eastern sanctuaries, Inca temples were not open to the faithful. They were the refuge of priests and the Virgins of the Sun, chosen from the purest young girls of the empire and educated at state expense in order to become either vestals or second wives of great dignitaries or of the emperor himself. If the emperor happened to "sin" with a vestal, the matter was settled if he admitted his transgression, but anyone else caught in the same situation was killed together with his consort.

The Sun was represented in temples by anthropomorphic statues and huge golden disks. The emperor was the Son of the Sun, the empress was Daughter of the Moon, the sister-wife of the Sun, worshiped in temples in the shape of silver anthropomorphic statues. The Incas would commonly use both a lunar and a solar calendar.

Other important divinities were Pachacamac, god of the earth, with his infernal wife Pachamama, and Illapa, god of the atmosphere and meteorological phenomena.

At the top of the church hierarchy was a high priest, closely related to the emperor, surrounded by a council of nine great dignitaries. Many priests were delegated to inspect the provinces, where religion was in the hands of the old keepers of the *huacas,* voluntary priests who were not on the central government's payroll.

The temple, as already mentioned, was not a place for public gathering; collective ceremonies took place in city squares, where animals were frequently sacrificed for propitiation or divination. Yet the most efficacious sacrifices were supposed to be those of ten-year-old children chosen according to their physical and moral perfection and happy to be directly dispatched to the other world, access to which was usually reserved for nobles. Inca human sacrifices were however less frequent than among the Aztecs or even the Maya. Even more seldom were the strongest war prisoners sacrificed, as they were according to Aztec custom.

Like their Egyptian homologues (10), Inca priests were the administrators of health, public and private, thus uniting the functions of sacrificer, diviner, and medicine man. Like the Babylonian *baru* (20), they carefully inspected the entrails of sacrificed animals, forecasting the future from such readings. But they also practiced healing by suction of an object supposed to represent the pathogenic agent that had produced organic imbalance. Moreover, they were skilled chiropractors, who treated dislocated organs by external manipulation, and excellent surgeons, able to carry out delicate operations such as skull trephination (perforation), for reasons which in most cases remain mysterious.

Unfortunately, the absence of written sources stemming from the Incas themselves makes impossible any serious understanding of their theologies. The existence of "monks" and "nuns" (the Sun vestals) as well as the practice of secret confession had impressed the Spanish missionaries. Yet the subtleties of Inca thinking, lost forever, only occasionally pierce through the hesitant, naïve, or unwittingly misleading phrases of alien informants, quite mistakenly convinced of their own superiority.

29.5 RELIGIONS OF THE TROPICAL FOREST. The huge jungle area of the Orinoco and Amazon rivers, which also stretches over the mountainous regions of Guyana, is inhabited by numerous tribes belonging to the linguistic families of the Arawak, Carib, Pano, Tukano, and Tupi. Although every group has its own religion or variant thereof, it is however possible to find common traits, both in their mythologies—studied in Lévi-Strauss's monumental *Mythologigues*—and in their ideas, practices, and institutions—studied in Lawrence E. Sullivan's *Icanchu's Drum* (1988).

The most important divinities of this area occupied an intermediate level between a Supreme Being and a culture hero, the latter's function being generally more precise. As already mentioned (6.2.1), the study of Indonesian peoples allowed the anthropologist Ad. E. Jensen to draw a distinction, which he believed to have universal validity, between two mythological archetypes of creation: that of the *dema*, primordial beings whose sacrificed body would give birth to tuberous plants like potatoes, and that of Prometheus, which applies in general to the secret of cereals stolen from heaven.

The lunar god Moma of the Witóto of northeastern Amazonia was a rather clear case of a *dema* divinity; he scarcely possessed the traits of a Supreme Being, which have been attributed to him by certain anthropologists. On the contrary, the mythology of the solar creator god Pura among the Warikyana of Guyana, with its periodical world destructions, is closer to the Supreme Being type. Another Carib tribe, the Munduruků, had a true Supreme Being: the *deus otiosus* (inactive deity) Karusakaibe. After having created the world of nature and the world of humankind, Karusakaibe was deadly offended by the humans, upon which he withdrew to the inaccessible regions of heaven. He would return at the end of time in order to destroy humankind by fire.

The religious experience of the Indians of the tropical forest was based on the existence of an invisible universe that overlapped with our world and could only be entered in altered states of consciousness such as dreaming, trance, and vision induced by inhaling hallucinogens or through mystical disposition, either natural or acquired by training. The worlds overlapped to such an extent that beings from the other world commonly took on the shapes of animals such as the caiman, the anaconda, the jaguar, or the eagle; only religious specialists were able to recognize their supernatural essence. Yet anything could have roots in the invisible; the Sanemá of the Brazilian-Venezuelan border could distinguish among eight categories of *hewkula,* or hidden beings.

Among these spirits, the Masters of Animals had a particular importance among certain groups, for they were supposed to regulate the wealth of game and fish coming into the world to be eaten.

The spirits of the Ancestors were equally important, for they took part invisibly in the social life of the living. One among the several human souls, that which continues to exist after physical death, could either haunt or bestow benefits upon the living. The conceptions of the soul of the South American Indians were different from the three main doctrines known both in the East and in Mediterranean religions: metensomatosis, traducianism, and neogenesis (or reincarnation, spiritual copulation of the parents, and new creation of souls). The Indians believed rather in a soul-stuff reservoir where the soul after death reverts to an indistinct state. The animation of a new human being occurs by apportioning him or her a piece of soul stuff. These ideas are similar to those held by certain gnostics who partially adhered to the Catholic doctrine of neogenesis of the soul; to those of the Andalusian philosopher Averroes (Ibn Rushd, 520–595 C.E.), who believed the Intellect to be one and indistinct, thereby rejecting the doctrine of the survival of every individual soul; and marginally to those of late Kabbalah, which admits the possibility that an individual has more than one soul and may incorporate as many famous souls as he or she wants to. Secularized, this idea became Benedetto Croce's reflection according to which the reader of Dante *is* Dante while reading the *Divine Comedy.*

More concretely, the Jívaro of eastern Ecuador distinguished among an "ordinary" soul, a "perfect" soul, and an "avenging" soul. The ordinary soul was common to all mortals; the perfect soul could only be obtained after the visionary experience of the invisible world. But the Jívaro was not supposed to make any use of the perfect soul, for it made him bloodthirsty. Another perfect soul would be added to the first when the Jívaro killed an enemy; being now in possession of two perfect souls, he would become invulnerable. And even if it was impossible to acquire more than two perfect souls, he could still extract the power contained in other souls.

The avenging soul appeared at the death of the possessor of a perfect soul and wished to take revenge upon his murderer. This was why the Jívaro practiced head shrinking, for they believed that the avenging soul would thus remain caught in the trap of their enemy's shrunken skull.

The religious specialist among South American Indians was the shaman (26), who fulfilled both the functions of healer of the body politic and physician of the human body when the body had been affected by a pathogenic agent from the invisible world.

It is easy to see that the religious system of the South American Indians is the most complex network of meaning that informs their culture; it would thus be quite impossible to distinguish the "profane" from the "sacred" side of their existence. After all, the world for any of us is nothing but one single mental operation, without any distinct compartments: there is no borderline where one stops thinking "profanely" in order to think "religiously," or vice versa. "Sacred" and "profane" naturally overlap: they speak the same language and are made of the same mind stuff.

29.6 GRAN CHACO RELIGIONS. The Gran Chaco (Chaco in Quechua means "hunting terrain") stretches between the Mato Grosso and the Pampas, in the middle of the South American continent. It is inhabited by the linguistic families of the Zamuco, Tupi-Guaraní Mataco-Makká, Guaiacurú-Caduveo, and Arawak. All tribes belonging to this area shared the institution of shamanism (26) and the belief in supernatural beings living in an invisible universe that interferes with ours. Among the supernatural beings, some were Supreme Beings mixed up with culture heroes or *dema* deities; Prometheuslike characters, thieves of cereals and/or fire; and Tricksters, whose creative functions could be more or less extensive. It is impossible to expand here on the individual aspects taken by all these mythical beings.

29.7 RELIGIONS OF THE PAMPAS, PATAGONIA, AND TIERRA DEL FUEGO. Now extinct, several tribes of the southern regions have been explored by anthropologists in the past. Tierra del Fuego Indians (Selk'nam, or Ona; Yahgan, or Yamana; and Alacaluf) have received special attention, especially because of their belief in a Supreme Being. The Selk'nam, for example, believed that the creator god Temakuel withdrew to the heavenly heights, leaving to the first ancestor Kenos the task of administering the world. The Selk'nam did not disturb Temakuel with frequent prayer, but would however perform daily food offerings in his honor.

29.8 THE MILLENARIAN MOVEMENTS of the Tupi-Guaraní of the Mato Grosso probably started shortly after the arrival of the

European colonists. In 1539 C.E. twelve thousand Tupis left Brazil in search of the Evilless Land; when they reached Peru, only three hundred of them were left. Illness and hunger had killed the others. In 1602 the Jesuits made an end to the exodus of three thousand Indians from Bahía, led by a *pagé* (prophet) in their search of the Evilless Land. Such episodes would continue to the twentieth century. Scholars gave these suicidal migrations different explanations that depict them either as local and acculturative "messianic" phenomena; as "movements of oppressed peoples" (which the Tupi were not); or as an internal mechanism by which society would commit self-destruction rather than becoming a State (P. Clastres).

29.9 BIBLIOGRAPHY. P. Rivière, "Indians of the Tropical Forest," in *ER* 13, 472–81; M. Califano, "Indians of the Gran Chaco," in *ER* 13, 481–86; O. Zerries, "South American Religions," in *ER* 13, 486–99; J. A. Vázquez, "Mythic Themes," in *ER* 13, 499–506; D. A. Poole, "History of Study," in *ER* 13, 506–12.

On the Incas, see J. Alden Mason, *The Ancient Civilization of Peru* (1968). On the mythologies of South American Indians, the most extensive work to date remains Claude Lévi-Strauss's *Mythologiques* in four volumes (1964–1971); see also his more recent *The Jealous Potter* (1987).

On Tupi-Guaraní millenarianism, see especially Hélène Clastres, *La terre sans mal: Le prophétisme tupi-guarani* (1975); Pierre Clastres, *La société contre l'État: Recherches d'anthropologie politique* (1974).

On South American religions in general, see the excellent book by Lawrence E. Sullivan, *Icanchu's Drum: An Orientation to Meaning in South American Religions* (1988).

30

Taoism

30.1 SOURCES. The classics of Taoism are the *Tao Te Ching,* attributed to Lao-tzu, the legendary founder of the Way (Tao), and the *Chuang-tzu,* so called after its presumable author. According to the legend, the birth of Lao-Tzu took place between 604 and 571 B.C.E. The dating of the *Tao Te Ching,* or "Classic of the Way and Virtue," is controversial; some scholars place it, according to tradition, in the sixth century B.C.E.; others, such as Arthur Waley, place its composition around 240 B.C.E. Chuang-tzu is said to have lived in the fourth century B.C.E.

However, to reduce Taoism to these two ancient texts would be worse than reducing Christianity to the four Gospels. For the hidden body of the Taoist iceberg is constituted by philosophico-medical and alchemical esotericism, and likewise by ritual, from the most popular to the most sophisticated. In a certain sense, Taoism is only comparable with that hydra-headed Platonic tradition that would now take on the shape of Philo's esotericism, then that of the theurgic rites of the *Chaldaean Oracles,* then that of Gnosticism, then that of the philosophical mysticism of Plotinus, then that of the luxuriant mythology and magic of late Neoplatonism, and then that of the orthodox doctrine of the church fathers.

The Taoist canon (*tao-tsang*) was printed in Shanghai in 1926 in 1,120 parts. In his book *The Parting of the Way* (1957), Holmes Welch counted thirty-six English translations of the *Tao Te Ching,* but no explanatory synthesis on Taoism whatever. The situation has undergone little change so far, yet recent generations of scholars have accomplished a few decisive steps toward understanding the esoteric aspects of Taoism.

30.2 ANCIENT MYTHOLOGIES. An ancient chronicle speaks about ten mythical epochs, after which the Yellow Emperor Huang Ti (ca. 2600 B.C.E.), associated with the element Earth and the making of silk, opened Chinese history. Culture hero and shaman, the Yellow Emperor's miraculous qualities fulfilled the expectations a founding character always raises in a historian of religions: like the Greek *iatromantes,* (12.3.2), Huang Ti frequently entered a state of catalepsy, during which he visited the distant provinces of the spirits who, like the inhabitants of the Isles of the Blessed in Plato, would walk on air and lie on bare space as if on a bed. The mythology of the Immortals was connected with the golden age of the Yellow Emperor, the sage and righteous ruler. The Immortals (Hsien) have mysterious relations with the joyful people of the fairies, to such an extent that sometimes the two species are mixed together. The territory of the Immortals is the Mountain (Hsien Shan) or the Nine Palaces (Chiu Kung), possibly the nine peaks of the mythical mountain Chin I. The land of the Immortals is often described as both mountainous and insular; the three Isles of the Blessed in the Eastern Seas are designated as San Hsien Shan, Insular Mountains. The emperor Shih Huang-ti in 217 B.C.E. sent an expedition to the islands in search of the elixir of long life; six thousand young people are said to have disappeared at sea.

Hsi Wang Mu, the mother of the fairies, gave the emperor Wu Ti of the Han dynasty (202 B.C.E.–220 C.E.) four miraculous peaches that grew every three thousand years. Therefore, peaches were often the symbol of the Immortals, a race that proudly stood next to the Perfect (Chen Jen) and the Saints (Shen). They drank a heavenly wine (*t'en-chin*), walked on the air, and used the wind as a vehicle. They pretended to die, but upon opening their coffins one would find no trace of corpses, only some symbolic object.

Based on these early legends, Taoism developed several doctrines concerning deified human beings, eternal representatives of the Way and warrants of its truth. Under Buddhist influence, the Immortals grew into a heavenly hierarchy. Yet according to another tradition, they continued to live on the Five Sacred Mountains, objects of pilgrimage, of which the most important was T'ai Shan in Shantung. And the deepest hope of the Taoist adept was to join one day the Immortals of the Western Mountain K'un Lun, the land of the cheerful queen Hsi Wang Mu, who rode geese and dragons; to feed on the plant of immortality and drink from the Cinnabar River, which, like the Platonic Acheron, one had to cross in order to reach the other world. The Heavenly Mountain and the Heavenly Caves lighted by their inner light, like Jules Verne's immense cavern in *Voyage to the Center of the Earth,* were the fantastic territory where the quest of adepts took place. Adepts entered this space supplied with magic amulets and formulae in search of the drug, the elixir, the universal panacea. Entering the Mountain, Taoists entered themselves, discovering the lightness of being that made them weightless. They relinquished all conventions, social and linguistic, and altered their consciousness in order to expel from it all acquired habits and obligations. Like Chuang Tzu, they dreamed of being a butterfly and upon awakening they did not any longer know who was dreaming whom: the butterfly or the Taoist master. The world was an illusory construction in which dream beings gave birth to the dreamer, even as Escher's hands, in the famous illustration, must draw each other in order to be able to draw.

30.3 THE THREE RELIGIONS. The idea of lightness of being and freedom from the heavy demands of the state was not likely to please Confucianism, which the Han dynasty had made into official ideology and which fulfilled this task until 1911. When Buddhism reached China (3.8), all Three Religions (Taoism, Confucianism, and Buddhism) were rivals for the hearts of the faithful. Methods used in this competition were sometimes excessively harsh, especially at the end of the T'ang dynasty (618–907 C.E.), when the most punished religion was also the most powerful: Buddhism. Since Buddhism's arrival, Taoism had suffered from an inferiority complex. Confucianism had already obliged it to disavow occult practices and popular gods; and now Buddhism submitted it to an intellectual pressure that Taoism was unable to withstand. On the other hand, the essential weightlessness of Taoist existence enclosed latent potentialities of utopianism and revolt. Only a strong organization was able to contain them. This organization, led by a Heavenly Master, appeared at the end of the Han dynasty (220 C.E.) and subsisted thereafter, always striving for credibility in the eyes of the state.

In her book *The Syncretic Religion of Lin Chao-en* (1980), Judith Berling shows that, starting about the eleventh century C.E., the religious life of the Chinese was dominated by an intellectual synthesis of the Three Religions. Yet this does not mean that political relations among Taoism, Confucianism, and Buddhism were ever peaceful. Emperors who favored Taoism would generally persecute Buddhism, and vice versa. It was under Buddhist influence that the Taoists adopted monastic institutions. From 666 to 1911, their mixed monasteries of monks and nuns were state supported. At least during the early period of Taoist monasticism, it is probable that the ancient sexual rituals performed in Taoist communities continued to exist, in spite of the Buddhist morality overtly professed by the monks. Yet the monastic movement never reached in Taoism the popularity it had in Buddhism. As far as the court was concerned, it readily adopted the universalistic spirit of Taoism, its minute and complex liturgy, its occult rituals, and its magic conjurations.

During the Ming epoch (1368–1644 C.E.), the Confucianist intellectual Lin Chao-en (1517–1598) felt the necessity to proclaim the unity of the Three Religions and constructed a synthesis in which the procedures of inner Taoist alchemy played an important part.

Taoism is still practiced in our time. Two recent books, *The Teachings of Taoist Master Chuang* (1978) by Michael Saso (concerning Master Chuang-ch'en Teng-yün of Hsinchu in Taiwan, who died in 1976) and *Taoist Ritual in Chinese Society and History* (1987) by John Lagerwey (concerning Master Ch'en Jung-sheng of Tainan in Taiwan), give us precious descriptions of contemporary Taoist practices in Taiwan.

30.4 DOCTRINE AND PRACTICE. The *Tao Te Ching* seems to proclaim at every step the supremacy of nothingness over being, of emptiness over fullness. Yet this should not be interpreted in simplistic terms as a negation of life. On the contrary, the ultimate goal of Taoism was the attainment of physical immortality. This goal was part of a complex theory of the cosmic body. Human beings were the image of the universe. They were enlivened by a primordial breath divided into *yin* and *yang,* female and male, earth and heaven. The phenomenon of life was based on this energy hidden in its manifestations. If the energy was preserved and increased, then the human being was able to attain immortality. There was more than one procedure to "nourish the vital principle": gymnastics, diet, respiratory and sexual techniques, ingestion of drugs, inner alchemy, and so forth. Meditation was a central part of Taoism and preceded Chinese Buddhism. It was based on a minute inner topography made of "palaces" where the adept installed the gods, visited them, worshiped them, and talked to them. Henri Maspero left us a remarkable description of these ancient Taoist techniques, whose importance gradually waned as soon as they became too formal, uniform, or monotonous.

On the contrary, the techniques of *t'ai hsi,* or embryonal respiration, based on a practice of breath suspension of ever-increasing length somewhat similar to yogic *pranayama,* as well as the *fang-chung shu,* or "art of the bedroom," which consists of suppressing ejaculation by blocking the seminal conduct, continued to exist as long as they did not stir the suspicion of the Confucian establishment. In both cases, the purpose was the attainment of physical immortality; and in both cases the "breaths"—respiration in *t'ai hsi* and spermatic breath in *fang-chung*—were redistributed in order to preserve or revive the vital principle. In his *Sexual Life in Ancient China* (1961), Robert van Gulik asserts that *fang-chung* was adopted by Confucian aristocrats, with no reference to Taoist ideology, out of the necessity of coping with the hardships of polygynous marriage, which would otherwise strain the male beyond his capacities. Many popular texts emphasized the idea of "sexual vampirism" on which many Chinese beliefs were based. Usually exerted by women, vampirism could change polarity and be used to the benefit of the male or of both partners in order to obtain physical rejuvenation.

The aim of Taoist alchemy was fabrication of the elixir of immortality. In the external procedures, the elixir was a potable substance; in inner alchemy, or *nei-tan,* which began in the T'ang epoch (618–907 C.E.), the elixir was the vital principle that all the techniques just mentioned wished to isolate, stir up, and increase. The vocabulary of inner alchemy was alchemical, yet its outcome was supposed to be the same as that pursued through embryonal respiration and *fang-chung:* through the *nei-tan* operations, the golden elixir climbed to the brain and from there it fell to the mouth. Swallowed, it became a Holy Embryo, which, after six months of gestation, transformed the adept into an Earthly Immortal. After nine years of practice, the Immortal would be perfect. The classics of inner alchemy are the collections *Tao-shu* ("Pivot of Tao," about 1140 C.E.) and *Hsiu-chen shih-shu* ("Ten Writings About Cultivating Perfection," after 1200). Master Chuang in Taiwan still claimed knowledge of the secrets of *nei-tan* and of Taoist magic, which consisted of conjurations of stellar spirits closely resembling practices of Western magic, according to Agrippa of Nettesheim (sixteenth century) and many a Renaissance handbook of magic. Master Chuang suggested that he could exact extraordinary performances from those spirits whose names and shapes were known to him; yet he would only enjoin them to respect heavenly Tao. Master Chuang likewise practiced Thunder Magic according to procedures of the Sung epoch (960–1279 C.E.) which seemed to be a kind of inner alchemy.

30.5 BIBLIOGRAPHY. See in general D. S. Nivison, "Chinese Philosophy," in *ER* 3, 245–57; D. L. Overmyer, "Chinese Religion: An Overview," in *ER* 3, 257–89; A. P. Cohen, "Popular Religion," in *ER* 3,

289–96; N. J. Girardot, "Mythic Themes," in *ER* 3, 296–305; Wing-Tsit Chan, "Religious and Philosophical Texts," in *ER* 3, 305–12; N. J. Girardot, "History of Study," in *ER* 3, 312–23; L. G. Thompson, "Chinese Religious Year," in *ER* 3, 323–28; D. S. Nivison, "Tao and Te," in *ER* 14, 283–86; F. Baldrian, "Taoism: An Overview," in *ER* 14, 288–306; J. Lagerwey, "The Taoist Religious Community," in *ER* 14, 306–17; J. Magee Boltz, "Taoist Literature," in *ER* 14, 317–29; T. H. Barrett, "History of Study," in *ER* 14, 329–32; N. J. Girardot, "Hsien," in *ER* 6, 475–77.

Classical works on Taoism: Henri Maspero, *Taoism and Chinese Religion*, English translation (1981); Max Kaltenmark, *Lao Tseu et le Taoïsme* (1965); Joseph Needham, *Science and Civilization in China*, 5 vols. (1954–1983).

Among recent works, see Michael Saso, *The Teachings of Taoist Master Chuang* (1978); Isabelle Robinet, *Méditation taoïste* (1979); Judith A. Berling, *The Syncretic Religion of Lin Chao-en* (1980); Kristofer Schipper, *Le Corps taoïste* (1982); Michel Strickmann (ed.), *Tantric and Taoist Studies in Honor of R. A. Stein*, 2 vols. (1983); F. Baldrian-Hussein, *Procédés secrets du Joyau magique: Traité d'alchimie taoïste de l'onzième siècle* (1984); Judith Magee Boltz, *A Survey of Taoist Literature, Tenth to Seventeenth Centuries* (1986); John Lagerwey, *Taoist Ritual in Chinese Society and History* (1987).

31

Thracian Religion

31.1 POPULATION. The word *thrakes* designated in Greek the inhabitants of the northeastern Balkan peninsula, including approximately two hundred tribes stretching west of the Scythians, east of the Pannonians, Dalmatians, and Illyrians, and south of the Balts and Celts. South of the river Danube was the borderline between two linguistic and cultural areas, occupied by the southern and by the northern (Geto-Dacian) Thracians.

31.2 SOURCES. The question of whether a Thracian writing exists is controversial. Even if such writing existed, which is unclear, we are not able to decipher the scant remains. Greek votive inscriptions acquaint us with some 160 names and epithets of gods of southern Thrace. All written evidence concerning the religion of the Thracians comes from Greek and Latin authors, from Herodotus and Plato (fifth century B.C.E.) to Jordanes (sixth century C.E.), the historian of the Goths, who was born on the western shore of the Pontus (Black Sea) in the ancient provinces of the pious Getae, and had ethnic reasons to resort to etymological fiction (Goths = Getae) in order to fabricate an illustrious ancestry for the Goths.

31.3 RELIGION. Thracian religion was divided by the same borderline that separated the south from the north. The reason for this division was the reform of Zalmoxis, which left an indelible imprint on northern beliefs. Yet all Thracian gods known by the Greeks in the fifth century B.C.E. (Sabazios, Bendis, Cotys), as well as characters such as Dionysus and Orpheus to whom a Thracian background was ascribed, came most certainly from southern Thrace.

31.3.1 Gods. According to Herodotus, the Thracians worshiped four divinities, correponding to Ares, Dionysus, Artemis, and Hermes; the cult of the last was reserved to the king. Ares-Mars was mentioned by Jordanes, but his local name is unknown to us; nor could the other three be safely identified.

Bendis, worshiped in Athens from the beginning of the fifth century B.C.E., was a nuptial goddess. She was identified with Artemis and Hekate.

Sabazios was a Thracian god who had early followers in Phrygia (Asia Minor). He was known in Athens during the fifth century B.C.E., where his nocturnal ceremonies included purification with mud. In the fourth century B.C.E., he came as far as Africa, where he became a sky god, probably identified with the Semitic Baal. He received the epithet *hypsistos* (supreme). There is no reason to suppose that there was anything Thracian in the mysteries of Sabazios during the Roman epoch (21.3).

Cotys or Kotyto had an orgiastic cult, including transvestism.

A male sky deity was important among the northern Thracians; in the southern area the sky deity was female, for she was identified with Hera.

Two practices were common to north and south: tattooing and burial or cremation of widows side by side with their deceased husband (the Thracians being polygamous). Yet tattooing did not have the same symbolic value: in the south, it was a mark of male aristocracy; in the north, only women and slaves were tattooed in memory of a suffering inflicted upon Zalmoxis.

Thracians practised either burial or incineration of corpses. Cremation was preferred in the north. Death was celebrated as a joyful event, but the sources disagree as to the reasons for such joy. For the northern Thracians, the reform of Zalmoxis gives it a coherent explanation.

31.3.2 Ascetics. The information offered by the geographer Strabo concerning the vegetarianism and sexual continence of the *theosebeis* (worshipers of the gods), *ktistai* (founders), and *abioi* (literally lifeless), who would feed only on cheese, milk, and honey, seemed to refer exclusively to the Getae inhabiting the province of Moesia. Some Thracians, nicknamed *kapnobatai* (those who walk on smoke), may have used the smoke of the cannabis plant as an intoxicating agent.

31.4 THE RELIGION OF THE NORTHERN THRACIANS is relatively well documented due to the attention paid by Greek and Roman literary sources to their reformer Zalmoxis, later divinized. In fifth century B.C.E. Greece, Zalmoxis was connected with Pythagoras and psychosomatic medicine, highly praised by Plato (*Charmides* 156d–57c).

31.4.1 Zalmoxis. According to Greek interpretation, Zalmoxis belonged to the special category of Apollonian seers and healers known as *iatromantes* (12.3.2). The principles of his religion—immortality of the soul, vegetarianism, and so forth—resembled those of Pythagoreanism. Originally, Zalmoxis seemed to have been a prophet and an associate of the Getic king. His legend contains episodes of occultation and epiphany vaguely reminiscent of the myths of dying gods such as Attis, Osiris, and Adonis.

Under the name Gebelizis, Zalmoxis was a sky god. Every four years the Getae sent a message to him through the intermediary of the soul of a brave warrior whose body was thrown on top of three spears. If the messenger did not die immediately, the procedure had to be repeated. Getic warriors were bold in the face of death. Zalmoxis had probably taught that the soul of the warrior would go to a paradise of which unfortunately we have no description.

31.4.2 Priesthood. Zalmoxis's cult was connected with Geto-Dacian kingship and aristocracy. The priests of Zalmoxis, whose list from around 80 B.C.E. to 106 C.E. is contained in Jordanes, were kings as often as not. The most important among them, Deceneus, was the counselor of the Getic king Burebista (ca. 80–44 B.C.E.). He taught the Getes cosmology, astrology, astronomy, and the rules of a mysterious calendar, the remains of which have been found in the ruins of the ancient capital of King Decebalus (d. 106 C.E.), Sarmizegetusa Regia, today Gradistea Muncelului in southeastern Romania. Another temple, belonging to the same complex, had a large underground room that may have represented the place where Zalmoxis withdrew for three years, pretending to have disappeared.

31.4.3 Kingship. The Jewish historian Joseph Flavius (first century C.E.) was already acquainted with the reputation for holiness of certain Dacians, whom he compared to the Jewish sect of the Essenes.

The name *pleistoi* he gave them must have indicated that they were using caps, a notice confirmed by Jordanes, according to whom Getic aristocrats wore headgear (*pilleus*), whereas common people went about bareheaded. We know that Geto-Dacian priesthood was closely connected with warlike aristocracy and kingship, to the point that two among Deceneus' successors, the priests Comosicus and Coryllus—Decebalus' predecessor if not father—had been kings.

31.5 BIBLIOGRAPHY. Recent bibliographical references and discussion of the extant documents and research hypotheses can be found in I. P. Couliano and C. Poghirc, "Geto-Dacian Religion," in *ER* 5, 537–40; "Thracian Religion," in *ER* 14, 494–97; and "Zalmoxis," in *ER* 15, 551–54.

32

Tibetan Religion

32.1 BON. A rather recent change of perspective has occurred in the interpretation of the ancient religion of Tibet, which scholars had traditionally identified with *Bon* (3.10). The autochthonous religion, called *mi-chos,* or "religion of the humans," actually preceded Bon and the coming of Buddhism, known as *lha-chos* or "religion of the gods." The sources for our knowledge of *mi-chos* are rather meager: fragments of myths, rituals, and divination techniques, inscriptions, refutations of the ancient religion compiled by the Buddhists, and some Chinese chronicles of the T'ang dynasty (618–907 C.E.). Ancient practices were assimilated by both Bon and Buddhism, yet it is almost impossible to extract them from the new structures into which they were inserted.

32.2 KINGSHIP. The central institution of the old religion was sacred kingship. The first king was supposed to have descended from heaven on the top of a mountain or with the aid of a rope or ladder. The kings of archaic times could return to heaven, like the Taoist Immortals (30.2), without leaving a corpse behind. But the seventh king was killed, and at his death the first funeral rites were established, consisting of the sacrifice of several animals supposed to serve the king as guides on the otherworldly routes. During the period of the immortal kings, the heavenly prototypes of plants and animals were transferred to the earth in order to be of help to humankind. Humans were constantly faced with a choice between the commandments of the heavenly gods and the evil advice of the infernal demons *klu,* who had already caused the world to decay. After the world destruction, a new cycle started from scratch. It is impossible to state how old these beliefs are; some scholars assume that they did not exist before the sixth or even seventh century C.E. and that they were created in order to justify the adoption of the royal cult from imperial China.

32.3 FOUNDER. Although the ancient religion was commonly designated by the word *bon,* today *bon* is only used in reference to *bon-po,* which did not become a religion until the eleventh century C.E., yet contained some pre-Buddhist elements. The founder of Bon was Shenrad-ni-bo, who came from a western land called Zhang-shung, or Tazig. His birth and career were miraculous. When he withdrew into nirvana, Shenrab left behind his son to preach the doctrine for another three years. The texts ascribed to Shenrad and allegedly translated from the language of Zhang-shung were inserted in the Buddhist collections called *Kanjur* and *Tanjur* during the fifteenth century, in a form that reveals powerful Buddhist influence.

32.4 BIBLIOGRAPHY. Eliade, *H* 3, 312–14; P. Kvaerne, "Tibetan Religions: An Overview," in *ER* 14, 497–504; M. L. Walter, "History of Study," in *ER* 14, 504–7.

33

Zoroastrianism

33.1 PRE-ZOROASTRIAN RELIGION. Iranian religion before the coming of the reformer Zarathushtra is not easy to reconstruct. It showed many traits in common with Vedic India, e.g., sacrifice (*yaz,* Sanskrit *yajña*) of animals whose soul was supposed to join the divine entity called Geush Urvan, or Bull's Soul, and use of the *haoma,* intoxicating or hallucinogenic beverage (Sanskrit *soma*). Divine beings belonged to two classes: *ahuras* ("Lords"; Sanskrit *asura*) and *daivas* ("Gods"; Sanskrit *deva*), both originally positive forces.

Pre-Zoroastrian religion corresponded to a form of society dominated by an aristocracy of warriors forming initiatory brotherhoods whose violent practices culminated in a state of murderous frenzy (*aēshma*). Sacrifice of animals such as the ox (*gav*) and consumption of *haoma,* which according to a passage of the the *Avesta* (*Yasna* 48.10; 32.14) may have consisted of the urine eliminated after ingestion of a drug that some have identified as being fly agaric, were at the center of the religious cult.

33.2 ZARATHUSHTRA. It is difficult to place in time the reform of Zarathushtra (Greek Zoroaster). When the reformer lived, somewhere in eastern central Iran, is varyingly placed between 1200 and 500 B.C.E. Zarathushtra's original message opposed bloody sacrifices and the use of *haoma* and brought about changes in the divine pantheon. Zoroastrian religion was *monotheistic* and *dualistic.*

33.3 ANCIENT ZOROASTRIANISM.

33.3.1 Sources. The sources of Zoroastrian religion were committed to writing starting in the fourth or fifth century C.E. They consist of several layers. The *Avesta* contains the following sections: *Yasna* (Sacrifices); *Yasht* (Hymns to the Deities); *Vendidad* (Purity Statutes); *Vispered* (Cult); *Nyāyishu* and *Gāh* (Prayers); *Khorda*, or Lesser Avesta (Daily Prayers); *Hadhōkht Nask* (Book of Scriptures); *Aogemadaēchā* (We Accept; containing instructions for afterlife); and *Nīrangistān* (Cultic Regulations). The most ancient part of the *Yasna*, the *Gāthās* (Hymns), are ascribed to Zarathushtra himself.

No less important than the Avestan sources, the Middle-Persian (Pahlavi) writings were compiled primarily during the ninth century C.E. They consist of the *Zand*, or Avestan, interpretation; the *Bundahishn*, or Zoroastrian Book of Genesis; the *Dēnkard*, a collection of religious data; the *Selections* of the priest Zātspram; the *Dādistān ī Denīg* of the priest Mānushcihr; the wisdom text (*Dādistān ī*) *Mēnōg ī Khrad;* the apologetic writing *Skhand-gumānīg Vizār* (Systematic Destruction of All Doubts); and the Book (*Nāmag*) of Ardā Virāz, a priest who performed an otherworldly journey. More recent Zoroastrian writings have been composed in Persian, Gujarati, Sanskrit, and even in English.

There is a wealth of Iranian monuments, from the inscriptions of the Achaemenids (Darius I: 522–486 B.C.E.; Xerxes, 486–465 B.C.E.; Artaxerxes II, 402–359 B.C.E.) to those of the Sassanian rulers Shāpūr I (241–272 C.E.) and Narses (292–302 C.E.). Without being typically religious, they shed some light on the status and character of religion in those times. Religiously more important are the inscriptions of the high priest (*mobād*) Kerdīr at the beginning of the Sassanian era.

Greek, Christian, and Arabic authors supply a wealth of information on Zoroastrianism, from the fifth century B.C.E. to the tenth century C.E.

33.3.2 Zarathushtra's reform represented, as already mentioned, a reaction against the orgiastic cult of male intiatory brotherhoods of warriors. Some scholars depicted it as a puritanical moral revolution, comparable to the Orphic revolution in Ancient Greece (12.3.6), meant to make an end to Dionysian orgies. From a religious angle, the most extraordinary innovation of Zarathushtra consisted of a system combining monotheism and dualism in an original synthesis. No matter how inadequate, this was an interesting solution to the fundamental question of theodicy: how can one reconcile the imperfection of the world with the existence of a good creator-god? Recourse to a form of rudimental free will was only one part of the Zoroastrian answer. Indeed, Ahura Mazdā, the Supreme Lord, was creator of all contrasts (*Yasna*

44.3–5), and his two twins Spenta Mainyu (the Beneficent Spirit) and Angra Mainyu (the Malignant Spirit) were supposed to choose between Truthful Order (*asha:* good thoughts, words, and actions) and Lie (*druj:* evil thoughts, etc.). Unfortunately, Ahura Mazdā was not thereby cleared of any relation with evil. On the contrary, logically he was twice creator of evil, for *druj* preceded the choice made by Angra Mainyu, and because the latter was Ahura Mazdā's son. This ethical dualism also contained theological, cosmological, and anthropological aspects.

During the common Indo-Iranian epoch, as well as in pre-Zoroastrian religion, the *daivas* (Sanskrit *devas*) and the *ahuras* (Sanskrit *asuras*) were divine beings. In Zoroastrianism, they underwent an evolution that was the opposite of what happened to them in India: the *ahuras* were the gods who chose *asha,* and the *daivas* the demons who chose *druj.*

The intermediaries between the Beneficent Spirit and humankind, which was continuously faced with moral choice, were the six Amesha Spentas, or Beneficent Immortals: Vohu Manah (Good Thought), Asha Vahishta (Perfect Truth), Khshathra Vairyia (Desirable Lordship), Spenta Armaiti (Beneficent Devotion), Haurvatāt (Plenty), and Ameretāt (Immortality). The six Beneficent Immortals were at the same time the retinue of virtues that surrounded Ahura Mazdā and the attributes of the human beings who chose the Truthful Order *asha.* The Truthful Being (*ashavan*), reaching a special state called *maga,* was supposed to join the Beneficent Immortals and become one with the Beneficent Spirit.

33.3.3 The priestly synthesis. First the eastern Avestan priests called *āthravans* (Sanskrit *atharvan*) and subsequently the western priests (Medes) known under the name of Magi submitted the puritanical message of Zarathushtra to a reinterpretation that reinstated pre-Zoroastrian customs and systematized traditional religion. The priestly synthesis addressed the ancient religion in its totality. Bloody sacrifice and the use of the *haoma* hallucinogen were resumed. The Amesha Spentas became full *yazatas,* or gods, while previously they had only been attributes of Ahura Mazdā and of the *ashavan.* Ancient gods such as Mitra became important again; others such as Indra were turned into demons. Two important divinities under the Achaemenids were Mithra (from the Indo-Iranian Mitra) and Ardvī Sūrā Anāhitā, a combination of the goddess whom the Indians called Sarasvati and a Near-Eastern goddess. In the Iranian pantheon, Mithra presided, with Sraosha and Rashnu, over the judgment of the dead. Other *yazatas* were Verethragna, god of victory; Vāyu, god of the wind; Daēnā, or the image of fulfilled religion; Khvarenah, or Royal Splendor; Haoma, and so forth.

33.4 ZURVANISM.

33.4.1 The problem. Under the Sassanians (third century C.E.), a religious reformation took place under the sign of intolerance. It is impossible to ascertain whether religious orthodoxy during the whole period was Mazdaean or Zurvanite (from Zurvan, the main character in certain dualistic mythos); yet, as R. C. Zaehner believed, Mazdaism must have been stronger, with minor episodes of Zurvanite preeminence.

Ardashīr (Artaxerxes) was the restorer of Zoroastrianism; yet what Zoroastrianism? Mazdaism or Zurvanism? Shāpūr I, probably a Zurvanite, had strong sympathies for Mani (9.6); his two brothers Mihrshāh and Pērōz converted to Manichaeism. His successor Hormizd I was favorable to the Manichaeans, but Bahrām II, supported by the fearsome Kerdīr, *mobadān mōbad*, or chief of the fire priests, jailed Mani, who died in prison, and persecuted his followers. Shāpūr II, who came to power in 309 C.E., continued Kerdīr's intolerant policy, which was maintained until the time of Yezdigird I, nicknamed "the Sinner," whose tolerance was praised by both Christians and non-Christians. Toward the end of his reign, his minister Mihr-Narsē was planning to send a religious mission to Armenia. It is possible that the myth of Zurvan, transmitted by two Armenian authors (Elishē Vardapet and Eznik of Kolb) and by two Syriac authors (Theodore bar Konai and Yohannān bar Penkayē), was an outcome of Mihr-Narsē's Armenian propaganda, once we admit that his three protectors—Yezdigird I, Bahrām V, and Yezdigird II—were all Zurvanites. Mihr-Narsē's firstborn, who became high priest (hērbadān hērbad), bore the name Zurvāndād, like a "heretic" (*sāstār*) mentioned in *Vidēvdāt* 4.49. It would be by no means impossible that the three rulers and their minister were Zurvanite. The emperor Kavād was favorable to the communist ideas of the reformer Mazdak, but his successor Xosrau I reverted to orthodoxy by having Mazdak and his followers slaughtered, by reinstating Mazdaean orthodoxy, and by having all "heretics" put in prison and all those who relapsed ruthlessly executed. After Xosrau I, the Persian Empire declined, and the Arabic conquest (mid-seventh century C.E.) was imminent.

33.4.2 The myth. In the version of the Armenian author Eznik of Kolb, the most complete among the four extant, the main myth of Zurvanism is thus exposed: Zurvan, an androgynous being whose name means Fate or Destiny, existed before anything else. Wishing to have a son, Zurvan offered sacrifice for one thousand years, but since nothing happened, Zurvan began to have doubts about the efficacy of sacrifice. At this very moment, two sons were conceived in Zurvan's maternal womb: Ohrmazd by virtue of the sacrifice, and Ahriman by reason of the doubt. Zurvan having promised to set in command of the world the first of the twins who entered before him, Ohrmazd revealed Zurvan's plan to Ahriman, who hastened to "pierce the womb" of Zurvan and make his entrance before his brother. Zurvan did not recognize him: "My son, he says, is scented and luminous, while you are dark and stinking." However, Zurvan was obliged by oath to give Ahriman the kingdom of the world; yet he did this for only nine thousand years, after which Ohrmazd would reign endlessly. Yet both brothers were able to create, and thus the world was split in Ohrmazd's creation, including "everything that is good and righteous," and Ahriman's creation, including "everything that is evil and tortuous."

Another Zurvanite myth recalls a Trickster story in which the Trickster is often wiser than the Creator. This was Ahriman's case, who knew a secret ignored by Ohrmazd, namely, how to make the heavenly bodies so that there would be light in the world. Speaking before his demons, Ahriman revealed to them that Ohrmazd could make the sun by having sexual intercourse with his mother and the moon by having intercourse with his sister. (Allusion was made here to the practice called in Pahlavi *xwētwodatīh*, Avestan *xvetuk das*, which, in its cultural setting, was very honorable.) The demon Mahmi ran to Ohrmazd and told him the secret.

A third myth narrates a property conflict between Ohrmazd and Ahriman: the element water in its entirety belonged to Ahriman, yet the animals created by Ohrmazd (the dog, pig, donkey, and ox) drank it. When Ahriman forbade them to touch his water, Ohrmazd was left speechless, until one of Ahriman's demons taught him to tell his evil neighbor: "Then withdraw your water from my land!" Unfortunately, the advice proved to be wrong, for Ahriman asked one of his creatures, the frog, to swallow all the water from Ohrmazd's land; eventually another Ahrimanian creature, the fly, came to the rescue of the helpless Ohrmazd by tickling the frog's nostril and thus forcing it to release the water.

33.4.3 Interpretations of Zurvanism. Despite the repeated attempts made by scholars such as H. S. Nyberg, E. Benveniste, and R. C. Zaehner, it is impossible to reconstruct a complete and coherent Zurvanite religion. However, Zurvanism certainly existed, possibly as a representative of sectarian doctrines that, for short periods of time, may have become official during the Sassanian era.

Strangely enough given the dualistic character of both religions, traces of Manichaean polemic against Zurvanism have survived. One of the hypotheses concerning the relationship between Zurvanism and Manichaeism is that during the reign of Shāpūr I Manichaeism and Zurvanism were close to each other and subsequently drew apart. The name Zurvan has been adopted in Manichaean cosmologies in Iranian languages.

33.5 THE MAZDAISM OF THE PAHLAVI TEXTS, the only coherent Zoroastrian system that survived, was unfortunately written down very late in time. However, some of the most influential scholars of the past were usually inclined to overstate the ancientness of Pahlavi mythology, making it more ancient than Plato and even than Moses! On the contrary, the present-day trend is more reasonable: any time a myth or mythical motif occurring in Judaism, Christianity, or Manichaeism would also occur in the late Pahlavi corpus and nowhere in Avestan literature, then the conclusion would obviously be that it is a recent borrowing from another religious tradition. Based on Avestan material, the only coherent cosmogonical and eschatological Zoroastrian narratives belong to the Pahlavi writings.

33.5.1 Cosmology. The Mazdaean Genesis (*Bundahishn*) took place in two forms of existence: the state *mēnōk,* or "spiritual," which was the seed of the state *gētīg,* or "physical." The latter was not entirely negative, as physical bodies were in Plato or matter was among certain Platonists. The *gētīg* state had *gumecishn* as a main feature, the "mixture" produced by the action of Ahriman, the Evil Spirit. Ahriman killed the Primordial Bull (Gaw-ī-ēw-dād) and the Primordial Man (Gayōmard); from the seed of the former all good animals were born, and from the seed of the latter the first human beings, Mashya and Mashyānag.

The parts of the world were created in six stages, from the crystal sky to human beings. At the center of the world there was the mountain Harā and all around the world the mountain chain Harburz (Avestan Harē Berezaiti). Human beings inhabited only one of the seven sectors (*kēshwar*) of the world circle, the Khvaniratha, south of which water streams stemming from Harā ended up in the Vurukasha Sea, whose center was a mountain made of heavenly crystal on which were the Archetypal Tree, the Tree of Immortality, and the White Haoma. Two rivers leave the Vurukasha sea, forming the eastern and western borders of Khwaniratha.

33.5.2 Collective eschatology. The state of gumēcishn was supposed to come to an end with the separation (*wisārishn*) of the creations of the two Spirits. World history had three main stages: the past, dominated by Gayōmard and his death; the present, dominated by Zarathushtra and his message; and the future, dominated by the Savior, or Sōshans (Avestan Saoshyant).

According to *Bundahishn*, the history of the world had four stages of three thousand years each, or a total of twelve thousand years. During the first three thousand years, Ohrmazd created the world in the state of *mēnōk* and Ahriman began his destructive activity. The following nine thousand years were a standoff between the two gods, marked by the mixture of their creation in the state of *gētīg*. Yet after three thousand years Ahriman attacked the world created by Ohrmazd, upon which the latter created the *fravashi*, or "soul," of Zarathushtra. After another three thousand years, the Prophet was revealed and began his triumphant mission in the world. During the last three thousand years, the three Sōshans, sons of Zarathushtra, would command the world, each of them for one millennium: Ukshyatereta, Ukshyatnemah, and Astvatereta.

Beginning with the Gāthās themselves, Zoroastrian collective eschatology was marked by purification of the world by fire and transfiguration of life (Frashōkereti; Pahlavi, Frashgird). A river of fire divided the Righteous from the evil. The dead were resuscitated in indestructible bodies through a sacrifice performed by the Savior. The latter were born from Zarathushtra's own seed, preserved in the waters of an eastern lake.

33.5.3 Individual eschatology. The judgment of the individual soul was an ancient Avestan motif, but its details became more precise in the later parts of the *Avesta* and especially in the Pahlavi texts. Three days after separation from the body, the soul reached the Cinvat Bridge, where it met a being representing the Daēnā, or image of religion as realized during her lifetime: a fifteen-year-old virgin for the good Mazdaeans and a terrifying old hag for the bad ones. After the judgment performed by the gods Mithra, Sraosha, and Rashnu, the souls of the good believers crossed the bridge, the bad ones fell into the pit of hell, and the lukewarm ones, who had been neither good nor bad, reached the purgatory called Hamestagan. The motif of the bridge that stretched to let the righteous pass and shrank to fling the sinners down to hell was a recent borrowing from Christianity, where it had been in use since the sixth century C.E.

The soul ascended to heaven in three stages: the stars, corresponding to "good thoughts" (*humata*); the Moon, corresponding to "good words" (*hūkhta*); and the Sun, corresponding to "good deeds" (*hvashta*)—eventually reaching the "Infinite Lights" (*anagra raosha*).

33.6 RITUAL. The Zoroastrian reform was initially antiritualistic, but it ended up reinstating animal sacrifice and the cult of the *haoma* in their previous rights. Temples and statues are unknown before the epoch of Artaxerxes I, who, under Near-Eastern influence, erected statues to Anāhitā. The "fire temples" were the centers of numerous fire rituals, among which the most important was the sacrifice of the *haoma* performed by two priests, the *rāspī* and the *zōt* (Avestan *zaotar;* Sanskrit *hotr*), who recited the text of the Avestan *Yasnas*.

Other rituals were seasonal, beginning with the New Year (*Nō Rūz*), a festival dedicated to the Fravashis (souls). The great Zoroastrian festivals were connected with the solstices and the equinoxes.

33.7 MODERN ZOROASTRIANS. Zoroastrianism—as Pahlavi literature bears testimony—survived the Islamic conquest. In the tenth century C.E., following their revolts against Muslim rule, most Zoroastrians left Iran and settled in northern India (Bombay), where to the present day they form a closed and rich community of Pharsees. On the contrary, the Mazdaeans who remained in Iran were poor and oppressed.

According to a 1976 poll, the total number of Zoroastrians in the world reached 130,000, of which 77,000 lived in India, 25,000 in Iran, 5,000 in Pakistan, and 23,000 in the United States.

33.8 BIBLIOGRAPHY. Eliade, *H* 1, 100–112 and 2, 212–17; G. Gnoli, "Zoroastrianism," in *ER* 15, 578–91; "Zarathustra," in *ER* 15, 556–59; "Iranian Religions," in *ER* 7, 277–80; "Zurvanism," in *ER* 15, 595–96. See also R. C. Zaehner, *Zurvan: A Zoroastrian Dilemma* (1955).

PART TWO

Annotated Index

Aaron: Older brother and spokesman of Moses and first priest of the Israelites depicted in Exodus and Numbers. He capitulated to the people's desire for an idol by making the golden calf of Exodus 32.

Abbasids: 17.5; 17.6

Abelard, Peter: 7.4.9

Abhidharma: 3.1; 3.4

Abhinavagupta: (ca. 975–1025 C.E.) Great Tantric Śaiva philosopher of Kashmir, author of the *Tantrāloka*. He professed a "supreme nondualism" (*paramadvayavāda*) meant to surpass Vedantic nondualism (*advaita vedānta*).

Abosom: 1.2.2

Abraham: Hebrew patriarch: father of Isaac and grandfather of Jacob and Ishmael and through God's covenant the ancestor of the Jews as told in Genesis. A pillar of Yahwistic monotheism, Abraham traveled with his wife Sarah from Mesopotamian Ur to Harran to the Promised Land at Canaan.

Abraham ben David: 19.8

Abraham ibn Daud: 19.7

Abū Bakr: 17.4

Abū Ḥanīfah: 17.7. (d. 767 C.E.)

Abulafia, Abraham ben Samuel: 19.8

Abyssinia: 1.6.1

Achilles: 12.3.7

Adad: 4.2.; 20.2 Babylonian-Assyrian storm and weather god, associated with Sumerian Ishkur and West Semitic Dagan. Connoted both virile, violent thunderstorms and fertilizing rain.

Adam: The first human being, created in Genesis 1 and 2; in the latter account, he was formed from the earth's clay (Hebrew *adamah*) and God blew into his nostrils the breath of life (Gen. 2:7). Adam, for centuries a symbol and paradigm of humanity, was expelled with Eve from Eden, lived 930 years, and fathered Cain, Abel, and Seth.

Adonis: 21.2. The handsome lover of Aphrodite/Venus, mutilated and killed by a boar in a situation akin to the Mesopotamian Dumuzi/Tammuz and Anatolian Attis. For the Greeks, Adonis was marked by unwholesome beauty and sterile sexuality, and withered from the world like seasonal vegetation.

Advaitavāda: 14.6

Aēshma: 33.1

Afkodré: 1.6.3

Aga Khans: 17.6.3

Āgamas: 14.7

Aghlabids: 17.5

Agni: 14.2. (Sanskrit: fire.)

Aher: 19.6.1

Ahiṃsā: 18.4. (Sanskrit: noninjury.) Avoidance of harm to any living thing is a Jain, Buddhist, and Hindu concept in harmony with the balanced workings of *karman* and compassion; Gandhi transformed and popularized the idea in the West.

Ahl-i Ḥaqq: 17.6.2

Ahriman: 33.3–33.5 (Pahlavi; Gathic-Avestan: Angra Mainyu, "Hostile Spirit.") Zoroastrian deity of falsehood and evil, paired in the Gāthās with twin brother Spenta Mainyu as good and evil twin sons of Ahura Mazdā; paired beginning in the sixth to fifth century C.E. with Ahura Mazdā (Ohrmazd) as poles in a dualist system.

Ahu: 23.2

Ahura: 14.2; 33.3.2. (Persian: lord.) In Zoroastrianism, the three good gods Ahura Mazdā, Mithra, and Apam Napat are the *ahuras.* In India, the (Sanskrit) *asuras* are the group of older, archaic gods.

Ainu Religion: Shamanistic, tribal religion of the native Ainu people of the northern Japanese islands. Their deities include goddesses of the sun, moon, and fire, and deities of water, woods, sky, and mountains; deities often come to the human world disguised as animals. The Ainu bear ritual entails the sacrifice of a domesticated bear—a divine soul—to evoke the god's blessings provided through the bears hunted by the tribe. Respect for ensouled creatures is emphatic; proper burial will keep a departed soul from returning as a malevolent spirit (see J. M. Kitagawa, "Ainu Bear Festival (Iyomante)," in H 1, 95–151).

Aiye: 1.2.1

Aka: 1.4.2

Akan: 1.2.2

Akhenaton: 10.6. Amenhotep IV, eighteenth dynasty king of Egypt (ca. 1360–1344 B.C.E.). He instituted a short-lived religious reform promoting the sun god Aton at the expense of the other gods, which also had political, artistic (the new naturalism), and linguistic (elevation of the vernacular) dimensions.

Akiba: See Aqiva ben Yosef.

Akitu: 20.5. Widespread ancient Mesopotamian festival, attested in written records as early as ca. 2000 B.C.E. (Ur III). In first-millennium B.C.E. Babylon, the festival is a New Year's celebration in the spring month of Nisan celebrating the city god Marduk's sovereignity, his victory over Tiamat as described in the *Enuma Elish,* and his sacred marriage to Sarpanitu.

Alakaluf: 29.7

Alalu: 15.2

Albert the Great: 7.4.9

Albigenses: 7.4.9

Alchemy: 13.2.5

Alchera (or alcheringa): 2.1

Alcuin: 7.4.8

Aleuts: 26.1.2

Alexander the Great: 13.1; 19.1

Algonquins: 22.2; 22.5; 26.1.2

ʿAlī: 17.4; 17.6

ʿAlī-ilāhī: 17.6.2

ʿAli Zain al-ʿAbidīn: 17.6.1

Allāh: 17.1

Allen, Prudence: 7.8

Almohads: 17.5

Almoravids: 17.5

Amar Das: 14.8.2

Amharghin: 5.4

Amaterasu Omikami: 27.4. The life-bringing goddess of the sun in Japanese mythology; her name means roughly "great goddess shining in heaven." Best known is the myth of her temporary cave retreat, which left the world in darkness until the antics of the other gods brought her forth. In later times she came to be associated with mirrors, seen as spirit-revealing objects.

Amaushumgalna: 20.2

Ambedkar, B. R.: (1891–1956 C.E.) Western-educated Indian reformer born into the untouchable caste, he was instrumental in the outlawing of untouchability and in the conversion of millions of untouchables to Buddhism.

Ambrose of Alexandria: 7.4.3

Ambrose of Milan: 7.4.6

Amenhotep IV: 10.6

American Colonization Society: 1.6.4

American Muslim Mission: 1.6.4

Amesha Spentas: 33.3.2. (Avestan: Beneficent Spirits.) A group of divinized concepts in the Zoroastrian *Avesta*, in which humans may partake, and which came to be associated with the elements. They are: Vohu Manah (Good Thought), Asha Vahishta (Perfect Truth), Khshathra Vairyia (Desirable Lordship), Spenta Armaiti (Beneficent Devotion), Haurvatāt (Plenty), and Ameretāt (Immortality).

Amidism: 3.8–3.9

Amitābha: 3.8–3.9 (Sanskrit: Immeasurable Light.) The Buddha who rules the western paradise Sukhāvatī in Mahāyāna tradition. From sixth-century C.E. China, the Pure Land sect that emphasized faith and reliance on Amitābha's merciful saving power and repetition of his name, spread gradually to Korea and Japan.

Amma: 1.2.3

Ammonius Saccas: 7.4.3

Amon: 10.6

Amoraim: 19.2. (Aramaic: speakers.) Babylonian and Palestinian rabbinical commentators who wrote on the Torah in Aramaic from the third to fifth century C.E., and whose legacy is to be found in the Midrash and the *gemara* of the Talmud.

Amorites: 19.1

Amos: 19.5. Prophet of eighth-century B.C.E. Israel, under King Jereboam II (ca. 787–747 B.C.E.). The Hebrew Bible's Book of Amos contains his condemnation of the luxurious vices and hypocrisy of the upper class and of the corruption of religious and cultic observance.

An: 20.2

Anabaptism: 7.4.13. A Protestant sect that broke from Zwingli's movement in Zurich in the 1520s, believing in life according to Jesus' life and the Gospels, the independence of church from state impingements, and baptism of confessing adults. Today's Anabaptists include Mennonites and Hutterians who emphasize pacifism and the Bible's ideals of social justice.

Anāhitā: 33.3.3. The great goddess of Achaemenid-Parthian-Sasanian Iran, related to Ishtar and other Near-Eastern goddesses. She played a role in royal coronation, and oversaw war and fertility associated with waters.

Analects: 8.1

Ānanda: 3.3

Anat: 4.2–4.4

Anatolia: 15.1

al-Andalus: 17.5

Andes: 29.2–29.3

Angad: 14.8.2

Angerona: 25.2.1

Anglicanism: 7.4.13. Henry VIII's split with the papacy and the work of his daughter Elizabeth I through the sixteenth century established the independent Anglican church, an institution of both Catholic and Protestant legacies. The Church of England is today one part of a worldwide federation of churches, noted for its ecumenical interests.

Angra Mainyu: 33.3.2

Angrbodha: 11.4.1

Anselm of Aosta: 7.4.9

Anthesteria: 12.5

Anthony: 7.4.8

Anu: 15.2

Anubis: Ancient Egyptian funerary deity. Embalmer of corpses and caretaker of the dead, this god originated early in Middle Egypt, with the shape of the dog or jackal that feeds on corpses.

Aṇuvrata: 18.4

Apaches: 22.2

Aphrodite: 12.3.4

Apo: 1.2.2

Apollinaris of Laodicaea (in Syria): 7.7.3

Apollo: 12.3; 12.7

Apollonius of Tyana: 13.2.4

Apsu: 20.5

Apuleius: 13.2.3; 21.3.2

Aqhat: 4.4

Aqiva ben Yosef: 19.1; 19.7. (ca. 50–ca. 135 C.E.) Early rabbinic commentator of Palestine who died during the Bar Kokhba Revolt. Famous for his inspired exegetical techniques and his influence on the Mishnah, Tosefta, and later Jewish intellectual traditions.

Aquinas, Thomas: 1.1; 7.4.9

Araucans: 29.1

Āraṇyakas: 14.3

Arawak: 29.1; 29.5; 29.6

Ardā Virāz: 33.3.1

Ardvī Sūrā Anāhitā: 33.3.3

Arhat: 3.3–3.4; 14.5. (Sanskrit: worthy; in Pali, *arhant*.) In Vedic usage, a meritorious person or deity; in Theravāda Buddhism, an enlightened person; in Jainism, a revealer of religion (Tīrthaṃkara).

Arianism: 7.7.2

Arikara: 22.2

Arinna: 15.1

Arioi: 23.2

Aristeas of Proconnesus: 12.3.2

Aristotle: 13.2

Arius: 7.7.2

Arjan: 14.8.2

Arjuna: 14.5. Third Pāṇḍava son, his mother Kuntī and his father the god Indra, in the *Mahābhārata*. The heroic Arjuna becomes Kṛṣṇa's interlocutor and disciple in the *Bhagavadgītā*, during the battle against the Kauravas.

Ars wa-Shamem: 4.2

Artemis: 12.2

Aryadeva: (1) Mādhyamaka Buddhist dialectician active in South India circa third to fourth century C.E.; a famous disciple of Nāgārjuna. (2) Tantric Buddhist teacher active in North India (the university at Nālaṇḍā) circa the eighth century C.E. The works and life stories of the two are much conflated in the Chinese and Tibetan Buddhist canons.

Ārya Samāj: 14.9. (Society of Honorables.) A reform movement breaking caste and gender barriers, grounded in the revealed Vedic hymns and emphasizing a monotheistic message. Founded by Dayananda Sarasvati in 1875, it remains a successful organization in India today.

Asaman: 1.2.2

Āsana: 14.4.2

Asaṅga: 3.5. (ca. 315–390 C.E.) North Indian Buddhist teacher who converted to Mahāyāna after ascending to the Tuṣita Heaven, where he was instructed by the Bodhisattva Maitreya. His explanations of Maitreya's teachings are sometimes attributed to Maitreya alone, who was said to have lectured on earth at Asaṅga's request. Asaṅga founded the Yogācāra school of Buddhist philosophy.

Asante: 1.2.2

Asantehene: 1.2.2

Asase Yaa: 1.2.2

Ases: 11.3.3; 11.4.1

Asgardhr: 11.3.3

Asha: 33.3.2

al-Ashʿarī, Abū al-Ḥasan: 17.8. (874–935 C.E.) Muslim theologian who lived in Basra and later Baghdad, and founded the most influential theological school in Islam, which set the tone that is still Sunni orthodoxy today: al-Ashʿarīyah. Renouncing rationalist Muʿtazilism, al-Ashʿarī worked from Qurʾān and sunnah toward an acceptance of theological paradoxes that elude human reasoning.

Ashavan: 33.3.2

Asherah: 4.2

Ashtart wa-Anar (Astarte): 4.2

ʿĀshūrāʾ: 17.6; 17.9. Day of mourning in Shiʿite Islam for the martyrdom of Imam Ḥusayn, son of ʿAlī and grandson of the Prophet, at Karbalā (Iraq) on the tenth of Muḥarram, 61 A.H. (10 October 680 C.E.).

Asklepios: (Latin: Aesculapius.) God of healing in the Greek and Roman worlds, recognizable by his kindly, bearded face, his (chthonic) snake, and sometimes his wife and daughters. At spalike healing precincts like Epidauros or the Isola Tiberina, sick people might be cured by the god's visit in a dream.

Askr: 11.3.1

Aśoka: 3.3.–3.4. Emperor of India (ca. 270–232 B.C.E.) in the Maurya dynasty, who converted to Buddhism and promoted nonviolence, religious tolerance (to an extent), and vegetarianism. He is known primarily through the edicts he had engraved on stone throughout his reign.

Āśrama: 14.4

Assassins: 17.6.3

Assiniboins: 22.2

Aṣṭapāda: 3.2

Astrology: 13.2.2

Asuman: 1.2.2

Asuras: 14.2; 33.1–33.3

Atahuallpa: 6.3; 29.3

Atargatis: 4.2

Athapascans: 22.2

Atharvaveda: 14.2

Athena: 12.3.4

Athirat: 4.2–4.3

Atisa: 3.10. (982–1054 C.E.) Northern Indian (Bengali) Tantric Buddhist monk, who later moved to Tibet. A devotee of the goddess Tara, he worked toward a reform of Tantric monasticism, wrote and translated texts, and founded the monastery of Rwa-sgren.

Ātman: 3.4; 14.3

Aton: 10.6

Atrahasis: 20.6

ʿAṭṭar, Farīd al-Dīn: 17.10. (ca. 1145–1220 C.E.) Persian Sufi and poet of Nishapur, best known today for his *Manṭi al-ṭayr* (*Conversation of the Birds*), a spiritual allegory of the journey of thirty birds (sī murgh) through seven valleys named for the stages of the soul's search, to find their divine king Simurgh.

Attis: 21.2

Atum: 10.3

Audhumla: 11.3.1

Augustine: 1.1; 3.9; 7.4.2; 7.4.7; 7.4.8

Aurobindo Ghose: 14.9. (1872–1950 C.E.) Indian spiritual leader and writer. After a childhood spent in England and a youth spent in nationalist political activity in India, Aurobindo developed a philosophy of consciousness evolution facilitated by "integral yoga", which, through his writings, has followers today in the East and West.

Aurr: 11.3.2

Avalokiteśvara: Bodhisattva of compassion in Mahāyāna Buddhism, known as Kuan-yin in China and Spyan-ras-gzigs in Tibet, he resides on the legendary Potalaka Mountain, seeing, hearing, and intervening in situations of suffering. He figures in the important *Lotus Sūtra, Flower Ornament Sūtra,* and *Pure Land Sūtra.*

Avatāra: 14.5. (Sanskrit: a descent.) In Hinduism, the appearance of a god on earth, usually in the form of an animal or person; usually the god Viṣṇu.

Averroes: 29.5

Avesta: 33.3.1. Collective name for the surviving sacred texts of Zoroastrianism, codified circa third to seventh centuries C.E.

Avidyā: 14.3; 14.6–14.7

Aymara: 29.1

Ayurveda: Hindu art of medical healing, which aims at the balancing of three "humors"—wind (*vāta*), bile (*pitta*), and phlegm (*kapha*) in differing human constitutions. Special foods and herbs, purgations, and ritual acts are often prescribed; techniques are of varying and uncertain antiquity, referring to texts that date from through out the first millennium C.E.

Azande: 1.1; 1.3

Azriel: 19.8

Aztecs: 6.1–6.5

Baal: 4.2–4.4

Baal Shem Tov: 19.10. (Hebrew: Master of the Good Name; also known by the acronym Besht.) Title of Yisra'el ben Eliʿezer (1700–1760 C.E.), Ukranian Jewish spiritual leader and Kabbalist, founder of East European Hasidism.

Bacchus: 12.6

Bādarāyaṇa: 14.6

Bahā'īs: World religion founded by the Persian aristocrat Bahā'u'llāh (1817–1892 C.E.), who endorsed the claim of the Persian religious reformer Bab (1819–1850 C.E.), executed in 1850 for having announced the imminent coming of the Messiah expected by the great world religions. In 1863 Bahā'u'llāh proclaimed himself the Messiah in

Baghdad. From his exile in Palestine, Bahā'u'llāh wrote letters to the chiefs of state of his epoch, announcing the emergence of a unified world civilization and calling upon them to establish universal peace. After his death, leadership of the religion passed on to his son 'Abdu'l-Bahā (1844-1921 C.E.), who proclaimed the Bahā'ī message in Europe and the United States. Upon 'Abdu'l-Bahā's death, his grandson Shoghi Effendi Rabbani (d. 1957) became Guardian of the Bahā'ī Faith. The headquarters of the religion are in Palestine; it has important Houses of Worship in all continents, and has undergone severe persecution, as in Iran. In the United States, the major Bahā'ī temple is near Chicago, Illinois.

Bahir: 19.8

Bahuśrutīya: 3.4

Bahya ibn Paquda: 19.7. Mid- to late eleventh-century C.E. Jewish philosophical theologian, probably from Saragossa (Spain), whose book *Guidance to the Duties of the Hearts* (written in Arabic) brought moderated Sufi themes into the Jewish *kalām* tradition epitomized by Saadia Gaon (882–942 C.E.).

Baka: 1.4.2

Baldr: 11.4.2

Bambara: 1.1; 1.2.3

Banisteriopsis caapi: 26.1.6

Bantu: 1.1; 1.3; 1.4.1; 1.5

Bar Kochba: 19.7

Baraka: 1.1

Baru: 29.4

Baruch: 19.6

Basil of Caesarea: 7.4.5 (ca. 329–379 C.E.)

Basmallah: 17.3

Bāṭin: 17.6.3

Beavers: 22.2

Beki: 26.1

Bektāshīyah: 17.10

Bell, Rudolph: 7.8–7.9

Bella Coola: 22.2; 22.7

Belobog: 28.1.1

Bemba: 1.2.3

Bendis: 31.3. South Thracian goddess, overseeing marriage.

Benedict of Nursia: 7.4.8. (ca. 480–547 C.E.)

Benin: 1.1; 1.2.1

Benveniste, Émile: 33.4.3

Benvenuta Boiano: 7.9; 7.11

Berbers: 1.1

Bereshit: 19.2

Bergelmir: 11.3.1

Bering Strait: 22.2

Berit: 19.4

Berling, Judith: 30.3

Bernard of Clairvaux: 7.4.9. (ca. 1090–1153 C.E.)

Berserkr: 11.5.2. ("bear-skinned.") In Norse mythology, theriomorphic (in the form of animals) warriors of the god Odhinn, characterized by wild, frenzied behavior in battle; associated with an ecstatic possession cult among Scandinavian warriors in pre-Christian times.

Besht: 19.7

Bestla: 11.3.1

Bhadrayanīya: 3.4

Bhagavadgītā: 14.5; 14.6. (Sanskrit: The Song of the Blessed.) One of the hundred books of the

Mahābhārata epic (incorporated ca. third century B.C.E.), this popular book grew to a status of sacred scripture for Hindus of many sects. Its heart is the dialogue between the hero Arjuna and the divine Kṛṣṇa, who had been disguised as Arjuna's charioteer. The god instructed Arjuna about the workings of the three *guṇas* (*sattva, tamas, rajas*), *karman*, and *dharma*, and how to detach oneself, transcend, and realize the divine, unbounded self.

Bhakti: 3.5; 14.6–14.7 (Sanskrit: devotion)

Bianchi, Ugo: 9.2

Big Drum Dance: 1.6.1

al-Bisṭāmī, Abū Yazīd: 17.10 (777–848 C.E.)

Bka-brgyud-pa: 3.10

Bka-gdams-pa: 3.10

Black Elk: (1863–1950 C.E.) Lakota Indian visionary influential through two books recounting his life experiences, including the oppression of the Indians and the Ghost Dance movement, and mystical participation in the divine forces and rituals of his people.

Blackfoot: 22.2; 22.6

Blavatsky, Helena Petrovna: (1831–1891 C.E.) Russian-born psychic and founder of the theosophical movement that arose in nineteenth-century Europe and America.

Boas, Franz: 22.1

Boccaccio, Giovanni: 7.4.11

Bodhidharma: 3.8. (Fl. ca. 480–520 C.E.) Indian-born founder of Chinese Ch'an Buddhism (Japanese: Zen); a revered figure in legend, as in the story of his sitting motionless before a wall for several years.

Bodhisattva: 3.5; 3.9. (Sanskrit: *bodhi* = enlightenment; *sattva* = being.) A being that delays its enlightenment to work for the salvation of all sentient beings.

Boehme, Jacob: 7.9. (1575–1624 C.E.) Lutheran mystical writer, who traced a complex cosmology from God to his creation, influential in seventeenth- to eighteenth-century Europe.

Boethius: (475–525 C.E.) Late Roman Neoplatonic philosopher and Christian theologian who translated some of Aristotle's logical work into Latin. His *On the Consolation of Philosophy* lays out his Neoplatonic world.

Bogazköy: 15.1

Bogomils: 7.4.9; 9.8

Bolthorn: 11.3.1

Bon: 3.10; 32.1–32.3

Bonaventura of Bagnoreggio: 7.9. (1217–1274 C.E.)

Bonhoeffer, Dietrich: (1906–1945 C.E.) Protestant theologian advocating active work for justice as opposed to theoretical Christian piety, killed for his resistance to the Nazis.

Boniface-Ulfila, Saint: 7.5. (673–754 C.E.) English missionary who worked to Christianize parts of Germanic Europe.

Bon-po: 3.10

Borr: 11.3.1

Bozo: 1.2.3

Brahmā: 14.8.1. Hindu creator god, sometimes grouped with Śiva (the destroyer) and Viṣṇu (the preserver); Brahmā is more significant in mythology than in cultic worship.

Brahman: 14.6. Sanskrit neuter noun for the supreme eternal principle underlying all.

Brāhmaṇas: 14.3

Brahmāsūtra: 14.6

Brāhmo Samāj: 14.9. (Society of Brahman.) Intellectual Hindu reform movement founded by Ram Mohan Roy (Calcutta, 1828) emphasizing monotheism at the expense of temple and image cult.

Brandon, S. G. F.: 7.2

Brazil: 1.6

Brighid: 5.3

Buber, Martin: (1878–1965 C.E.) Jewish philosopher and prolific author on interhuman and human-divine relations; influenced by European Hasidic tradition and by the world wars and the Jewish nationalist movement in which he participated.

Buddha: 3.2–3.3

al-Bukhārī, Muḥammad ibn Ismāʿīl: (810–870 C.E.) Great compiler and evaluator of *ḥadīth* (traditions of the life and sayings of the Prophet Muhammad).

Bundahishn: 33.3.1

Buri: 11.3.1

Buriats: 26.1.1

Buridan, John: 7.4.10

Burkert, Walter: 12.3.3

Bushmen: 1.1

Bu-ston: (1290–1364 C.E.) Tibetan Buddhist monk, famed especially for his translations of Buddhist texts from Indian languages and his mastery of Tantric thought.

Cabiri: 21.2

Caddoans: 22.2

Cain and Abel: In Genesis 4, the first two of Adam and Eve's three sons; Cain was the agriculturalist whose offering was rejected by God, Abel the shepherd killed by his brother.

Caitanya: 14.7.1

Cakchiquel: 6.2

Cakra: 14.4.2. (Sanskrit: wheel.) In Hinduism and Buddhism, energy centers where the channels of the subtle body converge. Varying in number, they are distributed from the base of the spine to the top of the head; they are visualized in meditation.

Cakravartin: 3.7. (Sanskrit: one who turns the wheel.)

Calakmul: 6.2

Calame-Griaule, G.: 1.2.3

Calvin, John: 7.4.13. (1509–1564 C.E.)

Campanella, Tommaso: 29.3

Candomblé: 1.6.2

Caribbean cults: 1.6

Cargo Cults: Multifaceted millenarian movement among the peoples of Melanesia resulting from the introduction of Western goods (cargo) into the islands from 1871 onward. Natives await contact with the cargo deity whose blessings the Europeans have monopolized.

Caribes: 29.1; 29.5

Cassian, John: (365–435 C.E.) Byzantine monk and theologian who moved to the West and wrote in Latin; his writings include an analysis of the ascetic life.

Cassiodorus: 7.4.8

Castaneda, Carlos: 22.1; 22.6

Castor: 25.2.1

Corpus Hermiticum: 13.2.6

Cortés, Hernán: 6.3; 6.4

Coryllus: 31.4

Cotys: 31.3

Cree: 22.2

Crescas, Hasdai: 19.7. (ca. 1340–1412 C.E.) Spanish Jewish philosopher who defended the Jewish faith and community against the assaults of the period, while formulating an anti-Aristotelian theology.

Cruce, Benedetto: 29.5

Crow: 22.2

Cú Chulainn: 5.4.2

Cybele: 21.2

Cyril: 7.5

Cyril of Alexandria: 7.6

Cyrus: 19.1

Dacian Rider: 21.3.4

Daēnā: 33.5.3

Dagan: 4.2–4.4

Daghdha: 5.4

Daimon: 12.3.6

Daivas: 14.2; 33.1–33.3 "Gods" of pre-Zoroastrian Iranian polytheism; vilified by Zoroaster, they became the maleficent demons of his religion.

Dalai Lama: 3.10

Dan Fodio, Usuman: (1754/1755–1817 C.E.) West African Islamic reformer who campaigned against the Hausa dynasty of Gobir and worked toward a more complete Islamization of the Hausa.

Dana: 5.4; 5.5

Daniel: 19.6. Visionary hero of the biblical *Book of Daniel*, a composite work in Hebrew and Aramaic pulled together in the Hellenistic period, whose overall message was of past and future Jewish triumph over oppression and martyrdom.

Dante Alighieri: 7.4.8; 7.4.9

Darśanas: 14.4

Datura stramonium: 22.8

David: 19.1. Early tenth-century B.C.E. king of Israel and Judah, who won Jerusalem and pushed back the Philistines; he was promised an eternal lineage by God, and his son Solomon built the Temple. Later tradition credited David with writing the Psalms.

Daʿwa: 17.6.3

Dayānanda: 14.9

Dead Sea Scrolls: 19.2. They are associated with the Qumran community (fl. ca. 135 B.C.E.–68 C.E.), thought to be Essenes.

Decebalus: 31.4.2

Deceneus: 31.4.2

Deghiga: 22.2

Deism: Term designating a late sixteenth- to eighteenth-century European rationalist religious position, which accepted the assumed existence of a God while remaining skeptical of religion, afterlife, and/or divine intervention in the world. This belief was held by many of the most prominent intellectuals of the eighteenth century, including "founding fathers" of America.

Delphi: 12.3; 12.7. Mountainous site of Greek Apollo oracle from the eighth century B.C.E. In the sanctuary, a woman, the Pythia, gave inspired utterances while seated on a tripod; these were versified by priests to answer inquiring embassies that made the pilgrimage to the holy place, which was adorned with rich, accumulated offerings.

Dema: 6.2.1; 21.1; 29.5; 29.6

Demeter: 5.5; 12.3.4; 12.6; 21.2. Greek goddess of fertility and grain, sister of Zeus and mother of Persephone (Korē); Demeter figures in the the Eleusinian Mysteries and the Thesmophoria festival.

Deus otiosus: 1.1; 1.2.1; 1.3; 1.4.1; 2.1; 4.2; 20.2; 29.5

Devas: 14.2; 33.1–33.3

Devī: 14.7.3

Dge-lugs-pa: 3.10. (Tibetan: virtuous way.) Tibetan Buddhist sect and comprehensive educational system founded circa 1400 C.E.; grounded in monasticism, it involved scriptural study, devotion, ritual, and intellectual discourse.

Dharma: 3.2; 3.4; 14.4.3. Sanskrit term used to signify, in Hinduism and Buddhism, truth and rightness, religion, and proper ways of life.

Dharmakīrti: (ca. 600–660 C.E.) South Indian Buddhist philosopher who wrote influential treatises on perception, cognition, and epistemology in the logical tradition of Dignāga (ca. 480–540 C.E.).

Dharmottarya: 3.4

Dhikr: 17.10. (Arabic: recollection.) Invocation of God, enjoined upon Muslims in the Qur'ān; practiced by Sufis in particular, who chant and meditate upon God's names to reach communion with him.

Dhyāna: 3.8; 14.4.2

Diana: 25.2.2. Roman goddess of the moon, early assimilated with the Greek virgin goddess Artemis.

Diego de Landa: 6.2.1

Dieterlen, Germaine: 1.2.3

Diggers: 22.1

Dighambara: 18.1; 18.3

Dignāga: (ca. 480–540 C.E.) South Indian Buddhist philosopher of the Yogācāra school, whose logical treatises dissected the mechanisms of causation and syllogistic proof.

Dinka: 1.1; 1.3

Dionysius the Areopagite: 7.9. (ca. 500 C.E.) Pseudonym of a Christian mystical writer whose Neoplatonic cosmologies emphasized the absolute transcendence and indescribability of God and the complex hierarchy of beings below, which participate by gradations in divine perfection.

Dionysus: 12.3.5; 21.3.1. Greek god of wine and divine madness; son of Zeus and Semele. Inspirer of female ecstatics (maenads, as in Euripides' *Bacchae*), he is an anomalous god associated with phallic processions and raw meat sacrifices, escape from social norms, and the Anthesteria and new wine festivals.

Divination: 1.1; 1.2.1; 1.3; 6.2.1; 6.3.1; 12.4; 15.1; 20.3

Djangwawul: 2.1

Docetism: 3.4

Dōgen: 3.9 (1200–1253 C.E.) Japanese Zen master especially influential in the Sōtō sect and through his most famous work, the *Shōbōgenzō*. He emphasized the attainability of enlightenment, which is one with the practice of *zazen* meditation, and the pervasive presence of the Buddha nature in the transient world and its inhabitants.

Dogon: 1.2.3

Dominicans: 7.4.9

Dominic Guzman: 7.4.9

Donatism: 1.1

Doniger, Wendy: 14.5

Douglas, Mary: 1.4.1

Dov Baer: 19.10

Drew, Timothy: 1.6.4

Druids: 5.2; 5.4.1

Druj: 33.3.2

Druze: 17.6.3

Duhkha: 3.2

Dumézil, Georges: 16.3; 25.2

Dumuzi: 20.2. Ancient Sumerian god, already mentioned around 3500 B.C.E.; Tammuz was his Akkadian name.

Duns Scotus, John: 7.4.10. (1266–1308 C.E.)

Durkheim, Émile: 16.3

Dyow: 1.2.3

Ea: 15.2; 20.2; 20.5; 20.6

Easter: (1) The Jewish Pesah is a mobile annual feast of seven or eight days starting on Nisan 15, in commemoration of the departure of the Israelites from Egypt. (2) Christian Easter, a mobile feast in commemoration of the Resurrection of Jesus Christ, should at least in theory be celebrated together with the Jewish Pesah. The Council of Nicea (325) decided that it would fall every new year on the first Sunday after the full moon succeeding the spring equinox. Differences in calendars and methods of computation explain the often considerable difference between the dates of Passover, the Orthodox Easter, and the Easter of Western denominations.

Ebionites: (Hebrew: Poor Ones.) Jewish Christians of the early centuries C.E. who believed in Jesus as Messiah (rejecting the virgin birth) and lived according to Jewish law, in contrast to St. Paul's attuning Christianity with a lifestyle lacking Jewish observances.

Ecclesiastes: 19.2

Eckhart, Meister: 7.9

Edda: 11.2; 11.4.1

Edwards, Jonathan: (1703–1758 C.E.) Presbyterian New England minister famed for his rousing sermons, which portrayed the utter sinfulness of humans and the redemptive salvation that comes from God.

Egungun: 1.2.1

Eisai: 3.9

Ekavyāvahārika: 3.4

El: 4.2–4.4

Eleazar ben Azariah: 19.7

Eleazar of Worms: 19.8

Eleusis: 12.6; 21.2

Eliezer ben Hyrcanus: 19.7. (First to second century C.E.) Conservative Jewish legal scholar at Lydda, whose strict views on purity and ritual were prominent in the Mishnah, and who was excommunicated for the intransigence of his opinions; teacher of Rabbi Aqiva.

Elijah: 19.2.4 (Ninth century B.C.E.) Hebrew prophet from Gilead who fought the Baal worship of Jezebel, wife of Ahab, and Baal's priests. Among his miraculous demonstrations of Yahweh's power,

Elijah ascended undying in a chariot of fire; he wandered through the world as a teacher of esoteric truths, and was a forerunner of the Messiah.

Elias, Saint: 28.1.1

Elijah Muhammad: 1.6.4

Elisha: 9.5; 19.2

Elisha ben Avuyah: 19.6.1. (First half second century C.E.) Palestinian Tanna who apostasized against Judaism and is portrayed in Talmudic sources as a persecutor of Jews.

Elohim: 19.2

Embla: 11.3.1

Empedocles of Agrigentum: 12.3.2

Enki: 20.2; 20.6

Enkidu: 20.6

Enlil: 20.2

Enoch: 19.2; 19.6

Enthusiasts: 7.4.13

Enuma Elish: 4.4; 20.3; 20.5

Epimenides of Crete: 12.3.2

Epona: 5.4.1; 5.5

Er: 12.3.3

Eros: 12.3.4

Esdras: 19.2; 19.6

Eskimos: 22.3; 26.1.2

Essenes: 19.2; 19.6.2

Esther: 19.2; 19.4. Heroine of the Jewish people; in the biblical Book of Esther, she was the Jewish wife of the Persian king Ahasuerus.

Esu: 1.2.1

Ethiopia: 1.6.1

Eucharist: 7.9

Euridice: 12.3.6

Eustachia of Messina: 7.9

Eutyches of Constantinople: 7.7.3

Evans, Arthur: 12.1

Evans-Pritchard, E. E.: 1.3

Evenki: 26.1.1

Ezekiel: 19.2–19.5. Biblical prophet, deported with the exiles to Babylon. His visions of the dry bones revivified (Ezek. 37) and the divine throne were central in later Jewish mysticism. He chided the people for their individual roles in the degradation of the community as a whole.

Ezra: Jewish prophet who reestablished and guided Jewish law and culture in Jerusalem after leading exiles back to their homeland.

Ezra ben Solomon: 19.8

Fang-chung: 30.4

Faqīr: 17.10

Faqr: 17.10

Fard, Wallace D.: 1.6.4

Faro: 1.2.3

Farrakhan, Louis: 1.6.4

Fāṭimah bint Muḥammad: 17.4; 17.6 (D. 633 C.E.)

Fenrir: 11.4.1

Fertile Crescent: 6.1

Ficino, Marsilio: 7.4.12; 12.3.3; 13.2.1

Filioque: 7.6

Fionn mac Cumhail: 5.4.2

Fiqh: 17.7

Flamen: 25.2

Fomhoire: 5.4. (Irish: *fobhar,* "spirit".) Evil demons of Irish mythology, accruing some of their traits in the Christian period. They are black with one arm, leg, and eye, and figure in the *Second Battle of Magh Tuiredh*.

Four Truths: 3.2

Fox, George: (1624–1691 C.E.) A founder and organizer of the Quakers in England and North America, he advocated in his teachings and in his many writings nonviolence and individual contact with the divine within.

Franciscans: 7.4.9

Francis of Assisi: 7.4.9 (1181–1226 C.E.)

Frank, Jacob: 19.7

Frashgird: 33.5.2

Frashōkereti: 33.5.2. Zoroastrian eschatological concept, involving a resurrection and final judgment and final obliteration of evil to come at the end of time.

Fravashi: 33.5.2. Good spirits in Zoroastrian tradition, present in the Avesta, often considered spirits of the dead.

Frederic II: 7.4.9

Freya: 11.3.3. Scandinavian fertility goddess. Sister of Freyr and wife of Odr, she was associated with cats, jewels, and magic, and was a bringer of prosperity.

Freyr: 11.3.3 Scandinavian fertility god and legendary king and warrior. Son of Njordr, brother of Freyja, his cult involved sexual practices, and animal and perhaps human sacrifice.

Frigg: 11.4.2

Frobenius, Leo: 1.5

Fujiwara Seika: 8.5

Gabriel: 17.2

Gamaliel II: 19.7

Ganda: 1.3

Gandhi, Mohandas Karamachand: 14.9; 18.3. (1869–1948 C.E.) Indian lawyer, theosopher, and politician, he led the nonviolent movement that achieved the independence of India. He was influenced by Westernized Hinduism, Jainism, and theosophy. In his action, he was inspired by the Jain concept of nonviolence (*ahimsa*).

Ganeśa: (Lord of the Group.) Hindu god, son of Siva and Pārvatī, who oversees obstacles, doorways, and success in various human activities; his head is an elephant's, his body squat and potbellied.

Ganges: Holy river and goddess (Gangā Mātā) of North India, and the site of pilgrimage for purification.

Gāthās: 33.3

Gauḍapāda: (ca. fifth to eighth century C.E.) Indian nondualist philosopher who held that causal origination is illusory and absolute unity is what truly exists. He is held to be the author of the *Āgama Śāstra* and the teacher of Sankara.

Gautama: 3.2

Gautama Indrabhūti: 18.3

Gayōmard; 33.5.1

Geb: 10.3

Genesia: 12.4

Gengis Khan: 26.1

Genshin: (942–1017 C.E.) Major thinker of Japanese Pure Land Buddhism. His influential work *Essentials of Pure Land Rebirth* (*Ojōyōshū*) delineated Pure Land cosmology and provided *nembutsu* meditations for salvation.

Geomancy: 1.1; 1.2.1; 1.3

Gerard of Cambrai: 5.4.1

Gerard of Cremona: 7.4.9

Gersonides: 19.7

Gētīg: 33.5.1

Ghana: 1.2.2

al-Ghazālī, Abū Ḥāmid: 17.10. (1058–1111 C.E.) Muslim religious thinker born in eastern Iran who mastered jurisprudence, philosophy, and theology, and, in a personal search for truth, embraced Sufi mysticism and wrote a refutation of the philosophers of his day.

Ghost Dance: 22.6. A regeneration movement originated by Paiute Indians of Nevada from 1870, but which spread through many western tribes. Men and women danced together in circle dances to hasten the return of the dead and the restoration of the Indian way of life. In some cases a messiah was expected; shamanic visions and conflict with opposing whites sometimes occurred.

Ghulat: 17.6

Gikatilla, Joseph ben Abraham: 19.8

Gilgamesh: 20.6. Hero of Sumerian and Babylonian epic, but based on a king of Uruk (ca. twenty-seventh century B.C.E.)

Giuliana, Orsola Veronica: 7.9

Gimbutas, Marija A.: 16.2; 24.2; 24.3; 28.1.1

Gisu: 1.3

Gnosticism: 9.3; 9.4

Gobind Rāi: 14.8.2

Gobind Singh: 14.8.2

Gogo: 1.3

Gokulika: 3.4

Gopis: 14.7.1

Gosāla, Maskalin: (ca. sixth to fifth century B.C.E.) Indian religious leader and ascetic. His sect, the Ājīvika, was known for its deterministic denial of free will, and was viewed as heterodox in the Buddhist and Jain writings that preserve fragments of their philosophy.

Great Basin: 22.2

Grant, R. M.: 7.4.4

Granth: 14.8.2

Great Goddess: 24.3

Great Lakes: 22.2

Greenberg, Joseph: 1.1

Gregory of Nazianzus: 7.4.5

Gregory of Nyssa: 7.4.5

Gregory Palamas: 7.9

Gregory VII: 7.4.8

Grenada: 1.6.1

Gromovnik: 28.1.1

Gros Ventre: 22.2

Gter-mas: 3.10

Guinea: 1.1

Gulik, Robert van: 30.4

Gumecishn: 33.5.1

Guṇas: 14.4.2. Inherent qualities, virtues, or strands that make up substances. In Hindu Sāṃkhya theory, they are *sattva* (light and clear), *tamas* (dark and heavy), and *rajas* (dynamic).

Gurdjieff, G. I.: (ca. 1877–1949 C.E.) Spiritual teacher and writer. Born in Russia, he traveled extensively in search of ancient spiritual truths, then acquired a following in Europe and America. His writings include an autobiography and musical scores for his dance techniques.

Gurus (Sikh): 14.8.2

Gwdyion: 5.5

Gylfaginning: 11.2; 11.3.1

Hades: 12.3.6; 12.6; 13.2.1

Ḥadīth: 17.2. Accounts of the sayings and actions of the Prophet Muhammad and certain early Muslims, passed down orally and in written form and collected in volumes for the guidance of the Muslim communities. Each report is accompanied by an *isnād* ("chain") listing the line of sources who transmitted the tradition. A science of *ḥadīth* criticism developed early on to judge the authenticity of the thousands of circulating reports, rejecting many dubious accounts composed to support various religious stances.

Haggadah: 19.2

Haida: 22.2; 22.7

Haile Selassie: 1.6.1

Hainuwele: 21.2

Haisla: 22.6

Haiti: 1.6.1

Ḥajj: 17.2; 17.9

Hako: 22.6

Halach Uinic: 6.2

Halakhah: 19.2. (Hebrew: law.) Comprehensive Jewish law, elaborated for centuries by rabbinical tradition; it is based on interpretation of written and oral sources and common custom, and resides in the Hebrew Bible, midrash, Talmud, Tosefta, and the ongoing conduct of rabbinical ajudication.

al-Ḥallāj, al-Ḥusayn ibn Mansūr: 17.10. (857–922 C.E.)

Han Yü: 8.4

Ḥanbal, Aḥmad ibn: 17.7

Hanukkah: 19.1; 19.4. (Hebrew: Dedication.) Eight-day Jewish festival honoring Judah the Maccabee's rededication of the Second Temple of Jerusalem in 165 B.C.E.. The lighting of the eight candles (or oil lamps) of the *menorah* (candelabrum) sequentially from the twenty-fifth of Kislev is the center of the celebration.

Hanumān: (Large-jawed.) Hindu god in the shape of a monkey, who figured prominently in the *Rāmāyana* epic; he was an auspicious god known for his ingenuity, eloquence, strength, and celibacy.

Haoma: 33.1–33.3. (Parallel to Hindu *soma*.) Organic substance crushed to yield a juice with ritual use in ancient Iran and India, personified as a deity. Its stimulative and perhaps hallucinogenic properties were praised in pre-Zoroastrian tradition.

Harappa: 14.1

Harivaṃśa: 14.5

Har Gobind: 14.8.2

Har Krishnan: 14.8.2

Har Rai: 14.8.2

Har Mandar: 14.8.2

Ḥasan: 17.6

Ḥasan al-Baṣrī: 17.10.1. (642–728 C.E.)

Ḥasan-i Ṣabbāh: 17.6.3

Hashemite al-ʿAbbas: 17.2; 17.6.1

Hasidei Ashkenaz: 19.8

Hasidism: 19.10. (Hasidim: Pious Ones.) Jewish mystical movement inspired by the Baal Shem Tov (1700–1760 C.E.) in the wake of the

Shabbetai Tsevi controversy, integrated an esoteric reading of the scriptures, personal pietism, intense prayer, and joyful realization of God's presence with a Kabbalistic outlook. Charismatic spiritual leaders (*tsaddikim*) assisted believers in their aspirations toward the higher world; some formed dynasties that continue today.

Haskins, Charles Homer: 7.4.9

Haṭha yoga: (Haṭha: forceful suppression.) System of exercises (such as breath control, postures, semen retention, meditation) that alter bodily processes and cause the serpent of Śiva's energy, Kuṇḍalinī, to rise through a channel in the subtle body to the crown cakra, bringing enlightenment and supernatural powers.

Hayashi Razan: 8.5

Head shrinking: 29.5

Heimskringla: 11.2

Hekate: Greek goddess of fertility, crossroads and transitions, and the dead, whose association with night, the moon, and the restless spirits of the dead grew into a link with witchcraft.

Hekhalot: 19.2

Hel: 11.3.2; 11.4.2

Helen: 12.3.7

Hera: 12.3.4; 12.3.7

Heraclides Ponticus: 13.2.1

Herbad: 33.4

Hermes: 13.2.6

Hermes Trismegistus: 7.4.12

Hermetism: 13.2.6

Hermotimus of Clazomenae: 12.3.2

Herodotus: 31.3

Herzel, Theodor: 19.7

Hesiod: 12.3.4

Hesychasm: 7.9

Hewkula: 29.5

Hidatsa: 22.2

Hijrah: 17.2

Hildegard of Bingen: 7.9

Hillel: 19.7. (Late first century B.C.E.) Influential rabbi and law interpreter in Jerusalem who emphasized love and leniency. His innovation of the *prozbul* (extending loan agreements through the sabbatical year) and his sagacious sayings had a lasting impact, as did his school, the Beit Hillel.

Hīnayāna: 3.3–3.4

Hine-nui-te-po: 23.3

Hinton, Charles Howard: 3.5

Hippolytus of Rome: 7.4.2

Hirayama Shosai: 27.6

Hmong: 26.1.4

Hodhr: 11.4.2

Hoenir: 11.3.1; 11.3.3

Hojas: 17.6.3

Holas, B.: 1.1

Homer: 12.3.4

Hōnen: 3.9

Honmichi: 27.6

Hopi: 22.2; 22.9

Hospital (of St. John of Jerusalem): 7.4.9

Horus: 10.2; 10.3

Hottentots: 1.1

Hsi Wang Mu: 30.2

Hsi-yu chi: 3.8

Hsien: 30.2

Hsien King: 30.2

Hsien Shan: 30.2

Hsüang-tsang: 3.8

Hsün-tzu: 8.4

Huacas: 29.4

Huang-ti: 30.2

Huascar: 29.3

Huayna Capac: 29.3

Huitzilopochtli: 6.3.1; 6.4. (Hummingbird of the South.) Aztec solar and warrior god, patron of Tenochtitlan. The cult of this supreme deity, who evolved from the tribal god of the Mexica, involved festivals and human sacrifices.

Hui-yüan: 3.8

Ḥujja: 17.6.3

Hunwe: 1.5

Hupa: 22.7

Hupashiya: 15.2

Huron: 22.5

Hus, John: 7.4.13

Ḥusain Ibn ʿAlī: 17.6

Hvergelmir: 11.3.1; 11.3.2

Iamblichus: 13.2.4

Iarovit: 28.1.1

Iatromantes: 12.3.2; 12.3.3

Ibn al-ʿArabī, Abū Bakr Muḥammad: 17.10 (1165–1240 C.E.)

Ibn Bājjah: (d. 1139 C.E.) (Latin: *Avempace*.)

Ibn Rushd: 29.5

Ibn Sīnā: 17.8

I Ching: 1.2.1; 8.1

Idel, Moshe: 19.8

Ifa: 1.2.1

Ifriqīya: 17.5

Ignatius of Loyola: 7.4.13

Ile: 1.2.1

Illapa: 29.4

Illuyanka: 15.2

Ilmarinen: Finnic god of air and weather, controlling sea conditions; a god of mythology (epic poetry) rather than cult.

Inanna: 20.2; 20.6

Inara: 15.2

Inca: 29.2; 29.4

Indra: 14.2

Ino: 1.3

Inone Masakane: 27.6

Inquisition: 7.4.9

Inti: Inca sun god, considered the father of the king. Maize and gold were especially important in his cult, which had a gilded temple complex (the Coricancha at the capital, Cuzco) with a powerful priesthood.

Inuit: 22.3; 26.1.2

Irenaeus of Lyons: 7.4.2

Iroquois: 22.2

Isaac: In Genesis, the son of Abraham and Sarah, husband of Rebecca and father of Jacob and Esau. His binding (*'aqedah*) by Abraham for sacrifice to God is one of the most celebrated and scrutinized of Bible passages.

Isaac the Blind: 19.8

Isaiah: 19.2–19.5. Jewish prophet (late eighth century B.C.E.) of the Jerusalem Temple; his wife was likewise a prophetess. He criticized religious relaxation and political institutions. The biblical Book of

Isaiah was mined by Christians as containing prophecies of Jesus, and by early Muslim theologians for prophecies of Muhammad.

Ishmael: Son of Abraham and the Egyptian slave Hagar during Sarah's time of infertility before the birth of Isaac, Ishmael and his mother were cast out by Sarah (Gen. 21). In Jewish and Islamic tradition, he is viewed as the ancestor of the Arabs, and Muslims see him as a prophet of monotheism for the ancient Kaʿba shrine at Mecca.

Ishtar: 20.2; 20.6

Isis: 10.3; 21.3.2. Queenly Egyptian goddess. The faithful wife of Osiris who gathered the pieces of her slain husband and conceived Horus. In the Hellenistic and Roman periods, her cult spreads through the Mediterranean world, her powers, attributes, and mysteries expanding, as seen in the *Isis Aretalogy* and Apuleius' *Metamorphoses.*

Ismāʿīl: 17.6.1

Ismāʿtli: 17.6.3

Iśvara: (The Powerful.) Hindu epithet for the highest god.

Ituri: 1.4.2

Itzam Na: 6.2

Ivory Coast: 1.1; 1.2.3

Izanagi and Izanami: 27.3. Father and mother gods of the world, they created the land and its gods. Active in mythology as well as cult, Awaji was an early cult place of Izanagi, and later Taga.

Izumo Oyashirokyo: 27.6

Jacob: Hebrew patriarch, son of Isaac and Rebekah, father of Joseph (Gen. 25–50). Jacob took his father's inheritance blessing from his brother Esau through disguise, and underwent a life of trials as ancestor of the Jews (he was named Israel in Gen. 32:29 after wrestling the mysterious being).

Jacques de Molay: 7.4.9

Jaʿfar al-Ṣādiq: 17.6.1. (702–765 C.E.) Shiʿite Imam, descendant of Fāṭimah bint Muḥammad and ʿAlī Ibn Abī Ṭālib through their son Ḥusain, revered by both Twelver and Sevener Shiites.

Jamaica: 1.6.1

Janus: 25.2.1. Roman god of passage, whose two faces represented the past and future, or opening and closing.

Jātakas: 3.1–3.2

Jean of Lugio: 7.4.9

Jehovah's Witnesses: Bible-based Christian sect of over two million members worldwide. Founded in 1872 in Pennsylvania by Charles Taze Russell. Expecting an imminent end to Satan's rule—a great judgment and reign of Christ over a perfected earth—the Witnesses maintain a moral and neutralist stance, refraining from saluting images or symbols and operating an active missionary and publications program (e.g., their magazine *The Watchtower.*

Jen: 8.2–8.3

Jensen, Ad. E.: 6.2.1; 21.1; 29.5

Jeremiah: 19.2; 19.5. (ca. 640–580 B.C.E.) Hebrew prophet of the beginning of the Babylonian exile.

Jerome: 7.4.7

Jerusalem: 7.4.9; 19.1; 19.6. A city sacred to Judaism since its adoption as the capital of David's kingdom (tenth century B.C.E.) and location of the ark of the covenant and Solomon's Temple. For Christians, it is the city of Jesus' passion and Resurrection. For Muslims, it is the first *giblah,* the Dome of the Rock that stands on the Temple Mount marks the place of Muhammad's ascent to heaven (*miʿrāj*).

Jesus Christ: 7.2; 7.7–7.7.3

Jikkokyo: 27.6

Jina: 18.2

Jingikan: 27.6

Jinja: 27.5

Jinn: 17.1

Jīvanmukti: (Sanskrit: liberation as a living being.) In Hindu thought, release from the cycle of rebirth (*saṃsāra*) during a human being's lifetime.

Jívaro: 29.5

Jñāna: 14.3. (Sanskrit: knowledge, cognition.)

Joachim of Flora: 7.4.9

Job: 19.2. Hero of the biblical Book of Job, which probably circulated as a folk tale from the second millennium B.C.E. It played out the dynamics of theodicy in the story of the stricken Job, his exasperated wife and three friends who blame him for his undeserved suffering (Eliphaz, Bildad, Zophar), and the God who speaks from the whirlwind.

Jōdō Shinshu: 3.9

Jōdo-shū: 3.9. Japanese Pure Land sect of Buddhism, founded by Hōnen.

John (Gospel of): 7.1

John of Damascus: 17.8

John of the Cross: 7.9. (1542–1591 C.E.) Spanish Christian mystical writer and monastic reformer. His influential poems with commentary, including *The Ascent of Mount Carmel, The Dark Night,* and *The Spiritual Canticle,* follow the course of human transformation toward union with God.

John the Baptist: 7.2

John XXIII: 7.6

Jomon: 27.2

Jonah: 19.2. Prophet of the biblical Book of Jonah (ca. fourth century B.C.E.), thought by some scholars to be a parody of the genre. Jonah fled his prophetic mission in Nineveh and was swallowed and regurgitated by a fish; God spared the repentant Ninevites and their cattle and sent Jonah the sign of the withering shade plant.

Joseph: 7.2. Son of Jacob and Rachel, whose rise in the court of the Egyptian king, after betrayal by his jealous brothers, was narrated in Genesis 37–50.

Joseph Caro: 19.7

Joseph Flavius: 31.4.3

Joshua: 19.2

Joshua ben Hananiah: 19.7

Jotnar: Giants of Germanic mythology, who battled the gods and could mate with gods or humans.

Judah ben Samuel: 19.8

Judah Halevi: 19.7

Judah ha-Nasi: 19.7

Julian of Norwich: 7.9

Julian the Apostate: 25.4

Julian the Chaldaean: 13.2.4

Julian the Theurgist: 13.2.4

Julius Caesar: 5.1–5.3; 11.3.4

Juno: 25.2.1. Roman goddess of birth, beginnings, and youth; related to the Etruscan goddess Uni, Juno became the wife of the high god Jupiter.

Jupiter: 25.2. (Indo-European: *dyeus pater:* Father of light) Highest Roman god, celestial and just king of the universe; from archaic times he formed a triad with Mars and Quirinus.

Jupiter Dolichenus: 21.3.7

Justin Martyr: 7.4.1

Ka. 10.7

Kaʿbah: 17.9. (Arabic: cube.) Granite house of the Black Stone in Mecca and focus of Muslim prayer (*ṣalāt*) and pilgrimage (*ḥajj*), when it is circumambulated and touched by the faithful. Islamic tradition recognized its central importance as a sanctuary in pagan times; it was profaned by idols in the centuries between Abraham's founding and Muhammad's cleansing, and has periodically been rebuilt.

Kabbalah: 19.8

Kabīr: 14.7.1; 14.8.2

Kachinas: 22.9

Kaguru: 1.3

Kaisān: 17.6

Kalām: 17.8; 17.10.3

Kam: 26.1

Kamba: 1.3

Kami: 27.3; 27.4; 27.5. Divine forces of Shinto religion, including ancestral and nature spirits.

Kamrushepa: 15.2

Kanjur: 3.1

Karaites: 19.7. Jewish scripturalist sect originating in the ninth century C.E. adhering only to the law of Moses: postbiblical elaboration and interpretation of the law is not recognized as authoritative.

Karanga: 1.5

Karbalā: 17.6

Karma-pa: 3.10

Karman: 14.3

Karok: 22.7

Karukasaibe: 29.5

Kaska: 22.2

Kāśyapīya: 3.4

Kawate Bunjiro: 27.6

Kele: 1.6.1

Kenos: 29.7

Kenya: 1.3

Kerdīr: 33.3–33.4

Keshab Candra Sen: 14.9

Ketuvim: 19.2

Kevala-jñāna: 18.2

Kevalin: 18.2

Key: 5.5

Khabirus: 19.1

Khakases: 26.1.1

Khalīfah: 17.4

Khanty: 26.1.2

Khārijīs: 17.4

Khasi: 26.1.4

Khmers: 26.1.4

Khors: 28.1.1

Kikuyu: 1.3

King, Noel Q.: 1.1

Kingu: 20.5

Kirta: 4.4

Kivas: 22.9

Knights of Malta: 7.4.9

Knossos: 12.1

Koan: 3.9

Kojiki: 27.2

Komi: 26.1.2

Konkokyo: 27.6

Kore: 1.2.3

Koriacks: 26.1.1

Koshitsu: 27.5

Kothar: 4.1; 4.4

Krochmal, Nachman: 19.7

Kromanti: 1.6.1

Kronos: 12.3.4

Kṛṣṇa: 14.5

Kuhn, Adalbert: 16.3

Kūkai: 3.9. (774–835 C.E.) Japanese master of Chinese Esoteric Buddhism and founder of the Shingon school in the Tantric tradition.

Kuksu: 22.8

Kukulkán: 6.2

Kule: 1.2.3

Kumārajīva: 3.8; 3.9 (Late fourth century C.E.) Central Asian Buddhist monk who translated a great body of Mahāyāna Buddhist thought, particularly Mādhyamika writings and the Sūnyavādin Sūtras, into Chinese; founder of San-lun (Mādhyamika) school.

Kumarbi: 15.2

Kumina: 1.6.1

Kunapipi: 2.1

K'ung Fu-tzu: 8.2

Kurahus: 22.6

Kurgan: 16.2

Kurozumi Munetada: 27.6

Kurozumikyo: 27.6

Kurumba: 1.2.3

Kwakiutl: 22.2; 22.7

Kyo: 3.9

Kyoha: 27.5

Lacandón: 6.2

Lagerwey, John: 30.3

Lamaism: 3.10

Lao: 26.1.4

Lao-tzu: 30.1. (sixth century B.C.E.) Divinized legendary sage venerated in the Taoist tradition; the *Tao Te Ching* is attributed to him.

Lapps: 11.1

Lares: 25.2.2

Laylat al-Qadr: 17.9

Lectisternia: 25.2.2

Leenhardt, Maurice: 23.1

Le Goff, Jacques: 7.8

Lele: 1.4.1

Lemures: 25.2.2

Leto: 12.3.4

Levenson, Jon: 19.3

Levi ben Gerson, 19.7

Lévi-Strauss, Claude: 27.3; 29.5

Liber: 25.2.1

Libera: 25.2.1

Liberia: 1.1

Lienhardt, Godfrey: 1.3

Lilith: (Female Demon.) Lilith was a Sumerian and Babylonian succuba demon, eventually conflated with

Lamashtu, the child-killing demon. Lilith has both these roles in postbiblical Jewish tradition. But in the *Alphabet of Ben Sira* (ca. seventh to tenth century C.E.) midrash, she is Adam's first wife in Eden, created from dust to be equal to him. She fled to escape domination by him, and was replaced by Eve.

Lin Chao-en: 30.3

Linga: (Sanskrit: phallus.) Phallic object usually symbolizing the creative power of Śiva.

Llwyd: 5.5

Lōdhurr: 11.3.1

Lokasenna: 11.4.1

Loki: 11.4. Impulsive companion of the Germanic-Scandinavian gods who acted as a trickster in mythological adventures of Thorr, Odinn, and Hoenir.

Lokottara: 3.4

Lollards: 7.4.13

Lombard, Peter: 7.4.9

Lophophora Williamsii: 22.6

Lorentz, Dagmar: 7.8

Lorenz, Konrad: 24.2

Lovendu: 1.5

Lucius: 21.3.2

Lugh: 5.4

Lu Hsiang-shan: 8.4

Luke (Gospel of): 7.1

Lull, Ramon: (ca. 1232–1316 C.E.) Catalan mystic and missionary, with philosophical and practical occupations as diverse as the art of memory, alchemy, and Christian-Muslim reconciliation.

Lupa: 25.2.3

Lupercalia: 25.2.3. Roman purificatory festival of 15 February, in which, with goat and dog sacrifices, a group of men called the Luperci (wolf-men) ran around the Palatine Hill; women they hit with goat-hide lashes were ensured fertility.

Luria, Isaac: 19.8. (1534–1572 C.E.) Jewish Kabbalist and mystical teacher who practiced in Safad. He elaborated the process of God's self-withdrawal, the imprisonment of divine sparks in the broken vessels of God's light, and the restoration of the light to unity through human piety and mystical practices.

Luther, Martin: 7.4.13. (1483–1546 C.E.) German theologian and catalyst of the Reformation of the Christian church. High points of his vision were his advocacy of scripturalism, justification by grace through faith, reduction of sacraments to baptism and nontransubstantial communion, and criticism of certain church practices such as the sale of indulgences.

Luzzato, Samuel David: 19.7

Lwa: 1.6.1

Mabinogi: 5.5. Eleven Middle Welsh stories (written form: late eleventh to thirteenth century C.E.), including the birth of the hero Pryderi, the rescue of Branwen by her brother Brān, and other supernatural adventures.

Maccabees: 19.1

Macrobius: 13.2.1; 25.4

Madhva: 14.6

Mādhyamika: 3.5

Maga: 33.3.2

Maggid: 19.10

Magh Tuired: 5.4

Maghrīb al-aqṣā: 17.5

Magi: 33.3.3. Priestly class of the ancient Medes, known as sacrificers and for their exposure of corpses; later, the learned, sacerdotal class of the Zoroastrians renowned in the Hellenistic world as wise men of occult knowledge.

Magli, Ida: 7.8

Mahābhārata: 14.5. Massive Hindu epic poem drawing on oral traditions, written down circa fifth century B.C.E. to fourth century C.E.; complex mythological themes were played out through the conflict between the Pāndavas and the Kauravas, in which many characters were incarnations of the gods, or demons.

Mahādevī: 14.7.3

Mahākāśyapa: 3.3

Mahāpuruṣa: 18.2

Mahāsāmghika: 3.1; 3.4

Mahāvīra: 18.2

Mahāvrata: 18.2; 18.4

Mahāyāna: 3.3–3.5

Mahāyuga: 14.5

Mahdī: 17.6

Mahmi: 33.4.2

Maia: 12.3.4

Maimonides: 19.7. Moses ben Maimun (ca. 1135/1138–1204 C.E.).

Maitreya: 3.5

Makah: 22.7

Malcolm X: 1.6.4

Mālik ibn Anas: 17.7

Malunkyaputta: 3.3

Mamluks: 17.5

Mana: 23.1

Manchus: 26.1.1

Maṇḍala: 14.7.4

Mandan: 22.3

Mandé: 1.1

Mandingo: 1.2.3

Manes: 25.2.2

Mani: 9.6

Manichaeism: 9.6

Manitu: 22.5

Mansi: 26.1.2

Mantra: 14.7.4. Meditational formula in Hinduism and Buddhism.

Māra: 3.2

Marabout: 1.1

Marcion of Sinope: 7.4.1; 9.5

Marduk: 4.4; 20.3; 20.5

Margareta of Cortona: 7.9

Mark (Gospel of): 7.1

Marpa: 3.10

Marranos: (Castillian from Arabic for "pig.") Contemptuous word that designated Jews and Muslims from Spain and Portugal accused of having converted to Christianity only pro forma (*conversos*), while in secret they were still faithful to the practices of their own religions. The existence of a crypto-Judaism has been contested (see Benzion Netanyahu, *The Marranos of Spain from the Late Fourteenth to the Early Sixteenth Century* [1966]). Evidence that Christopher Columbus was a *marrano*, or of Jewish descent, is compelling. The Spanish Inquisition zealously prosecuted suspects, submitting them to the humiliating trial called *auto da fe*. According to the recent statistics of Jaime Contreras and Gustav

Henningsen (1986), between 1540 and 1700 C.E. 4,397 (9.8 percent of the total) suspects of Judaism and 10,817 (24.2 percent of the total of tried) suspects of being crypto-Muslims underwent *auto da fes*. The general percentage of execution is, however, low (1.8 percent of the total: see J. Contreras and G. Henningsen, "Forty-four Thousand Cases of the Spanish Inquisition (1540–1700): Analysis of a Historical Data Bank," in G. Henningsen and John Tedeschi [eds.], *The Inquisition in Early Modern Europe* [1986], pp. 100–129).

Marrett, R. R.: 23.1

Mars: 25.2. Roman war god. His priest had the name *flamen martialis*. The god received the triple sacrifice of a boar, a ram, and a bull. His most important temple was the Ara Martis on the Martial Fields in Rome.

Mary: 7.2; 7.3

Masada: 19.1

Masai: 1.1

Mashya: 33.5.1

Mashyānag: 33.5.1

Maskilim: 19.7

Masoretes: 19.2

Maspero, Henri: 30.4

Mat' Syra Zemlia: 28.1.1

Math: 5.5

Matsuri: 27.5

Matthew (Gospel of): 7.1

Maui: 23.3

Mau Mau: 1.3

Māyā: 14.6. (Sanskrit: creative illusion.) A central concept of Hinduism, *māyā* meant different things according to the epoch: in the Vedas, it referred to the power of a god to create in the visible world; in common Vedānta, it indicated a process of illusion. The sensible world was said to be *māyā* in the sense that its multiplicity had a restricted ontological status and could be reduced to unity. Similarly, Western Neoplatonists used the negative concept of *goeteia*, "witchcraft," which was akin to *maya* to the extent that in both cases the result was an illusion.

Mayapan: 6.2

Mayas: 6.1–6.2.1

Mazdakism: 33.4.1. Communalist and pacifist religion founded by a certain Mazdak during the reign of the Sassanian sovereign Kawād (488–531 C.E.). First encouraged by Kawād, Mazdakism was abandoned under pressure from the aristocracy. The Mazdakites were massacred under Khosrau I (531–579 C.E.), but their influence was viable in the Islamic period.

Mbuti: 1.4.2

Medhbh: 5.4.2

Medici, Cosimo de': 7.4.12

Megillot: 19.2

Meillet, Antoine: 16.3

Melanchthon, Philip: 7.4.13

Melqart: (Phoenician: God of the City.) Patron god of the Phoenician city of Tyre. His cult, possibly introduced to Israel by Ahab and Jezabel (1 Kings 16) met the opposition of the prophet Elijah (1 Kings 17).

Mencius: 8.4

Mendelssohn, Moses: 19.7

Menelous: 12.3.7

Meng-tzu: 8.4. (Mencius.) Confucian philosopher (ca. 391–308 B.C.E.) to whom is ascribed an eponymous work in seven parts. He insisted on the inner education of the Confucian, who was supposed to repress selfishness.

Mennonites: 7.4.13

Mérida: 6.2

Merkabah: 19.2; 19.6.1

Merlin: 5.5. Magician and seer at the court of the legendary king Arthur. His name is late (Geoffroy of Monmouth, twelfth century, *Vita Merlini*), yet his prototype is ancient, probably Celtic.

Meslin, Michel: 7.9

Messiah: 7.2

Metatron: 19.6.1

Metensomatosis: 3.3; 12.3.3; 14.3; 17.6; 19.8; 29.5

Methodius: 7.5

Méxica: 6.3

Mexico City: 6.2

Miau: 26.1.4

Midewiwin: 22.5; 26.1.5

Midhard: 11.4.1

Midhgardhr: 11.3.1

Midrash: 19.2

Mihna: 17.8

Mi-la-ras-pa: 3.10. (Or Milarepa, 1040–1123 C.E.) Great Tibetan Buddhist ascetic, disciple of Marpa the Translator and one of the masters of the Bka-brgyud-pa school. His biography, compiled in the fifteenth century C.E. by Tsang Nyon Heruka, is one of the great edifying writings of Tibetan Buddhism.

Mīmāṃsā: 14.4

Mímir: 11.3.2–11.3.3

Minerva: Roman goddess of arts and skills. Adopted in the Roman pantheon in the sixth century B.C.E., she was largely a duplicate of the Greek goddess Athena.

Minianka: 1.1

Minkan Shinto: 27.7

Minos: 12.1

Miʿrāj: 17.9

Mishnah: 19.2

Misogikyo: 27.6

Mithra: 21.3.3; 33.3.3

Mitra: 14.2; 33.3.3

Mixtec: 6.1

Mobād: 33.3.1

Moche: 29.2.1

Moctezuma II: 6.3

Mohenjo Daro: 14.1

Mokosh: 28.1.1

Mokysha: 28.1.1

Mokṣa: 14.4.3

Moma: 29.5

Mongols: 17.3; 26.1

Mooney, James: 22.1

Monophysites: 7.7.3

Moorish Science Temple: 1.6.4

Moravian Brothers: The Moravian Brotherhood (Jednota Bratrská) was founded in 1437 C.E. in Bohemia and took inspiration from the religious and nationalistic ideas of the Czech reformer Jan Hus, burnt at the stake in 1415. His movement is interpreted today as a Czech revolt against German domination in Bohemia. Persecuted after the defeat of the Protestants in 1620, the Moravian Brothers continued their secret existence until 1722,

when their leader Christian David (1690–1751 C.E.) found refuge with the German Pietist count Nicholas Zinzendorf (1700–1760 C.E.). In 1727 Moravian Brothers and Pietists merged, forming a world movement.

Mormonism: The Church of Jesus Christ of Latter-day Saints and related sects have over six million members worldwide. Their founder was prophet and visionary Joseph Smith, Jr. (1805–1844 C.E.), whose First Vision in 1820 showed him the physical nature of God and his Son, and the inadequacy of the competing Christian denominations of his western New York State community. The scriptural *Book of Mormon* (1830) was his translation of the ancient gold tablets he unearthed with divine assistance. Its ancient compiler, Mormon, father of Moroni, tells the history of the North American descendants of wandering Israelites; the warrings of the Nephites and Lamanites (ancestors of the American Indians), sons of Lehi; and the ministry of the resurrected Christ among them. Smith sought to establish one true church under God. Baptism of the dead, eternal marriage, materialism of spirit, millennial/messianic expectations, the gradual divinization of humankind, and polygamy (in light of the neopatriarchal age dawning) were among his evolving tenets; God is a male being, material and physical, and Jesus Christ is his Son. When the jailed Smith was killed by an Illinois mob in 1844, he was a candidate for U.S. president.

The growing Mormonism saw in itself a unique revivification of apostolic early Christianity and the age of Hebrew patriarchs and kings. Under harsh persecution, an exodus led by Brigham Young (1801–1877 C.E.) brought Mormons to the Great Salt Lake, where a Kingdom of the Chosen People was founded. A division forming in the 1850s resulted in the "Reorganized" branch of the church (based in Independence, Missouri) accepting only the leadership of Joseph Smith III and his direct descendants thereafter, and disavowing polygamy.

Persistent attacks by the U.S. government culminated by 1890 with the Mormons' abandonment of independent political claims and polygamy. The modern Mormons, a "nation of behavers" (Martin Marty), maintains its apartness through lifelong church activities, dress and decorum codes, family orientation, and prohibitions of alcohol, tobacco, and caffeine.

Male authoritarian leadership is mandated. Boys above age twelve may enter the quorums of the Aaronic or Melchizedek priesthoods, reestablished in Joseph Smith's day, and may advance in the hierarchy. In the non-Reorganized church, women, and, until a 1978 revelation, black men, have been excluded from these lay priesthoods. Temple worship, community fellowship and education, missionary work, and a genealogy project facilitating vicarious immersive baptism of past generations in stone basins, toward a salvatory eschatological culmination, are among the present activities of the church. (See K. J. Hansen in *ER* 10, 108; J. Shipps, *Mormonism* (1985); for a Mormon perspective, see L. J. Arrington and

D. Bitton, *The Mormon Experience: A History of the Latter-day Saints* (1979).

Moses: 19.2. (Hebrew: Mosheh.) According to the Pentateuch (which is attributed to him), he was the liberator of the Jewish people from slavery in Egypt and mediator between God and the Jews. God gave the law to Moses on Mount Sinai (Exod. 19–20; Deut. 4–5).

Moses de León: 19.8

Mosi: 1.2.3

Mot: 4.4

Mo-tzu: (ca. 470–390 B.C.E.) Chinese philosopher and chief of the Mo-ist school, whose classic bears the title *Mo-tzu.* Universal love was the central doctrine preached by Mo-tzu, who was a pacifist during a period in Chinese history properly called "The Warring States Period" (403–221 B.C.E.). The Confucian philosopher Meng-tzu criticized Mo-tzu for ignoring the obedience that a son owed his father. According to Mo-tzu, the values of a patriarchal society inevitably led to war. To this extent, Mo-tzu was an early feminist thinker.

Muᶜāwiyah: 17.4

Mudra: (Sanskrit: seal.) Special positions of hands in the iconography and in certain meditative practices of Buddhism and Hinduism; especially developed in Indian dance, which uses over five hundred of them.

Mughal: 17.5

Muhammad: 17.2

Muhammad al-Bāqir: 17.6.1

Muhammad ibn al-Hanafīya: 17.6

al-Mukhtār: 17.6

Mūlasarvāstivāda: 3.10

Müller, Friedrich Max: 16.3

Munduruků: 29.5

Münzer, Thomas: 7.4.13

Mus, Paul: 3.8

Muses: 12.3.4

Muskogeans: 22.2

Muslim Mosque: 1.6.4

Muso Koroni: 1.2.3

Múspell: 11.3.1

Muᶜtazilites: 17.8

Myalists: 1.6.1

Nabu: Babylonian and Assyrian god of the first millennium B.C.E., scribe and eventually son of Marduk. His main temple was at Borsippa. His importance grew during the Assyrian Empire.

Nāgārjuna: 3.5. (Fl. ca. 150–250 C.E.) Great thinker of the Mādhyamika school of Mahāyāna Buddhism, known for his teaching on the "emptiness" (*śūnyatā*) of being. Powerful magician and yogin according to legendary tradition.

Nag Hammadi: 9.9.4. Village in upper Egypt, close to the ancient monastery erected by Pachomius at Khenoboskion, where in December 1945 thirteen fourth-century codices in the Coptic language were found, containing original Gnostic texts of which a number were previously unknown.

Nahmanides: 19.8

Nahuatl: 6.3

Nayakama Miki: 27.6

Na Khi: 26.1.4

Nālaṇḍā: 3.3

Nānak: 14.8.1 (1469–1539 C.E.) Founder of Sikh religion and first among the ten Sikh Gurus.

Nanays: 26.1.1

Nanmars: 14.4.2

Nanna: 20.2. Sumerian moon god. His Akkadian equivalent was Sin.

Naqshbandīyah: 17.10

Naram Sin: 20.3

Naropa: 3.10

Nasi: 19.7

Nathan of Gaza: 19.9

Nation of Islam: 1.6.4

Navajos: 22.2

Nawrūz: 33.6. (Nō Rūz.) Iranian New Year festival, celebrated during twelve days at the spring equinox. The *fravashis*, or souls of the dead, were supposed to be present at the beginning of the festival. Nawrūz continues to be celebrated in Muslim Iran.

Nazca: 29.2.1

Ndembu: 1.4.1

N'domo: 1.2.3

Nembutsu: 3.9

Neanderthal: 24.2

Nebiim: 19.2; 19.4

Nebuchadnezzar: 19.1

Nefertiti: 10.6

Nei-tan: 30.4

Nembutsu: 3.9

Nephthys: 10.3

Nergal: 20.2. Mesopotamian underworld deity. Also the malefic planet Saturn according to Babylonian astrology.

Nestorians: 7.7.2–7.7.3

Nestorius: 7.6

Nganasani: 26.1.1

Nguni: 1.5

Nichiren: 3.9

Nicholas of Cusa: 7.4.10

Nicole of Oresme: 7.4.10

Nidhoggr: 11.4.3

Niflheimr: 11.3.1

Nigeria: 1.2.1

Nihongi: 27.2

Nilotes: 1.1

Niman: 22.9

Ninhursag: Ancient Mesopotamian Great Goddess, member of the supreme triad of gods next to An and Enlil. Later on, she was replaced by the male god Enki.

Ninurta: (Sumerian: Lord of the Earth.) Mesopotamian god of storm and war, son of the cosmic god Enlil, worshiped in Nippur and Lagash.

Nirvāṇa: 3.3–3.5; 18.2. Sanskrit word of imprecise etymology. In Buddhism, it describes the ineffable condition of the Awakened One, in opposition to *saṃsāra,* the cycle of birth and death. In this sense, *nirvāṇa* is cessation of any phenomena and does not allow any positive description.

Nitta Kuniteru: 27.6

Nizaris: 17.6.3

Njordhr: 11.3.3. Father of the fertility god Freyr and one of the most important Vanes gods in Germanic mythology. Sent by Freyr to the Ases as warrant of the peace between the two races of gods. First mythical king of Sweden.

Nkore: 1.3

Noa: 23.3

Noah: In the biblical Book of Genesis, son of Lamech and father of Shem, Ham, and Japeth, chosen by God to survive the universal deluge and preserve in his ark all animal species that inhabited the earth.

Noble Drew Ali: 1.6.4

Nootka: 22.2; 22.7

Nō Rūz: 33.6

Nuadhu: 5.4

Nuer: 1.1; 1.3

Nuṣairī: 17.6.2

Nut: 10.3

Nyame: 1.2.2

Nyāya: 14.4

Nyberg, H. S.: 33.4.3

Obatala: 1.2.1

Odhinn: 11.3.1–11.5.3. Principal Ase god in Germanic mythology, patron of the *jarl* (nobles, as opposed to *karl*, freemen), god of war and brotherhoods of warriors, of poetry, magic, and runes.

Odudua: 1.2.1

Oedipus: 12.3.7

Ogboni: 1.2.1

Ogùn: 1.2.1

Ohenemmaa: 1.2.2

Ohrmazd: 33.4.2

Ojibwa: 22.2; 22.5

Oki: 22.5

Olmecs: 6.1–6.2

Olodumarẹ: 1.2.1

Olokun: 1.2.1

Olorun: 1.2.1

Ona: 29.7

Ongon: Mongol word designating certain objects in which dwell the spirits conjured by the shaman.

Onile: 1.2.1

Ontakekyo: 27.6

Orenda: 22.5

Origen: 7.4.3; 7.4.9; 21.3.3

Orisa: 1.2.1; 1.6.1–1.6.2

Oro: 23.2

Orochis: 26.1.1

Orpheus: 12.3.6. Mythical character associated with the land of Thrace and with a reform of the cult of Dionysus in the sixth century B.C.E.. His lyre charmed the rocks, the plants, the birds, the fishes, and even the formidable Thracian warriors; his song told the origin of the world, of gods and human beings. Other mysterious fragments of his myth showed him descending to the netherworld to recover his dead wife Eurydice and of his end, torn apart by the Thracian Maenads, like a Dionysiac sacrificial victim, for having rejected their sexual advances.

Orun: 1.2.1

Orungan: 1.2.1

Osiris: 10.3; 10.7; 21.2 Egyptian god, son of Geb (Earth), killed by his brother Seth. His wife Isis put together the pieces of the dead Osiris, who begot her Horus. Every pharaoh after death became Osiris, god of the dead.

Ostiaks: 26.1.2

Ottomans: 17.5

Pachacamac: 29.4

Pachacuti: 29.3

whose dialogues contained myths in which important religious knowledge was condensed concerning the survival of the soul after death, metensomatosis, cosmology, and cosmogony.

Plotinus: 7.4.3; 13.2.4; (205–270 C.E.) Platonic mystic and philosopher, whose interpretations we term Neoplatonist, a trend that after his death transformed Platonism into a religion, not only speculative but also having its rituals and mysteries.

Plutarch: 12.3.3; 13.2.1; 21.3.1

Poimandres: 13.2.6

Pomerium: 25.2.1

Pomo: 22.8

Pontifex: 25.2.3

Popol Vuh: 6.2.1

Porphyry: 13.2.4; 25.4

Poseidon: 5.5. Ancient Greek god, already present at Mycenae. During the classical period, he was the lord of the seas and fresh water. He is repeatedly linked with horses.

Potlach: 22.7

Potnia therōn: 12.2; 12.3.4

Powamuy: 22.9

Prajāpati: 14.3. (Sanskrit: Lord of Creatures.) In the ancient Indian Brāhmaṇas, he was the creator of the universe by self-sacrifice, and his primordial act was repeated in every fire oblation.

Prajñāpāramitā: 3.5

Prajñaptivāda: 3.4

Prakṛti: 14.4.2

Prāṇa: 14.4.2

Pratītya samutpāda: 3.3

Pratyeka Buddha: 3.5

Priapus: Minor Greco-Roman ithyphallic (with erect penis) deity.

Proclus: 7.9

Prometheus: 6.2.1; 12.4. Greek Titan, belonging to a generation older than the Olympian gods, Prometheus was known for his feats in favor of the human race (theft of fire in heaven, deception of Zeus at Mekone, where the latter chose the nonedible part of animal sacrifices to be the gods' share, etc.), for which Zeus condemned him to perpetual torture.

Prophet: 17.2–17.3

Proverbs: 19.2

Psalms: 19.2. Collection of 150 (151) biblical hymns belonging to the Ketuvim (Writings), of which seventy-two were attributed to King David (tenth century B.C.E.).

Psellus, Michael: 12.3.3; 13.2.4. (1018–1078 C.E.) Byzantine theologian fascinated by Neoplatonism—Proclus, in particular—and Hermetism. Great dignitary of the empire, he left the court in order to seek for spiritual truth and died in obscurity.

Psyche: 12.3.6

Ptah: 10.3

Ptolemy: 13.2.2

Ptolemies: 13.2

Pudgala: 3.4

Pueblos: 22.2; 22.9

Pūjā: 14.7. Offering for Hindu deities, made in front of the domestic altar or in the temple.

Pulque: 6.3.1

Pura: 29.5

Purāṇas: 14.5. Encyclopedic collection in Sanskrit including, according to tradition, eighteen major texts, or *Mahāpurāṇas*, redacted from the first century C.E. Contains the great myths of Hinduism.

Pure Land: 3.5; 3.8; 3.9

Purim: 19.4

Puritans: 7.4.13

Puruṣa: 14.2; 14.4. (Sanskrit: Man.) First Man in Vedic cosmogony (Ṛgveda X 90), in which he is archetype and creator of the social order, mentioned in the ancient Upanishads as well.

Pwyll: 5.5

Pygmies: 1.4.2

Pythagoras: 12.3.2. Greek religious innovator of the sixth century B.C.E., born in the Ionian island of Samos. At thirty, he left for Croton in southern Italy, where he organized a religious community based on an ascetic and mystical doctrine, paying special attention to sacred, archetypal numbers and cosmic harmonies. Legends made of him a "divine man" (*theios anēr*), capable of all sorts of prodigies.

Pythia: 12.7

Qādirīyah: 17.10

Qiblah: 17.2–17.3

Qilaneq: 26.1.2

Quamaneq: 26.1.2

Quechua: 29.1

Quetzal: 6.2

Quetzalcóatl: 6.2; 6.3.1. (Quetzal-feathered Serpent.) Aztec creator god of Toltec origin, worshiped by the Mayas under the name of Kukulkān.

Quichés: 6.2; 6.2.1; 6.4

Quileute: 22.7

Quirinus: 25.2

Qumran: 19.2; 19.5

Qur'ān: 17.3

Quraysh: 17.4

Quṭb: 17.10

Rābiʿah al-ʿAdawīah: 17.10

Rādhā: 14.7.1. In Vaiṣṇava Hinduism, young cow-girl passionately in love with Kṛṣṇa. Later on, she received the rank of heavenly spouse of Viṣṇu.

Ragnarok: 11.4.3

al-Raḥman: 17.1

Rainbow Serpent: 1.5

Rājagṛha: 3.3

Rāma: 14.5–14.7. Hero of the Hindu epic *Rāmāyaṇa*. In the more recent parts of the text, he was transformed into an avatar of Viṣṇu.

Ramadan: 17.3; 17.9

Ramakrishna: 14.9. (Gadâdhar Chatterjee, 1834/1836–1886 C.E.) Bengali Hindu mystic, worshiper (*bhakta*) of the Great Mother Goddess and militant advocate of the unity of all religions, founded in mystical experience. His message was essentially Vedāntist and is propagated by the Ramakrishna Mission, an international movement launched by Vivekananda (d. 1902) at the Parliament of Religions in Chicago (1893).

Rāmānuja: 14.6

Rāmāyaṇa: 14.5

Rām Dās: 14.8.2

Rashap: 4.2

Rashnu: 33.3.3

Ras Shamra: 4.1

Rastafarians: 1.6.1

Rasūl: see Muḥammad, 17.2

Ray, Benjamin: 1.1

Re: 10.3; 10.6. (Or Ra.) Ancient Egyptian sun god, worshiped at Heliopolis.

Remus: 25.2.3

Ṛgveda: 14.2

Rhiannon: 5.4.1; 5.5

Rifāʿīyah: 17.10

Rinzai Zen: 3.9

Rñin-ma-pa: 3.10

Rodrigo Ximénez de Rada: 7.4.9

Romulus: 25.2.3

Rosh Hashanah: 19.4

Roy, Rammohan: 14.9

Ṛṣi: 14.4.1

Rusalkas: 28.1.1

Russell, J. B.: 7.8

Ruth: 19.2

Ruusbroec, Jan van: 7.9

Saadia ben Joseph: 19.7

Saami: 26.1.2

Sabazios: 21.3.5; 31.3.1. Thracian and Phrygian god, identified by the Greeks with Dionysus. His nocturnal ceremonies were known in Athens from the fifth century B.C.E. During the Roman epoch, he became a mystery god.

Sacrifice: 6.2.1; 6.3.1; 12.4; 29.2; 33.1

Saddharmapuṇḍarika: 3.9

Sadducees: 19.7. (From Hebrew: *Tseduqim.*) Jewish theologians of the second century B.C.E. to first century C.E., literalist and conservative, who rejected oral tradition as well as the freer and more intellectual biblical exegesis of the Pharisees. They did not believe in the immortality of the soul, or in bodily resurrection.

Saicho: 3.9

Saint-Vincent: 1.6.1

Śaivism: Hindu devotional trend centered on the god Śiva and/or his Śakti (female power); divided in numerous sects, Tantric and otherwise.

Śakti: 14.7.3; 14.7.4

Śākyamuni: 3.2

Salish: 22.2; 22.7

Samādhi: 14.4.2. In Buddhism, concentration technique; in yoga, supreme stage of unitive contemplation.

Samaritans: People of the region of Samaria, north of Israel. They held themselves to be descendants of the northern Jewish tribes of Ephraim and Manasseh. They separated from the Jews after the return from Babylonian exile.

Sāmaveda: 14.2

Saṃgha: 3.2; 3.4. In Buddhism, community of believers established by the Buddha himself, consisting of four sectors (*parisad*): monks (*bhikṣus*), nuns (*bhikṣunis*), laymen (*upāsakas*), and laywomen (*upāsikās*).

Sāṃkhya: 14.4.2; 14.6. Hindu philosophical system, one of the six traditional schools (*darśanas*), forming a pair with yoga.

Sammitīya: 3.4

Samogo: 1.2.3

Samoyeds: 26.1.2

Saṃsāra: 3.5; 14.3; 18.4. Metensomatosis (incarnation of a preexistent soul in new bodies) in traditional Hinduism, paradoxically accepted in Buddhism. Conceived as negative. Different ascetic and/or mystical methods were devised in Indian religious history to obtain liberation (*mokṣa*) from karmic bonds and make an end to the descent of the soul in new bodies. A similar conception of metensomatosis was shared by certain Greek pre-Socratic philosophers and by Plato. In other religious contexts, metensomatosis can be positive.

Saṃskāra: 3.3; 3.4; 14.2

Samuel: 19.2. Jewish judge (*shofet*) and prophet of the eleventh century B.C.E., protector of David.

Samuel ben Kalonymus: 19.8

Sanhedrin: 19.7. (Hebrew and Aramaic, from the Greek *synedrion*, "assembly.") Supreme organ of Jewish administration and justice from the Roman occupation (63 B.C.E.) to the sixth century C.E. Its existence has been contested.

Śaṅkara: 14.6. Hindu religious master of southern India eighth century C.E.), commentator of the classics, and creator of nondualistic Vedānta (*advaita vedānta*).

Saṇṇagarika: 3.4

Sannyāsa 14.4.3. Fourth and last stage (āśrama) in the traditional life cycle of a Hindu male, it marked complete renunciation of the world after withdrawal in the forest (vānaprastha).

Sano Tsunehiko: 27.6

Santa Lucia: 1.6.1

Santería: 1.6.1

Saoshyant: 33.5.2. (Avestan, Pahlavi: *sōshans*.) World savior in Zoroastrianism. Late Mazdaism spoke of three Saoshyants. They would be born from Zarathushtra's seed, stored under the guard of 99,999 *fravashis* in Lake Kansaoya, when three immaculate virgins would bathe in the water of the lake. The last Saoshyant would appear at the final judgment (*frashôkereti*), defeating forever the enemies of the right order (*asha*).

Sappho: 12.3.4

Sarah: (Sarai; God changed her name to Sarah.) Beautiful half sister and wife of Abraham in the biblical Book of Genesis. Sterile at first, late in life she gave birth to Isaac.

Sarapis: 21.3.6

Sarasvati: 33.3.3

al-Sarrāj: 17.10

Sarvāstivāda: 3.4. Buddhist sect that split from the Sthaviravāda school at the time of the emperor Aśoka (third century B.C.E.), giving birth to three other Hīnayāna sects: the Sautrāntika, the Mūlasarvāstivāda, and the Dharmaguptaka.

Saso, Michael: 30.3

Śāstra: 3.1

Saul: 19.1–19.2

Saule: 28.2.1

Savitar: 14.2

Saxo Grammaticus: (ca. 1150–1216 C.E.) Danish historian, author of *Gesta Danorum*, one of the most important repertories of northern mythology.

Schechter, Soloman: 19.7

Schism (Eastern): 7.6

Schism (Western): 7.6

Schmidt, Wilhelm: 1.4.2

Scholem, Gershom: 19.9

Sedna: Goddess of sea animals among the Inuit (Eskimos).

Sefarad: 19.1

Sefer Yetsirah: 19.8. (Hebrew: Book of Creation.) Cosmogonic writing and first Kabbalistic treatise of uncertain date (second to eighth century C.E.).

Seidhr: 11.3.3; 11.5.1

Seljuks: 17.5

Selk'nam: 29.7

Semele: 12.3.4

Senegal: 1.1

Senge Takatomi: 27.6

Seniufo: 1.1

Septuagint: 19.2

Servius: 25.4

Seth: 10.2; 10.3.(1) Egyptian god, he killed and dismembered his brother Osiris. (2) In the biblical Book of Genesis, third son of Adam and Eve. In some Gnostic writings, he was the forefather of the race of the elect and the prototype of the Savior.

Sevener (Shiʿites): 17.6.3

Sgam-po-pa: 3.10

Shabbetai Tsevi: 19.6–19.7. (1627–1676 C.E.) Purported Jewish Messiah, he won many followers before his movement split as a consequence of his conversion to Islam. An antimonian revival of Shabbatianism was preached in Poland by Jacob Frank (1726–1791 C.E.).

Shādhilīyah: 17.10.2

al-Shāfiʿī: 17.7

Shakers: (1) Popular name of a Christian millennialist sect founded in England in 1747 and stemming from the Quakers. (2) 1.6.1.

Shaking tent: 22.5; 26.1.2

Shamash: 20.2

Shambhala: 3.10

Shango: 1.6.1

Shao Yung: 8.4

Sharīʿah: 17.7

Shavuot: 19.4. Jewish Pentecost, celebrated the sixth/seventh of Sivan, seven weeks after the first Sabbath after Easter in memory of the reception of the Law by Moses on Mount Sinai.

Shaykh: 17.10.2

Shekinah: (Hebrew: dwelling.) Presence of God in the Temple of Jerusalem; later, the female hypostasis of God, mediating between God and the world.

Shen: 30.2

Shevuot: 19.4

Shīʿat ʿAlī: 17.4

Shibata Hanamori: 27.6

Shih Huang-ti: 30.2

Shiʿites: 17.4; 17.6

Shilluk: 1.3

Shimoyama Osuka: 27.6

Shingon: 3.9

Shinran: 3.9

Shinrikyo: 27.6

Shinshukyo: 27.6

Shinto Shuseikha: 27.6

Shinto Taikyo: 27.6

Shinto Taiseikyo: 27.6

Shishino Nakaba: 27.6

Babylonian exile (sixth century B.C.E.) out of the necessity of performing the cult in a place remote from the Jerusalem Temple; subsequently, it came to designate religious facilities of the diaspora. After the destruction of the Second Temple in 70 C.E., the synagogues became centers for Jewish worship and scriptural readings.

Synesius of Cyrene: 13.2.4

Tagore, Devendranath: 14.9

Tai Chen: 8.4

T'ai hsi: 30.4

Taliesin: 5.5

Talmud: 19.2

Tammuz: 20.2; 21.2

Tanakh: 19.2

Tane: 23.3

Tangaroa: 23.2; 23.3

Tanhuma: 19.2

Tanjur: 3.1

Tanna: 19.2

Tantra: 14.7. (Sanskrit for "tissue.") Manual teaching a certain doctrine. In a more restricted sense, a work presenting Hindu or Buddhist esoteric doctrines sometimes employing sexual practices or allusions thereto.

Tantrism: 3.3; 3.6; 3.9; 3.10; 14.7.4

Tanzania: 1.3; 1.4.1

Tao: 8.3; 27.1

Tao-te King: 30.1

Tapas: 14.3; 18.4. (Sanskrit: heat.) Term corresponding to the Greek word *askēsis;* they both end up signifying the fire of asceticism. The practice of *tapas* produces accumulation of *siddhis,* or special powers.

Tapu: 23.1

Tārā: Buddhist goddess, especially from Tibet, forming a couple with Bodhisattva Avalokiteśvara or with Buddha Amoghasiddhi. There is a Green Tārā, symbolizing prosperity, and a White Tārā, symbolizing heavenly assistance and longevity.

Tartaros: 12.3.4

Taṣawwuf: 17.10

Tatian: 7.4.4

Tattvas: 14.4.2

Tauler, John: 7.9

Taurobolium: 21.3.3

Tazig: 3.10; 32.3

Tefnut: 10.3

Teg Bahādur: 14.8.2

Tel Amarna: 4.1

Telipinu: 15.1; 15.2

Temakuel: 29.7

Templars: 7.4.9

Temple of Jerusalem: 19.1

Templo Mayor: 6.3.1

Tendai: 3.8; 3.9

Tengri: Altaic word originally designating the physical appearance of the sky; heavenly divinity among Turks and Mongols.

Tenochtitlán: 6.3

Tenrikyo: 27.6

Teotihuacán: 6.2; 6.3.1

Tepehua: 6.4

Teresa of Avila: 7.9

Tertullian of Carthage: 7.4.2

Teshub: 15.1

Tezcatlipoca: 6.2–6.3. (Smoked Mirror.) Aztec creator god, opponent of Quetzalcóatl. Great wizard whose powers are contained in a magical obsidian mirror.

Theognis of Megara: 12.3.4

Theophilus of Alexandria: 7.4.4

Theotokos: 7.6; 7.7.2–7.7.3

Theravāda: 3.1; 3.4; 3.7

Thérèse of Lisieux: 7.9

Thesmophoria: 12.5. Greek autumn festival in honor of Demeter and Persephone, including exchange of obscene pronouncements, flagellation, and insertion of pieces of roasted piglet in the *megara,* or clefts, in the rock supposed to lead to the netherworld.

Thokk: 11.4.2

Thomas à Kempis: 7.9

Thorr: 11.3.3; 11.3.4–11.4.3. Powerful Germanic Ase god of war and storm, owner of the hammer Mjollnir, the terror of the Giants. Patron of the *karl* ("freemen," as opposed to the *jarl,* or aristocrats).

Thoth: Egyptian moon god of wisdom worshiped at Hermopolis in middle Egypt. Identified by the Greeks with their god Hermes (during the Roman period with Hermes Trismegistus).

Three Jewels: 18.2

Tiamat: 20.5

T'ien-t'ai: 3.8–3.9

Tikal: 6.2

Tillamook: 22.7

Tīrthaṃkara: 18.2–18.5

Titicaca: 29.4

Titus: 19.1

Tlingit: 22.2; 22.7

Todorov, Tzvetan: 29.3

Tojolabal: 6.2

Tollán: 6.2

Toloache: 22.8

Tolowa: 22.7

Toltecs: 6.1–6.2; 6.3.1

Tonantzin: 6.4

Topa Inca: 29.3

Torah: 19.2

Tosefta: 19.2

Transubstantiation: 7.6

Trickster: 1.2.1; 1.2.3; 9.2; 9.4; 11.4.3; 12.3.4; 14.2; 22.4; 22.7; 23.3; 29.6

Trinidad: 1.6.1

Tripiṭaka: 3.1

Triratna: 18.2

Tsimshian: 22.2; 22.7

Tsong-ka-pa: 3.10

Tswana: 1.5

Tuatha Dé Dananu: 5.4

Tukano: 29.1; 29.5

Tula: 6.3.1

Tulsīdās: 14.7.1

Tung Chung-shu: 8.3

Tungus: 26.1

Tupi-Guaranī: 29.8

Tupis: 29.1; 29.5

Turks: 26.1

Turnbull, Colin: 1.4.2

Turner, Victor: 1.4.1

Tuvin: 26.1.1

Tu Wei-ming: 8.4

Twelver (Shiʿites): 17.6.3

Tzeltal: 6.2

Vivekananda: 14.9. (Narendranath Datta; 1863–1902 C.E.) Disciple of Ramakrishna, he acquainted the Western world with his master's teaching and with Vedānta. Founder of the Vedanta Society of New York (1895).

Vladimir of Kiev: 7.5

Voguls: 26.1.2

Volos: 28.1.1

Voodoo: 1.6.1. Afro-Caribbean possession cult from Haiti; has male (*ungan*) and female (*manbo*) priests. Voodoo spirits are usually called *lwas* (from the Yoruba language).

Waldenses of Lyon: 7.4.13

Waley, Arthur: 30.1

Wali: 17.10

Walker, Caroline Bynum: 7.9

Wang Yang-ming: 8.4

Warikyana: 29.5

Warithuddin Muhammad: 1.6.4

Wawilak: 2.1

Welch, Holmes: 30.1

William of Ockham: 7.4.10

Wilson, E. O.: 24.2

Winti: 1.6.3

Witóto: 29.5

Wódhan: 11.3.4

World King: 3.2

Wounded Knee: 22.1

Wu Ch'eng-en: 3.8

Wu Liang: 3.8

Wycliff, John: 7.4.13

Xolotl: 6.3.1

Yagé: 26.1.6

Yahgan: 29.7

Yajña: 14.2; 14.7

Yajurveda: 14.2

Yakuts: 26.1.1

Yama: The first of the dead according to the Vedas; subsequently lord of the dead and finally sinister divinity of death and hell.

Yamana: 29.7

Yamm: 4.2; 4.4

Yang: 30.4

Yantra: 14.7.4. Geometric meditational figure in Hinduism and Buddhism.

Yasht: 33.3.1

Yasna: 33.3.1

Yazatas: 33.3.3

Yazīd: 17.6

Yellowknife: 22.2

Yemoja: 1.2.1

Yggdrasill: 11.3.2; 11.4.3

Yin: 30.4

Yishmael ben Elisha: (ca. 50–135 C.E.) Palestinien *tanna* (master), a contemporary of Rabbi Aqiva.

Ymir: 11.3.1

Ynglingasaga: 11.2

Yoga: 14.4.2; 14.5

Yogācāra: 3.5. Mahāyāna Buddhist school founded by Asaṅga (ca. 315–390 C.E.

Yohannan ben Zakkai: 19.7. (ca. 1–80 C.E.) Principal Jewish religious leader after the fall of the Temple in 70 C.E..